The
Soviet Union
& International
Oil
Politics

The Soviet Union & International Oil Politics

Arthur Jay Klinghoffer

Columbia University Press/New York/1977

Arthur Jay Klinghoffer is Associate Professor of Political Science, Rutgers University

Library of Congress Cataloging in Publication Data

Klinghoffer, Arthur Jay, 1941–
   The Soviet Union and international oil politics.

   Includes bibliographical reference and index.
   1. Petroleum industry and trade—Russia.
2. Russia—Foreign economic relations.   3. World
politics—1975–1985.   I. Title.
HD9575.R82K57   338.2'7'2820947   76–52411
ISBN 0–231–04104–7

Columbia University Press

New York   Guildford Surrey

TO JUDY AND JOELLA—the women in my life

Acknowledgments

Research for this book was carried out in Washington, D.C.; Ann Arbor, Michigan; Tel Aviv, Israel; and in my own home-base area, the environs of Philadelphia. The numerous geographical locales are more than matched by the large number of people who made substantial contributions to my research effort. Fundamental to the entire undertaking was Rutgers University's permitting me to take a year off, under the auspices of the Faculty Academic Study Program, to work on this project; so special thank you's must first be extended to my chairman, Harry Shapiro, and my dean, Walter Gordon. Their encouragement of my research was certainly crucial. In addition, the Rutgers Research Council provided some very necessary funds which helped defray the costs of mapmaking and of research in Washington. Fred Main, in particular, was of great assistance.

The key to my research in Washington was Ken Yalowitz, a State Department specialist on Soviet foreign trade who also served in a similar capacity at the Department of Commerce. Ken provided numerous insights into Soviet behavior and was also instrumental in setting up appointments with other officials who proved to be most helpful and informative. In this regard, the assistance of Robert Clarke and Marion Creekmore of the Department of State, Marc Coler of the Department of Commerce, and John Hardt and George Holliday of the Library of Congress was especially notable.

While in Israel, I was a Research Associate at the Russian and East European Research Center, Tel Aviv University. Yaacov Ro'i and Mati Mayzel helped make my stay at the university most pleasurable, while Eli Arom of the Israel Institute of Petroleum was most gracious in permitting me to use the research facilities at this excellent repository of information on the Middle East oil trade. He also spent numerous hours discussing oil with me, and his patience and erudition are clearly appreciated. Other Israelis who proved to be extremely knowledgeable on the subject of Soviet oil policies in the Middle East and who contributed significantly to my research were Aryeh Yodfat, well-known researcher and archivist on Soviet policy toward the Middle East; Moshe Neeman, Life Engineering Ltd., Haifa; Gideon Perlman, Israel Electricity Company, Haifa; and Emmanuel Racine, Delek Israel Oil Corporation, Tel Aviv. Although we never actually met, I would also like to thank Eliezer Shinnar, former Israeli ambassador to West Germany. Although confined to his home for medical reasons, he went out of his way to assist me in my research and he called me several times to give me further leads.

After my six months in Israel, I spent five months as a Visiting Research Associate at the Center for Russian and East European Studies, University of Michigan, Ann Arbor. William Zimmerman and his staff helped make my stay most productive and Morris Bornstein and Alan Deardorff, both of the Department of Economics, generously shared their expertise in the areas of economic theory and terminology. Frank Shulman of the Center for Japanese Studies made numerous bibliographic suggestions while Ken Stein of the Center for Near Eastern and North African Studies volunteered for the unenviable task of reading all sections of my handwritten manuscript dealing with the Middle East and North Africa. Ken's pertinent comments and criticisms were certainly appreciated when I went through the process of revision.

So many librarians facilitated my work that it is not possible to mention them all individually but I would like to convey collective gratitude to the staffs of Rutgers University Library, Camden; Van Pelt, Dietrich, Lippincott, Towne, and Biddle Law libraries of the University of Pennsylvania; the library of the Mobil Oil Corporation, Paulsboro, New Jersey; Elias Sourasky, Social Sciences, and Russian and East European Research Center libraries of Tel Aviv University; Abraham Friedman Library of the Israel Institute of Petroleum, Tel Aviv; Undergraduate, Graduate, and Center for Russian and East European Studies libraries of the University of

Michigan, Ann Arbor; and the Library of Congress, Middle East Institute, American Petroleum Institute, and Department of Commerce libraries, all in Washington, D.C.

In addition, a special salute must go to Sandi Fritz and Anita Grinvalds, who somehow managed to convert my handwritten manuscript filled with abundant additions and deletions into neat typewritten copy. They even managed to do it right on schedule, not being even one day late with the original draft. Marshall Shulman of Columbia University made many useful suggestions regarding possible improvements and Hannah McCullough then forged through the minefield of my revised draft in order to produce a most orderly final manuscript. Chuck Ogrosky of Rutgers College, New Brunswick, provided the expert mapmaking.

In a somewhat less academic vein, some endurance awards should be presented to my wife Judy and my daughter Joella. Judy went through childbirth in another country and was forced to set up a household in four different locations as the year of leave from Rutgers turned into a hectic packathon. She nevertheless found time to read each chapter as soon as I had completed it and she turned into a valuable, but hardnosed, critic. Joella never quite got her bearings straight. She was born while we were in Israel and even had to pose for a passport photo at the age of three months! Several flights and four pediatricians later, she finally arrived "home" in the Philadelphia area. She was a great inspiration throughout my research and successfully carried out the important function of making sure that I got an early start each day.

Many thanks to everyone who helped me during the course of my research, but it should be stressed that all viewpoints set forth in this book are my own and I alone should be held responsible for any inconsistencies, misinterpretations, or invalid deductions.

ARTHUR JAY KLINGHOFFER
Rutgers University
April 1977

Contents

Energy Conversion Factors

42 gallons = 1 barrel
7.3 barrels of crude oil = 1 metric ton
1 barrel per day = 50 metric tons per year
1 metric ton = 2200 pounds
35.3 cubic feet = 1 cubic meter

1/Foreign Trade and State Power

The Arab oil embargo of 1973–74 and the world "energy crisis" have helped focus attention on the strategic importance of oil in international political relations. The oil-exporting states now have a powerful political weapon at their disposal while the oil-importing states have come to recognize that plans for ensuring a stable oil supply must be given a high priority when they formulate their foreign policy.

Previous studies of oil politics have stressed the roles of the United States and Britain and the activities of the largest Western oil companies, the so-called Seven Sisters. Recently, as a consequence of the rising power of oil exporters, the emphasis has been on the confrontation between the members of the Organization of Petroleum Exporting Countries (OPEC), on the one hand, and Western Europe, the United States, and Japan on the other. Curiously, the role of the Soviet Union in international oil politics has been almost completely neglected, although this state is the world's largest producer of crude oil, a major exporter, and is also importing a growing quantity of oil. There appears to be close interaction between the oil trade and the implementation of Soviet foreign policy.

The Soviet Union has often resorted to the use of oil as an instrument of political pressure against other states, such as Yugoslavia, China, Ghana, and Finland, and it has additionally sought to limit Western power by encouraging the nationalization of Western oil properties in the Third World. The Soviets verbally supported the Arab embargoes of 1967 and 1973–74 and, with an eye on the containment of China, they have invited Japan and the United States to participate in the oil development of Western

Siberia. Of course, political motivation does not underlie all of the Soviet Union's international oil policies, as there is certainly a strong commercial element, especially regarding oil sales to Western Europe.

Any examination of Soviet oil policies must take natural gas into account since it is an alternative source of energy, it is usually found in the same locations as crude oil, and its price has recently been linked to that of oil in international markets. The Soviet Union has the world's largest reserves of natural gas and its exports of this fuel are rapidly increasing. As with oil, natural gas deliveries can be manipulated in a highly political manner and the Soviet Union has the potential to play a pivotal role in international energy politics.

Numerous intriguing questions come to mind when surveying Soviet energy policies: Why does the Soviet Union import both oil and natural gas if it is so rich in fuel resources? Did the Soviet Union reap any advantages from the Arab oil embargoes of 1967 and 1973–74? Is Soviet policy in the Middle East affected by the fact that the USSR is importing increasing amounts of oil from that area? How did the closure of the Suez Canal affect Soviet oil interests? Were Soviet energy policies in Siberia affected by the improvement in Sino-American relations? Has oil played a role in maintaining Soviet control over many other communist-ruled states? Was the Soviet "oil offensive" of the late fifties and early sixties precipitated by political considerations? Has the Soviet Union made any political inroads through its oil sales to Third World states? Has the Western use of oil politics against the USSR affected Soviet energy policies? Is it true that the Soviet Union scrupulously adheres to its oil export contracts? Do political relations between the Soviet Union and other states affect the price charged for Soviet oil? Will the Soviet Union and other Council for Mutual Economic Assistance (CMEA) states collectively become net importers of oil by 1980? I hope this book will provide the answers.

My analysis of Soviet oil policies proceeds from the vantage point of political science, rather than economics or petroleum geology. These latter two disciplines are certainly relevant, and must be taken into account, but my accent is on the politicization of Soviet foreign trade and the use of oil as a political weapon aimed at furthering Soviet foreign policy interests.

Some Theoretical Implications

Foreign trade has always been recognized as a major instrument of state power. Carthage, medieval Venice, and the seventeenth-century Dutch Republic derived their political strength largely from the successful manipulation and management of international commerce, and empires have frequently basked in glory as a result of their control over major economic commodities. Gold and spices once served as imperial foundations despite their non-essentiality; access to salt traditionally lay behind Saharan politics because of the vital importance of this commodity in a desert environment; and today oil has served as an impetus to political intrigue, interstate rivalry, and war. Control over oil has been used to further the ends of state power, and even though atomic power may eventually replace it as the prime source of energy, oil is still the strategic keystone of contemporary international trade relations.

Mercantilists of the seventeenth and eighteenth centuries, who believed that state power was based primarily upon economic wealth, advocated that foreign trade and internal economics be regulated by government, in order to harmonize political and economic interests. The state was to be responsible for the furtherance of economic welfare through the institution of protective tariffs, the encouragement of new industries, the maintenance of full employment, the training of labor, and the control of both economic consumption and the rights of the working class. Mercantilists believed that a positive trade balance would lead not only to an increase in wealth but also to the acquisition of greater power, since international trade was seen as an adversary relationship. As some states added to their wealth and power, other states necessarily had to suffer losses.[1]

Nineteenth-century advocates of free trade attempted to remove power competition from the international marketplace, arguing that all states could benefit from trade and that one's gain is not another's loss. They maintained that an extension of free trade could serve the interests of all states and therefore advance the prospects for peace. However, it should be pointed out that many states which supported the concept of free trade were themselves the masters of colonial empires over which they were clearly using their power advantage to practice economic exploitation. Free trade was therefore a policy to be practiced primarily within the European club of industrializing states, but it was also used as a rationale to secure access to the lucrative markets of China and Japan. In its purer sense, free trade led to economic interdependence and was therefore opposed by the protectionists who favored economic self-sufficiency as a stepping stone to increased state power.

The meaning of the term "imperialism" has become lost in an onslaught of epithet and descriptive nuance and, as professors Nye and Keohane assert, it has become broadened to such an extent that it now refers to any unequal power relationship across state boundaries.[2] However, "imperialism" does retain some specificity when viewed in a Marxist-Leninist framework, referring to the quest by advanced capitalist states for new markets in which to introduce their finance and industrial capital so as to secure markets for their exports and required raw materials for their imports. Marxist-Leninists clearly see a close relationship between foreign trade and state power in the policies of capitalist states, and they view such international economic transactions as inherently exploitive. British economist Peter Wiles maintains that all Marxists see any international exchange of goods as directly connected with international power politics, and Lenin has discussed the "advantages" accruing to those states which export capital.[3]

"Imperialism" derives great profits for monopoly capitalist enterprises, and the state often helps them acquire wealth overseas. Thus, there is some common ground with mercantilism but, viewed theoretically, "imperialism" somewhat diverges from mercantilism since the inflow of wealth does not serve the public welfare (through expenditures by royalty or maximization of employment opportunities owing to business expansion) but remains in the hands of a minority bourgeois class which economically exploits its own domestic proletariat. Observed in more practical terms, mercantilist entrepreneurs did accumulate great wealth without showing too much concern for the wages of their employees, and the proletariat in advanced capitalist states did gain access to some of the spoils of "imperialism" as a result of trade unionism and the purchase of stock. Mercantilism and "imperialism" were both based upon a perceived congruity between the desire of the state to increase its power and the desire of merchants to garner wealth through the expansion of international trade but, of course, their similarities in this one regard should not obfuscate their obvious differences and the distinct historical periods in which they were implemented.

Trade may be translated into power if a state stops exporting a commodity and the importing state can neither adjust its economy or secure the same product elsewhere. However, trade is related to power in many other areas than the denial of commodities, and economic analysts have delineated "supply effect" and "influence effect" aspects of foreign trade.[4] The supply effect is concerned with securing access to strategic materials and importing sufficient quantities as a contribution to war-making potential; the influence effect is based on the use of exports as an instrument of political pressure. The former can be furthered by stockpiling strategic materials, by trading with states which are unlikely to cut off supplies, and by controlling oceanic trade routes; the latter can be promoted by exporting products over which one has a supply monopoly, trading with states which are poorer than one's own, trading with states that cannot easily redirect their commercial patterns, and engaging in extensive bilateral trade and transit trade. Receiving, in return for one's exports, products for which there is little world demand or which the other state cannot absorb domestically also contributes to the influence effect, since a trading partner with an abundance of such apparently superfluous goods is placed in an inferior power position.[5]

Since trade can lead to an increase in power, autarkic economic policies may be counterproductive; but overreliance on trade can also reduce a state's power. Trading states are subject to the influence effect of others, and if they are dependent upon the import of vital commodities their power can be gravely affected by embargoes. Major industrial powers are now learning that because of their unwillingness to use force their access to key resources, such as oil, copper, and tin, is no longer guaranteed. Colonialism abetted a state's supply effect but its demise has led, paradoxically, to subjugation to the influence effect of former colonies which possess crucial mineral or raw material reserves.

Machiavelli saw a basic harmony between the state's wealth and power: with wealth, one could acquire an army and extend the state's power; with power, one could conquer other states and therefore acquire greater wealth. However, such an approach is overly simplistic: wealth and power are often in conflict, and their simultaneous maximization is an elusive goal of foreign policy. A state may attempt to increase its power by not becoming dependent on others for capital or technology and it may also refuse foreign aid.[6] Similarly, a state may seek political influence and power advantage by granting another state very favorable economic terms in aid or trade.[7] Domestically, expenditures on a higher standard of living and on armaments often create competition for scarce economic resources and, in a somewhat stranger light, inability to absorb capital can facilitate an increase in power via large investment in other states. Such a policy is now followed by many Arab states in which economic modernization is not far advanced.

The political and economic aspects of a state's foreign policy are so intertwined that debates about political or economic primacy, such as those between realists and Marxists, are neither instructive nor revealing.[8] In a specific situation, one of these factors can certainly be the basic determinant but, as a whole, attempts to delineate primacy lead to circular arguments, since economic power contributes to political power and political power in turn assists in the acquisition of economic power. In

1973–74, the Arab states had a political goal—Israeli military withdrawal from occupied territories. They used an oil embargo to pressure Western states to support the Arab political cause. Once this was accomplished and a partial Israeli withdrawal from Egyptian territory was facilitated, part of the Arab political goal was achieved, but at the same time great economic benefits were derived (other than added oil revenue), since plans were initiated to reopen the Suez Canal and Egyptian prospects for regaining control over the Sinai oil fields were enhanced. Going a step further, economic assets such as the Suez Canal and the Sinai oil fields will again contribute to an increase in Egyptian political power and the chain of events can go on indefinitely.

Leaving aside the question of primacy and looking at specific situations, it is apparent that economics can be a determinant of foreign policy or an instrument of foreign policy aimed at securing political advantage.[9] The degree to which the state controls industrial enterprises is certainly a key factor, but foreign policy interacts with the economic arena even in systems with a high degree of economic autonomy, since the state establishes tariffs and quotas on imports, probably sets limitations on strategic exports, and tends to protect overseas investments of private corporations.

In countries under communist rule, where all major enterprises are owned by the state, it is obviously rather easy to harmonize foreign policy with economic interests; but state and corporate interests may be similar even in capitalist societies, if the major corporations control or strongly influence the state's formulation of foreign policy. The Soviets contend that oil monopolies determine American foreign policy toward the Middle East and charge that the Standard Oil Company of New Jersey drew up the "Eisenhower Doctrine" and presented it to the State Department. The Doctrine was not really aimed at preventing the spread of communism but was actually a threat against Middle Eastern states which wanted to nationalize the properties of American oil companies.[10] Such an analysis is partially accurate; big business clearly influences policy in the United States, but portraying American foreign policy as the tool of economic interests is somewhat one-dimensional. In actuality, there is a complex web of interactions: corporations may influence state policies or the state itself may enact policies beneficial to them because it sees these policies as contributing to the state's interests; in addition, corporations may also carry out state policies, they may act independently of state policies, or the structure and personnel of the state and the major corporations may be so overlapping that no meaningful distinctions can be drawn.

Transnational organizations are nongovernmental structures that cut across state boundaries and clearly include multinational corporations. They are becoming increasingly significant in world affairs and are acquiring a political role for, as Nye and Keohane observe, they have substantial resources and can induce other international actors to perform differently than they would have in the absence of such inducement. They may influence states, constrain them, or create autonomous foreign policies.[11] Transnational economic forces are so powerful that analysts such as Edward Morse see a decline in the "state-centric" approach to international economics, but Werner Feld and Robert Gilpin both see the continuing importance of the state. Feld points out that state officials have a vested interest in maintaining their authority and that public pressure calls for some state control over transnational corporations while Gilpin believes that these transnational corporations generally serve the state's foreign policy interests.[12]

Accompanying the rising strength of transnational economic forces is an attempt to impose stricter state control—an attempt caused by more comprehensive state economic planning, a desire to use economics in support of international political programs (such as anti-communism or anti-imperialism), and growing concern about the public welfare. States are also finding it necessary to coordinate their policies as a result of increasing international economic interdependence and may therefore organize an effective counterbalance to international business cartels.

Trade and power must continue to interact in a multiplicity of forms, as Edward Morse asserts: "The politicization of economics and the creation of economic value for political goods are what transnational processes are all about. One can no longer be conceptualized independently of the other." [13]

Soviet Foreign Policy and Economic Interest

The Soviet Union can easily harmonize foreign policy with state economic interest as a result of state ownership of the means of production and a nationalized system of foreign trade. Not only can the full economic might of the Soviet Union be deployed in support of foreign policy goals but imports and exports can be closely integrated into a comprehensive economic plan, so that foreign trade is coordinated with domestic economic development. The Soviets therefore have a fundamental advantage over capitalist states, which often have difficulty in linking foreign trade practices with domestic economic requirements or national security interests. Long before the oil embargo of 1973–74, James Reston called upon the American government to coordinate national energy policies into a program consistent with U.S. security interests and he questioned the wisdom of importing oil and gas from the USSR. Reston, a columnist for *The New York Times,* maintained that private companies were negotiating with foreign states in order to conclude energy agreements that were not in accord with national strategic interest.[14]

In contrast to Western capitalist states, the Soviet Union rarely has to contend with nongovernmental, transnational economic actors, although domestic economic interest groups and state-controlled foreign trade corporations do have influence in the formulation of foreign policy. The Soviets are confronted with transnational forces in the ethnic, intellectual, and artistic areas, but when it comes to international economics the Soviet state is the prime actor. It is certainly true that Soviet foreign-trade policies are somewhat constrained by the integrative aspects of the CMEA, but the USSR is obviously dominant in that organization and most constraints are basically self-imposed. Also facilitating the Soviet Union's linkage of trade and power are the maintenance of a command economy, which can emphasize the development of an economic power base at the expense of a significantly higher standard of living, and the ability to use the pricing mechanism as a political instrument of foreign trade since the Soviet economy is not concerned with profits to the same degree as capitalist economies. The Soviet Union was largely autarkic during the later years of Stalinism but then turned toward more extensive international trade. However, the USSR possessed just about all basic economic resources and the ability to return to virtual autarky if necessary; it could therefore make greater use of the influence effect of foreign trade while not becoming quite so subject to the influence effect of other states.

The USSR has secured economic benefits through the use of military force, as in gaining control of joint stock companies in Eastern Europe at the end of the Second World War, and it has also used diplomacy, as in pressing for the reopening of the Suez Canal in 1974 and 1975. However, trade has been the prime method for promoting strategic economic interest and the Soviet Union has generally been well situated in regard to the supply effect. Due to possession of plentiful minerals, fuels, and raw materials, the USSR need not rely on other states in these areas, although it is partially dependent on the import of technology, equipment, and grains, which gives other states some influence effect over it. A history of autarkic policies and economic isolation from the major international capitalist markets contributed to this basic self-sufficiency, and attempts by the Western powers to ostracize the Soviet Union through discriminatory trade techniques only encouraged this tendency. Assisting in the furtherance of the supply effect are Soviet military control over Eastern Europe, which guarantees continued access to needed industrial commodities, and growing naval power, which protects vital commercial routes.

Especially in the field of energy, the Soviet Union can easily adjust its policies to counter any interruption of supply, since it can quickly revert to energy independence regarding oil and natural gas, and it has abundant coal and atomic energy resources as well. So far, there has been no major supply problem but the Soviets have shown a reluctance to import a greater quantity of oil from the Middle East, partially as a result of the political instability of the area and the possibility that the flow of oil could be disrupted. If a problem develops, the Soviets could balance any reduction in imports with a partial curtailment of oil exports. During the late thirties, the USSR did resort to decreasing oil exports, although the reason at that time was the need to stockpile fuel in preparation for a probable war.

As a major trading power, the Soviet Union can manipulate the influence effect to its political advantage. East European states have been placed in a position where they would have great difficulty in changing their trade patterns, and Third World states are often dependent on the Soviets for credits and spare parts. The Soviets also purchase products Third World states are unable to sell elsewhere. The Soviets have reaped advantages from their extensive use of bilateral trade arrangements (since the weaker trading partner has little leeway in seeking more favorable economic terms or other sources of supply) and from their growing use of transit and other forms of middleman trade, especially in the field of energy. The Soviets are also building up the potential for future use of the influence effect, since many NATO states are importers of Soviet oil and natural gas, and it is also possible that the United States and Japan will invest in Soviet energy development and increase their dependence on Soviet fuel supplies.

Since the Soviet Union is not very dependent on the import of crucial commodities, the likelihood that economic factors will serve as important determinants of foreign policy is not so great as the likelihood that these factors will serve as instruments of foreign policy. The ends of foreign policy therefore tend to be more political than economic while the means are frequently economic. This is commensurate with the Soviet Union's status as a powerful state, an active participant in trade, and yet an essentially self-sufficient economic giant. Such an approach can be contrasted to that of many West European states and Japan as they were faced with the 1973–74 Arab oil embargo. Because of their dependence on Middle East oil, economics clearly played a significant role in determining their political positions on the Arab-Israeli dispute.

In some specific cases, Soviet foreign policy is strongly influenced by economic considerations. Soviet support for Iraq against the Kurds, despite past sympathies for the Kurdish cause, is based partially on a desire to maintain the flow of oil from Kirkuk to the Soviet Union; the Soviets therefore seek to prevent the inclusion of Kirkuk in an autonomous Kurdish area. Similarly, the Soviets covet American technology and capital and the political détente with the United States is aimed largely at the extension of economic relations. The USSR even permitted the emigration of thousands of Jews, bowing to the pressures of those who linked increased trade and the granting of "most favored nation" status with the right of Jewish emigration. However, economics is more often an instrument used to further foreign-policy goals, although this need not exclude any accompanying economic benefit.

Among the techniques applied by the Soviet Union have been the cessation of exports to display political disfavor (as with oil shipments to Israel in 1956), the reduction of exports and the withholding of spare parts to apply political pressure (as with China in the early sixties), and the offer of a commodity at a low price to facilitate political entrée (as with the offer of oil to Cuba in 1960). The Soviets have also stopped importing commodities to accentuate a political protest (as with the import of wool from Australia after the defection of a Soviet spy in 1954), have intervened with trade offers to strengthen the hand of a state involved in a dispute with a major Western power (as with Iceland in its fishing dispute with Britain in the late fifties), and have delayed trade negotiations to influence a state's domestic politics (as with the selection of a Finnish cabinet in 1958). In the area of economic aid, they have tried to help a new government consolidate its position (Bangladesh), offered assistance following Western denial of such assistance (Aswan dam), helped secure the political power of "progressive" leaders (Nkrumah, Touré, Sukarno), and countered Western aid to one state (Ethiopia) with aid to its major rival (Somalia). In all of these cases, economics was an instrument rather than a determinant.

In its dealings with Third World states, Soviet policy aims at encouraging the growth of socialism and at reducing Western economic influence, which is seen as a lever of political control. Toward these ends, Soviet aid usually goes to state-owned industrial enterprises, thus strengthening the state economic sector and accelerating the growth of an industrial proletariat. Trade is also directed toward state corporations, and in many cases the Soviets have helped to break Western boycotts of nationalized firms by buying blacklisted products. The Soviets also offer aid to reduce a state's dependence on the West and they particularly assist Middle East and North African states in oil exploration and development to weaken the role of the Western oil cartel.

Ever since the clash with the Chinese at Ussuri in March 1969, the Soviet Union has accelerated its efforts to develop Siberia's economy to facilitate military preparedness against China. In addition, the Soviets have tried to attract Japanese and American investment to Siberia—partially because of obvious economic advantages but also quite importantly, it would give these states a stake in preventing any projected Chinese expansion into Siberia and would discourage them from joining with China in a loose anti-Soviet coalition. The Siberian situation has presented the USSR with diverse opportunities to use economics as an instrument of foreign policy. For example, the Soviets may encourage Japanese and American investment in order to help gain political support vis-à-vis China but they may also use the prospect of economic deals as bait to accomplish the same thing. The Soviets may also try to further economic ties with Japan to weaken the close Japanese-American political relationship or they may advocate foreign economic investment in the USSR as a means of obtaining political leverage, since the Soviets could hold back fuel and raw materials to press for political concessions.

For the Soviet Union, the growth of trade relations generally accompanies improved political relations and the volume of trade is therefore attuned to the vicissitudes of international politics. The Soviets see the present détente with the United States in both political and economic terms, and the history of Soviet trade relations with Yugoslavia clearly shows a quantitative fluctuation based on political considerations.[15] Similarly, the friendlier Soviet approach to the Third World initiated in 1955 had both its political and economic dimensions; policies toward Egypt and India are obvious examples.

In some cases, the Soviet Union strives to increase trade relations as a stepping stone to improved political ties, as has happened in Malaysia, Singapore, and the Philippines. Elsewhere, as in Iran, the sequence may be reversed, as a political rapprochement precedes extensive trade and aid agreements. However, the overall result is the congruence of commerce and diplomacy, for the Soviet Union is highly concerned about the long-term nature and reliability of trade ties. A planned economy, more than one based on free enterprise, must be assured of the timing, composition, and quantity of imports and exports, so the shifting of trade patterns can be highly disruptive. This is a major consideration behind the Soviet preference for trading with other communist-ruled states; political dislocation of trade is not likely to occur and economic integration and specialization help solidify bonds of longevity.

Although the Soviet foreign trade system is neither mercantilist nor "imperialist," some interesting parallels can nevertheless be drawn. Philip Buck has compared mercantilism to twentieth-century totalitarian systems, citing state attempts to control international commerce and internal economic forces with the aim of using economic development as a buttress for state power.[16] Both mercantilism and Soviet-style socialism emphasize economics as the key to political power and other factors are generally downgraded.

The Soviet system of trade and aid, particularly as it relates to Third World states, bears some resemblance to "imperialism" à la Lenin since the USSR seeks to find markets for its manufactured goods. The Soviets often stipulate that credits be spent on Soviet commodities, a practice certainly akin to that which Lenin attributed to the "imperialists" when he wrote: "The most usual thing is to stipulate that part of the loan that is granted shall be spent on purchases in the country of issue, particularly on orders for war materials, or for ships, etc. . . . The export of capital abroad thus becomes a means for encouraging the export of commodities." [17] Similarly, Soviet efforts to eliminate Western economic influence from the Third World have led to an Orwellian situation in which Soviet and Western policies are often indistinguishable. In such a vein, Soviet commentator V. Rymalov elliptically asserts that Third World states can reduce their dependence on the West by securing loans, credits, technical assistance, and machinery from the USSR.[18]

Soviet economic power has never been based on an overseas colonial empire, in the manner of Britain, France, or Portugal, and there has been no need to readjust in the face of rising anticolonialism. However, Soviet incorporation of the Transcaucasian, Central Asian, and Baltic republics has provided economic dividends and any potential separatism in these areas would surely prove disruptive. The strong Soviet influence over Eastern Europe and the economic integration of CMEA are also major pillars of Soviet economic strength, and it is the complex economic relationship between the Soviet Union and the East European states which proves the most elusive and difficult to define.

Soviet power in Eastern Europe has always been largely based on military force, as was shown in Hungary in 1956 and Czechoslovakia in 1968, but economic factors have also played a significant role. Stalin exploited the East European states economically in order to speed the Soviet Union's postwar recovery but, as polycentric tendencies developed during the Khrushchev period, a lessening of political controls was accompanied by expanded economic integration and reduced subjugation. The USSR is certainly the dominant member within CMEA; Rumania has objected to Soviet efforts to use CMEA integration as an instrument to further Soviet economic growth at the expense of other CMEA members. However, the Soviet desire to benefit economically from integration must be placed alongside the use of integration as a lever of power and the latter places certain economic constraints on the USSR.

If one looks at Soviet oil policies, it is apparent that control over the flow of oil to Eastern Europe can be used to further Soviet power interests, but the paradox is that continued Soviet influence is partially dependent on the maintenance of a near monopoly position as an oil supplier. Increased deliveries will therefore be required as Eastern Europe's energy needs rise dramatically. Just after the invasion of Czechoslovakia in 1968, the USSR increased oil deliveries in order to strengthen this means of control, and present policy is to keep up huge oil exports to Eastern Europe even though the Soviets are generally attempting to conserve their oil. No long-term financial loss is involved but the flexibility of Soviet oil export policies is clearly reduced. Therefore, if one thinks of colonialism, the concept is somewhat stood on its head when related to Soviet–East European economic relations. To preserve its power, the dominant Soviet Union exports fuel and raw materials while the subordinate East European states export machinery and equipment. Although this pattern bears little similarity to West European colonialism, it is certainly attuned to the new international tendency which features the shifting of power into the hands of those states possessing mineral or raw material wealth.

The Soviet Union uses trade for its own power advantage by keeping competition out of the fairly secure and closed CMEA system and it is also acting as a middleman in the flow of Middle East oil to Eastern Europe. Control of trade, particularly oil supplies, is a crucial component of the Soviet Union's hegemony. It may be instructive to point out that the only East European states self-sufficient in oil resources are Albania and Rumania; separatist actions in these states have probably taught the Soviets a valuable lesson.

In its attempt to use the economic instruments of aid and trade in pursuit of foreign-policy goals, the Soviet Union is faced with certain quandaries. Aid to a state may strengthen bilateral political ties, but at the same time antagonize a neighboring state which has also been friendly toward the USSR. For example, aid to either India or Pakistan is bound to have repercussions.[19] The influence derived from aid and trade can also be rather subliminal, as the overthrow of Sukarno in 1965 has shown, and constitute a waste of economic resources. It can also lead to political ties that are cordial but not quite influential enough at a time of crisis—witness Guinea's refusal to grant landing rights to Soviet planes bound for Cuba during the 1962 missile crisis. Extensive aid to China did not prevent a hostile schism and retaliatory withholding of aid and commodities, especially oil, only helped make China more self-sufficient and economically stronger. In the case of Yugoslavia, the application of extensive economic pressure after the rift of 1948 proved counterproductive, as Yugoslavia developed closer ties with the Western states. Thus, the political weaponry of aid and trade is conspicuously double-edged.

2/The Political Economy of Soviet Foreign Trade

The close connection between foreign trade and political interest is explicitly acknowledged by Soviet spokesmen; Nikita Khrushchev's comment that "we value trade least for economic reasons and most for political purposes" has become a classic.[1] Anastas Mikoyan made a similar observation when he said, "Just as economics are inseparable from politics, so the USSR's foreign political relations are inseparable from its foreign trade relations." Academician Abram Frumkin has written, "In the first place, a definite link between foreign trade and foreign policy exists not only in the Soviet Union but in the capitalist countries as well. What matters is the nature of the policy which the trade of a given country is called upon to promote."[2] Soviet commentators rarely provide details on the political uses of Soviet foreign trade, particularly in regard to oil, but when viewing international relations, they point out that "oil is the commodity most linked to politics."[3]

The linkage between foreign trade and foreign policy is not limited to Soviet actions vis-à-vis the West or the Third World but also extends to ties between the USSR and other communist-ruled states. The use of foreign trade as a political weapon has been obvious in the cases of China, Yugoslavia, Albania, and Cuba; one Soviet writer directly relates trade to politics when he asserts: "Underlying the growing economic strength of the socialist countries is fraternal mutual assistance. Consequently, any major economic or trade arrangement between them is of political importance also. Whether it is a matter of coordination and specialization or of increasing deliveries of raw materials in short supply, not only the economic effect is kept in mind but also the influence exerted on the socio-economic position of one or another country."[4]

Foreign trade gained added significance as an instrument of foreign policy with the advent of the Soviet Union's "peaceful coexistence" campaign in the mid-fifties; trade was able to serve as a nonmilitary means of struggle with the Western states. Economic competition largely replaced nuclear posturing, and in 1957 Khrushchev challenged the West: "We declare war on you— excuse me for using such an expression—in the peaceful field of trade."[5] The Soviets consistently emphasize economic competition, but at the same time they favor trade with the Western states as a means of furthering peaceful relations. Frumkin maintains that politics influences trade but that trade also influences politics since trade promotes peace.[6] A similar observation was made long ago by James Schlesinger, who later became the U.S. Secretary of Defense, when he asserted, "Aside from the economic advantages which trade conveys, the expansion of trade under present conditions is useful in that by creating interdependence it provides a medium for non-military deterrence."[7]

Although trade may serve the USSR's political purposes, it also serves basic economic needs and usually is justifiable in economic terms. There need be no contradiction between political and economic benefit, and the Soviet Minister of Foreign Trade, Nikolai Patolichev, is correct when he avers, "A certain element of politics does come into Soviet foreign trade. This does not mean, however, as is often alleged by the Western press, that the commercial activities of Soviet foreign trade organizations are entirely subordinated to political interests."[8] Some American political analysts contend that foreign trade is determined by a combination of domestic economic interests and foreign political interests while Milton Kovner, an American government specialist on Soviet foreign trade, writes: "Soviet foreign trade is as much a political as it is an economic phenomenon. It is essentially a question of political economy, a curious amalgam of politico-economic considerations which makes impossible any meaningful distinction between the two."[9]

Kovner maintains that certain decisions, such as the initiation of an economic offensive in the Third World during the mid-fifties, are based on political expediency but that the economic arrangements needed to implement such policy decisions are themselves based on sound economic reasoning.[10] However, Edward Taborsky argues that many Soviet economic activities in the Third World do not appear to make economic sense. This political science professor specializing in communist affairs asserts that the Soviet Union is deprived of a project whenever it agrees to build facilities in a Third World state and that the provision of loans or credits deprives the USSR of needed capital. He also points out that some loans and credits are never repaid and that when they are, the USSR often receives products that are not economically essential.[11]

It is basically true that Soviet trade relations with Third World states are more often based on political considerations than are their relations with Western states.[12] This may possibly be detrimental to Soviet economic interests and therefore tends to support the Taborsky viewpoint, but the difference between Kovner and Taborsky is really one of nuance rather than substance. It may certainly be true that political motivation leads the Soviets into some economic agreements which are not particularly beneficial to the USSR when analyzed in purely economic terms but, at the same time, the projects themselves may be developed efficiently and rationally so as to provide great economic benefit for the host states.

The Soviet Union, which maintains purely commercial relations with many states, does not always attempt to use trade for political purposes. Like any other trading power, it seeks markets for its products, strives to secure commodities to serve its domestic economic needs, and seeks to build up its reserve of hard currency. In many cases, it sets political reservations aside, as with Franco's Spain or with the pre-1974 military government of Greece. Overpoliticization of trade can be counterproductive, since other states may shy away from trade relations and as was indicated before a Congressional hearing in 1962, "Sustained trade is only entered into repeatedly if the trader brings himself under the discipline of the world market. Thus if the USSR does that, there will be a retreat from the autarchic and purely politically dominated trade of the past decades. If, on the other hand, Soviet trade continues to be primarily politically motivated, then it will be sporadic, and I would think much smaller in absolute volume." [13] This point is certainly valid if one is considering Soviet export policies, but it has lesser relevance to import policies. The USSR can continue to curry favor by buying products for which there is little world demand, or products which are being boycotted by traditional purchasers, without jeopardizing overall trade volume.

The Politicization of Trade and Aid

The Soviet Union has many means at its disposal to utilize economic pressure for political ends. Among them, as cited by political scientist Robert Freedman, are the withdrawal of advisers and technicians, the expulsion of students and trainees from the USSR, the expulsion of a state from CMEA, the cancellation of grants and loans, and the withholding of raw materials or spare parts. The manipulation of trade is also a major political instrument; the USSR can delay trade negotiations, refuse certain products as imports despite purchase agreements, reduce the quantity of an export particularly desired by another state, refuse to sell a product, delay specific exports, and reject a trade agreement already negotiated. [14]

Frequently, the Soviet Union decides to purchase products for political reasons and the timing is geared for maximum political impact. When Cuban-American relations deteriorated in 1960 following Castro's rise to power, the Soviets stepped in with a large sugar purchase deal. When many Western states were boycotting Iranian products during the oil nationalization dispute of 1951–54, the Soviets increased their barter trade with Iran. [15] When Egyptian–American relations were set back in 1955 and there was a reduction in Western purchases of Egyptian cotton, the Soviets (sometimes acting through Czechoslovakia) bought a large amount of Egyptian cotton, and by 1958 65 percent of the Egyptian crop was going to communist-ruled states.[16]

The Soviets also buy surplus commodities for which there is temporarily little world demand. Some of these commodities may be useful in terms of Soviet economic needs but they are often of marginal value or of no value at all. Included in this category would be Soviet purchases of Burmese rice in 1954–55, Greek tobacco in 1957, Algerian wine in 1968, Ghanaian cocoa during the Nkrumah period, Sudanese cotton, Colombian coffee, Icelandic fish, Cypriot citrus fruits, Ceylonese rubber, Brazilian coffee, and Uruguayan meat, wool, and hides.[17] In the cases of Greece, Iceland, Brazil, and Uruguay, the Soviets provided oil in return. Since the Soviets themselves become burdened with a surplus commodity, they often reexport it, generally at a lower price than they paid for it. This tends to place the Soviets in competition with the original supplier of the product and has the effect of bringing down world prices.[18] Among the products reexported by the USSR have been Burmese rice, Egyptian cotton, Turkish tobacco, Chinese tin, Indonesian rubber, Argentinian hides, and Brazilian cocoa.[19] Soviet motivation for the original purchase of surplus commodities is usually political, but sometimes the Soviets accept these commodities in exchange for their own exports, since no other products may be available for the purpose of repayment.

Foreign aid must be placed alongside trade in the Soviet political arsenal for, as George Liska indicates, aid is an important "instrument" of foreign policy and it becomes a "weapon" during "conditions of pervasive conflict."[20] Aid may be used to counter the influence of a rival state, it may be traded for rights to military bases, and it may be manipulated to affect the composition of a government. It may also be used to help keep a government in power or help consolidate the position of a new one. The withdrawal of aid is an obvious sign of political disapproval.[21] From the Soviet perspective, aid can further the growth of state corporations in Third World states, thus contributing to socialist development, and it can also help states become economically less dependent on the major Western powers.[22]

Soviet foreign aid usually forges close economic links between the recipient states and the USSR, since there is frequently a stipulation that credits must be spent on Soviet products. Furthermore, the aid is generally repaid with products rather than currency. Aid is thus repayable in trade and aid fosters the development of trade.[23] It is true that the maintenance of a large aid program deprives the Soviet Union and other communist-ruled states of additional projects and technicians, and it is also true that Soviet credit terms, frequently 2.5 to 3 percent, are more generous than those offered by the West.[24] However, it has been convincingly argued that the actual cost of Soviet foreign aid is quite low. Third World states, on the average, pay 15 to 25 percent more for Soviet products than do Western states, and the differential is even greater on the sale of machinery and heavy equipment. Therefore, when credits must be spent on Soviet commodities, the Soviets cut their costs because of the inflated prices attached to their goods.[25]

Soviet aid is often timed to take advantage of a Western setback, such as Iraq's withdrawal from the Baghdad Pact, or of Western policy decisions which irk Third World states, such as American withdrawal from the Aswan dam project in Egypt and American refusal to aid in the construction of the Bokaro steel mill in India. The Soviets have also used aid to strengthen the hand of "progressive" political leaders such as Nkrumah of Ghana, Touré of Guinea, Keita of Mali, Allende of Chile and Sukarno of Indonesia, and as was clearly shown in the latter two cases, aid was greatly reduced once the leaders fell from power.[26]

Among the actions that show a clear linkage between international economic policies and political interest are the Soviet Union's increase in sugar shipments to Iran in 1951 after Britain terminated her deliveries of sugar in protest over Iran's oil nationalization policies.[27] The Soviets also reduced trade with West Germany in 1964–65 because of a dispute over the status of West Berlin, and in 1958 they offered oil to Brazil in exchange for coffee, possibly in order to improve the chances of leftist candidates in an upcoming election.[28] In early 1971, when France and Algeria were engaged in a dispute over Algeria's nationalization of French oil properties, France retaliated by refusing to buy Algerian wine. On March 5, 1971, Radio Moscow then reported that the USSR had agreed to buy five million hectoliters of Algerian wine in 1971 and 35 million hectoliters over a seven-year period because Western states broke an import agreement "as a means of blackmail and pressure."[29] Politics was also partly responsible for the decline in Soviet–Ghanaian trade in 1966, following the overthrow of Nkrumah (see chapter 11).

An interesting case of trade politics took place in 1954 when Vladimir Petrov, the Third Secretary of the Soviet embassy in Australia, received political asylum and revealed information about Soviet espionage operations. The USSR broke diplomatic relations with Australia on April 23, 1954, not to renew them until March 17, 1958, and stopped buying Australian wool.[30] Instead, it purchased wool from South Africa, but in a peculiar twist it terminated such imports in 1960 in protest against that state's racial policies.[31]

In 1958, the Soviet Union and Finland had trade disagreements over Finland's economic ties with the West and her favorable trade balance with the USSR. The Soviets sought to ensure the formation of a Finnish Cabinet that would carry out economic policies more attuned to Soviet interests; they threatened not to renew their trade agreement with Finland, held up a loan, boycotted many Finnish exports, and withdrew their ambassador. They also stopped delivering oil to Finland after November 28. Finland succumbed to these pressures, and in December invested a Cabinet which was more pro-Soviet in its composition.[32]

The Soviet Union broke trade relations with Iceland in 1948 because it showed interest in joining NATO, which was then being organized, but by 1952 Iceland became involved in a fishing dispute with Britain and the Soviets soon reappeared on the scene.[33] Britain was unwilling to purchase Icelandic fish because Iceland had extended her territorial waters in March 1952, affecting British fishing interests, and the Soviets therefore renewed trade relations with Iceland in 1953 and began exchanging oil for fish. By 1957, the Soviet Union was Iceland's biggest trading partner, and by 1958 communist-ruled states were purchasing 35 percent of Iceland's total exports and 55 percent of her salt herring exports.[34] Iceland also received almost all of its oil products from the USSR.[35] On September 1, 1958, Iceland further extended her territorial waters and again became embroiled in a fishing dispute with Britain. Britain repeated its past policy of boycotting Icelandic fish and the USSR once more increased its purchases.[36] Soviet partisanship in favor of Iceland throughout the mid-fifties was aimed partially at securing the removal of American NATO forces from Icelandic bases, but the Soviet effort met with failure. Peter Wiles believes that the Soviet invasion of Hungary in 1956 influenced Iceland to maintain its strong NATO ties.[37]

Western Economic Tactics

Soviet use of trade politics has its counterpart in the economic tactics used by the Western states against the Soviet Union in order to register their political disapproval of the Soviet system. Among these tactics is the political use by the United States of "most favored nation" (MFN) trading status. The Soviet Union was granted MFN status during the period 1935–51 but that status was taken away during the Korean conflict. Then, in 1972–74, the United States was willing to reextend MFN status but, yielding to the pressure of the Jackson amendment, the administration asked for some Soviet concessions on the right of Jewish emigration. The U.S. also linked MFN with politics when it withdrew the staus from Cuba in 1962 and when it granted it to Yugoslavia and Poland as a sign of encouragement for their independence of action within the communist-ruled world.[38]

The United States has consistently embargoed the export of "strategic" commodities to the USSR, interpreting "strategic" rather broadly, and it has boycotted many Soviet products or has placed import quotas on them. The United States has pressured other Western powers to restrict their imports of Soviet oil and has encouraged some Third World states to refuse Soviet oil offers. Western oil companies have boycotted firms that distribute Soviet oil products and have blacklisted shipping companies willing to charter tankers to the USSR. The major attempts to blacklist shipping companies, in July 1960 and April 1962, were both highly unsuccessful, as the Soviets found many companies willing to do business with them.[39] American business firms have stayed away from Soviet trade fairs and have utilized other tactics in their anti-Soviet struggle.[40]

When Western states and corporations resort to denial and restriction in regard to Soviet trade, they are obviously rendering an anti-communist political protest and are attempting to hinder the development of certain sectors of the Soviet economy; additionally, they are striving to avoid any strategic dependence on Soviet products. Another major motivation is the protection of domestic industries and of overseas markets, therefore abetting Western business interests. In the sense that large corporations can serve as agents of a state's foreign policy, state power objectives are furthered as well.

The Soviet Union is extremely anxious to have the Western states eliminate their discriminatory trade practices, since the USSR wants to improve its technology by expanding trade. Soviet spokesmen frequently call for an end to strategic embargoes, import quotas, and credit restrictions; they claim that MFN is a "fundamental principle of international trade." [41] While many Western states see political détente, rather than a relaxation of anti-Soviet economic measures, as the key step toward increased East–West trade, many Western states have actually moved away from their negative trade policies of the past and have substituted positive incentives. Instead of stultifying trade with the USSR, they have gradually increased the volume and have attempted to derive political advantage from trade offers rather than trade denial.[42] Such a policy is also being applied to other communist-ruled states, as the West has realized that trade may encourage polycentric tendencies in the communist world.

The Soviet Foreign Trade Apparatus

The Soviet Union has an economic advantage over many Western states, since its industrial technology has developed somewhat later, permitting the USSR to cut costs by avoiding mistakes previously made by the West. Also, since all its basic economic sectors are state-owned, it has greater standardization of production and does not have to be overly concerned about rent or interest.[43] However, one of the most significant keys to Soviet strength is the nationalization of foreign trade, since foreign commerce and state strategic interests are brought into harmony and there is little of the dualism often prevalent in capitalist states. Since state interests supersede the profit motive, an element of politics is introduced alongside the mechanisms of the international economic order.[44]

The USSR nationalized foreign trade in April 1918, and political considerations are taken into account whenever decisions are made regarding trading partners, commodities, volume, and timing. State control of trade is essential in a centralized, socialist economy since imports and exports must be coordinated with the domestic economic plan.[45] Economist Nicolas Spulber relates the need to coordinate imports with internal planning to the protection of the domestic market from outside competition, and he maintains that a state monopoly over foreign trade is primarily a defensive political tool.[46]

All of the Soviet Union's trade is administered by the Ministry of Foreign Trade, and as indicated in a Soviet legal journal: "The most important questions of state direction of foreign trade are resolved by the USSR Council of Ministers." [47] These include what may be imported or exported, the source or destination, the quantity, the currency, and the transportation arrangements. Many of the details are handled by the State Planning Committee of the USSR Council of Ministers.

Although foreign trade is completely controlled by the state, the state itself does not engage in foreign trade. Transactions are carried out by independent trading corporations which receive state authorization to trade in specific commodities. As explained by Soviet legalists, Soviet foreign trade corporations are independent entities and the state bears no legal responsibility for their actions. It is asserted that "bourgeois courts" fail to understand their status and that "to confuse the relationships in which the state participates as the bearer of authority (relationships of international public law externally and relationships of administrative law within the country) and the civil-law relationships of business organizations can lead to many unfortunate consequences, including those of a political nature." [48] One such "unfortunate consequence" occurred in 1956 when the Soviet government withdrew the license of Soiuznefteeksport, the oil trading corporation, to trade with Israel. Soiuznefteeksport, organized in 1931, is licensed to handle the import and export of oil and oil products and it has a trading monopoly in these areas.[49] This was a political reprisal for Israel's participation in the Anglo-French attack on Egypt. Israel protested Soiuznefteeksport's breach of its trade agreement and a legal controversy over the status of Soviet foreign trade corporations ensued (see chapter 7). The legal independence of these corporations is not reflected in the realm of politics, as they are clearly subordinate to state dictates.

A good summary of the status of Soviet foreign trade corporations is offered by the United Nations Economic Commission for Europe: "The foreign trade corporations are independent juridical entities enjoying legal and contractual capacity. They are the exclusive property of the State, but this does not affect their legal autonomy. They own and dispose of property and they have the right to contract obligations. Within the limits laid down in their statutes, corporations are empowered to conclude trade deals with foreign organizations." [50] There are approximately fifty foreign trade corporations in the USSR and they account for 100 percent of imports and 95 percent of exports, some exports being handled directly by the Ministry of Foreign Trade.[51]

Soviet Trading Techniques

The Soviet Union's imports and exports are geared to fulfill the domestic economic plan, so its international commercial transactions should be analyzed as part of a broader economic framework rather than individually. Considerations of the cost of a transaction should also be subordinated to the question of its usefulness to the plan, as the USSR sometimes seeks to correct errors in economic planning by securing commodities vital to the plan or by disposing of surplus goods.[52] Soviet commentator B. Pichugin notes that there is also a political aspect to economic planning: "Planned foreign trade, since it is based on state monopoly, allows the USSR to make the most expedient and purposeful use of its export resources and satisfy its import requirements in accordance with its economic and political tasks at every stage of its development." [53]

Soviet economic planning usually emphasizes imports, as exports serve as the means of securing needed imports. Exports can earn the hard currency necessary to finance imports and, in barter agreements, can be exchanged for desired commodities. The Soviets explicitly recognize the preeminence of imports. The Minister of Foreign Trade, Nikolai Patolichev, has written: "Export is planned on the basis of the payments that have to be made for imported goods, and the necessity of creating currency reserves." [54] Prime Minister Alexei Kosygin also touched upon this theme in his April 5, 1966, address on the 1966–70 Five-Year Plan. Kosygin maintained that increased exports were a major goal of the Five-Year Plan since the USSR had to secure foreign currency.[55] This currency was to be used for the purchase of industrial equipment and sophisticated technology from the Western states for, as one Soviet journal acknowledged, "the growth of trade [with the West] helps the Soviet Union solve a number of important economic problems." [56]

The Soviet Union (as well as the East European states) does not have large reserves of hard currency and therefore prefers "compensatory trading" in which the expenditure of foreign exchange is unnecessary.[57] Switch trading accomplishes this goal as the Soviets can sell to state A a commodity that has traditionally been supplied by state B. At the same time state B sells the same quantity to state C, which has in the past received its supply from the USSR. Such trading often results in reduced transportation costs and has been practiced by the Soviets in conjunction with Middle East oil producers, particularly after the Suez Canal closure of 1967. The Soviets also practice transit trade, but the major forms of "compensatory trading" in which they are engaged are barter trade and balanced bilateral trade. Barter trade is the exchange of goods without any transfer of currency. Balanced bilateral trade is the exchange of goods within a given time period, with the overall volume of such trade being roughly predetermined. Payment is basically a matter of bookkeeping rather than currency transfer since each trading partner is exporting goods with a similar monetary value.

The Soviets have traditionally favored barter deals because they can acquire commodities without the expenditure of hard currency; this policy strongly appeals to many Third World states, since they too are short of hard currency and wish to receive barter goods. The Soviets therefore have a trade advantage over most Western states, since the latter usually insist on hard currency in exchange for their commodities.[58] Balanced bilateral trade also appeals to many Third World states, again because of the nonessentiality of hard currency.

The planned economy of the USSR cannot rely on free unregulated trade, since timing, volume, and the composition of imports and exports must be stipulated in advance if the plan is to be fulfilled. Many world markets are chaotic, but bilateralism contributes a degree of security and is well-suited to a planned economy.[59] James Schlesinger also points out that bilateral trade can be an effective political weapon since negotiations are required to determine the volume of trade.[60]

Bilateral trade binds trading partners to the Soviet Union, because their export earnings must be spent on Soviet products; they are therefore unable to seek out the lowest market price or the highest-quality item.[61] It has also been argued that bilateral trade is actually carried out at the level of the weaker trading partner since the stronger economy must accept commodities it does not particularly need just because no other products are available.[62] Even Soviet economic analysts have come to recognize this problem, with G. Mazanov claiming that creditors import goods they don't need just to balance trade. He also complains that creditors cannot use their export earnings to buy goods from third parties or to pay debts to other states and he asserts that there is little inducement to deliver goods promptly since money never changes hands but is only transferred in the books. Mazanov is referring specifically to Soviet trade with other members of CMEA and he calls for the replacement of bilateral trade with multilateral trade. He recommends yearly multilateral balancing of deliveries and payments among CMEA members and claims that increased trade will ensue once there is no longer a need to balance each trade transaction.[63]

Soviet trade emphasizes long-term agreements so that the economic plan will not be disrupted. Among CMEA members agreements are usually for five years, which coincides with the five-year economic plans and also fixes commodity prices for the length of the trade agreement.[64] When analyzing the issue of prices in Soviet foreign trade, one must realize that the price of an exported item often bears little resemblance to the domestic price of the same product as the Soviet economy is largely insulated from world market prices.[65] Low export prices on some Soviet products do not imply that the USSR is suffering an economic loss; overall trade profits and losses are crucial, not the profitability of one particular deal. Furthermore, prices can be raised on domestic products or on imports to subsidize any financial loss on exports.[66] The insularity of the Soviet economic system is further illustrated by the fact that other states may not interfere with the protected price structure of the USSR by offering commodities for sale at prices lower than those authorized by the Soviet government, whereas the USSR may intervene in the economies of other states with the entreaty of reduced prices (see chapter 5). Price cutting on oil was used as a political instrument to enter West European markets, causing dissension within NATO and lessening the predominance of the Western oil cartel, and offers of low-priced Soviet oil to Cuba and India helped make these Third World states less dependent on Western sources of supply.

The Soviets emphasize their reliability as a trading partner, generally with justification, since the Soviet Union would find difficulty maintaining its role as a trading power if its customers were not satisfied.[67] However, the Soviets obviously did not prove their reliability in the cases of China, Yugoslavia, and Albania, and in the area of oil they have occasionally proved unreliable for an assortment of reasons (see chapter 9). Sometimes technical problems are the root cause; production or pipelines may prove insufficient or weather conditions may hamper transportation. It is possible that such problems led to the shortfall to Greece in 1961.[68] A tanker shortage can also cause problems (as with India in 1969) or the closure of the Suez Canal can disrupt deliveries (as with Ceylon in 1969).[69] The tanker shortage and the Canal closure really amounted to the same thing, since Soviet tankers had to travel around Africa, which necessitated the use of additional tankers in order to deliver the same quantity of oil.

Price considerations may also lead to a shortfall in oil deliveries and probably underlay the West German situation in late 1973. The USSR was trying to pressure the Germans into paying considerably more for their oil under an agreement which was then being negotiated; at the same time, the oil diverted from West Germany was sold to other West European states at a more favorable price.[70] Politics can also be a major factor in causing reductions in oil deliveries (as with China in the early sixties) or in causing curtailment of deliveries (as with Israel in 1956).

Soviet Commercial Relations

The Soviet Union engaged in extensive trade during the twenties to help rebuild after a destructive civil war, and it also encouraged peaceful relations with the Western capitalist states to avoid international conflict during the rebuilding period. Foreign trade was instrumental during the years of the New Economic Policy (1921–28), when the Soviets secured Western products and investments, and it also contributed to the successes of the First Five-Year Plan (1928–32). The Soviets were aiming at economic self-sufficiency, largely because they did not want to risk dependence on outside sources of supply; but they needed Western technology and industrial goods to achieve this self-sufficiency. Once the USSR was on a more solid economic footing, Stalin adhered to a fairly autarkic development program, but his successors quickly moved to expand the Soviet Union's foreign trade.

One of the reasons for increased trade was that the USSR wanted to acquire more Western technology, and this could be accomplished by selling exports for hard currency. Furthermore, the USSR had been the victim of Western economic warfare and therefore desired to break out of its isolation into the world trading markets. The Soviets also realized that it was cheaper to import certain products than to produce them domestically, and international trade came to assume a larger role in the furtherance of political goals. As explained by a Soviet economist, the rapid growth of the Soviet economy did not contribute to a return to autarky but actually increased the prospects for trade.[71]

Soviet trade is equal to about 5 percent of GNP and approximately one-fifth of this trade is with Western states.[72] The USSR had an overall favorable trade balance every year during the period 1965–73, except for 1972, but had a trade deficit with the Western states every year but 1967.[73] The Soviet Union buys technology and machinery from the Western states but the inferior quality of Soviet products in these areas prevents the West from accepting them in return. The Soviets therefore sell the West raw materials and fuels and export their own technology and machinery to Third World states in return for raw materials and some fuels. The Soviets are thus at the hub of a triangular trade relationship.[74] More than two-thirds of Soviet exports to the West are raw materials and fuels but less than 4 percent is machinery. Soviet imports from the West are comprised of more than one-third each of machinery and manufactured goods.[75] Soviet earnings from oil and oil products are second to those derived from the export of machinery but are the largest in trade with the West.

The USSR sells to the Third World products the Western states would probably not buy anyway, and it receives needed products from the Third World without the expenditure of hard currency. The Third World states also have products most Western states do not want (oil is an obvious exception) and they can sell them only in payment for the industrial goods they buy. There is a somewhat natural economic fit between the USSR and many Third World states, and the Soviets claim that they carefully choose exports that will not compete with local Third World industries. They also point out that Third World states can export their traditional products to the USSR in exchange for Soviet machinery and manufactured goods without having to spend hard currency or gold.[76]

The economic fit between the USSR and many Third World states is still holding in place, but in regard to oil-exporting states it is beginning to come unglued. There have always been the problems of the USSR buying commodities it did not really need and of Third World complaints about the quality of Soviet merchandise; now additional factors have come to the fore. Third World oil-producing states are now in a position to make barter deals for superior Western machinery and technology and some of the states exporting oil to the USSR are now demanding hard currency. The Soviets are in turn requesting hard currency rather than products for their arms deliveries to Middle East states. There is also some concern about the Soviets' middleman role for small quantities of Middle East oil, as well as some apprehension that Soviet oil and gas exports are moving into traditional markets of the Middle East exporting states.

The Soviet Union's main trading partners are other CMEA states, as economic leverage is used to further political power, but the Soviets also benefit by receiving essential manufactured goods and by having a secure market for their own exports. The Soviets recognize the great political and economic importance of continued trade relations with the CMEA states and are willing to provide huge quantities of oil and gas to maintain their integral ties. The other CMEA states derive certain advantages as well, for they have long-term markets, generally stable prices, and do not have to spend hard currency. They also have a reliable source of fuel and raw materials, receive patents and designs free of charge from the USSR, and are able to dispose of manufactured goods the West would probably not buy. Furthermore, their close economic ties with the USSR help them secure favorable terms of trade from Western states anxious to break into socialist markets, for if they were to have a significantly larger volume of trade with the West, terms would most likely be less generous.[77]

CMEA states are subjected to some price descrimination by the Soviet Union and the Soviets receive goods frequently substandard by Western terms; but the overall economic interaction is largely beneficial to both parties.[78] Describing the position of the CMEA states, one specialist on East European economics asserts:

> It is likely that, by market economy standards, most CMEA countries' terms of trade with the USSR have been worse than those with the West (although less so in recent years as compared with the 1950s). . . . Socialist countries take a broader view of foreign trade—they are guided more by macrosocial long-run cost-benefit considerations than by immediate commercial terms of trade. Apart from ideological and political hostility, such realities as instability and discrimination in Western markets are significant factors to be taken into account.[79]

Looking at Soviet trade relations with Western capitalist states, the USSR desires technology, machinery, and capital and offers fuel and raw materials in return. The decision to seek trade collaboration with the West to modernize the Soviet economy was largely the work of Khrushchev. The Seven-Year Plan of 1959–65 stressed technological improvements through international commerce.[80] However, the worsening of Soviet–Chinese relations, particularly the battle at Ussuri in March 1969, led the USSR to stress Siberian economic development and to strengthen trade ties with the West even further. A few days after the March 1969 clash, Brezhnev attended a Warsaw Pact meeting in Budapest; the final communiqué showed moderation toward the West. At the same time, the Soviets frequently cited Lenin to justify close economic relations with the West.[81]

Trade with the West gives the USSR a technological short cut, since time and money are not spent on experimentation and development. Readymade technologies can be bought and the prototypes acquired can serve as models for future expansion and replacement.[82] Additionally, the purchase of sophisticated technology and machinery from the West permits the USSR to avoid domestic economic reforms that would be necessary were these items to be produced at home.[83] Wolfgang Leonhard, an astute observer of Soviet politics, argues that since early 1969, the USSR has been moderate toward the West but rigid in terms of domestic political and economic controls. He avers that the Soviet opening to the West was an alternative to domestic economic reforms, as the latter could lead to a weakening of political controls. Leonhard maintains that Soviet trade ties with the West are also aimed at neutralizing Western Europe and at counteracting the potential threat from China.[84]

Soviet spokesmen claim that because of scientific and technological advances international economic cooperation is now essential; they therefore advocate an "international division of labor," since even the largest states cannot be self-sufficient in research and production.[85] One writer asserts: "In this age of explosive scientific and technical development, no country, however high its scientific and technical level, can progress without participating in international cooperation." [86] Seeking to assure the West that such participation does not benefit only the Soviet Union, it is maintained that the West can receive Soviet natural resources in return for technology and it is pointed out that Western states are suffering from an energy shortage.[87] Soviet remarks generally indicate that it is the USSR which is to be the recipient of scientific and technical assistance but the Soviets dangle the enticing carrot of energy supplies as an inducement to the West.

The Soviets see their trade with the West as a source of contradictions between capitalist states, and believe these contradictions should be utilized to the Soviets' advantage. There is friction between those states which favor trade with the USSR and those which do not, and there is also American pressure against some of the former states.[88] The Soviets also argue that they can manage without trade relations with the West but, that because trade improves political relations and the prospects for peace, it should be encouraged.[89]

In order to allay American fears, the Soviets stress the long-term nature of the trade relationship they desire with the United

States and indicate that "the idea of adapting to various short-term considerations is alien to our state." They also attack those who see the extension of Soviet-American trade ties as a "gift" to the USSR and warn that no political concessions will be granted in return for American trade participation.[90] As indicated by American Sovietologist Mose Harvey, the Soviets believe that American businessmen are very influential in the formulation of American foreign policy, and they therefore want to gain the support of these businessmen in order to lobby on behalf of increased Soviet-American trade.[91] The Soviets feel that the United States will engage in expanded trade because profits are to be derived, the USSR is a reliable trading partner, past American embargoes and boycotts against the U.S.S.R. have resulted in failure, and other Western states have extensive trade relations with the USSR so the U.S. does not want to be shoved aside by her Western allies.[92]

Economic cooperation with the West offers many benefits to the USSR and, as itemized by one Soviet journalist, they include greater exploitation of Soviet raw material wealth, improved technology, increased hard currency earnings, more rapid development of Siberia, the North, and the Far East, and faster growth of Soviet agriculture. This journalist also reassures his Soviet readers by indicating that projects in which the West participates are all owned by the Soviet state and that the socialist basis of the economy is in no way affected.[93] Prime Minister Kosygin has also stressed the importance to the USSR of East–West economic cooperation and he has called for expanded trade with capitalist states. Kosygin asserted in 1966: "In the past five years, foreign trade helped us solve a number of important economic problems. But we are still not making the most of the opportunities that the development of foreign economic relations offers us." [94]

Foreign trade is clearly functional to the Soviet economy, but as trade expands so do the opportunities to use it as a political instrument of foreign policy.

3/ Domestic Foundations of Soviet Energy Policies

The Soviet Union, a net exporter of oil and natural gas, is among the world leaders in the size of its reserves of these crucial fuel resources. It is the only major industrial power that can boast of energy self-sufficiency and ranks first in the world as a producer of crude oil. *The Economist* notes that the USSR, with only 7 percent of the world's population, consumes 18 percent of the world's energy and possesses 55 percent of all known energy resources.[1] Despite such a favorable position, Soviet domestic energy programs have been beset by numerous problems in recent years and yearly production of oil and natural gas has often not lived up to expectations. With domestic consumption generally rising faster than production, some important constraints must naturally be placed on Soviet export policies.

Historically, Russia has been a major oil power. At the turn of the century it produced more than half of the world's oil. In 1902 it was surpassed by the United States, but it continued to be the chief oil exporter since domestic demand was rather low.[2] Russian oil exports were generally controlled by foreign firms; before the Bolshevik revolution, 60 percent of Russia's oil was owned by outside interests.[3]

Following the Bolshevik seizure of power, the Council of People's Commissars of the Russian Soviet Federated Socialist Republic nationalized the oil industry within its borders (June 20, 1918) and the Council of People's Commissars of Azerbaijan, the main oil producing area, followed suit. However, the Civil War led to efforts by the interventionists to seize the oil fields in Azerbaijan, and production was severely disrupted. Effective nationalization did not actually take place until May 28, 1920.[4] Western oil companies were unwilling to accept Soviet nationalization of their holdings. They lobbied against recognition of the Bolshevik government, subsidized anticommunist activities in Georgia, and tried to organize other creditors who were attempting to collect compensation from the Soviet government. They were also instrumental in setting up a boycott of Soviet oil, although it was unsuccessful owing to a world-wide oil shortage. Nevertheless, there was still a reduction in Soviet oil exports as a result of increased domestic consumption.[5]

Western intervention during the Civil War was partially aimed at regaining control over the nationalized oil properties; the Anglo-French assault in the south had this as an objective. There was also considerable turmoil around Baku in Azerbaijan, with both the British and the Turks playing a role, and the British also set fire to the oil fields at Groznyi in the Caucasus.[6]

Oil production and exports stagnated during the Civil War, but production and exports increased significantly as the Soviet Union began to rebuild during the twenties. Although the USSR fell to second place among oil exporters, after Venezuela, oil was still of great importance and constituted 13.5 percent of Soviet exports in 1928.[7] The Soviets used profits from the sale of oil to help finance the First Five-Year Plan (1928–32) and some of these profits were reinvested in the oil industry. The Soviet Union supplied 14.3 percent of the oil imported by Western states during the period 1926–35, 19 percent during 1930–33.[8] From 1926 to 1935, Italy received 48 percent of its oil from the USSR (68 percent in 1931), Spain 39 percent, Belgium 27 percent, Germany 17 percent, Denmark 17 percent, Sweden 15 percent, France 18 percent and Britain 7 percent.[9] Turkey also imported large quantities of oil from the Soviet Union.[10] Soviet oil was in great demand among states trading with the USSR because its quality conformed to international standards, whereas the quality of other Soviet products was suspect.

Beginning in 1933, Soviet oil exports began to decline, partially because production failures held back the growth rate, and also as a result of domestic need for fuel to further the industrialization process. By the late thirties, the USSR was a net importer of energy, as it began to stockpile in anticipation of a war.[11] Following the Nazi–Soviet pact of 1939, the Soviets assisted their German ally by delivering sixteen million barrels of oil between January 1940 and June 1941. According to a memorandum from Hitler to Stalin (May 23, 1941), the Germans also hoped to join in the exploitation of Soviet oil fields, but Stalin rejected this suggestion. The Germans were anxious to secure access to more oil and when they launched their attack on the Soviet Union in June 1941, the Caucasian oil fields were a prime objective.[12]

At the time of the German invasion, 80 percent of Soviet oil production was concentrated in the Caucasus. Although the Germans were unable to capture the key oil fields at Groznyi and Baku, the war led to decreased production, and geopolitical considerations were instrumental in the Soviet decision to emphasize production in the less vulnerable Volga-Ural region. Both distribution and Soviet strategic defense were thereby facilitated.[13]

During the war, Soviet oil production was severely disrupted by equipment and labor shortages and by the German occupation; the United States delivered oil to the USSR from 1941 to 1947.[14] Soviet refinery capacity was also increased thanks to U.S. assistance under the Lend Lease program.[15] In addition, the Soviets received oil from Iran.[16] When the war ended, the Soviet Union incorporated the oil-producing areas of southern Sakhalin (acquired from Japan) and Droholycz-Borislaw (acquired from Poland) and gained control over many oil fields in Rumania, Hungary, and Austria. All of these areas taken collectively contributed five million extra tons per year for Soviet use.[17]

Rebuilding the Soviet oil industry proved to be time-consuming; the USSR remained a net importer of oil until 1954. In 1950, oil accounted for 1.5 percent of Soviet exports and 5.5 percent of imports; by 1954, the figures were 4.2 percent and 3.3 percent; by 1957, they were 9.1 percent and 3.0 percent.[18] The so-called Soviet "oil offensive," with an emphasis on exports, gathered momentum in the mid-fifties and the USSR has continued to be a net exporter of oil ever since.

Oil and Gas Resources

It is difficult to estimate reserves of oil and natural gas owing to differing standards such as "proven," "probable," and "estimated" as well as to subjective application of these standards, but no matter what criteria are used the Soviet Union is clearly well-endowed. It ranks second in the world, after Saudi Arabia, in the size of its oil reserves and ranks first in gas reserves. "Giant" oil fields, each with reserves of at least 500 million barrels, constitute less than 5 percent of the world's oil fields but produce 85 percent of the oil, and the USSR has more giants than any state outside of the Middle East.[19] As indicated in the *International Economic Report of the President* (February 1974), the USSR has 6.3 percent of the world's "proven" oil reserves, as compared to 6.1 percent for the United States, but R. M. Burrell attributes 12 percent of "discovered" reserves to the USSR.[20] According to the United Nations Statistical Office, "estimated" reserves stand at 8.2 billion metric tons while the Economist Intelligence Unit cites 5.6 billion tons of "proven" reserves.[21] A pair of American energy

Table 3.1. Soviet Crude Oil Production, 1918–1954 (in millions of metric tons)

1918	4.146	1931	22.392	1944	18.300
1919	4.448	1932	21.414	1945	19.400
1920	3.851	1933	21.489	1946	21.746
1921	3.781	1934	24.218	1947	26.022
1922	4.658	1935	25.240	1948	29.249
1923	5.277	1936	27.427	1949	33.444
1924	6.064	1937	28.501	1950	37.878
1925	7.061	1938	30.186	1951	42.253
1926	8.318	1939	30.259	1952	47.311
1927	10.285	1940	31.121	1953	52.777
1928	11.625	1941	33.000	1954	59.281
1929	13.684	1942	22.000		
1930	18.451	1943	18.000		

SOURCES: United Nations, Statistical Office, *Statistical Yearbook 1948* (Lake Success: United Nations, 1949), p. 135; United Nations, Statistical Office, *Statistical Yearbook 1953* (New York: United Nations, 1953), p. 111; United Nations, Statistical Office, *Statistical Yearbook 1961* (New York: United Nations, 1961), p. 139; Robert Ebel, *Communist Trade in Oil and Gas* (New York: Praeger, 1970), pp. 20, 28, and 31.

specialists presents the astounding statistic of 400 billion barrels, which is roughly equivalent to 55 billion metric tons.[22] The Soviets are not willing to supply any precise statistics on oil reserves.

In the area of natural gas, Soviet gas minister A. K. Kortunov claimed in 1970 that the USSR had 35 percent of the world's gas reserves and *The Economist's* figure of 33 percent in "proven" reserves, cited in 1974, is fairly similar.[23] The Soviet Union also has the world's largest individual gas field, Urengoi in the northern part of Western Siberia. Kortunov placed Soviet "proven" re-

Table 3.2. Soviet Oil Exports, 1921–1940, Including Crude Oil and Oil Products (in millions of metric tons)

1921	0.031	1928	2.787	1935	3.368
1922	0.170	1929	3.625	1936	2.665
1923	0.383	1930	4.712	1937	1.930
1924	0.815	1931	5.224	1938	1.400
1925	1.505	1932	6.011	1939	0.500
1926	1.685	1933	4.894	1940	0.900
1927	2.097	1934	4.315		

SOURCE: *Vneshniaia torgovlia SSSR: statisticheskii sbornik* (Foreign Trade of the USSR: Statistical Compendium 1918–1966) *1918–1966* (Moscow: Izdatel'stvo "Mezhdunarodnye otnosheniia," 1967), pp. 18–19.

Table 3.3. Soviet Imports and Exports of Oil, 1946–1954 (in thousands of metric tons)

	Imports		Exports	
	crude oil	oil products	crude oil	oil products
1946	9.1	900.0	0.0	500.0
1947	74.9	500.0	0.0	800.0
1948	74.0	800.0	0.0	700.0
1949	131.9	1700.0	100.0	800.0
1950	336.6	2300.0	300.0	800.0
1951	59.9	2600.0	900.0	1600.0
1952	197.6	3600.0	1300.0	1800.0
1953	104.6	4600.0	1500.0	2700.0
1954	193.0	3800.0	2100.0	4400.0

SOURCE: *Vneshniaia torgovlia SSSR: statisticheskii sbornik, 1918–1966* (Moscow: Izdatel'stvo "Mezhdunarodnye otnosheniia," 1967), pp. 80–81 and 102–5.

serves as of the end of 1967 at 325 trillion cubic feet (9.2 trillion cubic meters) and "estimated" reserves at 2471 trillion cubic feet (70 trillion cubic meters) while the United Nations Statistical Office indicated over 18.6 trillion cubic meters in "estimated" reserves as of the end of 1972.[24] The Soviet Union is obviously rich in oil and natural gas resources and its energy problems are not due to any quantitative deprivation.

An analysis of Soviet economic geography, petroleum geology, or petroleum engineering is beyond the scope of this study but the reader is advised to look at the works of Robert Campbell, Theodore Shabad, Violet Conolly, and Robert Ebel, as well as relevant journals such as *Oil and Gas Journal* and *The Petroleum Economist.*[25] However, some comments on the location of major oil and gas fields is probably in order, since such information is vital to an understanding of Soviet domestic energy policies as well as to an analysis of fuel export planning.

As has been indicated previously, before the Second World War 80 percent of Soviet oil production was concentrated in the Caucasus, especially around Baku, but the German attack spurred an effort to develop alternative oil fields in the Volga-Ural region or "Second Baku."[26] This region came to be the focus of the Soviet oil industry and was responsible for 80 percent of output during the fifties. Statistics from as late as 1967 show the Volga-Ural region contributing 68 percent of production, as compared with Western Siberia's 2 percent, Sakhalin's 1 percent, Azerbaijan's 8 percent and the Northern Caucasus' 9 percent.[27] However, since many wells in this region did not keep up their production as long as expected and marginal wells stayed in production, there was a slowdown in the growth rate.[28] The average yearly growth rate fell from 15.9 percent during 1955–60 to 10.4 percent in 1961–65, and to 7.7 percent in 1966–70. Today, Volga-Ural is becoming less important; the center of oil activities is shifting to Western Siberia.[29] Soviet oil minister Valentin Shashin complains that only 11 of 26 oil-producing areas are providing growth, and this tends to support the view of a respected Western oil analyst who predicts that the combined oil production of the European USSR and the Caucasus will decline from 281 million

Baltic
Sea

Ventspils
Klaipeda

U.

Ur

TIUME
REGIO
WESTERN

S.

SIBERIA

VOLGA – URAL

REGION

Odessa

Black

Sea

Feodosiia

Novorossisk

Tuapse

CAUCASUS
Batumi

Azerbaidjan

Caspian

Sea

Mangyshlak
Peninsula

CENTRAL

ASIA

0   500   1000 KM

IRAN

MAP 1. THE SOVIET UNION

tons in 1970 to 265 million in 1980.[30] He sees Central Asian and Far Eastern production rising from 41 to 75 million tons and Western Siberian production increasing astronomically from 31 to between 260 and 300 million tons.[31]

The first major oil field in Western Siberia was discovered in the Tiumen region in 1961 and production began in 1965. The Tiumen region may contain one-third of all Soviet oil reserves and the huge Samotlor oil field has contributed significantly to Soviet production. In 1970, 9 percent of Soviet production was already coming from Western Siberia and both the Ninth Five-Year Plan, approved at the 24th Congress of the Communist Party of the Soviet Union in 1971, and the Tenth, approved at the 25th Congress in 1976, emphasized the exploitation of Western Siberian oil.[32] In 1973, Western Siberia accounted for 87 million tons of oil, and in 1974 production was 116 million tons, which represented approximately 25 percent of the national total. In 1975, production was 148 million tons, thereby constituting about 30 percent of the national total.[33]

Western Siberian production is expected to contribute most of the Soviet Union's oil growth during the seventies, and in December 1973 the Volga-Ural region was supplanted as the leading oil-producer.[34] There are various estimates of Western Siberian production as of 1980, ranging from 230 to 300 million tons, and it is evident that this region will come to produce more than half of the Soviet Union's oil in the 1980s.[35]

In addition to the major oil fields in Western Siberia, Volga-Ural and the Caucasus, the USSR is rapidly developing the Mangyshlak Peninsula of the Kazakh Republic, situated on the eastern shore of the Caspian Sea. Oil is also found in Turkmen, Uzbek, Kirghiz, Tadzhik, Byelorussia, and Sakhalin. Offshore oil under the Caspian Sea, off Sakhalin, and in the Arctic and Baltic areas is also due for more extensive exploitation.

The Soviet Union has the longest coastline in the world, and it naturally is endeavoring to expand offshore oil production; but huge sections of this coastline are in the Arctic area, where oil exploitation presents problems of cost and technology.[36] Anxious to protect its offshore mineral and fuel resources, the USSR seeks a definition of the outer limits of the continental shelf that would be favorable to its interests, but it also desires cooperation with neighboring states. Agreements have been reached with the United States, Japan, Finland, and Poland.[37] Since the USSR has a shallow coastal margin, it advocates that states should own mineral resources out to a depth of 500 meters or a distance of 100 miles, whichever is greater, but at the 1974 "Law of the Sea Conference," the USSR supported the proposal of many Third World states which called for an offshore economic zone extending 200 miles.[38] The Soviet position is complicated by the fact that the USSR would like to be highly protectionist regarding mineral and fuel rights, but as a major fishing power it wants fewer restrictions in the area of fishing rights.

Oil and natural gas are often found at the same locations, with the possibility of striking gas increasing with depth; it is therefore not surprising that the largest gas reserves in the world are in Western Siberia, especially in the Tiumen region.[39] This region is fast becoming the prime producer of natural gas and may account for as much as 50 percent of production by 1980.[40] Other major gas-producing areas are in Uzbek, Turkmen, and the southern Urals, with the Yakutsk region of Eastern Siberia having great potential.

The Energy Usage Pattern

Soviet energy usage has gradually shifted from an emphasis on coal to accelerated utilization of oil and natural gas. As of 1950, 66.1 percent of Soviet energy was derived from coal, 17.4 percent from oil, and 2.3 percent from natural gas; but the reliance on coal then began to decrease—a trend which has continued ever since.[41] Economic geographer Theodore Shabad maintains that the Soviets had stressed coal as an energy source largely for strategic reasons. Since oil installations in the Caucasus were vulnerable to ground attack, there was a desire to decentralize fuel resources, but the advent of the missile age lessened the importance of decentralization, facilitating the shift toward oil.[42] The growth of the oil industry in the well-protected Volga-Ural region was also a probable factor. Economist Robert Campbell, evaluating comparative transportation costs, points out that the use of coal had been more economical than the use of oil or gas. The latter two energy sources were generally located far from the major areas of consumption but the development of pipelines made their usage more economical by the 1950s.[43] During the late 1950s oil was clearly on the upswing, and it constituted 26.1 percent of energy usage by 1960.[44] Natural-gas consumption was also rising, but the Soviets were a little slow in deriving maximum use out of their gas reserves, partially because they lacked knowledge about natural gas.[45] Between 1959 and 1965, 45 billion cubic meters of natural gas were wasted through flaring.[46]

Statistics on Soviet energy consumption unmistakably show the rising importance of oil and natural gas and the decline, percentage-wise, in the usage of coal. However, there appears to be great disagreement over the precise statistics. According to a 1971 study undertaken by the U.S. Department of the Interior, Bureau of Mines, oil accounted for 29.5 percent of Soviet energy usage in 1965; Shabad attributes 35.9 percent to oil, 15.6 percent to natural gas, and 42.9 percent to coal in that year. Soviet energy specialist Leonid Tomashpol'skii cites 33.2 percent, 14.6 percent, and 40.2 percent as the correct figures. Further confusion is caused by John Hardt's figures of 39.6 percent for oil and 18.6 percent for gas as of 1970, Hardt and Holliday's figures of 33 percent for oil, 22 percent for gas and 44 percent for coal as of 1971, and A. F. G. Scanlan's figures of 32.7 percent for oil and 19.8 percent for gas as of 1972. A Soviet figure for oil cited in 1974 is 44 percent. Looking toward the future, Scanlan sees 37.9 percent of energy usage coming from oil in 1980 and 28.4 percent from gas, and the study conducted by the U.S. Department of the Interior, Bureau of Mines, cites 36.5 percent as an estimate on oil. Tomashpol'skii sees greater reliance on atomic energy, predicting it will constitute 4.4 percent of usage in 1980 and 19.6 percent in 2000, and his figures for 1980 show 30.8 percent for oil, 27.8 percent for gas and 29 percent for coal.[47]

Soviet energy usage roughly conforms to the world pattern, which shows oil and gas contributing 61 percent of world energy consumption. However, the USSR has consistently lagged behind the United States in converting its energy system to an oil and gas base; the United States now derives 78 percent of its consumption from oil and gas.[48] Although the late Soviet shift to oil and gas was often perceived by outsiders as an economic drawback, the energy crisis has changed the perspective of many observers. Soviet conservation of oil and natural gas resources and heavy utilization of coal may, in retrospect, have been extremely wise.

As the Soviet Union modernizes, it is almost inevitable that per capita energy consumption will rise, and this is borne out by United Nations statistics. In 1960, the USSR used 2847 kilograms per capita and this figure rose to 4436 in 1970.[49] In 1972, per capita consumption ws 4767, which was greater than Western Europe's 4000 but far behind the United States' 11,611.[50] Until the late 1960s, the Soviets managed to hold down energy consumption by strictly limiting the number of motor vehicles; but vehicle production then increased dramatically and now far exceeds the increase in oil production.[51] The Ninth Five-Year Plan (1971–75) called for a 270 percent increase in car production, but only a 40 percent increase in oil production as the USSR was scheduled to produce one million cars per year by 1975.[52] The use of fuel by airlines and trains is also expected to rise, so the Soviets will surely be faced with a burgeoning energy demand. They are therefore experimenting with propane-powered vehicles, which save on fuel and are not highly pollutant, and they are beginning to mass-produce cars which run on liquefied natural gas.[53]

Soviet oil consumption can be determined by subtracting net exports from production and by assuming that no significant amounts are being stockpiled.[54] Analyzing in this manner, it becomes evident that in recent years consumption has been increasing faster than production and is generally advancing at a rate of approximately 8 percent per year. It seems likely, as predicted by The Economist, that this 8 percent yearly increase will be maintained at least until 1980; with a modest growth rate in production and large export commitments to the East European states, the USSR is therefore faced with an oil squeeze that can seriously affect oil export policies.[55]

Oil and Gas Production

Soviet oil production continues to increase but the rate of growth is clearly slowing down. During the five-year period 1959–63, production increased by 82 percent but the increase dropped to 50 percent during 1964–68 and 36 percent during 1969–73. The yearly increases for 1971, 1972, 1973, 1974 and 1975 were 5.7 percent, 5.9 percent, 6.6 percent, 9.0 percent and 7.0 percent, but growth during the latter half of the decade is expected to be no more than 5 percent per year.[56]

The Soviets realized that oil production would present some growth problems, and in the late sixties they scaled down their output projections for 1975.[57] However, 1970 proved to a banner year for the oil industry, with production surpassing the plan and growth advancing by 7.5 percent, so by 1971, sights were set higher than originally anticipated for the 1971–75 oil plan. The boom in Western Siberian oil production also helped to encourage the Soviets' optimism. Therefore, the Ninth Five-Year Plan called for an average yearly growth rate of 7.1 percent and production for 1975 was estimated at 480–500 million tons.[58] This goal was reached; production was 491 million tons.

Production at Baku and Groznyi did not live up to expectations, and the oilfield equipment plan was underfulfilled by 15.4 percent, thus producing a huge oil production shortfall in 1972. This was the largest shortfall since the Second World War and it forced the Soviets to lower their oil target for 1973.[59] In December 1972, the original estimate of 429 million tons was revised downward to 424 million tons but production for 1973 was only 421 million tons.[60] The 1974 target was supposed to be 461 million tons, but in December 1973 economic planning director Nikolai Baibakov indicated that production would increase by only 7 percent during 1959–63, to 88 percent during 1964–68, and to 39 percent during 1969–73 and this is understandable since gas production began increasing rapidly from a rather small original base. However, the yearly growth rates for 1971, 1972, and 1973 were 7.3 percent, 4 percent, and 6.8 percent, as compared with the Ninth Five-Year Plan's projection of almost 10 percent annual growth. The shortfall in 1972 was the largest since the Second

Table 3.5. Soviet Natural Gas Production, 1940–1973 (in billions of cubic meters)

1940	3.219	1957	18.583	1966	142.962
1945	3.278	1958	28.085	1967	157.445
1950	5.761	1959	35.391	1968	169.101
1951	6.252	1960	45.303	1969	181.121
1952	——	1961	58.981	1970	197.945
1953	6.384	1962	73.525	1971	212.398
1954	7.512	1963	89.832	1972	221.000
1955	8.981	1964	108.566	1973	236.000
1956	12.067	1965	127.666		

SOURCES: United Nations, Statistical Office, *Statistical Yearbook 1966* (New York: United Nations, 1967), p. 200; United Nations, Statistical Office, *World Energy Supplies, 1961–1970,* Statistical Papers, series J, no. 15 (New York: United Nations, 1972), p. 254; United Nations, Statistical Office, *Statistical Yearbook 1970* (New York: United Nations, 1971), p. 211; United Nations, Statistical Office, *Statistical Yearbook 1972* (New York: United Nations, 1973), p. 183; Robert Ebel, *Communist Trade in Oil and Gas* (New York: Praeger, 1970), p. 128; J. Richard Lee, "The Soviet Petroleum Industry: Promise and Problems," in *Soviet Economic Prospects for the Seventies* (Washington: U.S. Government Printing Office, 1973), p. 284; "Rethinking Soviet Policies," *The Petroleum Economist* 41, no. 3 (March 1974): 100; Iu. Kazmin, "Neft' i gaz Severa," (Oil and Gas of the North) *Pravda,* February 8, 1974, p. 2.

World War, which caused a downward revision in the estimated production for 1973 from 250 billion cubic meters to 238 billion cubic meters; actual production turned out to be only 236 billion cubic meters.[63] Kosygin indicated that planned production for 1974 was 256 billion cubic meters, but a sizable increase of 10.6 percent brought production to 261 billion cubic meters.[64] Production for 1975 amounted to 289 billion cubic meters, an increase of 11 percent, so the 300–320 billion cubic meter goal of the Ninth Five-Year Plan was far from realized.[65]

cent in 1974, therefore bringing it to slightly over 450 mi
Baibakov did not sound very optimistic when he asserte
1974 plan "insures in the main" the delivery of fuel
statement on January 7, 1974, helped confirm a 1974 e
450 million tons, as did remarks made by Kosygin in Ji
minister Shashin, writing in April, cited a figure of 458
Moscow had even gone as high as 460.[62] Soviet oil
boomed during the last quarter of the year and actual
was 459 million tons.

The natural gas industry has also been problem
Soviets in recent years. The rate of growth declined fr

Table 3.4. Soviet Crude Oil Production, 1955–1973[a] (in mil
tons)

1955	70.793	1962	186.244	1968
1956	83.806	1963	206.069	1969
1957	98.346	1964	223.603	1970
1958	113.216	1965	242.888	1971
1959	129.557	1966	265.125	1972
1960	147.859	1967	288.068	1973
1961	166.068			

SOURCES: United Nations, Statistical Office, *Statistical Ye*
York: United Nations, 1961), p. 139; United Nations, Statistical
Yearbook 1966 (New York: United Nations, 1967), p. 202; Unite
cal Office, *World Energy Supplies, 1961–1970,* Statistical Pape
(New York: United Nations, 1972), p. 112; United Nations, *S*
1970 (New York: United Nations, 1971), p. 213; United Nation:
Statistical Yearbook 1972 (New York: United Nations, 1973), pp
Lee, "The Soviet Petroleum Industry: Promise and Problems,"
Prospects for the Seventies (Washington: U.S. Government Pr
p. 284; "Russian Oil: Where Will They Get It From?," *The Econ*
(December 1, 1973); 40; *Soviet Oil to 1980,* QER Special,
(London: The Economist Intelligence Unit), p. 18; Iu. Kazmin,
(Oil and Gas of the North) *Pravda,* February 8, 1974, p. 2; "S
tion Below Target," *The Petroleum Economist* 41, no. 2 (Feb

[a] There were discrepancies between the various statistical
offered by *Soviet Oil to 1980* and *Petroleum Press Service* b
than those of the United Nations, those of Lee being conside
of *The Economist* being tremendously lower. Statistical disp
differences in accounting for waste and spillage. This table
United Nations statistics.

The Pervasive Energy Problems

There are numerous causes for the difficulties confronting the Soviet oil and gas industries, among them problems of geography, transportation, pipeline construction, equipment shortages, cost, labor, and planning. The Soviet Union's major concentrations of oil and gas resources do not correspond to the centers of population.[66] Sheer distance contributes to increased transportation costs and, since much of the fuel is in northern Siberia, problems are caused by the cold climate, the difficulty in attracting workers, and the lack of adequate housing or food-distribution facilities which are necessary to support drilling operations in such remote areas.[67] The Soviets must also develop specialized oilfield technology for dealing with the frigid climate.

Soviet oil and gas exports are also affected by the geographical conditions, as the exploitation of these resources generally occurs far distant from the point of export. Oil exports leave from the Black Sea ports of Odessa, Batumi, Novorossisk, Feodosiia, and Tuapse, the Baltic ports of Ventspils and Klaipeda, and via pipelines to Eastern Europe; the bulk of the oil must therefore be transported thousands of miles from Western Siberia and the Volga-Ural region. Furthermore, the low level of economic development in Eastern Siberia and the Far East mitigate against exporting large quantities of oil from Pacific ports, even though the USSR has export commitments to Japan and other Asian states. As of now, the majority of the oil shipped to Japan leaves from Black Sea ports. Natural gas requires lengthy pipelines for transportation from Western Siberia to both Eastern and Western Europe and the Soviets even find it more efficient to import gas from Iran to serve the Caucasus than to transport Western Siberian gas to the Caucasus. Despite its oil fields, the Caucasus has depleted its reserves of natural gas and is an energy-deficient area.[68]

About 40 percent of Soviet oil is still transported by railroad, which is three times more expensive than pipeline transport.[69] The Soviets are anxious to increase the use of pipelines, but they have a pipe shortage, as well as insufficient capital.[70] They therefore seek pipe from West European states and Japan in return for Soviet oil and gas exports and they hope to acquire both pipe and credits from the United States and Japan to assist in Siberian pipeline development. The Ninth Five-Year Plan made oil and gas pipeline construction a top priority item, calling for an additional 60,000 kilometers during 1971–75, and, to lend further emphasis, a new Ministry of Oil and Gas Industry Construction, headed by Alexei Kortunov, was created in 1972 to spur pipeline construction. However, problems persist and there are delays in building the oil pipeline from Tiumen in Western Siberia to Eastern Europe.[71] It should also be pointed out that Soviet oil refineries were at one time located near the oil fields but are now generally built in the consuming areas, necessitating longer pipelines from the source of exploitation to the refineries.[72]

Production costs must be weighed against another consideration when analyzing Soviet exports: it might be cheaper to produce the imported commodity rather than to trade for it. High production costs for an exported item may be worthwhile if the savings on importing, rather than producing, the commodity received in return are considerable. Costs are of more direct concern in regard to commodities produced for domestic consumption, since no exchange of goods is involved and it is obviously beneficial to reduce costs as much as possible. Since the overwhelming majority of the oil and natural gas produced in the USSR is consumed domestically, cost considerations do present a problem for the Soviets.

The average yield of oil wells in Azerbaijan has been decreasing, as is true for the Volga-Ural region as well. Therefore more capital investment is necessary to produce the same quantity of oil, and so the relatively new and underexploited Western Siberian oil fields look rather promising.[73] There, oil can be removed from the ground at a rather low cost per unit because the wells have not been drilled before and oil is close to the surface. But appearances can be deceiving; although the oil can be obtained more easily than in Azerbaijan or Volga-Ural, the total cost of extracting and transporting the oil is actually higher per unit.[74] The primary reason is that both equipment and oil must be transported over such great distances. One Soviet fuel specialist, T. Khachaturov, even suggests that the use of Siberian oil should be limited owing to cost. He advocates increased use of coal in the European regions of the USSR.[75]

Difficulty with costs is often due to geographical factors. For example, the Soviet Far East must import oil from elsewhere in the USSR but its geographical isolation makes this task rather costly. Oil from Western Siberia could be sent eastward by pipeline as far as Irkutsk and then proceed by train to the Far East, but this turns out to be too expensive. Instead, oil from Sakhalin is sent by underwater pipeline to be refined on the mainland at Komsomolsk. From there, it is distributed throughout the Far East. This is cheaper than pumping oil eastward to Irkutsk but is still extremely costly, since operational costs of the Sakhalin oil industry are higher than the national average and worker productivity is lower.[76] In addition, the Soviets ship oil to the Far East all the way from the Black Sea.

Oil is produced more cheaply in the Soviet Union than in the United States but less cheaply than in the Middle East.[77] One way to reduce the cost of production is to import advanced Western oil technology, and the Soviets are doing so. They are negotiating with both the United States and Japan for credits to cover the purchase of equipment and pipe and they are buying it from other Western states as well. To defray costs, the Soviets are also encouraging East European states to join them by investing in oil and gas production within the USSR. These states are to receive increased deliveries of oil and gas in return.[78]

Attracting labor to the harsh climate of Western Siberia is a major problem for the Soviets. Labor turnover is notably high, especially in the Tiumen region. Students are therefore being recruited to work in the Tiumen oil industry and prisoners "on parole" are also being used as laborers. The latter receive a salary, may bring their families, and have their sentences reduced by one year for each year of work.[79]

Planning failures, waste, and inefficiency also plague the Soviet fuel industries. One of the main bottlenecks results from poor coordination of equipment deliveries with transportation. Equipment often piles up where it isn't needed while production in other areas is held back as a result of equipment shortages. On a national scale, the production of oilfield equipment frequently falls behind the production of oil, necessitating increased imports of the former. In both 1970 and 1971, the USSR doubled its import of oilfield equipment.[80] Planning problems also arise with attempts to extend transportation and pipelines to keep up with expected increases in fuel production, and it has always been difficult to expand refinery capacity as quickly as crude oil production. Sometimes, mismanagement leads to wasted time, as was indicated in a *Pravda* article which attacked the oil industry in the Komi autonomous republic for excessive delay between exploration and production for commercial use.[81]

Looking at the Soviet Union's plethora of oil and gas problems, one could wonder whether the Soviets are in fact faced with an "energy crisis." Speaking in Minsk in November 1973, Prime Minister Kosygin described the fuel situation as "tense" and he called for economizing and a search for new sources of energy. He indicated that neither oil nor gas production would reach its target in 1973 and that the same could easily happen in 1974. The Soviet press began to call for the conservation of fuel and new government committees were formed to study Soviet energy usage. In June 1974, Kosygin returned to the theme of energy problems and indicated his concern about rising consumption, but he declared that socialist economies do not experience major upheavals like the capitalist "energy crisis." [82]

Because of its ample reserves of oil, gas, coal, and hydroelectric power—and the great potential for atomic power—the Soviet Union has no shortage of energy. However, shortages of technology and capital and a need to reduce production and transportation costs do create major, although not insurmountable, problems and do not constitute a crisis in the Western sense. The Soviets clearly have sufficient resources and, as net exporters of energy, if faced with energy deficiencies they can cut back on exports.

Various energy difficulties in recent years have led the USSR to energy conservation and to the import of Western capital and technology. Small quantities of oil have also been imported since the late sixties, even though the USSR remains a net exporter of oil. The Soviet Union was actually a net importer of gas, despite its huge reserves, until very recently. Problems in increasing oil production have placed constraints on exports, particularly to Western Europe and Third World states, and deliveries to these areas probably will not increase substantially during the remainder of the decade. However, the Soviets do not really have an "energy crisis" but rather policy and organizational dilemmas over choosing the most efficient methods of fuel development. Production, consumption, transportation, equipment, imports, and exports must be made to fit together in a coherent pattern, and in contrast to Western Europe, Japan, and to some extent the United States, the Soviet Union is not worrying about a scarcity of fuel or a possible cutoff of its major sources of supply.

4 / Development of the Soviet Oil Trade

The Soviet Union is both an exporter and an importer of oil. Substantial exports during the late fifties and early sixties frightened the Western states, as they perceived both a political and economic challenge in the so-called Soviet "oil offensive." At that time, Soviet imports were negligible, but by the late sixties and early seventies exports to noncommunist states leveled off and the USSR became an importer of increasing quantities of Middle East and North African oil. Paradoxically, the Soviet threat to Western interests has now shifted from that of an exporter seeking additional markets to that of an importer, middleman, and cheerleader acting to restrict the flow of Arab oil to Western states and to reduce Western control over production in the Middle East. This can be facilitated by the USSR's purchasing some of the oil itself or encouraging the embargoes and nationalization policies of the oil-producing states. The source of Western oil supplies has evolved as the prime target, rather than the markets in which the Western oil companies make their sales. According to a British specialist on Soviet policies in the Middle East, the Soviets used to criticize Western oil interests as "nonparticipating onlookers" but now they are themselves customers for Middle East oil and are deeply involved in the oil politics of the area.[1]

Political and Economic Rationales

Since production far exceeds consumption, the Soviet Union is naturally one of the world's largest exporters—but why does it import oil as well? [2] If it encounters oil shortages, why doesn't it just

decrease exports? The answer to these questions is multi
and must take economic, political, and geographical factor
account. First of all, it is usually cheaper to import Middle East or
North African oil than to produce the same amount in Western
Siberia and then transport it to the populated western areas of the
USSR. The Soviets also resell some of this imported oil at a profit
and an additional advantage is the conservation of Soviet oil resources. Politically, the Soviets can assist the nationalization policies of oil-producing states by providing a market for oil from nationalized fields and their role as middleman for some Middle
East oil gives them greater opportunities for the use of oil as a
lever of power. Geographically, the Soviets are able to save on
transportation costs by reselling Middle East oil to some of their
European and Asian customers rather than exporting oil directly,
and switch deals involving Middle East oil have the same result.
The key geographical advantage may lie in the future, if the
United States and Japan become purchasers of Siberian oil. The
Soviets could then import oil from the Middle East and North
Africa and export Siberian oil via the Pacific, cutting down on
lengthy and expensive transportation routes from Siberia to the
western part of the Soviet Union. Overriding all of these considerations, however, is the fact that when faced with a need to augment their oil supply, the Soviets prefer to increase imports rather
than reduce exports since the latter play a pivotal role, both economically and politically, in Soviet foreign trade.

Although the figures fluctuate from year to year, oil accounts
for approximately 12 percent of the total value of Soviet exports,
and 30 percent of exports to Western states; the USSR provides
somewhat less than 4 percent of the world's oil imports.[3] There is
great demand for Soviet oil because its quality conforms to international standards and helps states reduce their dependence on
the Western oil monopolies. In addition the Soviets are anxious to
export their surplus production despite Western charges that they
do not retain enough oil at home, thus holding back the standard
of living of the Soviet people.[4] The USSR exports both crude oil
and oil products, but since 1960 crude oil has predominated and
the margin is constantly widening. Profits could probably be in-

creased if a higher percentage of refined oil products were exported, but Soviet production has generally outstripped refinery capacity and most states now prefer to save money by refining the oil themselves.[5]

One of the basic motivations underlying Soviet oil exports is the desire to acquire Western products in return, thus aiding the domestic economy.[6] Soviet oil analyst Boris Rachkov indicates that the USSR is willing to sell oil to states, irrespective of their political or economic systems, because it seeks needed goods, particularly machinery. He writes: "The Soviet Union sells oil in order to buy the goods it needs. . . . On the whole, exports of Soviet oil serve as an important means of paying for Soviet imports."[7]

In exchange for their oil, the Soviets are willing to accept either goods or hard currency. Permitting the oil importers to pay with goods makes Soviet oil very attractive since limited hard currency or gold reserves can be conserved and it gives the Soviets an important selling advantage over the major Western oil companies. These companies are generally under private ownership, and thus rarely able to engage in a barter exchange. They have no use for goods and insist on payment in hard currency, partially in order to acquire the necessary funds for tax and dividends payments. From the Soviet point of view, certain goods are at least as valuable as hard currency. Usually, the USSR is more concerned about the amount of pipe and technology received in return for its oil than it is about the sale price of this oil, and in some cases the export of oil helps further additional oil exports since tankers or pipe are received as payment. The Soviets bartered oil for Japanese tankers in 1958, 1960, and 1961 and for Swedish steel pipe in 1961.[8]

The Soviet Union needs hard currency to purchase much of the technology offered for sale by Western firms and for its recent large grain imports. The Soviets find it beneficial to export oil to the West even if this may cause some domestic shortages, since the acquisition of hard currency is vital and the USSR cannot always sell gold on a consistent basis.[9] In 1972, the Soviets garnered $570 million from oil sales to the West, making oil the largest earner of hard currency, and hard currency income has increased greatly since that time because of high oil prices.[10]

Samuel Nakasian, testifying before a Congressional committee in 1962, said that Soviet oil exports to the "free world" were aimed at "strategic procurement" but he also saw elements of "political penetration." [11] It seems as if Nakasian's reference to "political penetration" was somewhat accurate when applied to Third World states but less appropriate in regard to Western Europe. Soviet oil sales to Western Europe, excluding Finland, have never led to increased leverage in the domestic politics of these states but important political consequences have resulted nevertheless. By supplying oil to NATO states, the USSR is in a position to terminate or slow down deliveries as a method of political pressure, and in the event of East-West military conflict the Soviet oil lever can be a major strategic instrument. Soviet oil sales also serve to divide the Western alliance, with some members opposing large purchases from the USSR and warning against strategic dependence (see chapter 10).

Political motivation generally plays a lesser role in Soviet oil policies toward the West than toward the Third World. There is obvious economic benefit in exporting to the West, since crucial goods and hard currency are received in return, but there is little economic rationale in exporting to Third World states which often repay the USSR with nonessential goods.[12] The introduction of Soviet oil into Cuba and India in 1960 was primarily a political move and *World Petroleum* points out that the low price attached to these sales and the great distances over which the oil had to be transported made economic motivation highly unlikely.[13] By exporting oil to Third World states, the USSR hopes to acquire political leverage, reduce the power of Western oil companies by providing an alternative source of oil, and, indirectly, assist these states in divesting themselves of unwanted Western influence.[14]

Soviet oil is used as an instrument of pressure and control vis-à-vis other communist-ruled states (even though such an approach proved to be unsuccessful in the cases of China and Yugoslavia) and the Soviets are unwilling to relinquish their role as the predominant oil exporter to CMEA states.[15] When faced with numerous policy options regarding their growing oil squeeze, the Soviets have clearly ruled out any cut in their exports to other communist-ruled states (other than Cuba) and the percentage of exports directed toward these states has been rising in recent years. In 1955, at the beginning of the Soviet "oil offensive," communist-ruled states were receiving 58.8 percent of Soviet oil exports, but increased exports to Western and Third World states brought about a decline in the percentage going to communist-ruled states. By 1959, they were receiving a minority of Soviet exports and this situation continued until the late sixties. At that time, the Soviets developed a problem in extending their large oil export program and they opted to continue sizable deliveries to communist-ruled states and to hold back the rate of increase in shipments to Western and Third World states. East European states in particular were asked to secure some of their oil from other sources, but the USSR retained its role as the major supplier. As a result of this decision, the percentage of oil exported to communist-ruled states began to increase, again becoming a majority of total exports, and the trend is continuing. In 1971, 52.7 percent of oil exports went to other communist-ruled states, in 1972 it was 56.3 percent, and in 1973 it was 57.2 percent.[16] It has been estimated that during the period 1971–75, there will be an average yearly increase of 12 percent in Soviet deliveries of crude oil to CMEA members, but only a 4–5 percent increase in deliveries to the West.[17]

Communist-ruled states have traditionally been the major recipients of Soviet oil but, beginning in the late fifties, a number of West European states and Japan began importing large quantities and became prime customers. Italy has been one of the Soviet Union's largest customers since 1959 and Finland and West Germany have consistently bought large supplies. As of 1973, Czechoslovakia, East Germany, and Poland were the largest recipients of Soviet oil, with Finland ranked fourth, Italy sixth, West Germany ninth and France tenth.[18] Finland is politically neutral but has extensive economic ties with its neighbor. It is not surprising that Finland has become the largest noncommunist importer of Soviet oil. Soviet oil sales to Italy, West Germany, and

Japan have been counterweights to the dominant American influence in these states. After suffering defeat in the Second World War, these states were brought, under American tutelage, into the Western camp and the Soviets may have been using economic enticement while attempting to slow their military and economic integration into the Western sphere of influence. In 1960, these three states were the largest noncommunist importers of Soviet oil. The Soviets sought close economic ties with France during the late sixties and early seventies in order to encourage and show support for France's maverick role within the Western alliance.

Since the Soviet Union began substantial oil sales during the late fifties, it has exported crude oil and refined products to at least thirty customers per year; in 1973, forty-one states imported Soviet oil.[19] Communist states have been the largest recipients but considerable quantities have also gone to Western Europe. Third World states, particularly India, Sri Lanka (Ceylon), Egypt, Ghana, and Guinea, have received oil, as have Argentina, Brazil and Uruguay. The Soviets often use oil as a political weapon but they are additionally interested in profitable economic transactions and this leads them into some curious oil export deals. Setting aside any qualms about the domestic political systems of certain states, the USSR consistently sold oil to Franco's Spain and it also supplied Greece during the period of military rule, 1967–74. The Soviets even exported oil products to the United States during the early seventies and increased deliveries in early 1974 when the U.S. was suffering from the effects of the Arab oil embargo (see chapter 8). The Soviet Union has at times exported oil to Arab states which are not oil-rich, such as Morocco, Lebanon, Tunisia, Yemen, Egypt, and Syria, and has also provided oil for Israel.

Most communist-ruled states, including Yugoslavia, are greatly dependent on Soviet oil, but Rumania, China, and Albania are exceptions; this has assisted them in their independent stances toward the USSR. Outside of the communist world, a number of states developed a significant dependence, but the degree of dependence generally declined during the sixties—par-

Table 4.1. Soviet Oil Exports, 1955–1973 (in millions of metric tons)

year	crude oil	oil products	total exports	year	crude oil	oil products	total exports
1955	2.9	5.1	8.0	1965	43.4	21.0	64.4
1956	3.9	6.2	10.1	1966	50.3	23.3	73.6
1957	5.9	7.8	13.7	1967	54.1	24.7	78.8
1958	9.1	9.0	18.1	1968	59.2	27.0	86.2
1959	12.5	12.9	25.4	1969	63.9	26.9	90.8
1960	17.8	15.4	33.2	1970	66.8	29.0	95.8
1961	23.4	17.8	41.2	1971	74.8	30.3	105.1
1962	26.3	19.1	45.4	1972	76.2	30.8	107.0
1963	30.2	21.1	51.3	1973	85.3	33.0	118.3
1964	36.7	19.9	56.6				

SOURCES: *Vneshniaia torgovlia SSSR: statisticheskii sbornik, 1918–1966* (Foreign Trade of the USSR: Statistical Compendium, 1918–1966) (Moscow: Izdatel'stvo "Mezhdunarodnye otnosheniia," 1967), pp. 80–83; *Vneshniaia torgovlia SSSR za 1967 god: statisticheskii obzor* (Foreign Trade of the USSR for 1967: Statistical Abstract) (Moscow: Izdatel'stvo "Mezhdunarodnye otnosheniia," 1968), p. 26; *ibid.* 1969 (1970), p. 25; *ibid.,* 1971 (1972), p. 27; *ibid.,* 1973 (1974), p. 27.

Table 4.2. Soviet Oil Imports, 1955–1973 (in millions of metric tons)

year	crude oil	oil products	total imports	year	crude oil	oil products	total imports
1955	.6	3.8	4.4	1965	.0	1.9	1.9
1956	1.5	3.8	5.3	1966	.0	1.7	1.7
1957	1.3	2.9	4.2	1967	.1	1.4	1.5
1958	1.1	3.2	4.3	1968	.1	1.1	1.2
1959	1.1	3.3	4.4	1969	1.5	1.1	2.6
1960	1.2	3.2	4.4	1970	3.5	1.1	4.6
1961	.9	2.7	3.6	1971	5.1	1.5	6.6
1962	.5	2.3	2.8	1972	7.8	1.3	9.1
1963	.5	2.3	2.8	1973	13.2	1.5	14.7
1964	.0	2.1	2.1				

SOURCES: *Vneshniaia torgovlia SSSR: statisticheskii sbornik, 1918–1966,* pp. 102–5; *Vneshniaia torgovlia SSSR za 1968 god,* pp. 39 and 264; *ibid.,* 1969, p. 38; *ibid.,* 1970, p. 39; *ibid.,* 1971, p. 41; *ibid.,* 1972, p. 41; *ibid.,* 1973, p. 41.

tially as a result of these states' efforts to diversify, and also because Soviet exports to Western Europe leveled off. Between 1961 and 1968, the percentage of Iceland's import dependence fell from 79 to 74, Austria's from 24 to 18, Greece's from 42 to 18, and Italy's from 17 to 12. The percentage of Sweden's and Finland's dependence increased somewhat during this period, the former rising from 18 to 19 and the latter from 70 to 84. In 1972, the percentage of Iceland's dependence was 88, Austria's 12, Greece's 29, Italy's 6, Sweden's 15, and Finland's 66. Yugoslavia was 66 percent dependent.[20]

The "Oil Offensive"

Following the Second World War, the Soviet Union was a net importer of oil, but policy changes began to take shape following the death of Stalin in 1953. Exports increased sizably in 1953, even though the USSR remained a net importer, and in 1954 the USSR became a net exporter and has been one ever since. In 1954, exports were 6.5 million metric tons and imports stood at almost 4 million while in 1955, exports climbed to 8 million metric tons and imports were 4.4 million. The export drive, or "oil offensive," was underway.

The Soviet decision to become a major oil exporter was based on four important considerations, which became linked together in a comprehensive policy. First of all, Soviet oil production, which had been greatly affected by the war, was on the rise; the steady increase that had begun in 1949 (when prewar levels were again reached) became a dramatic one beginning in 1955. Greater production, coupled with lagging refinery capacity, was therefore an important ingredient in the Soviet export formula.[21] At the same time, the Soviets were faced with a shortage of pipe suitable for oil and gasline construction, and one of the aims of the oil export program was to secure pipe in return for oil.[22] Italy was willing to enter into such an arrangement and many other West European states and Japan followed suit.

Also influencing the Soviet decision was Khrushchev's desire to modernize the Soviet economy. One of the means by which he hoped to do so was through the purchase of sophisticated technology from Western states, and for this purpose he needed the hard currency that could be acquired from oil sales. His "peaceful coexistence" campaign coincided with the oil export push and was probably aimed at setting the stage for expanded trade ties with noncommunist states. Finally, the Soviet Union wished to use trade to improve its image, especially in Third World states. Expanded oil exports to Asia and Africa accompanied the new, friendlier political line initiated in 1955. The Soviets began to woo Third World nationalist leaders and deemphasized the prospects for communist-led revolutions in these states. Soviet oil was frequently welcomed since it led to lessened dependence on Western oil companies, reduced oil prices, and increased opportunities to pay for oil with goods rather than hard currency. From the Soviet side, oil sales served as a political instrument aimed at abetting the Third World states' efforts to pull away from the dominant Western influence; in the Third World, the Soviet "oil offensive" was not primarily undertaken to provide economic dividends.

Soviet oil exports increased every year during the period 1955–61 and so did exports to noncommunist states.[23] Oil constituted 10 percent of total Soviet exports (20 percent of exports to Third World states) and by 1962 the USSR was responsible for 2.2 percent of the world's oil exports. The value of Soviet oil shipments to Western states increased from $45.1 million in 1955 to $214 million in 1961, while the figures for the Third World were $36.2 million and $119.8 million.[24] The growth rate of Soviet oil exports slowed during the early sixties. The percentage of production converted into exports remained fairly steady at about 27 percent, but the overall growth rate of both production and exports decreased. This was a rather natural occurrence, since the production and export growth rates for the late fifties had been distorted by the fact that the Soviets had started from such a low original base.

Many Western states, especially the United States, viewed large Soviet oil exports as both an economic and political threat and saw them as an instrument of international communist expansionism. The U.S. Congress sought ways of dealing with the Soviet "oil offensive" and Secretary of the Interior Stewart Udall warned states not to rely on Soviet oil because of military dependence during wartime, contaminants in the oil, which could necessitate equipment changes, and because the low price could not be counted on in the future.[25] The United States pressured states to limit their imports of Soviet oil, to embargo the export of pipe to the USSR, and to ban the leasing of oil tankers to the Soviet Union (see Chapter 10). The Soviets protested that political factors were hindering East–West trade, particularly regarding oil, and at the Second Arab Petroleum Congress, held in Beirut in October 1960, they attempted to reassure the West and Arab exporters about the motivation underlying their oil export drive.[26] Evgenii Gurov, the chairman of Soiuznefteeksport, claimed that the USSR was just trying to return to its traditional, prewar role as an oil exporter and that it was seeking to regain its share of the Western oil market. He indicated that there was no cause for alarm, since only 4 percent of Western oil imports came from the USSR.[27] Gurov hoped to ease Western fears and blunt the U.S.-led counteroffensive.

Despite American efforts, Western states became major purchasers of Soviet oil. In addition to the attractive price, they wanted to diversify their sources of supply since the Suez War of 1956 had demonstrated that Middle East shipments could potentially be disrupted.[28] Italy was especially concerned about the dominant role of the "Seven Sisters," and hoped to use the import of Soviet oil as a weapon against their monopolistic methods, so she took the lead in exchanging pipe for oil, disregarding American objections. Other West European states also exported pipe to the USSR and the rationale for the pipe embargo largely disappeared with the completion of the Druzhba (Friendship) Pipeline from the USSR to four East European states in 1963.

Western states opposed the Soviet oil export program because their security could possibly be jeopardized by Soviet oil leverage; also, they did not want the USSR to take over oil markets from Western companies. The most important reason for the opposition, however, was that the price of oil was being driven downward. The "Seven Sisters" feared that their profits would be reduced and, as indicated in *World Petroleum,* the Soviet threat was really related to prices, not to volume, since the Soviet share of the world market was minimal.[29] The "oil offensive" coincided with increased exports by other producing states and this caused a glut on the world oil market, lowering prices.[30] The Soviets managed to increase their sales, despite the abundance of oil, because of their price-cutting tactics. They generally sold oil at 10–20 percent below world prices and the huge deal with the Italian firm ENI in 1960 was at the rock-bottom sale price of one dollar per barrel f.o.b. at Black Sea ports, which amounted to $1.40 per barrel delivered in Italy.[31]

The Soviets denied that they were flooding the world oil market but they also indicated that they would not help maintain artificially high prices.[32] The addition of considerable quantities of Soviet oil, coupled with low Soviet prices, certainly contributed to the decline in prices, but the Soviet role should not be exaggerated since the world surplus was driving down prices anyway.[33] Roger Hilsman, a former government adviser on international and security affairs, asserts that the Soviets were exporting oil in order to finance necessary imports and that they were not trying to disrupt world markets and Willard Thorp, another contributor to a government study of the Soviet economy, concurs, indicating that market disruption was unintentional and that it hurt Third World oil exporting states more than the West.[34] In response to falling prices, many of the major oil exporters banded together, in August 1960, to form OPEC, the Organization of Petroleum Exporting Countries. The original members of OPEC were Saudi Arabia, Kuwait, Iran, Iraq, and Venezuela.

By contributing to lower prices, the Soviets posed a threat to the high profits of other oil-exporting states and they also moved into some of the latter's traditional markets. At the same time, these states were not permitted to compete within the closed oil markets of the communist-ruled states. Paradoxically, Soviet actions aided West European states because they were able to purchase low-priced Soviet oil but the interests of Third World oil exporters were harmed as a result of reduced world oil prices.[35] The Soviets certainly did not want to incur the wrath of the Third World oil exporters, particularly those in the Middle East, since Soviet policy was to befriend these states and weaken their links with the West. As a consequence, they were careful to point out that world oil consumption was rising and that the larger market allowed room for Soviet exports without affecting the quantity supplied by other exporters. Although Soviet exports were rising, they were not in competition with other exporters, since the Soviet share of the total market remained constant.[36] The Soviets tried to place the blame for reduced oil prices at the door of the Western oil companies charging that they were using lower Soviet prices as a pretext to maximize their profits by paying Arab states less money for their oil. They denied any link between low Soviet prices and the world price of oil.[37] The Arab oil exporters were reluctant to blame the USSR because many of them were recipients of Soviet aid and arms so they tried to raise oil prices by pressuring Western oil companies. Benjamin Shwadran, a specialist on Middle East oil politics, maintains that the Soviets were pushing down world oil prices in order to cause dissension between Arab states and Western oil companies. This certainly occurred, but it seems more probable that the lower prices were more of a side-effect of Soviet export policies than a conscious goal.[38]

Problems and Priorities

Soviet oil exports continued to increase substantially into the mid-sixties; the export growth rates for 1965 and 1966 were a healthy 13.8 percent and 14.3 percent. The Soviets were anxious to secure hard currency to pay for their large wheat imports. They also had extra oil available because they had stopped almost all deliveries to China.[39] However, the oil export program ran into great difficulty beginning in 1967, owing to a domestic production slowdown. The Soviets continued to export about the same percentage of their oil production (26.5 in 1965 and up slightly to 27.1 in 1972) but the slower growth rate in production had to affect total exports as well. During 1955–59, exports increased by 291 percent; in 1960–64 the increase was 123 percent. On the other hand, the growth rate for 1965–69 was only 60 percent and it increased at an even slower pace during the following three years (7.1 percent in 1967, 9.4 percent in 1968, 5.3 percent in 1969, 5.5 percent in 1970, 9.7 percent in 1971, and 1.8 percent in 1972). Since they did not have large quantities of oil available, the Soviets took only minimal advantage of the 1967 Arab oil embargo, and in 1968 oil exports to Western states even fell to 32 million metric tons from a total of 34 million in 1967.[40] In 1972, the increase in exports was so small that net oil exports decreased for the first time since the Second World War, falling from 98.5 million metric tons in 1971 to 97.9 million in 1972.[41] (Net exports are determined by subtracting imports from exports.)

To compound the Soviets' problems, the East European states, whose need for oil had significantly increased, were seeking greater supplies from the USSR. Since the Soviets wanted to preserve their dominant oil role, partially because of its usefulness as a political instrument, they increased their exports to the East European states. Shipments to Western Europe and the Third World leveled off.[42] However, the Soviet oil supply was not sufficient to meet all of Eastern Europe's burgeoning needs, unless exports to Western Europe and the Third World were reduced dramatically. The Soviets, unwilling to take such a drastic step, advised the East European states to supplement their imports with purchases from the Middle East and North Africa. While such a step might possibly have lessened Soviet political leverage, the East European states in fact remained highly dependent on Soviet oil deliveries. In any case, the Soviets were willing to take the risk, because the alternative would have been to relinquish some of the political influence and good will they already gained in many Third World states.

On November 23, 1969, the Deputy Chairman of the Czechoslovak Committee for the Chemical Industry, Vlastimil Plechac, indicated that the Soviet Union had asked its allies to seek Middle East and North African oil. He said that Soviet oil development was shifting more toward Siberia and that the cost of exporting to Eastern Europe was increasing.[43] This was certainly true, but the nonavailability of oil for export was also a major factor. The East European states quickly took up the Soviet cue and began to import considerable quantities of Middle East and North African oil (they had been importing small amounts since 1966).[44] An editorial in *The New York Times* attacked the Soviets for asking Czechoslovakia to look elsewhere for oil while they were arranging to export natural gas to West Germany, via Czechoslovakia.[45] Such an arrangement made economic sense for the Soviets since they preferred to export energy in return for hard currency rather than inferior East European manufactured goods. The editorial portrayed these actions as the application of a "double standard," since the Soviets were acting niggardly in regard to their supposed ally but were planning to sell natural gas in order to acquire hard currency from a Western state. The editorial was making a valid point but was somewhat unfair to the Soviet Union since the Soviets did greatly increase their oil shipments to Eastern Europe, including Czechoslovakia, during the same period when they were asking these states to seek additional sources of supply. Furthermore, Soviet deliveries of natural gas rose substantially at the same time.

The USSR itself became a purchaser of Middle East and North African crude oil. The growth rate of Soviet oil exports was decreasing at the time, and to avoid cutting it even further, the Soviet Union decided to import crude oil. Exports remained at about 27 percent of production, but with the import of crude oil the growth rate of net exports had to decline. In fact, net exports even decreased from 1971 to 1972. After importing no crude oil at all during 1964–66, the Soviets began importing Algerian crude in 1967 and reached a tentative import agreement with Iraq in December, 1967. Eventually, crude oil came from Libya, Syria and Egypt as well and the total import of crude oil rose to 13.2 million metric tons in 1973.

The Soviets had consistently imported small quantities of refined oil products from East European states, and such deliveries continued, but the need to import crude oil represented an important change in Soviet policy and it bore ramifications fundamental to Soviet interests in the Arab world (see chapter 7). Imports of crude oil prior to 1964 were comprised of war reparations from Austria, which ceased in 1964, and small quantities from Albania, which ceased in 1961, and the total yearly volume of crude oil imports was much lower than that received during the period 1969–73.[46]

The Soviet Union activated an oil import program for a variety of reasons. Production growth was slowing down, the consumption rate was increasing, East European states were requiring more Soviet oil, and the USSR was unwilling to reduce its exports to Western Europe and the Third World. In addition, the purchase of oil from Arab states was aimed at encouraging the nationalization of Western oil properties, since the Soviet Union was displaying interest in buying the oil produced from nationalized oil fields. In case of a Western boycott of nationalized oil production, the Arabs could turn to the USSR as a market. Furthermore, the purchase of Arab oil served as a stopgap measure until the Western Siberian oil fields could start producing their expected huge volume.

However, the question of costs was also an important consideration affecting the Soviet decision to import crude oil, as it was cheaper to import from the Middle East and North Africa than to exploit the oil resources of Siberia.[47] In fact, two Western analysts estimated the cost of importing Middle East oil at only half that of using Siberian oil.[48] Even the Soviets explicitly recognized the economic savings, with Boris Rachkov writing: "It would seem that under certain favorable conditions, oil imports may even be profitable for the USSR." Referring to unequal oil resources distribution within Soviet territory, Rachkov stated: "Importation of oil and gas from neighboring or nearby countries will enable the USSR to endure this injustice of nature." [49]

It is highly expensive to transport Siberian oil to the Western part of the USSR and to the East European states, but the Soviets do not have more conveniently located domestic sources of supply, particularly since production at Baku is not expected to increase in the future. It therefore makes economic sense to import Middle East and North African oil for use in the Western areas of the Soviet Union and to export Siberian oil, via the Pacific, to Japan and other customers. Therefore, negotiations with Japan were carried out simultaneously with the oil import drive. At the same time, the Soviets saved on transportation costs by reselling some of their purchased oil to East and West European states; another advantage was that the prices paid for the oil were generally favorable, since the oil was usually repayment for Soviet credits.

The Oil Resurgence

The years 1967–71 were not very good for Soviet oil production and exports, and 1972 was disastrous; but 1973 was an excellent year and the prospects improved for 1974 and the near future. In 1973, the USSR exported 28.1 percent of production, exports rose by 10.6 percent, and net exports increased from 97.9 to 103.6 million metric tons. However, the key events were the Western "energy crisis" and the Arab oil embargo, since they led to an increase in the world price of oil, thereby contributing to added Soviet earnings. The Soviet Union did not have much oil available at the time of the Arab embargo, and its room for maneuver was therefore limited, but it did manage to take advantage of the new price structure, even though its exports did not increase that significantly. Although exports of oil products went up 7 percent in 1973 and those of crude oil rose 12 percent, Soviet income from oil sales increased by 20 percent. Windfall profits thus contributed substantially to the Soviet coffers.[50] After 1973, the Soviet Union benefited enormously from the high world oil prices, which were generally quadruple the pre-embargo level.

The Soviets do not have too much oil to spare, but because of its high price they can greatly increase their hard currency reserves without any increase in exports.[51] Soviet oil sales to the West are based upon the fluctuating world price of oil and sales to Third World states are sometimes tied in as well. The Soviets therefore benefit from the actions of OPEC in raising world prices, even though the USSR is not a member of OPEC and has no direct role in hiking up prices. The Soviet Union wants to take advantage of the present price boom by selling oil to the West at high prices but the price increase directed at Third World states has been somewhat lower, probably for political reasons.[52] As a major oil exporter, the Soviet Union is anxious to keep world prices as high as possible.

Thanks to higher oil prices during the last quarter of 1973, the Soviet trade deficit was converted into a positive balance of trade. In 1972, the Soviets had a deficit of 575 million rubles ($701,500,000 if the ruble exchange rate is calculated at $1.22), and for the first three quarters of 1973 there were deficits of 580, 282 and 127 million rubles but the surplus of 996 million rubles for the last quarter was so great that the Soviets emerged with a yearly positive balance of 261 million rubles ($360,180,000 if the ruble exchange rate is calculated at $1.38).[53]

The Soviet Union did manage to increase exports somewhat to take advantage of the high oil prices during the winter of 1973–74, and it also diverted some supplies to more profitable markets; however, the Soviet profits bonanza was due mainly to prices and not to additional exports. If the Soviets had more oil available, they probably would have sold it; but they had none. Ivan Semichastnov, First Deputy Minister of Foreign Trade, indicated in December 1973 that the USSR would honor its oil commitments to the West during the Arab embargo but he said that there were no plans to increase supplies.[54] Of course, his comments were partially aimed at appeasing the Arab states, but they were basically true nevertheless. In January, the Minister of the Oil Extracting Industry, Valentin Shashin, stated that Soviet oil exports to the West would not rise very much as a result of increased domestic consumption and heavy export commitments to Eastern Europe. Prime Minister Kosygin made similar remarks in late May of 1974.[55] There were even reports of Soviet shortfalls in late 1973, which included deliveries to Norway, France, and Finland, and there was a major shortfall to West Germany in late 1973 and early 1974.[56] However, the former shortfalls may have been exaggerated and the latter was probably due to a combination of oil diversion and price haggling rather than to an actual shortage of supply. The Soviets can usually live up to their commitments but their supply is indeed limited; they are unable to provide the quantities wanted by Finland and by the Idemitsu Company in Japan. In Finland's case, the Soviets agreed to deliver additional natural gas rather than extra oil; in Japan's, they claimed that they could only deliver somewhat less than the two million tons of crude oil wanted by Idemitsu, even though they had sold that full amount to the corporation in 1973.[57]

While the Soviet Union was accumulating greater profits from oil sales, there were grumblings from some of its customers over the high prices. West Germany and France registered complaints and Finland joined in when prices were trebled to $17.38 per barrel.[58] This price was to fluctuate with the Rotterdam market price of oil. The Idemitsu Company, which had imported Soviet oil for thirteen years, temporarily decided not to buy any more, mostly because of high prices but also because of a dispute over the quantity.[59] Thus, the charges of price-cutting leveled against the USSR during the late fifties and early sixties had now shifted into a chorus of complaints about high Soviet prices. The Soviets had joined the Western oil companies as international profiteers. However, the pricing mechanism proved to be double-edged, as Iraq and Libya raised the price on their crude oil exports to the USSR and they demanded hard currency instead of goods as payment.[60] This led to a decline in Soviet imports of Iraqi oil from 11,010,000 tons in 1973 to 3,888,000 in 1974 and the Soviets will have to reconsider their oil import policies in light of this new development.[61]

Emerging from the 1973 and 1974 oil price increases in the best temporary position was Eastern Europe, which in the past had generally paid high prices for Soviet oil although it was insulated from world market fluctuations, since its contracts with the USSR were for five-year periods at fixed prices (see chapter 5). One such five-year period was to extend to the end of 1975 and the price for the 1976–80 period was to be negotiated one year before the expiration of the previous contract. A hefty price increase was certainly anticipated, but during the latter part of 1973 and all of 1974 the East European states were paying some of the world's lowest oil prices. Despite Soviet pressure, East European states were able to hold the line on prices until early 1975 and they then agreed to pay approximately double for Soviet oil for the remainder of the year.[62]

High oil prices contributed substantially to the Soviet Union's favorable economic position in late 1973 and early 1974 but there were other important factors. The USSR had to spend a great amount of hard currency for American grain in 1972 but the 1973 Soviet harvest was a record 222.5 million tons and purchases were greatly reduced.[63] The situation in 1974 was not quite so rosy; the grain target was only 205.6 million tons and actual production may have fallen below 200 million tons. But the Soviet position was still stronger than it had been in 1972, despite the need to turn to purchases from the United States again.[64] Also helping to fill the Soviet coffers were arms sales to Middle East states. The Arabs traditionally have not had the hard currency to pay for Soviet weapons deliveries and they usually have given goods to the Soviet Union in return. The Soviets have often taken an economic loss, as the Arabs were unable to repay the full cost. However, the rising price of oil in 1973–74 increased the wealth of many Arab states and they could now pay for Soviet weapons with hard currency. Egypt and Syria were financially aided by richer states, such as Saudi Arabia and Kuwait, and Soviet hard currency reserves increased dramatically.[65] Further providing hard currency were the large sales of natural gas to West Germany, which began in 1973, and the sale of 300 tons of gold in 1973, which brought in a billion dollars.[66]

Much of the Soviets' income from oil sales was nevertheless in goods rather than hard currency. However, high oil prices enabled the USSR to receive more goods in return than before. As a result of the changing economic realities, the Soviet Union began to reassess some aspects of its oil policies. Since it was no longer deficient in capital, the acquisition of American and Japanese credits was not so necessary as it once appeared, and the Soviets entered into negotiations with these two states from a much stronger bargaining position. They were capable of being more self-sufficient in the development of Siberia, and oil minister Shashin so indicated in his May 1974 press conference.[67] Taking a hard line, Shashin claimed that there would not be joint agreements for the development of Siberian oil and gas resources and he indicated that there would be no deal with Japan on a Tiumen oil pipeline—at least until 1980. Instead, the USSR was planning to build a railroad from Western Siberia to the Pacific.[68] Shashin was exaggerating the Soviet position—some agreements for Siberian development probably will be forthcoming—but the gist of Shashin's message was basically accurate since Soviet hard currency reserves encouraged energy self-sufficiency and made the USSR less anxious to conclude agreements with the United States and Japan. The Soviets had the funds to buy Western oil equipment and this permitted them to develop Siberia without Western credits or investment. A shortage of hard currency led to reductions in the purchase of Western oil equipment in both 1972 and 1973 but the Soviets then went on a shopping spree in the West. During that previous two-year period, the USSR had turned toward communist suppliers, particularly Rumania, since hard currency was not necessary in communist markets.[69]

The Soviet Union is now in a position to derive large profits from oil exports, and these profits can be used for the purchase of Western oil equipment, which will in turn increase their exports further. It therefore is in the Soviet interest to increase exports at this time, and Theodore Shabad writes that this is indeed the Soviet plan. Oil export facilities are being developed to handle a greater volume and, during the 1976–80 Five-Year Plan period, refinery capacity will continue to lag behind production. He indicates that the export capacity at the port of Ventspils in Latvia is being doubled to 30 million tons per year and that oil pipelines from both Western Siberia and Kuibyshev to Novorossisk on the Black Sea are being completed.[70] However, increasing exports to Western Europe and the Third World will be a difficult task as communist-ruled states are making greater demands on the Soviet oil supply.[71] If the Soviets resort to larger imports in order to build up their export capability, they will have to spend more hard currency than in the past. To further complicate their oil bind, Western Siberian production may not accelerate so rapidly as expected in the absence of American and Japanese assistance.

The Natural Gas Trade

The Soviet Union has consistently exported natural gas, but imports began in 1967 and the Soviet Union temporarily became a net importer in 1970. It again became a net exporter in 1974. Although experiencing problems with domestic production, the Soviet Union should substantially increase its gas exports in the coming years, partially as an alternative to greater oil exports, since the supply of oil will be tighter.[72] Gas exports are often paid for with pipe, which assists the Soviets in "speeding up" domestic conversion to greater gas use. Leslie Dienes, an analyst of Soviet energy resources, believes that the desire for this conversion is a significant motivating factor in the gas export program.[73]

Table 4.3. Soviet Imports and Exports of Natural Gas, 1955–1973 (in billions of cubic meters)

year	imports	exports	year	imports	exports
1955	0	.139	1965	0	.392
1956	0	.136	1966	0	0.828
1957	0	.170	1967	.207	1.291
1958	0	.206	1968	1.500	1.729
1959	0	.222	1969	2.030	2.664
1960	0	.242	1970	3.551	3.300
1961	0	.272	1971	8.100	4.600
1962	0	.300	1972	11.000	5.100
1963	0	.301	1973	11.400	6.800
1964	0	.295			

SOURCES: Robert Ebel, *Communist Trade in Oil and Gas* (New York: Praeger, 1970), p. 138; United Nations, Statistical Office, *World Energy Supplies, 1961–1970,* Statistical Papers, series J, no. 15 (New York: United Nations, 1972), p. 27; *Vneshniaia torgovlia SSSR za 1972 god, statisticheskii obzor* (Moscow: Izdatel'stvo "Mezhdunarodnye otnosheniia," 1973), p. 41; *ibid.,* 1973, pp. 27 and 42.

Soviet natural gas exports go to Czechoslovakia, Bulgaria, Hungary, East Germany, Austria, West Germany, Italy, and Finland; they will soon be sent to France and Yugoslavia (and probably Sweden) as well. It is possible that Japan and the United States will also buy Soviet gas. Imports come only from Iran and Afghanistan and a web of political and economic factors is involved in each trade relationship.[74] Gas imports make economic sense. The imports will save on pipeline construction, alleviate gas deficiencies in the Caucasus, and generally contribute to Soviet energy usage until the expected upsurge in Western Siberian gas production. Price considerations are also relevant; in 1973 the Soviets paid Afghanistan 18 cents per thousand cubic feet of gas and Iran 29 cents, but they sold gas to Austria at 39 cents, Poland at 52 cents, and Czechoslovakia at 55 cents.[75]

Soviet gas sales are assuming greater importance since the ability to increase oil exports is limited by the slow growth in production. Illustrative is the Soviet decision not to deliver additional oil supplies to Austria in 1974 but to provide an extra half billion cubic meters of natural gas.[76] Gas and oil are also interrelated in the sense that greater domestic use of gas can eventually free more oil for export.[77] In early November 1974, Moscow apartments began receiving Western Siberian gas supplies, and the use of gas is due to expand rapidly. Foreign sales of gas and greater domestic usage may occur simultaneously since, as already indicated, sales are often paid for with pipe, and this pipe may be used to accelerate the growth of the gas industry.

In a financial sense, gas exports are as profitable as oil exports. The world trend is to dissociate gas from supply and demand considerations and instead link price increases to those of the main alternative fuel—oil. As oil prices rise so do gas prices, and the Soviet Union intends to take advantage of this development. The Minister of Foreign Trade, Nikolai Patolichev, has called for a linkage between gas and oil prices and he has indicated that it should be applied to any gas agreement with the United States.[78]

As a political instrument, gas exports have certain advantages as well as disadvantages. It is much more difficult for the purchaser of gas to shift his buying pattern than is the case with oil, which provides the seller with added political leverage. Oil can be bought in numerous markets and is easily transported by tanker; gas requires extensive pipeline construction or the building of expensive facilities for the processing of liquefied natural gas. Liquefied natural gas tankers are also very costly.[79] On the other hand, the seller may not be very anxious to cut off gas supplies after he has invested heavily in pipelines or liquefied natural gas tankers and his ability to shift exports to take advantage of temporarily opportune situations is highly restricted. A natural gas trade relationship therefore encourages long-term cooperation and is not so fickle as one based on the sale of oil.

Soviet oil and gas programs are marked by a number of contrasts. Although a large exporter, the USSR must continue to import oil and gas in order to help meet export commitments. The Soviets also have huge oil and gas reserves, but they are faced with production problems and must seek outside technology. Furthermore, the Soviet economy is based on socialist principles, but the USSR has nevertheless become an international marketer of fuel interested in maximizing profits.

The Soviet Union is confronted with numerous policy dilemmas regarding its external fuel programs and the decisions reached will strongly affect its foreign relations in the years to come. Should the USSR divert exports from elsewhere in order to increase hard currency sales to West European states? Should the USSR bear the burden of supplying most of the fuel requirements of its East European allies, Rumania excluded? Should the USSR continue to sell fuel to Third World states even though prices may be somewhat lower than in Western Europe and payment is rarely in hard currency? Should the USSR continue to import Middle East and North African oil since prices are rising and payment is shifting to hard currency? Should the USSR encourage American and Japanese investment in Siberian fuel projects even though its basic self-reliance would be jeopardized? All of these dilemmas are fraught with political implications, as the future of détente with the West, containment of China, and relations with Middle East oil-producing states hang in the balance.

5 / The Strategy and Tactics of Soviet Oil Politics

The economic and political aspects of Soviet oil policies are usually inseparable. At the end of the Second World War, the Soviet Union incorporated additional oil-producing regions, secured oil reparations from Rumania and Austria, and created joint-stock companies to exploit East European resources. These acts brought economic benefits, but they contributed to the spread of Soviet political power as well. When the USSR decides to sell oil in order to display political support, as to Iceland and Egypt during the fifties and Cuba during the sixties, politics and economics are clearly intertwined. When the USSR encourages Arab embargoes, cuts off the oil supply to China or Israel, or buys blacklisted oil from nationalized oil fields in Iraq and Libya, its actions have obvious political consequences. Even oil prices are inherently political; low prices are often used to gain political entree or to undercut the influence of Western oil companies. Through most of the fifties and sixties, the Soviet Union charged high prices to its East European allies. Some Soviet oil practices, particularly in Third World producing and consuming states, carry indirect political overtones since they serve to reduce Western power, which is partially based on oil dominance. Oil may be an economic commodity but it helps lubricate the wheels of political power.

The Soviet Union has ample oil resources to run its industries, transportation, and military, and its geographical dispersal of reserves is an asset during times of war. Oil exports permit the USSR to acquire equipment, technology and hard currency which can be used to build up the domestic economic base and the Soviets can hold back their oil exports in a wartime emergency and divert the oil to internal use. The fact that the USSR is a large oil exporter furthers the Soviet power potential and also provides an opportunity to terminate deliveries to Western customers and thereby reduce their power capability as well.[1]

Power is relative and cannot be measured in absolute terms. Soviet actions aimed at weakening Western power, such as those seeking to limit access to oil supplies in the Middle East, therefore increase Soviet power vis-à-vis the West. The use of oil as an instrument of pressure or influence against a customer state gives the USSR a power advantage, and states which are dependent on Soviet oil deliveries are potentially somewhat subservient to Soviet power interests. The growing role as an oil middleman also improves the Soviet power position while entailing little power risk and Soviet interest in purchasing Middle East oil is due largely to a desire to serve as middleman, rather than to any internal Soviet need for additional oil.[2] The Soviets could certainly eliminate these purchases and reduce their exports by a corresponding amount but they would thereby lose a potential lever of power. Much of this oil is resold to East European states, a good part is shipped to Soviet customers in Asia, and some is resold to West European states. The Soviets derive economic benefit from these transactions since they often sell at higher prices than they pay for the oil, and they save on transportation costs as shipment from the Middle East to Soviet customers is sometimes less expensive than transporting the oil from the Volga-Ural region or Western Siberia. The Soviets also make profits out of their refining and distribution systems in Western Europe, again playing the role of oil middleman, for, as economist Marshall Goldman points out, the Soviets buy Middle East oil, ship some of it to their Nafta marketing network in Britain, and then sell it at a profit.[3] Economic advantages certainly influence the Soviet desire to serve as middleman, especially in Western Europe, but considerations of power are also fundamental; the USSR would like to control the East European oil tap without having to expend its own resources. In another sense, the middleman role could adversely affect Western power interests since the large oil monopolies are losing their grip over international marketing operations.

The Soviets use both the supply and influence effects of foreign trade to bolster their power position. Indicative of the supply effect have been the use of military occupation to secure oil reparations from Rumania and Austria; the export of oil to acquire the equipment, pipe, and tankers necessary for the growth of the Soviet oil industry; the creation of a naval presence in the Indian Ocean to protect Soviet Interests In the crucial oil sea lanes; and the diplomatic effort to have the Suez Canal reopened, thereby facilitating Soviet oil imports from Iraq. In addition the USSR assumes no risks when it provides equipment and technicians to Middle East and North African states in return for crude oil deliveries. The Soviets are repaid in oil even if there is little or no production in the Soviet-assisted oil fields, as the USSR usually receives a specific stipulated volume rather than a percentage of the production. In the unlikely case that production is less than the amount due to the Soviet Union, these states can supply the Soviets from more prolific oil fields. Finally, all of the states exporting crude oil to the USSR are partially dependent upon the Soviet Union for the provision of arms, which reduces the possibility that oil deliveries will be slowed down or terminated.

Soviet actions in regard to the influence effect have been diversified and numerous. For example, the Soviets have used oil to gain political entree and reduce the influence of Western oil companies (as in Cuba, India, and Ceylon) and they have also cut off oil deliveries to Israel to make a political point. They reduced the quantity supplied to China because of its independent stance within the Soviet bloc and they disrupted shipments to Ghana until it agreed to release two Soviet trawlers and their captains, which had been detained for violating Ghana's territorial waters and for possible gun-running violations. The Soviets delayed the completion of an oil agreement with Finland in order to influence the cabinet selection and they made veiled threats to Czechoslovakia in 1968 pertaining to its dependence on Soviet oil supplies.

Oil has been an effective political weapon and a financial asset at the same time.

In analyzing the Soviet oil trade, some distinction should be drawn between strategy, which rarely changes and is based on long-term considerations, and tactics, which frequently adjust to take advantage of short-term situations in the most expedient and opportune manner. Soviet strategy is to export large quantities of oil, even if some imports may be necessary to keep up the volume of exports. Exports are valuable in acquiring imports needed for the growth of the domestic oil industry, in keeping the East European states in line, and in reducing the power of Western oil companies. They are also instrumental in furthering political influence and in obtaining hard currency. Soviet tactics are subject to rapid change and opposite tactics may be applied contemporaneously in different states. The Soviets may cut prices to gain political good will or to take part of a market away from Western oil companies or they may charge high prices to acquire hard currency or to take advantage of a captive market. Other tactics may include verbal and diplomatic support for Arab embargoes but with behind-the-scenes oil sales to the embargoed states or they may feature increased or decreased deliveries to customers, based in either case on the vagaries of political relations.

Soviet policy may be directed at the acquisition of oil, such as the reparations from Rumania and Austria, but it may also be aimed at the denial of oil to Western states. During the forties and fifties, most Soviet actions in northern Iran fell into the latter category. Not only was the USSR concerned with limiting Western access to oil resources but it was also wary about the establishment of a Western presence so close to the Soviet border. Oil may be used as an instrument of political pressure, but political benefits may also be accrued as a natural outgrowth of oil policy. In such a manner, the sale of oil makes the customer state partially dependent on the Soviet source of supply and also prompts good will toward the USSR. Whereas the sale of oil is often used as a diplomatic wedge, the opposite may occasionally take place, as pressure is applied to secure a market for Soviet oil. In 1964, the

Soviets attempted to sell oil to Canada by threatening not to buy wheat unless Canada purchased oil in return.[4]

Sometimes, oil policies lead the USSR to tread a precarious political tightrope. The Soviets sold oil to Israel in 1955 and 1956—at a time when Soviet foreign policy was clearly pro-Arab. They explored for oil in Pakistan during the early sixties at the risk of antagonizing India, and they built an oil refinery in Ethiopia even though Soviet policy generally tilted toward support for Somalia. The Soviet Union also increased its oil sales to the United States at the height of the 1973–74 Arab embargo, while they were lending strong verbal support to the Arabs. While economic profit is occasionally a consideration in cases such as these, it is often absent as a motivating force (as in Pakistan and Ethiopia), and Soviet actions probably are taken in an effort to hedge bets and keep a foot planted in the enemy camp. So far, the Soviets have been very adept at this maneuver.

Soviet oil policies have not always been successful. Although the USSR offered Japan the allure of joining in the exploitation of Western Siberian oil resources in order to short-circuit any rapprochement between Japan and China, the Japanese eventually renewed ties with China and began importing increasing quantities of Chinese oil. The Soviets also met with failure in their campaign to remove NATO bases from Iceland, as they apparently expected that Icelandic dependence on Soviet oil would be sufficient impetus. They may also have miscalculated in the case of crude oil imports from the Middle East and North Africa. These imports were usually repayment for Soviet credits, and the USSR was able to secure oil at low cost and without the expenditure of hard currency; but the buoying of Arab fortunes as a result of the 1973–74 boost in oil prices has led to demands by Iraq and Libya that the USSR pay high prices with hard currency for their oil. Soviet policy may sometimes be so successful that it begins to become counterproductive. This has occurred in Eastern Europe and Cuba where oil has proved to be an important instrument of political control. As the demand for oil has risen in these states, the Soviets have had to supply such large quantities that their export program has become an economic burden. The Soviets have therefore been encouraging these states to seek oil from other sources as well.

When one speaks of Soviet oil strategy and tactics, there should be no implication that the Soviet Union is forever the perpetrator and the other states the victims. The oil relationship need not be one of subject-object, as Soviet trading partners have their own strategy and tactics and their own reasons for dealing with the USSR. In many cases, both sides derive benefit. Many states like low Soviet prices and others see an advantage in acquiring oil by barter rather than by expending hard currency. Barter also adds to self-esteem, since a state feels that it is paying for the oil with its own goods. This is psychologically preferable to a price discount. Many states are anxious to buy Soviet oil because it permits them to diversify their supply in case the flow of oil from the Middle East is disrupted. Soviet assistance in building refineries, in supplying equipment and technicians, and in oil exploration is particularly crucial to Third World states, and oil exporters are thankful for Soviet credits, diplomatic support, and the market the USSR provides. It is certainly true that the Soviet Union uses oil to further its power interests, but the oil trade can often be quite harmonious and based on mutual self-interest.

The Tactics of Oil Pricing

Oil pricing is an important part of the Soviet tactical arsenal. In a manner which appears to be inverse price discrimination, Third World and Western states have generally paid less for Soviet oil than have communist-ruled states. There is even a further paradoxical twist: Third World states which are politically closest to the USSR pay more than Third World states which are less pro-Soviet. It is evident that the Soviet Union uses low prices so that it can enter the oil markets of many Third World states, and then raises prices once some of these states move in a more pro-Soviet direction. Cuba once paid a fairly low price for Soviet oil, but as it moved into the Soviet orbit and joined CMEA, prices rose. Egypt, which was one of the Soviet Union's closest Third World allies at the time, paid a higher price for Soviet crude oil in 1967 than any Third World, or even any communist-ruled, state.[5] Moskoff and Benz have shown that the closer the political relationship between the Soviet Union and a Third World state, the higher the prices paid by this state for Soviet exports.[6] The authors are unable to explain this phenomenon but it is conceivable that the USSR no longer needs to woo its closest friends by offering goods at low prices and instead seeks to take economic advantage of cordial political ties. It is also possible that the exports of these Third World states to the Soviet Union may be overvalued and may therefore balance the high oil prices. Moskoff and Benz indicate that the prices paid by Third World states for Soviet crude oil in 1967 displayed a 73.4 percent gap between the highest and lowest prices and it seems as if political considerations were at least partially responsible.[7]

From the beginning of the "oil offensive" in 1955 until late 1973, the Soviet Union usually charged noncommunist states from about 50 percent to more than 100 percent less for crude oil than it charged communist-ruled states.[8] In 1959 Argentina paid only 44 rubles per ton, Japan and West Germany 49 rubles, but Mongolia paid 102 rubles and Poland 95 rubles. In 1967, France paid 8.5 rubles per ton and Italy 9.5 rubles but Hungary paid 15.3 rubles and Czechoslovakia 15.4 rubles.[9] Soviet prices for East and West Germany are rather revealing since transportation costs cannot be very different. In 1961, East Germany was charged 17.2 rubles per ton but West Germany only 8.4; in 1967 the figures were 13.4 and 9.2.[10] As indicated previously, West Germany was one of the prime targets for Soviet oil sales, since the USSR hoped to reduce West Germany's reliance on the United States. Another state that received favored treatment was Japan. The Soviets wanted to drive a wedge between Japan and the United States, but as the Sino-Soviet dispute became more virulent during the early sixties, the USSR also attempted to give Japan a little push in the Soviet direction. In 1963, Japan paid the lowest price for Soviet crude oil of any state in the world but, even during the late fifties, Japan was paying only slightly more than half the price charged to China.[11]

The Soviets derive lesser profits from the sale of oil than they do from the sale of machinery since capital investment in the oil industry is very high.[12] They also produce an average of less oil per well than do Middle East states, but the Soviets still place a high priority on oil exports and frequently undersell their competitors.[13] The reasons for oil sales have already been discussed but some explanation of low Soviet prices is necessary. One contributing factor is the Soviet desire to break into markets that have long been controlled by the major Western oil companies. The best means of entree is attractive prices, and an American specialist on Soviet foreign trade writes of Soviet behavior: "They have learned the classic strategies of marginal suppliers who sell in oligopolistic markets: to cut the price only to the point at which retaliation will not be provoked, lest the reaction wipe out the oligopoly rent that was being shared by all the sellers." [14]

The Soviets manage to sell oil at bargain prices and yet still make a profit. Much of the profit is in the savings on the imports received in return for the oil, compared with the domestic cost of producing the same items. Also, when the Soviets sell for hard currency, they usually come out ahead financially. High prices charged to communist-ruled states do not really subsidize the low-priced oil exports to noncommunist states, since the Soviets make a profit on the latter sales as well.[15] Perhaps there may be a financial loss on a specific transaction—when oil is bartered for nonessential goods, for example—but overall the Soviet oil export program is profitable. The USSR imposes no oil export taxes, which helps keep prices low, and, if ever desired, the Soviets can easily raise the price on domestic oil sales in order to subsidize low-priced exports.

American economist Paul Marer maintains that CMEA states often export goods to the West at low prices because they may be of inferior quality; because exports are based on a plan and this limits flexibility in taking advantage of periodically high prices; because high Western tariffs on communist goods force the communist-ruled states to sell for low prices so their products can be competitive in Western markets; and because communist-ruled states are in great need of hard currency and are therefore willing to sell at low prices to encourage the conclusion of trade agreements.[16] Marer's points are very well taken when considering communist exports in a broader context, but when focusing on the Soviet oil trade it appears that his first three points are not directly relevant. Nevertheless, Soviet oil is sold for low prices in Western markets and the key question is whether or not this constitutes "dumping."

Dumping generally means that a commodity is sold abroad for less than it is sold at home. It helps remove overstock, secures hard currency, introduces a product into a new market, drives a competitor out of a market by underselling him, retaliates for dumping activities of other states, and creates political good will by offering merchandise at an attractive price. Dumping may also imply that the market mechanism is being intentionally disrupted by the introduction of a large quantity of low-priced goods. Dumping is therefore rather broad in scope. As Marer indicates, it is difficult to apply such a concept to state-controlled barter economies because the export price of an item secured in return for oil may cost less than the price of domestic production of that item.[17] The Soviets certainly sell goods at low prices but ambiguity clouds the question of whether they actually dump commodities such as oil.

According to Soviet oil specialist Boris Rachkov, the Soviets do not dump oil, but they do sell at prices lower than those fixed by the major Western oil monopolies. The Soviet Union, along with independent capitalist firms, participates in the non-monopolized oil market, where prices are generally 30 to 40 percent lower than those set by the monopolies; even the monopolies sell at these prices when they have an oil surplus. Rachkov asserts that the Soviets sell at "normal market prices." [18] M. A. Adelman, a noted analyst of the international oil trade, also does not portray Soviet tactics as dumping since he believes that the Soviets lower prices only as far as is necessary in order to secure a sale.[19] Western observers such as Willard Thorp, Roger Hilsman, and Samuel Pisar all maintain that the Soviets do not intentionally disrupt world oil markets, but that their real aim is to finance imports.[20]

Although the Soviets generally underprice their competition when they are anxious to make a sale, they have been underbid on a number of occasions. In 1962, *Oil and Gas Journal* reported that BP had underbid the Soviets and had won the crude oil delivery contract for a new Moroccan refinery at Mohammedia.[21] The Soviets were also underbid for a Swiss contract and Boris Rachkov accuses the Western oil monopolies of underpricing the Soviets in Japan, Italy, Brazil, and some African countries.[22] Rachkov is apparently referring to surplus oil sold at reduced prices.

Until late 1973, Soviet oil sales to communist-ruled states were at higher than world prices. The Soviets took economic advantage of their privileged position but other factors also were involved. Since trade between the Soviet Union and other communist-ruled states was on a barter basis, the exporter usually charged a high price, but this was balanced by the high prices charged for the imports he received in return. Furthermore, a hypothetical transport cost was added to the price of a commodity, based upon what it would have cost to transport that commodity from a Western state.[23] It was also true that the USSR had to invest more capital into fuel production than the East Europeans needed to invest into the equivalent amount of machinery used as payment.[24]

The Soviets profited from oil sales to communist-ruled states but they received barter goods rather than the hard currency they could have received by exporting this oil to the West.[25] The industrial products received as barter were generally inferior to those produced in the West so the Soviets could therefore afford to sell oil to the West at low prices because they received either high-quality goods in return or the hard currency needed to buy such goods.[26] Another explanation of the higher prices to communist-ruled states was offered by Soviet economic analyst Y. Shiryayev. He wrote: "The establishment of higher prices for certain raw materials and scarce manufactured goods than those prevailing in the world market stimulates their production for export and to some extent compensates for their high cost." [27] Shiryayev was indicating that the high prices charged to East European states were spurring on Soviet raw material development and assisting the Soviet export program but that the East European states were benefiting equally, as they were charging high prices for the machinery and equipment exported to the USSR.

Soviet price discrimination against communist-ruled states was most marked before 1965; during the 1965–73 period, the price differential between sales to noncommunist and communist-ruled states narrowed. Paul Marer has determined that the price of goods imported from the USSR by other CMEA states during the years 1965–67 fell by 10 percent, while the price of Soviet imports from CMEA states went down by only 2 percent.[28] Marer's calculation is based on the total value of trade and does not apply specifically to oil, but the pricing advantage previously enjoyed by the Soviets in the area of oil was also reduced in a similar manner. To some extent, the Soviets were succumbing to East European charges of price discrimination, but they were also trying to organize CMEA into an effective and mutually advantageous economic grouping so that integration between communist-ruled states would be based less on coercion and more on a solid economic basis. The invasion of Czechoslovakia certainly represented a policy aberration, but the Soviets felt that force was the answer since the cohesion of CMEA and the Warsaw Pact were at stake.

The Suez Canal's closure in 1967 led to less discriminatory oil prices, as the disruption in oil shipments pushed up the world price of oil. However, the average price paid by communist-ruled states for Soviet oil actually fell from $2.18 per barrel in 1966 to $2.10 per barrel in 1967 while Soviet oil exports to noncommunist states rose from an average of $1.39 in 1966 to $1.50 in 1967. Italy, Japan, and Spain received the largest price increases.[29] The prices charged to communist-ruled states did not rise, because they were fixed for the five-year period, 1966–70, whereas Soviet exports to other states were almost always tied to world fluctuations in the price of oil.[30] The slight reduction in price to CMEA members was probably a minor Soviet gesture of good will in order to eliminate the bitter taste of past discrimination but even the somewhat more equitable pricing system of 1965–73 produced some ferment in Eastern Europe. After all, CMEA members were still paying more than Western or Third World states and Czechoslovakia complained that the Soviet Union was continuing to take economic advantage of her. She charged that the price of Soviet oil exceeded world prices by a greater amount than did the price of Czechoslovak machinery sold to the USSR.[31] The Soviets countered Czechoslovak criticism, with one writer maintaining: "Lastly, if one takes into account the real expenditure of home products in payment for imports, one would see that Czechoslovakia, for instance, pays less for Soviet oil than she would have to pay for oil bought from capitalist countries." [32]

The CMEA states were protected from the 1973–74 quadrupling of oil prices by their five-year agreements running through 1975. The Soviets were not at all pleased with this new situation and tried to secure "voluntary" price increases which could be applied retroactively. The CMEA states resisted until early 1975, when they did reluctantly agree to pay approximately double for Soviet oil for the remainder of 1975.[33] This meant that they were still paying considerably less than the world market price but a stiff increase for the new Five-Year Plan period, 1976–80, was surely anticipated. Normally, oil prices for a Five-Year Plan are based on the average world price during the first three years of the last plan, in this case 1971–73, but such an approach in this situation would not have taken into account the worldwide major increases. The Soviets wanted a somewhat higher price than one based on the 1971–73 average, and they also pushed for greater East European investment in the production and transportation of Western Siberian oil. They buttressed their pricing argument with the fact that more of the oil to be exported to CMEA states would be coming from Western Siberia, thus driving up transportation costs.[34] The CMEA oil importers were willing to go along to some extent with the Soviets on prices and investments, but they advocated a fixed price for the 1976–80 period, since they did not want to be subjected to world market fluctuations.[35] The final solution was basically favorable to the USSR. It called for prices to be based on the world average of the previous five years, and there were to be yearly price adjustments. Despite their loss of the protection the five-year fixed prices had provided, as of 1976, CMEA states were nevertheless paying only $7.50 to $8.00 per barrel of crude oil—about three or four dollars less than the prevailing world rates. However, they were required to invest heavily in the Soviet oil industry and their oil price was almost certainly to rise to the world level by 1979, owing to the yearly adjustments.[36] Although Soviet oil exports to CMEA states were not much of a financial blessing to the USSR in 1974–75, the higher prices of 1976 put the Soviets on a much more profitable footing.

Some Comparisons with the West

Because it is self-sufficient in oil, the USSR's oil strategy necessarily differs from that of Western states and Japan. Soviet trade features the export of oil and the import of technology (just the reverse of the Western powers) and Soviet policies are strongly influenced by a perennial shortage of hard currency. This last distinction is now losing some of its validity, as the Soviet Union and other oil exporters are building up their hard currency reserves as a result of high world oil prices while most Western oil importers are confronted with a hard currency crisis. Another element which sets Soviet strategy apart from that of the United States, Britain, or France is that the USSR has not occupied a colonial or semicolonial position in Third World states and does not have a history of oil exploitation either in terms of controlling their production or dominating their oil import markets and refining operations. While the West seeks to retain its oil influence in the Third World, the USSR acts in a largely negative manner by trying to hasten its demise.

Tactically, the Soviet Union and the West are similar in the sense that prices may be raised or lowered, or the supply may be increased or decreased, to suit political purposes. On the other hand, Soviet oil tactics are often linked with barter trade while Western companies have always engaged in cash transactions.

Since the Arab embargo of 1973–74, many Western states have sought to barter their technology in return for oil, so Western practices are clearly changing in this regard. One of the main distinctions between the USSR and the West is that Soviet tactics serve the political cause of the state whereas Western policy is sometimes bifurcated, as oil companies and the state have different inherent interests. During the Arab embargo, Western oil companies prospered financially while Western states were faced with an energy shortage. At the same time, the tactics applied by these companies often ran counter to the security interests of their own states; for example, American oil companies in Saudi Arabia withheld oil supplies from the U.S. military because this was demanded by the Saudis. Western governments now seem to be moving quickly into the area of energy policy so that this past duality can be eliminated. Another fundamental difference between the Soviet Union and the West is that the Soviet Union emphasizes the influence effect, since it is primarily an oil exporter, while Western states are much more concerned with the supply effect, particularly at this time of rising OPEC power. Western states, using oil companies as intermediaries, certainly do take advantage of the influence effect, but the energy crisis and Arab embargo actions have made accessibility to oil supplies the top priority.

The strategy and tactics of oil make up one part of Soviet foreign policy and the selective emphasis of my study should not imply a unicausal approach to Soviet policy analysis. What is especially interesting is that Soviet foreign policy does include the aspect of oil politics, since the Soviets have always attributed such politics exclusively to the Western powers and even past Western studies of oil politics have usually neglected the important role of the USSR.

6/The Geopolitics of Middle East Oil

Oil and oil products make up more than half the physical volume of world trade and the considerable distances between producing and consuming states add an important geopolitical dimension to the international flow of oil.[1] The sale of oil brings huge profits to many states, but part of the world has been thrown into economic chaos as it endeavors to pay the spiraling oil prices. Oil is the energy backbone of most industrialized societies and is crucial in terms of military capability so its strategic relevance is of utmost importance. The power of major Western consuming states is highly dependent on continued access to oil supplies while the power of the largest exporting states lies in their control over oil resources. The focus for the strategic interplay between producers and consumers is the Middle East—the world's greatest storehouse of oil reserves and a vital hub of the export trade. In recent years, the political volatility of the area and the importance of certain waterways and pipelines have combined in a geopolitical amalgam which has often erupted into crises of major proportions.

The Soviet Union began playing a significant role in the Middle East following World War II, but its involvement was somewhat secondary when compared with that of the United States, Britain, and France. Gradually, the Soviets fostered extensive economic, political, and military ties with the Arab and Northern-tier states (Turkey and Iran), and by 1967 they were deeply enmeshed in regional affairs. The closing of the Suez Canal became an impediment to the realization of Soviet strategic goals in the area, and the USSR actively pressed for the Canal's reopening.

The Suez Canal

During the first half of 1956, oil was transiting the Suez Canal at an annual rate of 77 million tons and oil tankers made up 63 percent of the tonnage passing through the Canal. Oil was also reaching the Mediterranean via the IPC (Iraq Petroleum Company) pipeline from Iraq at a rate of 25 million tons and via the Tapline from Saudi Arabia at a rate of 16 million tons.[2] However, oil transit was disrupted by the Arab-Israeli war, as the Egyptians blocked the Suez Canal with scuttled ships on October 31, 1956, and the Canal did not reopen until March 1957. In addition, Syria destroyed the IPC pumping stations in her territory on November 3, bringing about unemployment and a revenue loss for herself, Iraq, and Lebanon, but the major outcome was the stoppage of the oil flow from Iraq.[3] Syria did not sabotage the Tapline, which transits her territory, but Saudi Arabia embargoed the export of oil to Britain and France from November 6, 1956 to March 9, 1957, because of their role in the attack on Egypt.[4]

Had oil transport not been disrupted, Western Europe would have received 105 million tons of oil from the Middle East in 1956, representing 90 percent of her oil imports. As it turned out, the Suez Canal was closed, oil was not flowing through the IPC pipeline, and only Tapline was providing oil for West European states—other than Britain and France. Some oil was rerouted around Africa, but the overall shipment of oil from the Middle East to Western Europe fell by 70 percent following the war.[5] Nevertheless, the effect was not that disastrous for the West European states since the United States, Canada, and Venezuela helped out by providing oil and warm weather and rationing contributed to reduced consumption.[6]

In 1956, the Soviet Union was not importing any oil from the Middle East, but the closure of the Suez Canal still created a problem. The Soviets shipped oil from the Black Sea southward through the Canal in order to supply China, and even the Soviet Far East received most of its oil via this route.[7] Nevertheless, the Canal closure generally worked to the advantage of the USSR, thanks to the lift given to the Soviet sales drive in Western

Europe. At this time, the Soviets were in the early stages of their oil offensive and they were looking for new markets. The events in the Middle East therefore provided a helpful impetus. Many West European states had previously shied away from Soviet oil because they were influenced by the Cold War attitudes then prevalent, but the cutoff of most Middle East deliveries led to a reassessment of past positions and West European states did slightly increase their purchases of Soviet oil. The rapid energy recovery of Western Europe probably prevented these states from seeking even more Soviet oil but the key point was that tho insecurity of Middle East supplies was recognized and Western Europe therefore sought to diversify its sources.[8] By 1960, the Soviet Union was a major supplier and the taint of "communist" oil had largely been erased by the realities of geopolitics.

By the time of the 1967 Arab-Israeli war, the Suez Canal's importance had increased even more. In 1966, it handled 20 percent of the world's oil cargo tonnage, and oil made up 176 million tons of the 242 million tons of freight passing through the Canal.[9] Of the ships traversing the Canal in that year, 75 percent were oil tankers.[10] The Soviet Union ranked as the seventh largest user of the Canal in terms of cargo tonnage and it was rapidly increasing its usage.[11] It shipped oil southward through the Canal on its way to Asian states and 62 percent of the oil passing in that direction was sent by the USSR.[12] Of course, the main flow of oil went northward from the Middle East producing states to Western Europe and the United States.

The 1967 closure of the Suez Canal proved to be much more than temporary; it did not reopen until June 1975. During this lengthy period, the Soviet Union managed to make the most out of a disadvantageous situation, but it still advocated the reopening of the Canal since its strategic position was likely to improve, particularly in regard to naval strength. The Soviet oil trade was also expected to benefit from the Canal's reopening but some of the oil practices based on post-1967 improvisation are now being continued because they have proved their utility.

With the Canal closed, the transport of oil from Black Sea ports to Asian states was severely disrupted. In 1967, Soviet oil

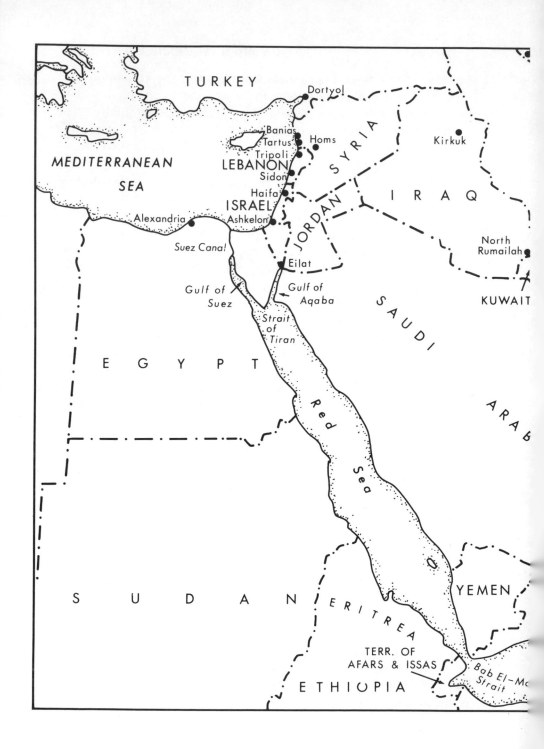

MAP 2. THE MIDDLE EAST

exports to Third World states and Japan fell by 32 percent, with Asian customers suffering the greatest deprivation.[13] Although Soviet oil deliveries to Japan were up 11.3 percent during the first half of 1967 as compared with the same period in 1966, the yearly total went down from 2.786 million tons in 1966 to 1.798 million tons in 1967.[14] Similar drops were recorded for India and Ceylon, the former falling from 1.214 to .469 million tons and the latter from .645 to .565 million tons.[15] However, the Soviet Union did manage to keep the oil flowing to North Vietnam. The 7000-mile sea journey from Odessa to Haiphong increased to 14,000 miles once the Canal was closed and this lengthened the trip for an average cargo ship from slightly over a month to 72 days.[16] Consequently, the number of Soviet ships traveling this route decreased after the 1967 Arab-Israeli war but North Vietnamese oil product imports from the USSR rose from 85,700 tons in 1966 to 214,400 tons in 1967.[17] Apparently, oil was given top priority among cargoes sent to North Vietnam at this time and it is also possible that much of the additional oil was delivered before the Canal closure.

Since oil exports to Asia were being reduced because of the high cost of transportation, the Soviet Union sought to increase its oil sales in Western Europe. In 1967, oil exports to noncommunist states fell by .1 percent, but sales to Western Europe went up by 17 percent.[18] Oil originally earmarked for Japan was sent instead to Italy, France, West Germany, and Spain as deliveries to regular European customers increased.[19] This sales upswing continued in 1968 but Western Europe's oil needs were rising too and Soviet oil's percentage of the market actually fell from 4.5 percent in 1967 to 4.2 percent in 1968.[20] It should also be pointed out that in addition to the Middle East transportation problems, West European oil supplies were also affected by the Nigerian civil war which began in mid-1967.[21] Furthermore, the reduced oil flow of this period led to a rise in world oil prices and the Soviet Union therefore benefited from its sales to noncommunist states.[22]

Soviet oil deliveries to Asian states were disrupted by the Canal closure, but the USSR partially overcame this problem through switch deals. In 1968, the Soviets worked through a

Swiss oil broker in order to arrange a switch of Abu Dhabi and Black Sea crude oils. Three and a half million barrels of crude oil from the Black Sea was to be sold to the French company Compagnie Française des Pétroles (CFP) for resale in Italy while CFP was to supply the same amount of crude oil from Abu Dhabi to Soviet customers in Japan and Burma. The deal began in June 1968 and was completed by the end of that year.[23] Another switch deal involving Abu Dhabi also took place in 1968 as the Soviet Union supplied British Petroleum's customers in Western Europe with Soviet crude, and in return BP supplied Abu Dhabi crude to the Soviets so they could fulfill their commitment to Japan.[24] In October 1970, the Soviets arranged a switch deal with the Kuwait National Petroleum Company under which the USSR made refined oil available to Kuwait's customers in Western Europe in exchange for Kuwaiti oil which was sent to Soviet markets in Ceylon and India.[25] Switch deals should continue even though the Suez Canal has reopened because of the transportation savings involved.

The Suez Canal closure greatly affected Soviet oil relations with Egypt. The Egyptians were unable to transport any of their Gulf of Suez crude oil to the Mex refinery near Alexandria on the Mediterranean coast, and this situation became even more accentuated in 1969 when the Suez refinery complex was heavily damaged during the War of Attrition with Israel and had to close down.[26] The refinery reopened with only partial operations just before the 1973 Arab-Israeli war and did not begin normal operations until 1974. Egypt thus had in the Gulf of Suez area surplus crude oil that it was unable to refine and it had on the Mediterranean a refinery that was not receiving an adequate supply of crude oil. This happened to correspond with the Soviet Union's problem in transporting oil to Asia, so the USSR and Egypt practiced what was equivalent to a switch deal. The Soviets sent crude oil to the Mex refinery and then received a similar amount from Egyptian stocks in the Gulf of Suez for export to Soviet customers in Asia. This switch arrangement worked smoothly until its disruption by the 1973 Arab-Israeli war. At that time, Egyptian crude oil production in the Gulf of Suez declined precipitously. There was no damage to the oil fields, but the military situation made Egypt fearful. Little oil was exported from the Gulf. Since the USSR was not receiving much oil from the Egyptians, Soviet deliveries to Egypt were also reduced and the total volume of Soviet-Egyptian oil trade fell considerably in 1973.[27]

The 1973 war also interfered with Soviet oil imports from Iraq and Syria. Part of the oil purchased in Iraq is sent to Soviet customers in Asia, and of the amount transported to the Mediterranean Sea for resale or actual import by the USSR, some is shipped from the Persian Gulf around Africa and the rest is pumped through the IPC pipeline, which runs from Kirkuk in Iraq, to Mediterranean terminals in both Syria and Lebanon. It would probably be more economical for the USSR to receive all of its Iraqi oil through the IPC pipeline and to dispense with the Cape route around Africa, but the IPC pipeline is unable to handle the total volume bought by the USSR, because much of its capacity is committed to the supply of the IPC's West European customers. Even after Iraq nationalized the British-owned IPC and its pipeline in 1972, it continued to export oil through the pipeline to IPC and its customers in order to pay for the properties acquired by nationalization. Thus the Soviet Union purchases Iraqi oil, which is transported along with oil bound for Western Europe and it can suffer the same fate in case of pipeline disruption.

During the 1973 Arab-Israeli war, the IPC terminal in Banias, Syria, was damaged during an Israeli attack and oil tankers were unable to load for several weeks.[28] Soviet oil supplies were therefore delayed. At the same time, Soviet imports of Syrian oil were interrupted by war damage at the port of Tartus; in addition, a Soviet oil tanker was damaged by the Israelis. Oil from the Karachuk and Suwaidiyah oil fields in Syria goes by pipeline to the Homs refinery and then that part which is to be exported continues to go through the pipeline to Tartus.[29] Not only did the war cause some destruction at Tartus but the Homs refinery was heavily damaged as well. Syria occupies a crucial geographical location which can affect Soviet oil imports from both Syria and Iraq, and it is not surprising that the USSR is attempting to exert a strong influence over Syrian affairs through its provision of economic and military assistance, plus thousands of Soviet advisers.[30]

The Soviet Union consistently pressed for the reopening of the Suez Canal and tried to enlist the support of West European states. The Soviets maintained that the Canal closure benefited the United States and Israel while Western Europe suffered the most because of the Canal's importance as an oil route. According to the Soviet argument, the United States was not highly dependent on oil which could possibly be sent through a reopened Canal, and American oil companies were able to increase their profits while the Canal stayed closed. First of all, these companies owned numerous supertankers which transported the oil around Africa; secondly, they had raised the price of oil since the Canal closure.[31] As for Israel, it derived profits from the Eilat–Ashkelon pipeline and from the Eilat–Ashdod overland cargo transport route, and these sources of revenue were generally expected to disappear when the Canal was reopened to traffic.[32]

The Soviets used the theme of West European dependence on Middle East oil supplies to encourage these states to exert pressure on Israel. They maintained that because an Israeli withdrawal from occupied Arab territories would lead to the reopening of the Canal, it was in the interest of West European states to seek an Israeli pullback to the pre-1967 borders.[33] The Soviets also asserted that a reopened Suez Canal would still be a major transit route for oil tankers and that the projected Suez–Mediterranean (Sumed) pipeline through Egypt would be an additional route, not a substitute.[34] This emphasis on the importance of the Suez Canal was aimed at building up diplomatic support for an Israeli withdrawal, but the Soviets probably had their own naval interests uppermost, not the convenience of the oil flow to Western Europe.

The Soviet Union stood to benefit from a reopened Suez Canal, as it would derive naval and oil-transport advantages, and one Western analyst suggested that the Soviets could possibly save money when using the Canal since the tolls could be deducted from the large Egyptian debt owed to the USSR.[35] The Soviets tried to downplay their interest in the Canal but it clearly was a top priority, as was shown during the diplomatic maneuvering following the 1973 Arab-Israeli war. The Soviets supported efforts to have the Canal cleared of debris and wreckage and prepared for reopening and, as maintained in the *Middle-East Intelligence Survey,* this was their main strategic objective. They briefly practiced the politics of conciliation to achieve this objective, but once a Canal agreement was reached the Soviets hardened their position on other issues. They took a more militantly pro-Palestinian stance than ever before, obstructed Secretary of State Kissinger's peace initiatives, particularly in Syria, and strongly encouraged the continuation of the Arab oil embargo.[36]

The Soviet Mediterranean fleet was greatly expanded after the 1967 Arab-Israeli war and the Soviets secured the use of port facilities in Latakia, Syria; Alexandria, Port Said, and Mersa Matrûh, Egypt; and Algiers, Bône and Mers el-Kébir, Algeria.[37] Soviet naval might become an important power factor in the area and increased the possibility of Soviet intervention in an Arab-Israeli conflict. Growing communist strength in Portugal, Spain, Italy, and Greece also alarmed many Western states, as they saw Soviet influence expanding throughout the Mediterranean region. The Soviet fleet did not intervene in the 1973 Arab-Israeli war, nor in the 1974 Cyprus dispute, and its role has so far been cautious. However, with the Suez Canal now reopened, the fleet will be able to expand its activities into the Red Sea, Indian Ocean, and Persian Gulf and add a new dimension to the oil geopolitics of the area. While the Canal was closed, ships from the Soviet Pacific fleet, based in Vladivostok, occasionally visited the Indian Ocean, but, now ships from the Mediterranean fleet based in the Black Sea port of Sevastopol can make the journey with a saving of 2800 sea miles.

With the Suez Canal reopened at its old width and depth, all Soviet naval vessels are capable of fitting through, including the USSR's first aircraft carrier, the *Kiev.*[38] This gives the Soviets a naval advantage over the United States, as many American ships are too large or deep in draft to transit the Canal.[39] Perhaps this is one of the major reasons why the United States is so interested in widening and deepening the Canal.

South and East of Suez

Since 1967, the Soviet Union has become deeply involved in Middle East affairs.[40] It has improved relations with the Northern tier states of Iran and Turkey and has extended substantial economic and military assistance to Egypt, Libya, Syria, and Iraq. The Soviets may also see the Middle East as an important link with India, as naval access to the subcontinent requires a network of intermediary port facilities. The Soviets have additionally developed an economic stake in the Middle East as they buy crude oil from Egypt, Libya, Syria, and Iraq, and natural gas from Iran and the extension of Soviet naval influence into the Indian Ocean and Persian Gulf is clearly related to the importance of these waters for the oil trade. The Soviets want to protect their own interests but they also want to be in a position to interfere with Western oil supplies in case such a course of action is chosen during a crisis. The fleet may protect Soviet oil supplies but oil is also needed to run the fleet. The Soviet Union may be able to secure Egyptian oil refined in South Yemen in order to fuel its naval vessels in the Indian Ocean area.[41]

As Soviet ships once again sail into the Red Sea and then out into the Indian Ocean through the Bab el Mandeb Strait, they will be able to obstruct the oil traffic of Western states; in the immediate future, however, a more likely target could be Israel. Israel imports a considerable percentage of its oil from Iran and the tankers must pass through the Bab el Mandeb Strait, as well as the Strait of Tiran, on their way to the Israeli port of Eilat.[42] Egypt has previously blockaded both locations, and on June 11, 1971, members of the Popular Front for the Liberation of Palestine damaged a tanker bound from Iran to Eilat while it was passing through the Bab el Mandeb Strait. The tanker, the *Coral Sea,* was registered in Liberia but was chartered by Israel and it carried

30,000 tons of crude oil. It was damaged by bazooka fire but still managed to reach Eilat.[43] If there is another Arab-Israeli war, the Arab states may make a concerted effort to prevent the flow of oil to Israel and whatever role the Soviet fleet may decide to play in such an action is purely speculative at this time.

In order to enhance its naval power, the Soviet Union has fostered cordial political relations with the states along the Red Sea and those adjacent to the Bab el Mandeb and it has secured some significant strategic rights. The Soviets have the use of port facilities at Hodeida, Yemen; Aden, South Yemen and Berbera and Mogadishu, Somalia and they have anchorages off the island of Socotra, South Yemen. They enlarged the ports of Hodeida, Berbera and Mogadishu and they have the use of airfields in Somalia from which the Indian Ocean can be patrolled. As reported by *Middle-East Intelligence Survey* in June 1974, the Soviet Union sent a naval mission to Somalia and South Yemen to ask for increased port rights and this mission also looked into the possibility of building a submarine dock in Somalia.[44] The Soviets, in recognition of the strategic importance of Somalia and South Yemen, may even have wiped out debts of $45 million and $15 million respectively owed by these two states to the USSR, even though this was contrary to usual Soviet practices.[45] Furthermore, in 1971 the Soviets reduced the price of oil for Somalia after complaints from the Somali Finance Secretary, Ibrahim Megag Samatar. A delegation dispatched to the USSR was able to secure the reduction.[46]

The Soviet Union has developed close ties with Somalia and has provided sizable arms shipments. This strengthens the Somali position in the Somalia–Ethiopia disputes over the Ogaden region of Ethiopia and the French-controlled territory of Djibouti (formally known as the Territory of the Afars and Issas). If Somalia ever gains control of Djibouti, it can join with South Yemen in controlling the Bab el Mandeb and this would threaten the interests of both Ethiopia and Israel.[47] These latter two states would prefer to see French or Ethiopian control of Djibouti so that their naval rights of passage will be respected, and Ethiopia also needs

Djibouti as a vital transportation link to the sea since its major railroad runs from Addis Ababa to Djibouti. Ethiopia and Israel also have a common interest in preventing the secession of Eritrea from Ethiopia. The Eritrean Liberation Front receives backing from many Arab states and a Moslem-dominated Eritrean state could help disrupt Israeli shipping in the Red Sea. Ethiopia obviously does not want the dismemberment of its state, but it is also concerned about being landlocked, since with the loss of Eritrea it would have no access to the sea and would have to depend upon possible transit rights through Eritrea or Djibouti. The Soviet Union has generally maintained correct relations with Ethiopia, despite the deep Soviet involvement in Somalia, and ties could possibly become more extensive now that the Ethiopian monarchy has been overthrown. The USSR has not supported the Eritrean secessionists and Soviet technicians are still serving at the Soviet-built oil refinery at Assab on the Eritrean coast. The Soviets have also shown interest in forging strong ties with the Sudan. The Soviet Union did have access to some port facilities at Port Sudan, but its ambitions were set back after the unsuccessful, communist-supported coup against President Numeiry in 1971. Soviet relations with Yemen have usually been close. Overall, the USSR carefully laid the necessary political and strategic groundwork in preparation for the reopening of the Suez Canal. It is now operating from a position of power in a vital oil route but whether it will seek to capitalize on this asset is still subject to question.

Much of the oil produced in the Persian Gulf is exported by tankers which must sail through the Indian Ocean after exiting the Gulf via the Strait of Hormuz, and this has brought about an East–West naval rivalry in the area. Britain served warning of its continued interest in the Indian Ocean, despite its previous naval withdrawal from the Persian Gulf, by staging a joint exercise with South Africa off Simonstown in early November 1974, and France also plans to conduct exercises with South Africa and to build a naval base at Mayotte in the Comoro Islands. In November 1974, the largest CENTO naval exercises ever were held in the Arabian

Sea, with American and British ships participating, and the American aircraft carrier *Constellation* was briefly sent into the Persian Gulf for a "familiarization" visit, the first to that area by an American carrier in 26 years. The United States is also constructing a naval base on the British-owned island of Diego Garcia (it has also acquired airfield rights on the Omani island of Masirah), although it may have preferred a base in Pakistan. The American "tilt" toward Pakistan during the Bangladesh crisis may have been motivated by strategic considerations, since Pakistan is very close to the entrance of the Persian Gulf, but India objects to the granting of such a base to the Americans and the U.S. has settled on Diego Garcia instead so as not to offend India more than necessary.[48] The U.S. may also have feared that were it to establish a base in Pakistan, India would permit the Soviet Union to have a similar facility on her territory.

The U.S. decision to develop a base on Diego Garcia will probably increase Soviet pressure on India for naval-base rights. The Soviet fleet already enjoys some port privileges in India, particularly at Vishakhapatnam and also at Bombay, but it would like a more extensive base of operations. As reported in *The Washington Star-News,* Soviet requests for a base were made in November 1973, during Brezhnev's trip to India, and again when an Indian delegation visited the USSR in January 1974; but India turned down the Soviets on both occasions.[49] The Soviets may keep on trying but now, in light of the overthrow of the Rahman government in Bangladesh, they will have to push aside any serious thoughts about seeking naval facilities at Chittagong, Bangladesh as well. They already have a strong naval presence at Umm Qasr, Iraq and their ships make calls at Bandar Abbas, Iran.

Soviet naval strength in the Indian Ocean may limit the possibilities for armed intervention by the United States or other Western powers in case there is another oil embargo and the Soviets can then posture as the defenders of Arab oil interests. Furthermore, Western apprehension about growing Soviet influence in the Indian Ocean area seems to be pushing the Western states into closer collaboration with anticommunist South Africa.[50] This strains their relations with Third World states and comes at an inopportune time diplomatically since the decolonization of Southern Africa and sanctions against South Africa have become top-priority international issues.

The Persian Gulf

As the Soviet fleet extends its activities in the Indian Ocean, it also plays a somewhat greater role in the Persian Gulf, where a partial vacuum has been created by the British military withdrawal. On January 16, 1968, the British government announced that all of its troops and naval vessels would be removed from the Persian Gulf by the end of 1971, but the Soviets felt that the Federation of Arab Emirates being organized by the British was a cover for retention of British influence in the Gulf. They also did not want the United States to replace Britain as the dominant military force in the area and they feared that there could be an attempt to create a military bloc to protect American oil interests.[51] In addition, they may have been concerned about their own security since IRBMs launched from the Persian Gulf are capable of reaching the Soviet Union's missile and space installations in Central Asia. Therefore, the Soviets were anxious to deny the Persian Gulf to Western navies.[52]

In order to minimize Western anxieties about the potential Soviet role in the Gulf, the USSR decided to keep a low profile. It was very difficult for the Soviets to bring ships to the Persian Gulf from their Pacific or Mediterranean fleets; in addition, they did not want to alarm the West and thereby abet an American naval buildup. The U.S. did not seek a naval race, which might have led to a direct confrontation with the Soviets, so both sides soft-pedaled the issue and established a modest presence in the Gulf. Soviet warships paid occasional visits to Umm Qasr and to Bandar Abbas, Iran, and the United States maintained a minimal naval facility at Bahrain. In a strange manner, Soviet and American policies coincided, since both states desired stability in the Gulf and wanted to restrict the other's role. The USSR and the U.S. there-fore stepped aside and permitted Iran to build up its fleet in order to enhance its role as guarantor of Persian Gulf tranquility.

The Soviet Union wants a stable Persian Gulf to protect its own oil supply route from Iraq and it does not want to have to choose sides in the event of an Iran–Iraq conflict. Furthermore, the Soviets can hurt the West without threatening the stability of the area since they can encourage the nationalization policies of oil-producing states or support future oil embargoes. Such steps can be just as effective as the naval interdiction of tankers. In order to undercut Western influence, the Soviets have been im-proving relations with states which were previously viewed as "re-actionary." [53] Contacts with Kuwait, Saudi Arabia, and Abu Dhabi have increased and arms may be sold to Kuwait. The USSR even purchased oil from Saudi Arabia in 1969 and moderated its criti-cism of King Feisal once he became instrumental in the 1973–74 Arab oil embargo. Abu Dhabi may initiate trade relations with Hungary.[54]

The Soviet Union is willing to let Iran play a major role in the Persian Gulf, even though it is a member of CENTO, because this provides some stability and is certainly preferable to a large American presence.[55] One Soviet commentator called for "peace and safety" in Iran since it is on the southern frontier of the USSR. He indicated that a strong Iran could resist imperialist pressures and he wrote: "In such a situation, Iran can only have a favorable influence on neighbors in the region." [56] The Soviet Union has consistently maintained that Persian Gulf states should be left to handle their own regional problems without outside in-terference, and such a position really acknowledges Iran's lead-ing role among Gulf states. It was enunciated when the Shah vis-ited the USSR in October 1972 and reiterated numerous times such as when Kosygin went to Iran in March 1973, when Iranian premier Hoveyda came to the USSR in August 1973, and when the Shah was in the USSR in November 1974.[57] When Iranian troops occupied the three islands of Abu Musa and the two Tumbs on November 30, 1971, the Soviets tacitly accepted this action.[58] These strategic islands help control egress from the Persian Gulf and the Iranian use of force against territories previously claimed by Arab emirates (Abu Musa by Sharjah and the Tumbs by Ras al-Khaima) was roundly condemned by the Arab states.

The Soviet Union would like to reduce American influence in Iran and weaken CENTO and it has therefore been furthering economic, and even military, contacts with Iran (see chapter 7). From the Iranian perspective, economic ties with the USSR can be profitable and Iran would also like to display some independence toward the United States. However, an important motivating factor for the Iranians is the desire to foster a moderate Soviet policy in the Gulf so that the USSR does not take a pro-Arab position and is at least willing to acquiesce while Iranian naval might is expanded.[59]

There is one significant exception to Soviet-Iranian harmony in the Persian Gulf and it relates to the continuing struggle being waged against the Omani sultanate by the Popular Front for the Liberation of the Occupied Arabian Gulf (PFLOAG), operating in the Dhofar region. The Soviets supply some arms to the guerrilla movement as they portray Sultan Qabus as an agent of British imperialism who is trying to suppress "patriotic forces."[60] They also charge that Britain has not really withdrawn its troops from the Gulf but has just redeployed them in Oman in order to continue the exertion of military and political pressure on other Gulf states.[61] Iran wants to prevent the radicalization of Oman and has sent troops to support the antiguerrilla effort. Both the Soviet Union and Iran have strategic considerations in mind since Oman sits astride the Strait of Hormuz and can play an obstructive role in regard to Persian Gulf traffic.[62] Radio Moscow has alluded to Oman's strategic importance for the oil trade, claiming that the British are trying to gain control of Oman in order to serve the interests of the oil monopolies.[63]

The Soviet Union wants to maintain its very close relationship with Iraq but it simultaneously hopes to continue its rapprochement with Iran. Therefore, prior to the 1975 Iran–Iraq accord, the Soviet Union sought to prevent any confrontation between these states over the Shatt al-Arab waterway, since it could have been pressured to take sides and its own oil imports from the Iraqi port of Fao could also have been disrupted. The Soviet Union constantly called for friendship between Iraq and Iran and pointed out that neither had a territorial claim against the other.[64] This was technically true, but there had certainly been a riparian dispute and border skirmishes occurred frequently.

Posing an even greater problem for the USSR was the Kurdish issue in northern Iraq. After the Second World War, the Soviets supported the Kurds as they fought to create their own state, or at least to create an autonomous unit within Iraq, and the Kurdish leader, Mustapha al-Barzani, lived in the Soviet Union for many years.[65] The situation changed during the late sixties, when the Soviet Union found an ally in the Baathist government of Iraq and then began importing oil from the Kirkuk oil fields in northern Iraq. The USSR came to desire stability in the area and a peaceful resolution of the Kurdish issue. It therefore supported the 1974 Iraqi plan for Kurdish autonomy and called upon the Kurds to accept its provisions; but the Kurds balked, partially because the oil-rich Kirkuk region was not to be included within the Kurdish autonomous zone and the Kurds were not to receive a large share of the oil revenue.[66] Kirkuk had been a Kurdish city, but many Arabs were moving into Kirkuk to work in the oil industry. The Soviet Union imported Kirkuk crude oil, which flowed out through the IPC pipeline to Syria, and hoped to forestall any turmoil which could impede its oil supplies. It also wanted Iraq, not the Kurds, to control Kirkuk, since the Kurdish leadership had turned anti-Soviet and might have terminated oil exports to the USSR were it able to incorporate Kirkuk into Kurdestan. Thus the USSR supported the Iraqi military efforts against the Kurds, which began after Kurdish refusal of the autonomy offer, and the Iraqi forces were equipped with Soviet weapons. It is likely that the dozen MiG–23s provided by the USSR were flown by Soviet pilots.[67] Complicating the Soviet role in the Kurdish–Iraqi conflict was Iran's support of the Kurds; deep Soviet involvement could have caused a rift in Soviet–Iranian relationships. However, the Iran–Iraq accord of early 1975 simplified the situation for the Soviets. It led to an Iraqi victory over the Kurds and a settlement of the Iran–

Iraq dispute along the Shatt al-Arab. Iran also discontinued its support for the Iraqi Kurds.

The Soviet Tanker Fleet

In order to assess Soviet interaction with the geopolitics of Middle East oil, some knowledge of the Soviet oil tanker fleet is essential. There was a tanker shortage during the late fifties and early sixties, but the USSR became basically self-sufficient by the late sixties. Now, the USSR is in a very favorable position, since most of its tankers are small enough to pass through the Suez Canal. Most Western states rely on supertankers which are too large to transit the Canal.

As of 1960, the USSR and 123 tankers with a total deadweight tonnage of 1,040,000 and its tanker fleet was the eleventh largest in the world. Its average tanker size of 8455 deadweight tons was very small (in 1959, the entire tanker fleet of all communist-ruled states except Yugoslavia made up only 1.53 percent of the world total).[68] The USSR was faced with a tanker shortage and, despite Western efforts to impose a tanker chartering embargo on her, she managed to charter tankers. There was a tanker glut at the time and many tanker owners were anxious to lease out their ships.[69] The Soviets transported more than half of their oil imports and exports in chartered tankers, many of them coming from Norway, Greece, Sweden, Italy, and Britain.[70] In one deal, Greek shipping magnate Stavros Niarchos agreed to transport two million tons of Soviet oil from Black Sea ports between August 1960 and the end of 1963.[71] The Soviets bought tankers as well—from Japan, Yugoslavia, the Netherlands, Italy, Sweden, Finland, Poland, Britain, France and Denmark.[72]

The Soviet Union concentrated on building up its tanker fleet and became basically self-sufficient by 1965.[73] As of 1970, the USSR had 192 tankers with a total deadweight tonnage of 4.449 million; when the tankers of other CMEA states were added, the total tonnage was 5.28 million.[74] The Soviets had enough tanker capacity so they could even afford to charter out tankers on a number of occasions. They did so in 1967 following the closure of the Suez Canal and they have been leasing tankers to Iraq in order to transport North Rumailah crude from the Persian Gulf.[75] They also lease a tanker, the *Azov,* to a Canadian company in order to carry Libyan crude oil to Quebec.[76] Now that the Suez Canal is again open, the Soviets may have ships available for charter, as the reduced sailing distance between the Black Sea and Asia will mean that fewer Soviet ships will be at sea at any one time.[77]

Most Soviet tankers are between 18,000 and 36,000 deadweight tons; as recently as 1968 the Soviets had no tanker larger than 40,000 tons. The USSR has not followed the world trend toward supertankers because it does not have sufficient port development and since most supertankers cannot fit through the Bosphorus and Dardanelles on their way in or out of the Black Sea.[78] The Soviets are now testing some tankers as large as 150,000 deadweight tons, but the USSR will generally stick with smaller tankers.[79]

After the 1967 closure of the Suez Canal, world construction of supertankers was accelerated in order to transport oil from the Persian Gulf to Europe and North America via the Cape route. At the beginning of 1968, there were 66 tankers of at least 100,000 deadweight tons but the number rose to 112 by 1969, 184 by 1970, and 244 by 1971. In 1973, 35 to 40 percent of crude oil transport was in tankers of more than 150,000 deadweight tons.[80] The Suez Canal can only handle tankers of up to 60,000 deadweight tons and yet just 30.9 percent of world tanker tonnage now falls into that category and only 4.1 percent of the tankers on order do so.[81] It should be pointed out, however, that some empty supertankers are able to transit and that the Canal will probably be enlarged in the near future.

With the Suez Canal reopened, the Soviet Union will be in a most advantageous position for a number of years, since it will have a fleet of small tankers capable of passing through the Canal while most countries will be burdened with supertankers. Eventually, the advantage will dissipate as the Canal is widened and deepened and as the Sumed pipeline is constructed. This pipeline will enable supertankers to send their oil from Ain Soukna on the Gulf of Suez to a terminal on the Mediterranean, west of Alexandria. It will then be picked up by other tankers. The Suez Canal will therefore be bypassed, as it is already by Israel's Eilat–Ashkelon pipeline. It is possible that the importance of the Suez Canal as an oil artery will someday decline as oil pipelines proliferate.[82] The IPC, Tapline, and Israeli pipelines will be joined by the Sumed pipeline through Egypt, as well as by a planned Iraq–Turkey pipeline from Kirkuk to Dortyol. In addition, it is already apparent that cost factors are making shippers reluctant to shift from supertankers to smaller tankers which are capable of transiting the Canal, and oil traffic through the Canal is below pre-1967 levels. In the meantime, the USSR will effectively utilize the Canal for its oil imports and exports and it may lease some of its tankers to other states.

The Soviet Union's geopolitical position in regard to Middle East oil is strong, as it possesses naval power, an adequate tanker fleet, and useful political influence in key geographical locations where the possible obstruction of oil traffic could take place. Although a major oil exporter, the Soviet Union has jumped into Middle East oil politics alongside the superpower oil importers and an active Soviet role can be expected for many years to come.

7/The Middle East and North Africa

Soviet oil policies in the Middle East and North Africa are aimed primarily at limiting Western power in the area and secondarily at extending the influence of the Soviet Union. The latter can be accomplished through Soviet diplomatic maneuvering on Arab-Israeli issues and the provisions of military assistance to Arab states, while the use of oil as a lever of political influence would probably prove counterproductive and lead to the impression that Soviet and Western policies are both exploitative and manipulative.

Western power is directly related to the accessibility and security of oil supplies and to the influence that can be exerted through the control of production, refining, and marketing operations. The Soviet Union can undercut the Western position by encouraging the nationalization of Western oil properties and embargoes on exports to major Western states; the Soviets can also purchase and market more of the oil themselves, thus weakening the Western marketing network. In addition, the Soviets can help develop the potential for obstructing the flow of oil to the West by supporting the efforts of regional states to wield more effective control over vital waterways and pipelines.

The Soviet Union has often served as an exporter of oil to Middle East and North African states lacking self-sufficiency, but the Soviets have traditionally denied any desire to import oil from Arab states. The Soviets began to purchase Algerian oil in 1967 and Egyptian oil in 1969, and imports from other Arab states followed; but even in late 1967 the Soviet journal *International Affairs* could declare: "The rationalization for U.S. policy in the Middle East is the alleged threat of a Soviet takeover of the area's oil.

Imperialist spokesmen know, of course, that the USSR, a large oil exporter, has no need of Middle Eastern oil and does not take control of other peoples' resources in the imperialist manner." [1] Since imports from Arab states were initiated, the Soviets have been reacting very defensively when questioned about their motivation. It is maintained that the Soviet Union has no oil shortage and is importing Arab oil because the Arab states desire to repay Soviet credits in this manner. It is also averred that the Soviet delivery of Arab oil to communist-ruled states has been approved by the Arabs.[2] The point about credits seems to imply that the Soviets are doing the Arabs a favor by importing their oil. The Soviets use a similar line of reasoning when they discuss their purchases of oil from nationalized oil fields; they claim that by doing so they are providing a market for oil which may be blacklisted by Western oil companies.[3] Furthermore, the Soviets assert that Third World states are exporters of raw materials because of their colonial heritage and that the USSR helps them out by buying these raw materials. One Soviet writer indicates that 73 percent of Soviet imports from Third World states consist of raw materials and that fuel is representing an increasing percentage of these raw-material imports.[4]

It is true that Arab states derive advantages from their oil exports to the USSR, but the Soviet desire to import is not based on sheer magnanimity. It is cheaper to buy oil in the Middle East and North Africa than to produce it in Western Siberia and these oil purchases can also serve as a margin of supply security until Western Siberian production achieves its expected lofty level. The Soviets also save on transportation costs since they can resell Middle East oil to Asian customers or Algerian oil to Cuba, rather than directly export their own oil from Black Sea ports. Oil purchases enable the USSR to maintain large export commitments (thereby furthering the Soviet influence effect) and they additionally serve as a convenient means of repayment for Soviet arms or industrial credits. Frequently, the Soviet Union receives oil as part of a barter arrangement and thus is able to find markets for its own machinery and equipment exports.

The USSR is playing the role of middleman with much of the

oil it purchases, since this oil is resold to East European and, to some extent, West European states. The Soviets are thus able to retain their strong grip over most of the East European energy supply and can also drive a small dent into the West European marketing operations of the major Western oil companies. Furthermore, the Soviets spur on the nationalization programs of Arab states as they buy oil from the state sector. The East European states also buy some Arab oil, and Iranian oil as well, but their motivation is much simpler than that of the USSR. They have an oil shortage and the Soviet Union is unable to supply all of their needs.

Soviet oil relations with Middle East and North African states are multifaceted, as the USSR is an importer, an exporter, and a middleman and it also lends assistance in prospecting, production, refining, and marketing. Furthermore, the USSR helps orchestrate anti-Western actions such as nationalizations and embargoes and it seeks to establish geopolitical influence at key points in order to weaken the West's strategic position. The thrust of Soviet policy is to end Western control over large sectors of the oil industry, and to reverse the situation so that oil becomes the Achilles heel of Western states. As access to oil supplies is made more difficult, as the security of oil routes becomes questionable, and as Western economies are disrupted by an energy shortage, the Soviet Union gains a strategic advantage without much effort or risk.

The Soviets believe that control over oil has been the key to Western influence in the Middle East and North Africa and that the demise of Western oil hegemony is leading to a reduction of influence as well. According to the Soviet interpretation, the West uses its hold over the foreign exchange earnings of oil-producing states in order to influence their foreign policies and, at the same time, it economically exploits these states.[5] It is maintained that more than half of the capitalist profits derived from the Third World come from oil and that 15 percent of all American overseas profits are based on oil.[6] Profits are maximized since Western companies do not permit the oil-producing states to refine much of the oil, instead reserving the refining operations for themselves. They also pay low wages to oil workers and do not pay enough in oil taxes.[7] Their dominance over marketing in the non-communist world also adds to their profits. Another Soviet charge is that part of the Western oil profits are used to support Israel against the Arab states. Radio Moscow declared: "An important part of this profit goes into the pockets of Western oil kings who, at the same time, represent Zionist big capital. Here the Arabs are faced with a glaring reality—money from exploitation of Arab oil and the labour of Arab workers subsequently finds its way into the pockets of the Israeli extremists. The money is used to buy Phantom aircraft and other weapons for the Israeli armed forces while Israel is encouraged in its expansionist, criminal policy against the Arab countries. This is food for thought." [8]

The Soviets make no distinction between oil companies and Western states, since they believe that both serve the same imperialist interests. Oil companies put pressure on states so that the policies they desire will be enacted and oil company officials are given high state positions.[9] *Izvestiia* has pointed to the oil company–state relationship as one in which oil companies supply fuel for the army and the army controls other states in order to protect the interests of the oil company.[10] One Soviet writer even claims that when the three Kennedy brothers tried to bring about greater state regulation of the oil companies, the companies hatched a plan to silence them.[11]

The Soviets maintain that Western oil interests in the Middle East were concerned with preserving the status quo, and therefore their oil concessions, and this brought about their collaboration with "reactionary" governments.[12] As Middle East states have moved to limit the power of Western oil companies, the latter are ending their internecine struggles and are cooperating in order to hold onto their privileged position.[13] The attempts by oil-producing states to restrict the activities of the oil companies have led to extreme counterattacks by the companies. The Soviets charge that the Suez War of 1956 and the American and British interventions in Lebanon and Jordan in 1958 were aimed at protecting Western oil interests.[14] The 1967 war resulted from oil company retaliations for restrictions placed on them by "progressive" Arab states. These states wanted a greater share of the profits and Syria demanded high transit fees for the Iraq Petroleum Company pipeline. The oil companies therefore encouraged Israeli aggression as one of the aims was the overthrow of the "progressive" governments of Syria and Egypt.[15] An article in *International Affairs* discussed the 1956 and 1967 wars and declared: "The essential object in both wars was to reverse the revolutionary trend and to preserve the area for imperialist oil companies." [16]

The Soviets believe that their assistance to oil-producing states can weaken the influence of Western oil companies. As the oil-producers become less reliant on the West, they can more easily nationalize oil properties, raise prices, or pursue more independent foreign policies; the USSR contributes to this effect by prospecting for oil, providing equipment and credits, training oil specialists, building refineries, and drilling wells. It also constructs storage facilities, provides technicians, and helps with the development of pipelines and tanker fleets. It is asserted that the main obstacle to further nationalization is the lack of personnel to run the oil industry but that the communist-ruled states are now training such cadres.[17] The Soviets also send their own technicians and oil minister Valentin Shashin claimed that there were 775 Soviet oil experts in Algeria, Egypt, Syria, Iraq, and India as of January 1971.[18]

Most Middle East and North African oil-producers refine very little of their own oil. The Western companies dominate refining operations, which deprives the producers of greater profits. Occasionally, they do not even have enough refined oil for their domestic needs.[19] Soviet writers concede that Western companies share some of the profits from crude oil with the producing states but they point to refining as a major area of economic exploitation. Western control of transportation and marketing is also decried and the Soviets particularly want to assist the oil-producers in these three areas so that the Western position can be undermined.[20]

The Soviets would like to see the nationalization of all Western oil holdings in the Middle East and North Africa and they would prefer state control of marketing operations. The Western companies could then be bypassed, with deals being made directly with the consuming states. However, the development of state oil corporations and marketing networks will take time, so some ties with Western oil companies will be necessary. It is therefore advisable to deal with small, independent Western companies rather than the large monopolies.[21] In order to eliminate Western oil influence, the Soviets obviously advocate socialism and they assert that independence from the oil monopolies is greatest in states such as Iraq, Egypt, Syria, and Algeria, which follow a non-capitalist path.[22] State-controlled oil corporations can be strengthened, and Western concessions weakened, if new oil fields are developed under state aegis and the Soviets therefore assist in exploration and oilfield development.[23] They also encourage socialism by providing advisers for state-run oil corporations and they buy oil only from the state sector, thus facilitating its growth.

The Soviets maintain that their willingness to buy oil from nationalized fields, as in Iraq and Libya, greatly assists the nationalization process and prevents any effective Western boycott.[24] They assert that the boycott of Iran in 1951–53 was successful because the Iranians could not find markets for their oil but now that the communist-ruled states provide a market, boycotts are doomed to failure.[25] The Soviets always advocated nationalization but, for practical reasons, they believed that it must occur gradually. One commentator suggested partial nationalization and the creation of "mixed" companies in partnership with Western interests. He pointed out that the oil-producing states had insufficient funds to pay for complete nationalization.[26] Ruben Andreasyan, a journalist who frequently writes about oil, wanted the Western oil companies to appoint more nationals of the oil-producing states to their directorial boards, to share profits more equitably, to share profits earned outside of the Middle East, and to train a greater number of local personnel.[27] The Soviets recognized the problems inherent in any nationalization action, such as a shortage of capital, technicians, and tankers. They also believed that even if a bourgeois state were to nationalize its oil industry, the

workers would still be exploited; they claimed that this had occurred in Iran during the early fifties.[28] However, as the power of
the oil-producing states increased in 1973 and 1974, the Soviets
somewhat radicalized their stand by rejecting "partnership" or
reforms and they began to call for rapid nationalization.[29]

The Soviet position on the quantity of oil production in the
Middle East and North Africa has changed with the times. Until
mid-1973, when the availability of oil was not a problem and
prices were generally low, Soviet writers charged that Western oil
monopolies were keeping production low and depriving the producing states of extra income.[30] Even as late as April 1973, Ruben
Andreasyan was claiming that Western oil companies were decreasing production in "progressive" states as a pressure tactic
while they were increasing production in "pro-imperialist" countries.[31] However, the producing states then decided to limit production in order to help support higher prices and the USSR has
praised this action. Soviet writers do not fail to point out that nationalized oil companies can facilitate the fixing of extraction
quotas and prices.[32] In regard to prices, the Soviets feel that large
increases are justifiable because of past exploitation and the de-
valuation of the dollar, but they certainly derive a profit bonus for
themselves as well.[33] As the Arab states build up their currency
reserves through oil sales, the Soviets are encouraging them to
spend the funds in the Middle East and to develop their own
banking systems. The Soviets do not want the funds to flow back
to Western states as investments or bank deposits.[34]

Soviet–Iranian Energy Relations

The Soviet Union and Iran have had a long relationship in the
areas of oil and natural gas as strategic considerations and geographical proximity have fostered a high degree of economic interaction. Iran adjoins the Soviet Union's southern border and the
Russian attempts to keep Western influence out of Iran go back
to Czarist times. The Russians have tried to deny northern Iran to

outside powers while establishing some control there themselves. Russia, and then the Soviet Union, obviously did not want major Western powers to have a position of strength on its border. In addition, the Baku oil fields are located near the border. The Russians feared that foreign powers might seize Baku and deprive Russia of its prime oil-producing area. In addition to strategic defense, Russia traditionally sought to extend its influence southward toward the Persian Gulf, possibly securing the use of warm-water ports in the process. In World War II, the Soviet Union indicated to Germany that its main expansionist interest was southward through Iran. The Soviet Union temporarily occupied northern Iran at the end of the Second World War and it also encouraged Kurdish and Azerbaljani separatist movements against the Iranian state. Although the Soviet Union has often cooperated with Iran, it has always looked somewhat askance upon its monarchical government. And anticommunist Iran is perpetually wary about its powerful neighbor to the north.

One of the first episodes concerning Russian–Iranian oil relations took place in 1916 when Russian troops entered northern Iran and some Iranian cabinet ministers granted an oil concession without seeking parliamentary approval. The recipient of the concession was a Georgian, Akakii Khoshtaria, but he was a Russian subject. He was unable to exploit his concession in northern Iran because of the war, and with the advent of the new Bolshevik government, which opposed the concept of concessions in other states, Khoshtaria (in 1920) sold his interests to the British-owned Anglo-Persian Oil Company. However, the Soviets did not want a British concession so close to their border and Iran was also distrustful of British involvement. Accordingly, the Soviets and Iranians agreed to a treaty on February 26, 1921, which stipulated that all Soviet concessions in Iran were renounced but that Iran could not grant any of these concessions to another party. This treaty effectively eliminated any claim by Anglo-Persian and the Soviets were successful in keeping northern Iran free of big power influence.[35] The Soviet Union generally cooperated with the Iranian government and did not press for its own sphere of influence in northern Iran, but the Soviets did acquire a majority of shares in the Kavir-Khurian oil company which was granted a concession near Semnan in 1925, despite the 1921 treaty.[36]

Overall, Soviet activities in northern Iran were not extensive until World War II, when the flow of oil to Allied forces was severely disrupted and the Soviet Union experienced an oil shortage owing to logistical difficulties resulting from the German occupation. To solve both of these problems, Britain and the USSR occupied Iran in 1941, exploiting its oil resources for the Allied cause and using it as a gateway for sending supplies to the USSR.[37] The Anglo-Soviet intervention was also based on the fear that pro-German groups in Iran might gain control and deny oil to the Allies.

The Soviets tried to take advantage of their occupation status by pressing for oil concessions in northern Iran. To some extent, the Soviets wanted to make sure that neither the United States nor Britain would be able to establish oil concessions in northern Iran but the Soviets, in addition, probably wanted Iranian oil since their own oil industry was heavily damaged during the war.[38] George Lenczowski, an American specialist on Middle East oil politics, writes that the Soviets may have thought that if their effort to gain concessions failed, at least Iran may have refused to grant concessions to Western states as well.[39]

In September 1944, Soviet Assistant People's Commissar for Foreign Affairs, Sergei Kavtaradze, arrived in Teheran with an oil delegation. He was supposedly in Iran to discuss Soviet exploitation of oil as part of the Kavir-Khurian concession but, on October 2, he asked for exclusive Soviet oil rights in northern Iran. Iran did not want to grant such a request and stalled for time. The Soviets encouraged demonstrations within Iran to support their position and they obstructed commerce in and out of their occupation zone. On October 16, the Iranian cabinet declared that no oil concessions would be granted until after the war, but Kavtaradze still continued his effort. On December 2, the Iranian legislature (the Majlis) passed a law stating that no oil concessions could be granted without its approval. This measure was introduced by Mohammed Mossadegh, who later became known as the main champion of Iranian economic nationalism.[40] Rebuffed again, Kavtaradze returned to the USSR in December 1944.

Soviet troops remained in northern Iran after the war ended, and when Stalin met with U.S. Secretary of State James F. Byrnes on December 19, 1945, he linked the occupation of northern Iran with the protection of the Baku oil fields. He explained that the 1921 Soviet–Iranian treaty permitted Soviet intervention in northern Iran if there were a threat to Soviet security.[41] In February 1946, the Soviets renewed their request for oil concessions but also indicated a willingness to accept majority control of a joint Soviet–Iranian oil company. Iran refused. At the United Nations on April 3, 1946, Andrei Gromyko claimed that the question of withdrawing Soviet troops and the issuance of oil concessions were unrelated, but the Soviet military presence obviously provided the USSR with added leverage. In fact, the very next day the USSR agreed to withdraw its troops in return for the creation of a joint Soviet–Iranian oil company. The USSR was to have 51 percent control for twenty-five years and 50 percent for the ensuing twenty-five years.[42] This oil arrangement was made explicit in an exchange of letters between the Iranian Prime Minister, Qavam Saltaneh, and the Soviet ambassador, Sadchikov.[43] The Soviet withdrawal was not entirely the result of successful oil negotiations; the Americans and the United Nations exerted pressure. The Soviets carried out their half of the bargain, but Iran did not want a joint oil company with the Soviets and had only agreed to it because of the Soviet military occupation. Therefore, Iran managed to back out of the deal with the USSR, using the legislature's action of December 2, 1944, as a legal basis. Since its approval was needed for any oil concessions granted to foreigners, the legislature accordingly voted on October 22, 1947, to reject the deal with the USSR, thus nullifying the action already taken by the Prime Minister.

During the Iranian oil nationalization dispute of 1951–54, the Soviet Union verbally supported Iran against Britain and other Western powers, and at the United Nations the Soviets backed up the Iranian position during the 1951 Security Council debate. Britain had protested Iran's action in expelling British personnel from

Abadan oil installations, in violation of an interim decision made by the World Court.[44] However, the Soviet Union lent little direct assistance to Iran and failed to take advantage of a golden political opportunity. The Western powers were refusing to buy Iranian oil, thereby attempting to reverse the nationalization decision, and the Soviet Union could have offered to purchase some of the oil, or at least to provide technical assistance for the nationalized oil industry. Instead, the Soviets indicated that they were considering intervention in Iran in order to remove any British threat and they also encouraged Azerbaijani separatism.[45] Iran became wary of Soviet intentions and the USSR did not manage to further its role in Iran, either politically or economically.

While the West was boycotting Iranian oil, Western oil companies were increasing their production in Saudi Arabia and Kuwait in order to make up for the oil shortage. Nevertheless, Britain in particular did experience a supply problem and it received help from an unlikely source, the Soviet Union. In September 1951, Sovrompetrol agreed to deliver oil to Britain.[46] Sovrompetrol was a joint Soviet-Rumanian company operating in the latter state but it was dominated by the USSR and clearly could not make any deal without the approval of the Soviet government. The Soviets were thus deriving economic benefit out of Britain's oil plight and political considerations were thrown by the wayside. On the other hand, Czechoslovakia (in December 1951) and Hungary (in January 1952) agreed to buy oil from Iran.[47] Neither of these states would have acted without Soviet consent and their purchases helped Iran with its oil marketing problem. Soviet policy throughout the Iranian crisis was on the whole ambivalent and ineffectual, despite some indirect actions carried out by her East European allies. Once the oil nationalization dispute was resolved, Iran remained politically and economically linked with the Western states.

The USSR had possessed a majority of shares in the Kavir-Khurian joint stock oil company ever since 1925, and the original agreement was supposed to extend until 1995. Nevertheless, in order to further "good neighborly relations" with Iran, the USSR gave up its holdings in the company in 1956. (The Kavir-Khurian company was fairly inactive and had not found any substantial quantities of oil in the test wells it had drilled.) The USSR turned its equipment over to Iran and did not seek any compensation for its stock. However, the Soviets did attach the provision that no foreign concerns could replace the USSR in searching for oil in northern Iran.[48] The Soviet good-will gesture was probably aimed at improving political relations, since Iran had become affiliated with the anticommunist Baghdad Pact, but the Soviets were also continuing their traditional policy of opposition to any Western oil interests in northern Iran. This policy was reiterated in March 1957, when the Soviet Union warned Iran against admitting any Western oil companies into the northern region.[49] Paradoxically, one of the motivations behind the Baghdad Pact may have been the perceived need to protect Western oil interests in southern Iran from any Soviet encroachments.[50]

As Iran became a member of the Western alliance system, the USSR tried to steer her toward a more neutral position. In late 1959, the Soviets offered to search for oil in northern Iran and to give Iran 15 percent of the oil found. In return, Iran was to refuse permission for any foreign military bases on her soil.[51] Iran rejected this proposal, as it was anxious to retain its ties with the Baghdad Pact (which by then had been reconstituted as CENTO) and did not want Soviet oil interests to return to northern Iran, from which they left three years earlier.

Gradually, Iran sought to improve its ties with the USSR so that it could become somewhat independent of Western control and benefit economically from improved trade with the USSR. Iran signaled its intentions in 1962 when it indicated that no nuclear missiles could be stationed on its territory and this led to a visit from Leonid Brezhnev, then chief of state, in 1963.[52] In 1965, the Shah returned the visit. The Soviet Union and Iran made numerous economic agreements during the late sixties, especially in the area of energy, and in January 1967, the Soviets sold Iran $100 million worth of arms in return for future deliveries of natural gas.[53] This was the first time that the Soviet Union and Iran had ever concluded an arms agreement and it took place despite Iran's continuing participation in CENTO. Soviet–Iranian relations have stayed fairly cordial but Iran is still basically pro-Western and anticommunist and the Shah has in no way fallen under Soviet influence. In fact, it has been Iran, rather than the USSR, which has generally set the standards for their oil and gas collaboration. The Shah has warned the Soviets: "I even serve notice that if our present friends do not respect Iran's rights in the Persian Gulf, they must expect Iran to take the same attitude toward them." [54]

Soviet-Iranian oil contacts are minimal and many Western reports of Soviet oil exploration in Iran and Soviet purchases of Iranian crude oil have been highly exaggerated. Actually, the Soviet Union has periodically sold small quantities of oil products to Iran and the issues of Soviet exploration and Iranian oil sales have been discussed, but not acted upon. In April 1967, the USSR offered to prospect for oil in Iran, and in April 1968 Prime Minister Kosygin visited Iran and inquired about a possible oil search in southern Iran along the Persian Gulf.[55] The Soviets may also have proposed that they prospect for oil in the southern part of the Caspian Sea, in return for the delivery of some Iranian crude oil.[56] However, Iran did not really want Soviet involvement in its oil affairs and gave noncommittal responses. Discussions are still going on, and the Soviets seem to be focusing their attention on northern Iran and the southern part of the Caspian Sea. In 1974, a Soviet delegation went to Iran to look into oil and gas prospecting in these areas. The Soviets analyzed energy prospects and submitted recommendations to the Iranians but no prospecting agreement was reached. The USSR has indicated its interest in reaching an agreement that would include the use of Soviet oil specialists and equipment and has also shown a willingness to provide floating drilling platforms for work in the Caspian Sea.[57]

The Soviet Union probably does not import crude oil from Iran; Soviet and Iranian trade statistics do not indicate that any such transaction is taking place. Yet many Western sources claim that there are such sales. In 1967, *Oil and Gas Journal* maintained that Iran had agreed to sell "surplus" crude oil to the USSR,[58] and in 1970 *Middle East Economic Digest* even furnished statistics, purporting to show that the USSR imported 5000 barrels per day of Iranian crude in 1968 and 20,000 barrels per day in 1969.[59] It is possible that these figures should have been attributed to East European allies of the USSR rather than to the USSR itself, since there were East European purchases at that time. In 1970 Australian international relations specialist T. B. Millar wrote that Iranian oil was being piped to the USSR but there was surely no such pipeline, and in 1972 economist Marshall Goldman mentioned planned oil deliveries from Iran to the Soviet Union.[60] In 1973 political scientist Charles McLane indicated that the USSR had an oil import agreement with Iran, and in 1974 oil analyst Frank Gardner asserted that the Soviets were buying oil from Iran during the Arab embargo and reselling it in Western Europe at a 300 percent profit.[61]

When there is so much smoke a fire is certainly possible, but I have been unable to verify any of the claims made above. Perhaps Iranian oil is transported across the border to outlying areas of the USSR, or perhaps it is involved in switch deals, with the Soviets reselling it to Asian customers; it cannot come from the southern part of the Caspian Sea, because the oil fields there are not yet in production. In any event, if there are oil sales, why should both sides hide such a fact? After all, Iranian gas sales to the USSR are highly publicized. Some suggest that the oil is shipped to the USSR and is piped through Israel's Eilat–Ashkelon pipeline en route. This would explain the secrecy but it is unlikely that the Soviets would risk antagonizing the Arabs just to transport a small quantity of crude oil. Rumania does use the Israeli pipeline for its transport of Iranian crude but Rumania has diplomatic ties with Israel and has a more evenhanded policy in the Middle East than does the USSR.

In April 1970, the Soviet Union and Iran discussed the building of an oil pipeline from Bushir, on the Persian Gulf, to Astara, on the Soviet border.[62] It was to have a capacity of 1.4 million barrels per day and was to transport Arab oil, mostly from Iraq.[63] The Shah indicated that although the pipeline was his idea, he expected Arab states to finance the project since it was their oil that was to be transported.[64] Had there been a pipeline agreement, the Soviet Union would have imported large quantities of Arab oil, thus freeing more of its own production for export, and the Soviet role of middleman would have been enhanced. However, no agreement was ever reached. Iraq probably did not want to export oil through the territory of its chief rival, Iran, preferring instead to develop an additional pipeline to the Mediterranean via Turkey. Iran too may not have been particularly interested in its own proposal. It may have feared such close collaboration with the USSR, and possibly floated the pipeline idea to pressure potential Western investors into an alternative Iran–Turkey pipeline. Iran was having difficulty in attracting funds for the plan, but the threat of a pipeline project with a communist-ruled state could have served to open up some Western pockets for the Turkey route. If that was the Iranian ploy, it was unsuccessful; there is still no Iran–Turkey oil pipeline.

The Soviet–Iranian gas relationship has proved to be mutually beneficial. The Soviet Union secures a gas supply for Azerbaijan, which lies alongside the Iranian border, and thereby overcomes the gas deficiency of this republic. Although Azerbaijan still produces a sufficient quantity of crude oil, its natural gas deposits are almost depleted.[65] Also, by importing gas from Iran, the Soviets can save on the pipeline construction that would have been necessary to link Azerbaijan with Soviet gas-producing areas.[66] The Soviets benefit financially since they pay Iran less than they charge for their own gas exports to Western and Eastern Europe. In 1973, they paid Iran 29 cents per thousand cubic feet but received 39 cents from Austria, 52 cents from Poland, and 55 cents from Czechoslovakia.[67] The Soviet claims that they do not actually resell any Iranian natural gas are apparently true.[68]

From the Iranian perspective, it makes sense to export natural gas to a neighboring state since gas is transported through pipelines that are very expensive to build if they must extend over great distances. The alternative, shipping liquefied natural gas, also involves very high investment costs. In return for its natural gas, Iran has received industrial plants and arms. It is also allowed to siphon off some of the gas from the pipeline to the USSR. The Iranians also had the northern half of the pipeline constructed for them by the Soviets and there is a spur line connecting the major pipe with Teheran. Gas sales help Iran overcome an unfavorable balance of trade with the USSR, and it is expected that Soviet credits for the gasline project will be repaid with gas exports by 1985.[69] On the negative side, Iran does not receive a good price from the Soviet Union and there has been much haggling in recent years. Iranian gas sales to France and Japan are far more profitable.[70]

In late 1965, the Soviet Union and Iran agreed on the construction of a gas pipeline from near Ahwaz, Iran, to the Soviet border at Astara. The arrangements were formalized in January 1966.[71] The Soviets were to build the northern half of the pipeline and a connecting spur to Teheran and Iran was to make agreements with Western companies for the construction of the southern half. Iran then contracted with the British firm of Costain-Press and with Williams Bros. of the United States.[72] Although the Soviets were to build half of the pipeline, Iran was to provide the pipe. Iran was to pay for Soviet construction work with future deliveries of natural gas and the Soviets were to construct a steel mill near Esfahan and other industrial facilities, also in return for gas. Before the Soviet gas deal, Western oil companies had generally wasted Iranian natural gas by flaring it and the West had been reluctant to assist Iran with industrial projects, but collaboration with the USSR provided a solution to both problems.[73]

The Soviet–Iranian pipeline was to supply the USSR with six billion cubic meters of natural gas per year, rising to ten billion by 1974, and deliveries thereafter would be ten billion per year through 1985.[74] Subsequently, there were agreements to more than double the intended gas flow during the 1974–85 period.[75] Deliveries began on October 1, 1970, and on October 28, ceremonies were held at the Soviet–Iranian border, with Soviet chief of state Podgorny and the Shah participating.[76] The quantity delivered was 964.9 million cubic meters in 1970, 5.623 billion in 1971; 8.197 billion in 1972; and 8.679 billion in 1973.[77]

The USSR and Iran have frequently clashed over the price paid by the Soviets for Iranian gas. When the gas first started flowing in 1970, the Soviets paid 18.6 cents per thousand cubic feet but there were provisions for increasing the price in the future. The gas price was to be linked with the oil price, specifically that of Bunker C fuel at Bandar Mahshahr, and it was to change automatically whenever there was an oil price fluctuation of no more than 30 percent. However, when the oil price rose or fell by more than 30 percent, the price of gas was to be renegotiated.[78] In 1973, negotiations were held to raise the price, and on July 19, 1973, agreement was reached on a 35 percent increase to 25 cents per thousand cubic feet. This increase was to be retroactive to January 1.[79] By the end of 1973, the price had risen further to 30.7 cents but the spiraling of world oil prices during the winter of 1973–74 drastically changed the pricing structure for natural gas as well, and Iran demanded a hefty increase. At first, Iran wanted $1.20 per thousand cubic feet but this turned out to be a bargaining price and Iran then asked for 62 cents, retroactive to January 1, 1974.[80] Paradoxically, the USSR was being charged a higher gas price because of oil price increases and yet the USSR had encouraged the Arab oil embargo and pushed for higher world oil prices.

The Soviet Union imports natural gas from Iran as part of a series of barter agreements under which Iran receives industrial goods. The Soviets do not pay any hard currency for the gas and can therefore raise the prices on their industrial goods to match any Iranian gas price increase. The Soviets threatened to do just that. Equal price increases on opposite sides of the ledger obviously cancel each other out, but a gas price increase does have broader ramifications.[81] The prices the USSR charges its own gas customers are, to some extent, related to the price paid to Iran. They are already considerably higher but should go up even more as the Iranian price rises. France began receiving Soviet natural gas in 1976 and it is expected that the Iranian price will affect the price which the Soviets charge France.[82]

When Iran asked for the price increase to 62 cents the Soviets claimed that they had just raised the price they were paying Afghanistan from 19.7 to 34 cents and that this should serve as a guideline for negotiations with Iran.[83] Discussions were held in Moscow, but they broke down in early July. Iran then announced a unilateral price adjustment to 62 cents, retroactive to January 1, and asserted that it would continue to charge this price until a new agreement was reached. The Director of the National Iranian Gas Company, Taghi Mossadeghi, explained that such a step was necessary, because even by January 1, 1974, there should have been a 305 percent price increase since the last adjustment in 1973. It was generally expected that arbitration would be needed to arrive at a new gas price, but in early August Deputy Minister of Foreign Trade Nikolai Osipov arrived in Teheran to renew negotiations. His mission was successful and a price of 57 cents was agreed upon, retroactive to January 1.[84]

The Soviet Union and Iran discussed the possibility of Iranian gas exports to West Germany, with the Soviet Union serving as the intermediary, and preliminary agreements were reached on October 24, 1973, and January 18, 1974. A final twenty-year agreement, calling for the sale of 13.4 billion cubic meters of Iranian gas per year, was then reached on November 30, 1975. Iran is to pipe the gas from Kangan, on the Persian Gulf, to the Soviet border at Astara. The pipeline should be completed by 1981 and foreign firms will probably join with Iran in the pipeline investment. In return for its receipt of Iranian gas, the Soviet Union will export an identical amount of its own gas to West Germany and one-third will then be passed on to France and one-sixth to Austria. West Germany will therefore consume half of the total quantity.[85] Perhaps Czechoslovakia will participate in this arrangement as well.

For its part as the middleman, the USSR may receive its choice of hard currency or extra Iranian gas.[86] If it is permitted to choose gas, it will probably be three billion cubic meters per year out of the more than thirteen billion involved in the three-way transfer.[87] If hard currency is the means of payment, the Soviets will receive it from West Germany as part of that country's payment to Iran.[88] Iran would also receive industrial goods from West Germany.[89]

By acting as a gas middleman, the Soviet Union can possibly earn hard currency and also increase its potential for political leverage over the West European gas-importing states.[90] Iran, of course, will be placed in a position in which the Soviet Union can cut off some of its gas exports to Western Europe, but it is giving serious thought to the construction of another pipeline through Turkey to the Mediterranean port of Iskenderun. Such a pipeline would be capable of transporting up to forty billion cubic meters per year, which is greater than the capacity of the projected pipeline to the USSR.[91] Iran could also ship liquefied natural gas to Western Europe via the Suez Canal and it has attempted to improve relations with Egypt.[92] Iran has contributed money for the restoration of the Canal area but Iranian–Egyptian relations could suffer if Egypt aligns with Saudi Arabia on any Iranian–Saudi disputes in the Persian Gulf.

In recent years, Soviet oil and gas relations with Iran have been marked by their businesslike atmosphere and have focused on truly economic questions. Political considerations have certainly influenced Soviet behavior, particularly the desire to draw Iran further away from the Western camp, but the Soviets have neither used political pressure to secure economic advantages nor economic pressure to secure political advantages. Even the gas price dispute did not bring about any political recriminations or threats. Soviet policy toward Iran has come to feature an absence of oil or gas politics, as secure economic ties are stressed. After all, it is the Soviets who want Iranian gas, and who may possibly want Iranian oil, while Iran is easily capable of finding alternative markets. The Soviets also know that if they try to press Iran too hard, Iranian anti-Soviet feelings will rise to the surface and help push Iran more firmly into the arms of the West. From military intervention and the quest for oil concessions, the Soviets have turned to political cordiality and economic correctness and they have derived greater energy benefits in the process.

Oil Ties With The Arab World

IRAQ: Soviet interest in Iraqi oil is predicated on both political and geographical considerations. Ever since the overthrow of the monarchy in 1958, Iraq has exhibited strong anti-Western tendencies and it has wanted to oust Western oil companies from their dominant position in the Iraqi oil industry. This has been made possible by large-scale Soviet assistance. The Soviets have a special interest in Iraq because of its position on the Persian Gulf and the USSR has been granted extensive naval facilities at Umm Qasr. The Soviets have always been interested in having a foothold on the Persian Gulf and no other state is likely to oblige them. Additionally, Iraq has turned out to be a natural source of oil once the Soviet Union decided, in the late sixties, to turn toward the import of crude. Iraq is the Arab state geographically closest to the Soviet Union and, among the major Middle East oil exporters, it was the state most willing to get deeply involved economically with the Soviet Union. At the time, Saudi Arabia and Kuwait were basically pro-Western and the Libyan monarchy was still in power.

Soviet oil technicians started working in Iraq in 1958 and the USSR and Iraq concluded an oil prospecting agreement on April 4, 1960.[93] However, close oil collaboration did not really begin until 1967. The Arab states had just lost another war with Israel and the Soviets registered a dramatic political coup in the Arab world by agreeing to assist Iraq with many facets of its oil industry. In September, Soviet–Iraqi negotiations began in Baghdad and a letter of intent was signed on December 24. The Soviet Union was to provide the Iraqi National Oil Company with equipment and technicians and it was to aid in drilling, transport, exploration and marketing in return for crude oil. Exploration was to be primarily in northern Iraq and drilling in the south.[94] This was the first time that the USSR had agreed to participate so extensively in the oil production of an Arab state and the promise of Soviet help in transporting and marketing the oil made sure that the increased production could be efficiently exported.

It was not until a year and a half later that the Soviets turned the letter of intent into specific aid commitments and agreements. It seems likely that the Soviets were stalling because they were not adequately prepared to receive Iraqi oil exports. They lacked a sufficient number of tankers to transport the oil and Soviet refinery capacity was limited and not geared toward handling imports. This extra time gave the Soviets a chance to make the necessary preparations and, by June 1969, they were ready to go ahead with Iraqi oil projects.

On June 21, 1969, the USSR agreed to provide a $72 million credit for oil equipment. It was to be used for development in the Halfayah area and the contract was made between Mashinoeksport and the Iraqi National Oil Company.[95] On July 4, there was another agreement with the USSR, giving a loan of $70 million, repayable at 2½ percent interest in crude oil. The loan was to cover Soviet aid in oil production at North Rumailah and Ratawi, Soviet help in preparing five other oil fields in southern Iraq for production, and the construction of an oil pipeline from North Rumailah to the Persian Gulf port of Fao.[96] North Rumailah was already known to have proven reserves so the Soviets were sure that Iraqi repayment with crude oil would not constitute a problem.

On August 30, 1970, the Soviets agreed to increase their development efforts at North Rumailah and on the Fao pipeline in return for additional deliveries of crude oil but the next major step in Soviet involvement came on April 8, 1971.[97] On that date, representatives of the two states signed an agreement according to which the Soviets would provide a $222 million loan, again repayable at 2½ percent interest in crude oil by the Iraqi National Oil Company.[98] The Soviets were to help finance a refinery at Mosul and an oil pipeline from Baghdad to Basra and they were to build industrial projects unrelated to oil as well.[99] Many other Soviet–Iraqi oil agreements have followed and the Soviets have provided arms to Iraq in exchange for oil.[100] They have also agreed to accept crude oil as payment for all of Iraq's debts up to 1980.[101]

On April 9, 1972, the USSR and Iraq concluded a "Treaty of Friendship and Cooperation," and at about the same time Iraq began its export of crude oil to the Soviet Union.[102] It came from the North Rumailah oil fields and was piped to Fao, where it was placed on Soviet tankers. The destination of the first two tankers may have been Rostock, East Germany, as the Soviets did resell much of the Iraqi oil to its East European customers.[103] Iraq was to supply the USSR with 1 million tons of North Rumailah crude oil in 1972 and 2 million tons per year during the period 1973–75.[104] Actual production at North Rumailah rose to 7 million tons per year by 1974 and may eventually reach 18 million tons.[105]

Buoyed by the friendship treaty with the USSR and by the initiation of exports from North Rumailah, Iraq felt strong enough to take its most far-reaching step against the Western oil interests— the nationalization of the Iraq Petroleum Company, on June 1, 1972. Iraq nationalized the Kirkuk oil fields, the pipeline to the Mediterranean, and all other assets of IPC.[106] However, Iraq did not nationalize two of IPC's susidiarios, Mosul Petroleum and Basra Petroleum, which were producing one-third of Iraq's oil. Simultaneous with the Iraqi nationalization action, Syria took over that part of the IPC pipeline which passes through its territory. The Soviet Union applauded the steps taken by Iraq and Syria and began to purchase Kirkuk crude oil which flowed through the IPC pipeline to the Mediterranean.[107] Soviet purchases began as early as July 8 and they helped Iraq overcome a Western boycott of nationalized Iraqi oil.[108] Iraq's problems with Western oil companies were not really resolved until February 28, 1973, when a compensation agreement was reached with IPC.[109]

Immediately after the nationalization of IPC, Iraqi foreign minister Murtada Said Abd al-Baqi went to Moscow to discuss the ramifications of the nationalization action. He was in Moscow from June 3 to June 8 and he secured promises of further Soviet assistance in the areas of transportation, prospecting, and refinery construction. The USSR was thus instrumental in helping Iraq carry out its nationalization program.[110]

The Soviet Union claimed that the friendship treaty enabled Iraq to nationalize IPC and that the Soviet Union had been largely responsible for breaking the oil boycott of Iraq. The Soviets also pointed to the role of other communist-ruled states, such as East Germany and Bulgaria, which bought Iraqi crude and supplied tankers at the Banias terminal as well.[111] Soviet actions in support of Iraq were important, particularly in a political sense, but the ability of the USSR to market Kirkuk crude oil was indeed limited as the Soviets could only make a symbolic dent when purchasing oil flowing from the IPC pipeline.[112] In 1972, such purchases could not have been more than three million tons, while the pipeline capacity was approximately twenty times that amount.

As the price of oil began to rise in early 1973, Iraq had misgivings about its barter arrangements with the Soviet Union. It decided to honor all of its commitments with the Soviets but to demand hard currency in any future deals.[113] This might easily dampen Soviet enthusiasm about importing large quantities of Iraqi oil in the future. Later in 1973, Iraq went further with its nationalization policies, taking over the American and Dutch shares of the Basra Petroleum Company, but not the British or French shares. This nationalization took place during the course of the Arab-Israeli war and was meant to punish the United States and the Netherlands for their support of Israel. Iraq did not completely adhere to the ensuing oil embargo because it did not have the large currency reserves possessed by many other oil-exporting states, but it did verbally support the embargo action.[114]

Soviet crude oil imports from Iraq totaled 4.084 million metric tons in 1972; 11.010 million in 1973; but only 3.888 million in 1974.[115] Most of this oil is not actually brought to the USSR, but is instead resold to fulfill Soviet export commitments. Oil bought by the USSR at the Persian Gulf port of Fao is used to supply Soviet customers in Asia and is also shipped directly to Poland and East Germany. Deliveries are additionally made to Hungary and Czechoslovakia.[116] A portion is sold to West European states and the Soviets have in many cases sold Iraqi crude oil for less than Iraq's normal export price, thereby driving down the price of Iraqi oil. On one occasion, the Soviets arranged to sell Kirkuk crude to Spain on this basis but a strong Iraqi protest forced the Soviets to back down. Iraq already had an oil export contract with Spain and the price structure would have been undercut by the Soviet action.[117]

The construction of an oil pipeline from Iraq to the Mediterranean coast in Turkey would increase Iraq's ability to export oil to Europe, including the Soviet Union. Such a pipeline was seriously discussed in May 1957, when representatives of Western oil companies met in London and sought a way to avoid reliance on the

IPC pipeline through Syria. Syria had interrupted the flow of oil on previous occasions and a pipeline from Kirkuk to Iskenderun was therefore proposed as a more secure route.[118] Plans for the pipeline fell through when Iraq decided not to participate. Arab states, especially Syria, put pressure on her not to find an alternative to the Syrian route, and there was domestic opposition to the project as well.[119] However, the pipeline proposal was resurrected many years later and on August 27, 1973, Iraq and Turkey agreed on a Kirkuk to Dortyol (near Iskenderun) pipeline. It is supposed to open in 1977 with a capacity of 25 million tons, rising to 30 million in 1983.[120] Disruption in the Kurdish areas of northern Iraq delayed construction plans but, should the oil begin flowing on schedule, the Soviet Union's potential for purchasing Iraqi oil will be increased.[121] On the other hand, Iraqi–Syrian differences over transit fees on the IPC pipeline could lead to the termination of Iraqi exports via that route.

The bulk of Soviet oil imports comes from Iraq, and the Soviets also desire to maintain a strong position there, but the key to Soviet oil policies in Iraq is probably the support given to its anti-Western actions. At one time, Iraq was the headquarters of the anticommunist Baghdad Pact and the center of British oil operations in the Middle East; now, Iraq has a treaty relationship with the USSR, participates in some of the activities of CMEA, extends naval facilities to the USSR at Umm Qasr, equips its armed forces with Soviet weapons, and collaborates with the USSR in running its oil industry. If the removal of Western influence from the Middle East lies at the heart of Soviet oil politics in the area, Iraq represents the clearest example of Soviet success.

ALGERIA: The Soviet Union has lent assistance to Algeria in order to make it self-sufficient in oil production and to encourage its nationalization policies. On the other hand, the Soviets point out that Algeria's chief energy resource is natural gas and Western states are still influential in the Algerian natural gas industry.[122] Since its independence in 1962, Algeria has tried to maintain close relations with the Soviet Union in order to balance out its ties with France and other Western powers. In August 1963, the

Soviet Union agreed to develop a petroleum research institute, and in May 1964 it lent its support for an oil and gas institute. Both facilities were opened in September 1964—staffed with Soviet specialists.[123] The Soviets were training Algerian petroleum technicians both in Algeria and the USSR, and by late 1966 there were also 200 Soviet technicians in Algeria.[124] Furthermore, the Soviets were supplying oil-drilling equipment and they were prospecting for oil. Commitments were made to develop an Algerian tanker fleet; by March 1974 three tankers had been provided.[125]

Soviet imports of Algerian crude oil began in 1967 and extended through 1972.[126] A Soviet–Algerian trade agreement (July 1968) indicated that deliveries would continue through 1975, but it seems that Algerian debts to the USSR, payable in oil, had been repaid by the end of 1972 and Algeria then preferred to sell its oil to other customers for higher prices.[127] When the Soviets first decided to buy Arab oil, they turned to Algeria—which was willing to sell at that time and had a geographical location convenient for shipping oil to Cuba. About half of the oil Spain purchased from the Soviets also came from Algeria.[128] An official document from the Algerian Ministry of Finance in 1967 maintained that Algeria was intentionally not competing with the USSR for European oil markets but that Algeria continued to be irked by Soviet sales of natural gas to Western Europe.[129] The Algerians want to sell large quantities of gas themselves and are worried that Soviet competition will tend to lower the price.[130]

EGYPT: Egypt has imported Soviet oil products ever since the thirties but did not begin to purchase Soviet crude until 1955.[131] Since then, Egypt has imported both crude and other oil products from the USSR. In a strange twist dictated by the closing of the Suez Canal, Egypt began to sell crude oil to the Soviets in 1969. In recent years, imports and exports have gone on simultaneously, but there has been an evolving quantitative reduction in the Soviet–Egyptian oil trade, paralleling the cooling political relations.

The Egyptian decision to import Soviet crude oil was based on both economic and political considerations. Egypt had been engaged in a price dispute with Western oil companies and was therefore very satisfied when it arranged a barter transaction with the USSR—cotton for oil.[132] Not only could Egypt acquire oil without paying hard currency but it could also find a market for its cotton, a difficult task at that time. Politically, Egypt was having its differences with the United States, Britain, and France over the issues of the Baghdad Pact, the Aswan dam, and the Suez Canal, and in 1955 it turned to the USSR for both armaments and oil. Egypt's conflicts with the Western powers coincided with the beginning of Khrushchev's policy of collaborating with Third World nationalist leaders, such as Nasser, and the Soviet "oil offensive" was gathering steam as well. The Soviet Union and Egypt thus had a clear mutuality of interests.

Egypt, which is just now reaching oil self-sufficiency, was a net importer of oil during the fifties and sixties. It was anxious to develop its oil resources and was able to secure some Soviet assistance in exploration and the building of refineries, plus the provision of technicians and equipment.[133] Most notable of the Soviet projects was the search for oil in the Siwa oasis area of western Egypt. Egypt had hoped to find extensive oil deposits in this desert region near Libya but the Soviet effort resulted in failure. Soviet prospecting began in 1968, and in 1969 there was some discussion about the Soviet Union's receiving some crude oil in return for its aid in the oil search. By August 1973, no significant quantity of oil was found and the Soviet specialists returned home.[134]

The Soviet Union began buying Egyptian crude oil in 1969 so that it could resell this oil to its Asian customers. The Suez Canal was closed but the Soviets were able to receive Egyptian oil at the Gulf of Suez, on the far side of the Canal. In 1972, the amount purchased by the Soviets dropped considerably and there was another large decline in 1973. This development was closely related to the decrease in Soviet oil exports to Egypt in those years since the Soviet Union and Egypt were, to some extent, really practicing a Mediterranean–Gulf of Suez switch deal.[135] The reasons for the Soviet–Egyptian oil slide are multiple and complex but most of the responsibility seems to belong to Egypt rather than the Soviet Union. Soviet–Egyptian relations deteriorated in 1972, culminating in the expulsion of Soviet advisers from Egypt, and such a political atmosphere was obviously not conducive to close trade relations. Also, Egypt did not want to sell much oil to the Soviets because of the low price it received. The Soviets insisted on the receipt of crude oil at low prices as partial repayment for Soviet aid but Egypt rebelled at such transactions. In 1972, Egypt was paid only 9.73 rubles per ton, in 1973 only 6.68 per ton. This was the best economic arrangement the Soviets had since, in 1973, they were paying Syria 10.55 rubles per ton, Iraq 16.90, and Libya 17.72.[136]

In addition, Egypt did not want to buy such a large quantity of oil from the Soviet Union. It was wary about reliance on the USSR, owing to the political situation, and it was able to purchase oil from Iraq and Saudi Arabia at a better price. In 1973, Egypt was paying the Soviets 27.57 rubles per ton, but this statistic is difficult to analyze since it includes both crude oil and oil products in an unknown mix.[137]

Some other factors are also relevant to the decline in oil trade. During the Egyptian cotton season ending on March 31, 1974, production went down 19 percent and sales to the USSR fell from 203,143 bales during the 1972–73 season to 117,000 during the 1973–74 season.[138] This may help explain the reduction in Soviet oil sales to Egypt since the bartering of cotton for oil has long been part of the Soviet–Egyptian trade relationship. Also having an effect on oil exchanges was the 1973 Arab–Israeli war, when Egyptian production in the Gulf of Suez was disrupted and exports declined.

SYRIA: Syria was traditionally a net importer of oil, but with Soviet help it became self-sufficient and is now a net exporter. Soviet oil sales to Syria began in the mid-fifties, and by 1959 Syria was 58.4 percent dependent on Soviet oil supplies.[139] Soviet deliveries continued, but by 1971 they had fallen to an infinitesimal level as Syrian oil production had increased.[140] In 1972, Syria began to sell crude oil to the Soviet Union, supplying

315,000 tons in 1972 and 247,000 in 1973.[141] Some of this oil was marketed by the Soviets in Western Europe.[142]

The Soviet Union assisted in the development of the Syrian oil industry, with the aim of reducing Western economic control. At the same time, socialism was encouraged. Oil enterprises in Syria and the IPC pipeline are now state-owned. In 1957, the USSR agreed to drill test wells, provide equipment, and train Syrian technicians while Czechoslovakia contracted to build the Homs refinery.[143] In 1959, the Soviets found oil at Karachuk and some new deposits at Suwaidiyah, and in 1964 they agreed to build oil storage tanks in Damascus, Aleppo, Latakia, and Homs.[144] In 1965, they contracted to develop the Suwaidiyah oil fields and production began in 1968.[145] By 1971, there were 200 Soviet oil experts in Syria, and Soviet involvement has remained at a high level.[146] Soviet–Syrian oil relations have grown alongside the very close political ties between these two states, and Soviet oil assistance to the Syrians is based more on good will than on any desire by the Soviets to import Syrian oil. The amount purchased by the USSR is minimal and unnecessary but, for the Syrians, Soviet aid in transporting and marketing oil is of much greater importance.

LIBYA: Soviet–Libyan political relations have often been poor because of the strong anticommunist feelings of Libya's leader, Colonel Muammar al-Qaddafi and this had hindered cooperation on oil projects. On September 9, 1970, the Libyan News Agency announced that the Soviet Union would provide oil specialists to estimate Libyan reserves and well capacities, but the first major breakthrough in oil ties did not occur until early 1972.[147] Libya had nationalized the BP-owned Sarir oil fields in December 1971, and was having trouble managing them. On top of this, many Western companies were boycotting Libyan oil in retaliation for the nationalization action. The Soviets then stepped in and an agreement on March 4, 1972, provided for Soviet assistance in prospecting, extracting, and refining, plus the training of Libyan oil specialists.[148] On May 13, the Libyan News Agency announced that the USSR was to buy Libyan crude as well.[149] Soviet technical assistance and oil purchases enabled Libya to carry off the Sarir nationalization successfully and Soviet behavior in Libya was similar to that shown in Iraq at about the same time, as the Soviets were abetting the nationalization of IPC. It has even been suggested that Soviet commitments to Libya were actually arranged before the Sarir nationalization.

Soviet aid to the Libyan oil industry did not reach its expected level because of political differences and Soviet imports of Libyan crude oil did not rise to the anticipated 2.5 million tons per year.[150] In 1972, the Soviets bought 1.867 million tons from Libya, and in 1973, 1.713 million.[151] During 1973, the amount fell each quarter from 50,620 barrels per day, to 42,220, to 38,790, to 10,200.[152] This fall was due primarily to Soviet unwillingness to pay the higher oil prices demanded by the Libyans. Of the Libyan oil purchased by the USSR, some is shipped directly to East European states for resale.[153]

OTHER ARAB STATES AND TURKEY: The Soviet Union has sold small quantities of oil to Lebanon, Yemen, Tunisia, and Cyprus. But one of the main recipients ever since the late fifties has been Morocco. In 1973, Morocco received 943,000 tons of crude oil and oil products which, according to Soviet claims, represented 60 percent of Morocco's needs.[154] The Soviets prospected for oil in Morocco in 1968 and they are now prospecting for shale oil.[155]

The Soviets have tried to maintain proper relations with Turkey in order to encourage some weakening of its strong ties to the West and because they want no navigational disputes that can impede the movement of their warships between the Black Sea and the Mediterranean. On June 12, 1967, the Soviet Union agreed to build an oil refinery at Izmir. It offered a loan of $60 million, payable in 15 years at 2½ percent interest, and the payment was to consist of Turkish products, many of them agricultural.[156] The refinery opened in April 1973.[157] The Soviet Union also sold oil to Turkey, but these sales decreased to a minimal level after 1971.[158] Before the 1974 Cyprus crisis, the USSR basically supported Turkey in its offshore oil dispute with Greece.[159]

The Soviet Union has bought small quantities of oil products from South Yemen ever since 1969 and the Soviets are assisting South Yemen with oil prospecting.[160] South Yemen also figured in Soviet plans during the Yemeni civil war, since Soviet tankers took Egyptian oil from the Gulf of Suez to Aden, South Yemen, for refining. This refined oil was used to fly Soviet aircraft in Yemen in support of the Republicans and against the Royalists.[161] The Soviet Union has also purchased small quantities of diesel fuel from Kuwait, and in 1969 it even bought 19,700 tons of crude oil from Saudi Arabia.[162] The Saudi Arabian oil was actually purchased from a European oil broker as part of a switch deal, and it seems likely that the Saudis did not even know about the transaction. Saudi Arabia is strongly anticommunist and does not want to export oil to the Soviet Union. On the other hand, the Soviets have been encouraging a thaw in their relations with the Saudis. The Soviets may therefore have listed the oil purchase in their foreign trade yearbook to lend publicity to the transaction.[163] A slight warming of Soviet–Saudi relations has taken place since 1967, and in November 1969 the Soviet Union sold oil-drilling rigs to Saudi Arabia.[164] The Soviets also tried to develop closer contacts with Jordan, extending a credit for oil exploration in 1972.[165]

Soviet–Israeli Oil Relations

One of the most interesting chapters in Soviet oil politics is the little-known history of Soviet oil relations with Israel.[166] When Israel's independence was declared in May 1948, its oil supply was completely cut off. Palestine had received its oil via the IPC pipeline from Iraq, as an arm of the pipeline brought crude oil to Haifa for refining. The refinery was owned by British interests, largely affiliated with the Shell group. As soon as Israel was created, the Iraqis refused to send oil through the pipeline, Britain closed the Haifa refinery, and Western oil companies embargoed deliveries to Israel. Iraq's action was due to Arab objections to the establishment of Israel while Britain and the Western oil companies expected an Arab victory and feared Arab reprisals against their interests if they were to assist Israel. For example, Shell stopped all deliveries to Israel on the day it was founded, asserting that it was in a "war zone." American oil companies also had an interest in keeping the Haifa refinery closed since they were planning the Tapline from Saudi Arabia to the Mediterranean and it was to be in competition with the IPC pipeline and Haifa refinery. Thus Israel was faced with the prospect of fighting a war without a sufficient supply of oil, while at the same time, the Haifa refinery stood idle.

Into the situation stepped the Soviet Union and Rumania. The Soviets were anxious to have the British removed from Palestine, so they set aside their traditional aversion to Zionism, and backed the United Nations' partition plan which included the creation of a Jewish state. The Soviets believed that the Jews were better organized than the Arabs, and they also perceived some British machinations behind the founding of the Arab League. Accordingly, the Soviet Union was the first state to extend de jure recognition to Israel, and Czechoslovakia, acting on Soviet instructions, supplied arms for the Israeli war effort.

As soon as Israel announced its independence on May 15, 1948, Rumania indicated its willingness to provide Israel with all the oil products it needed.[167] At that time, Israel's oil needs for industrial purposes were not very great because the war was disrupting the economy but oil was certainly necessary for military use and total need for 1948 was about 400,000 tons.[168] Israel and Rumania made a number of short-term agreements calling for the delivery of oil products, but no crude oil was included since Israel had no refining capacity while the Haifa refinery was closed. Israel paid with dollars and deliveries continued throughout 1948. Many of the details were arranged in July 1948, when Israeli diplomat Mordechai Namir was dispatched to Rumania. He negotiated with the Rumanian foreign minister, Anna Pauker, and agreements were reached on the emigration of Rumanian Jews and on the supply of oil products, particularly those for military use.[169] These oil deliveries must have been approved by the Soviet Union, as Rumania's oil industry was closely directed, and partially owned, by the USSR.[170] Namir also had oil discussions with the Soviets when he visited the USSR in October, but his account of these meetings is sketchy and no deal was reached, possibly because Israel was not satisfied with the amount of credit offered by the Soviets.[171]

In addition to supplying oil products, Rumania indicated an interest in delivering crude oil to the Haifa refinery. The surplus oil products produced there were to be sent to East European states.[172] The refinery had the capacity to produce ten times the amount needed by Israel so the Rumanian offer made economic sense.[173] However, the refinery was closed and could only be opened with the approval of the British interests in Shell, an approval which was unthinkable since the war was still in progress and since oil from a communist state was to be used. As a result, Rumanian crude oil was never sent to Israel.

By October 1948, both Shell and some American oil companies realized that Israel could possibly win the war and they ended their oil embargo. Shell still refused to reactivate the Haifa refinery but Israel began to receive oil products from it and other companies.[174] Israel wanted to buy oil from Western companies to strike some balance between them and Rumania and also to get the refinery opened. Israel began to receive the bulk of its oil supplies from the West and there were no deliveries from Rumania after 1948. By August 1950, with Israel having been successful in its war with the Arabs, Shell reactivated the refinery and began importing crude oil from Venezuela.[175] The IPC pipeline linking Iraq with Haifa was not reopened and remains closed to this day.

Shell, Mobil, and Esso dominated oil marketing operations in Israel but they agreed to the creation of an Israeli oil company—under one significant condition. It was to be allowed only 20 percent of the Israeli market, but its share could eventually rise to 30 percent. Delek Israel Fuel Corporation was founded in November 1951 and it operated under this restriction. Ownership was 10 percent by the government, 45 percent by the Histadrut (the labor federation), and 45 percent by private interests. However, it was under effective government control because the Histadrut had very close ties with the ruling Mapai party. The British interests which controlled the Haifa refinery agreed to refine the oil to be marketed by Delek.

Israel continued to receive most of its oil from Western companies, paying them the highest prices charged to any of their customers, and its hard currency reserves were dwindling. In order to maintain its oil purchases, Israel reached an agreement with West Germany, according to which 30 percent of the reparations payments from West Germany were to be used for oil supplies. West Germany was to pay Shell with British pounds on Israel's account and Shell was to provide oil for Israel.[176] Shell accepted this arrangement in September 1952, and the first payment from West Germany to Shell was in March 1953.[177] This assistance from West Germany was helpful to Israel but was not enough to solve the payments problem. Israel was therefore anxious to diversify its oil sources, relying less on Western companies, and the Soviet Union conveniently reentered the Israeli oil market.

It is generally believed that the Soviet Union and Israel began their oil relations in 1953, after the death of Stalin, but they actually started in 1952 while Stalin was still in power. Israel imported Soviet paraffin, an oil byproduct, and discussions on crude oil sales were carried on through a London broker. The Soviets even sent a sample of their crude oil to Israel for examination. Delek wanted to buy Soviet crude but preferred dealing directly with the Soviet Union rather than working through a broker. Delek approached the Israeli foreign ministry about this matter, and the foreign ministry indicated that if the price and quality of the oil were satisfactory, it would have no political objections to such an agreement. It pointed out, however, that Israel did not have enough tankers to import Soviet oil.

In late 1952, the Soviet government supposedly uncovered a "doctors' plot" aimed at the murder of top officials; most of the doctors arrested were Jewish; these doctors were accused of working for the United States and Israel. The whole affair led to a deterioration in Soviet–Israeli relations. On February 9, 1953, a bomb exploded at the Soviet legation in Tel Aviv and this led to a breaking of diplomatic ties. Stalin died in April, bringing an end to the "doctors' plot" charges, and the doctors were released. On July 20, diplomatic relations were restored.

As a result of the political difficulties, oil contacts had been broken off since late 1952, but they were renewed in mid-1953. An Israeli communist, speaking in the Knesset (the Israeli parliament), inquired of the finance minister why Israel did not buy oil from the Soviet Union. Believing that he may have been acting on a cue from Moscow, government officials questioned him and this resulted in the dispatching of an Israeli delegation to the USSR. Israel also sent a representative to Paris to discuss oil with the Soviet ambassador to France. By December, an oil agreement was reached.

At first, the Soviet Union provided only fuel oil but crude oil deliveries began shortly thereafter. Israel received between 300,000 and 400,000 tons of oil per year, which was a very large amount when one considers the small volume of Soviet oil exports at that time (Soviet exports of crude oil and oil products in 1954 totaled 6.5 million tons). The Soviets were willing to supply even more, but Delek's agreement with the Western companies restricted her to 30 percent of the Israeli market and all of the Soviet oil sent to Israel was marketed by Delek. Israel, which relied on oil for 100 percent of its energy needs, was glad to decrease its dependence on the Western oil companies; it was especially pleased with the low Soviet price. Israel paid the USSR less than it paid any of its other oil suppliers, and payment was with citrus fruit, which permitted Israel to conserve its hard currency resources. Although the Haifa refinery was in operation, there was no Soviet request that Israel refine Soviet oil for reexport, since Soviet and East European refinery capacity was sufficient for its needs.

Most of the oil was transported from Odessa to Haifa by the hastily assembled Israeli tanker fleet; when Israel could not provide enough tankers, Soviet tankers were used. Israeli ships were given a highly preferential tariff rate in Soviet ports, thus facilitating the oil deliveries. Some of the oil was actually picked up in Rumania, which owed oil to the Soviets as part of their share of Sovrompetrol, the joint Soviet-Rumanian oil company.

As of 1953, the Soviet Union was neutral in the Arab–Israeli dispute, not shifting to a clearly pro-Arab position until 1955, so politics did not present much of an impediment to oil trade. From the Soviet point of view, it was convenient to sell to Israel since it was so close geographically to the Soviet Union's oil export facilities on the Black Sea. The Soviets also hoped that Israel would encourage West European states to buy Soviet oil, and they specifically asked Israel to use her influence in this manner. Many of the salesmen for Soiuznefteeksport, the Soviet oil trading corporation, were Jewish and this may have helped in the development of smooth oil relations with the Israelis. However, the prime interest of the Soviets was in reducing the power of Western oil companies in Israel and this concern was frequently conveyed to the Israelis. The act of selling oil to Delek had this effect and the Soviets did not use oil to pressure Israel on political issues.

On November 1, 1955, the Soviet Union and Israel renewed their contract for the delivery of crude oil, and another contract on May 29, 1956, extended deliveries through the end of the year.[178] On July 17, there was an additional two-year contract increasing Soviet shipments to 700,000 tons per year, but possibly rising to one million tons per year during the 1957–58 period.[179] The Soviets also agreed to supply Israel with drilling equipment and to send Soviet experts to Israel to teach drilling techniques. With this additional export commitment, the Soviet Union was to be providing about 40 percent of Israel's oil needs, which was 10 percent more than Delek was permitted under its quota agreement with Western companies. Delek solved this problem in two ways: it stockpiled oil, thus exempting it from the quota on marketing; and it sold some Soviet oil to Shell and Mobil for them to market in Israel.

Increased oil sales to Israel angered the Arab states, but the Soviets tried to reassure them by claiming that the USSR was a friend of the Arabs, despite its deals with Israel. Foreign Minister Shepilov, trying to justify Soviet secrecy about the transactions, said that the Soviet Union did not publicize its agreements with Israel because it did not want to attach any political significance to them.[180] By 1956, the Soviet Union had adopted a strongly pro-

Arab position on Arab–Israeli issues, but oil sales to Israel were probably related to a Soviet desire to keep all options open. At the risk of antagonizing the Arabs, the USSR wanted to keep a foot in the Israeli door, partially in order to encourage Israel's independence from Western economic control. The Soviets also had their own economic interests in mind, since oil sales to Israel were geographically convenient and the Soviet Union did have a need for citrus fruit.

The advent of a new war in the Middle East on October 29, 1956, caused a major change in the Soviet position. A delegation from Soiuznefteeksport was in Israel for a few weeks just before the war, as the guest of Delek. When the war broke out, the Soviet Union labeled Israel an aggressor—a political stance that had its effect on economic relations as well. On November 6, Soiuznefteeksport sent a cable to Delek indicating that its export licenses for the delivery of crude oil to Israel had been canceled by the Ministry of Foreign Trade. The contracts of November 1, 1955, and May 29, 1956, were therefore voided and no contract would be issued for oil deliveries in 1957 and 1958, as provided in the agreement of July 17, 1956. Soiuznefteeksport asserted that the actions of the Ministry of Foreign Trade were in accordance with the principle of *force majeure.* Delek replied on November 12 that no provision in the previous contracts could justify the Soviet action and that Soiuznefteeksport would be held liable for all losses and damages. In February 1957, the Israeli government protested against Soviet behavior, declaring: "The attitude of the Government of the USSR, particularly towards a small nation, conflicts with the numerous statements made by Soviet representatives in condemnation of restrictive practices in international trade and of embargoes motivated by political reasons. . . . It appears that their [Soviet State Companies] contractual obligations retain validity only as long as they suit the current requirements of Soviet policy." [181]

The Soviet Union's stoppage of oil deliveries to Israel represented one of the few times that the Soviets had failed to live up to their contractual obligations and the cancellation was obviously based on political considerations. Israel refused to accept the Soviet Union's actions and sought legal recourse against Soiuznefteeksport, although some leading Israelis believed the case was hopeless.

Most Soviet foreign trade contracts, including those with Israel, stipulated that disputes would be heard by the Soviet Arbitration Commission. Therefore, on November 1, 1957, Delek Israel Fuel Corporation and Jordan Investments filed suit against Soiuznefteeksport. Jordan Investments was an affiliate of Delek, with the specific responsibility of providing oil for Israel's electricity needs. The Israeli contention was that force majeure could not be applied in regard to Soiuznefteeksport's oil contracts with Israeli firms. Force majeure is a widely accepted principle in Western legal practice according to which a contract can be voided if events beyond the control of one of the parties prevent it from fulfilling its obligations. If a state decides that a contractual agreement entered into by a corporation is not in conformity with the state's interests, it can prevent that corporation from activating its contractual agreement with a corporation from another state and the former may not be held legally accountable because a force beyond its control, in this case a state directive, is responsible. Israel maintained that force majeure was not relevant to the Soviet situation, since the state trading corporations were really part of the state rather than independent entities, and that Soviet contracts with Soiuznefteeksport were in fact contracts with the state itself. Israel argued that state direction could not actually supersede the contractual obligations of Soiuznefteeksport since Soiuznefteeksport was itself a state agent.[182] On June 19, 1958, the arbitration commission ruled in favor of Soiuznefteeksport, holding that Soviet foreign trade corporations are independent legal entities which are covered by the principle of force majeure.[183]

The decision was not unexpected: a Soviet arbitration commission was hearing the case, force majeure was a generally accepted principle, and Soviet foreign trade corporations were independent legal entities distinct from the state. Of course, the Israelis were correct in pointing out the practical relationship between Soiuznefteeksport and the Soviet state (the former always functions on behalf of state policy interests and never initiates any independent actions), but legally the Soviets have a convenient structure to serve their political ends. The state can always take export licenses away from Soiuznefteeksport in order to make a political point with another state, but this other state has no legal recourse, as Soiuznefteeksport can always pass the legal buck.

Although the Soviet Union officially ended oil deliveries to Israel in November 1956, Soviet oil did find its way to Israel until the 1967 Arab–Israeli war. The USSR shipped large quantities of crude oil to Italy, which, after refining, sold some of the oil products to other states, including Israel. Soviet crude oil came to Israel via two secretive routes. One involved the use of Yugoslavia as an intermediary since part of the oil supposedly exported to Yugoslavia by the Soviet Union was actually sent to Israel instead. A large part of this oil came directly to Israel, never even entering Yugoslavia on its way. This arrangement lasted from 1957 to 1967, but the Soviets broke it off as a result of the 1967 war. The second route had Turkey playing the role of intermediary; again, much of the oil came directly to Israel. This Turkish connection existed only from 1965 to 1967. Israel wanted diversified sources of oil supply and it sought to arrange a direct deal with the USSR. The Soviet ambassador in Tel Aviv, Mikhail Bodrov, encouraged the Israelis and a delegation from the Citrus Marketing Board visited the USSR in February 1962, to disuss a citrus fruit for oil agreement.[184] However, the Soviets decided not to conclude a direct deal with the Israelis, since there were strong objections from Arab states.

Since 1967, there have been no oil ties between the Soviet Union and Israel, but there has been commerce between Rumania and Israel. Rumania's oil relations with Israel in 1948 could be depicted as those of a Soviet agent, but such an interpretation would not be valid for the current period. Rumania now exercises a degree of independence from the Soviet Union, and this is particularly evident in its Middle East policies. Rumania is alone among East European states in having diplomatic relations with Israel and it is attempting to take a somewhat neutral position on Arab–Israeli issues.

After the 1967 war, Rumania offered to sell oil products to Israel. Its move was probably an attempt to assert its independent stance on Middle East issues, but Rumania also had an economic rationale, since it had a surplus of certain oil products. Israel had no objection to buying from Rumania, but it did not happen to need the types of oil products offered for sale. Thus, no agreement was reached on oil products although Israel did buy some Rumanian oil byproducts.

Both Israel and Rumania import crude oil from Iran. It is shipped to the Israeli port of Eilat, where Israel's oil is piped to the refinery in Haifa while Rumania's is piped to the Mediterranean port of Ashkelon for shipment to Rumania. The Soviet Union has called upon Iran to stop supplying Israel with oil but apparently has not objected to Rumania's use of the Eilat–Ashkelon pipeline.[185] This pipeline opened early in 1970, and in 1971 37,000 barrels per day of Iranian crude was transported through it on the way to Rumania.[186] No other East European state uses the Israeli pipeline.

During the 1973 Arab–Israeli war, oil shipments from Iran to Eilat were disrupted and oil stopped flowing through the Eilat–Ashkelon pipeline. Rumanian oil imports suffered, and this is one of the reasons why Rumania had to introduce energy conservation measures at that time.[187] The Israeli pipeline is at present the most convenient transportation route for the Rumanians, but once Egypt builds the Sumed pipeline, it will provide an attractive alternative. The Rumanians have already promised the Egyptians that they will send 60,000 barrels per day through the Sumed line, and it appeared as if Rumania would terminate its pipeline arrangement with Israel when the current contract expired in July 1976.[188]

Another aspect of Rumanian–Israeli oil ties, but one which is conjectural and difficult to prove, was cooperation in marketing. Before the second stage Egyptian–Israeli agreement of 1975, Israel produced oil from Abu Rudeis and other fields in the occupied Sinai, but most of this oil was not used domestically. It was sent through the Eilat–Ashkelon pipeline and marketed in Western Europe. However, many customers may have been politically reluctant to acknowledge the purchase of oil from occupied Arab territories, so it is possible that some of this oil was marketed as Rumanian rather than as Israeli. The oil Rumania bought from Iran was also loaded on tankers at Ashkelon, so it would not have been very difficult for Rumania to assist the Israelis in this manner.

Soviet Energy Dilemmas

During the past two decades, Soviet policy in the Middle East and North Africa has been focused particularly on Egypt, but it is now shifting more toward Iraq and other oil-producing states.[189] To some extent, this is due to a deterioration in Soviet–Egyptian relations and to the political inroads in Egypt made by the U.S. after the 1973 Arab–Israeli war. However the oil factor is also highly significant. The Soviet Union is buying large quantities of Iraqi oil and also seeks to impede the flow of oil to the West from Middle East states. This latter goal may lead the Soviets into warmer relations with Saudi Arabia and Kuwait, as the USSR would like to take advantage of the West's oil supply vulnerability in any manner possible.[190] Western Europe will continue to be greatly dependent on Middle East oil, despite exploitation in the North Sea, and the United States seems to be backing away from "Project Independence," thereby increasing its reliance on the Middle East. Furthermore, the United States and Soviet Union will probably not reach agreement on Tiumen oil deliveries to the United States, also causing an American turn to Middle East oil.

Middle East and North African oil producers are moving toward a position where they will be demanding high prices from the Soviets, to be paid in hard currency, and this affects Soviet plans for the development of Siberian oil resources.[191] The Soviet Union appears to be opting for a policy of oil self-reliance, based upon limited exports from Siberia and limited imports from the

Middle East and North Africa. It is clearly backing away from any large export agreements with the United States and Japan. These exports would have to be balanced against large Soviet imports, but high prices and the need for hard currency mitigate against such imports. Rather then use their hard currency reserves to buy more Arab oil, the Soviets will use them to buy Western technology to develop Siberian oil more quickly.[192] Soviet self-reliance in Siberia will mean a slower oil production growth rate than would be possible with American and Japanese assistance and this leads to a temporary need for Arab oil. In the long run, however, the Soviets will have more Siberian oil for their own use and will not have to depend on Arab supplies.[193] The Soviets recognize the potential instability of Arab oil deliveries as a result of the political volatility of many Arab states and the possibility of wartime disruption, so self-reliance is seen as the most secure policy, despite the slower exploitation of Siberian resources it engenders.

The Soviet Union will have difficulty in meeting the oil requirements of the East European states during the coming decade, and one solution would be to buy Arab oil and then control its delivery to Eastern Europe. This can be done by purchasing Arab oil and then exporting a similar amount or by reselling Arab oil.[194] However, large purchases from Arab states are unlikely, since the Arabs would probably prefer to deal directly with Eastern Europe.[195] This is somewhat problematic at the moment because marketing and transportation networks are not well developed, but it should become more feasible in the coming years.

The Arab states are now commanding high prices for their oil. They are able to secure Western arms and technology in return for this oil and the West is in a position to provide more hard currency than the Soviet Union. Only the poorest among the oil-producing states may still be interested in barter transactions with the Soviet Union, since the wealthier states can buy superior Western equipment with their large currency reserves or they can barter with the West.[196] As the price of oil rises faster than the price of Western goods, the Arabs have a reduced interest in exporting oil to the USSR.[197]

Sales competition with Arab states could conceivably lead to a deterioration in political relations between the USSR and many Middle East and North African states. The Soviet Union did increase its sales during the Arab embargoes of 1956, 1967, and 1973–74; in 1971, it replaced Algeria and Libya as the main oil suppliers of Morocco and Ghana respectively.[198] However, the likelihood of significant Soviet–Arab friction over oil marketing is not great, since the world demand for oil is so large. Soviet writers point out that the USSR lends assistance to Arab oil industries and that Soviet industrial aid to Third World states increases their need for oil and thus facilitates Arab sales.[199] Oil analyst Boris Rachkov maintains that as the consumption rates of the Soviet Union and Eastern Europe continue to rise, the Soviets will not be in a position to engage in a sales offensive.[200] Furthermore, it seems as if the Soviet Union will not be supplying large quantities of oil to the United States and Japan, thus reducing the possibility of conflict with the Arabs in these markets.

8/Oil Embargoes and the Energy Crisis

The Soviet Union verbally supports Arab oil embargoes against Western states but does not itself participate. The Soviet Union has actually increased its oil sales at the time of Arab embargoes, seeking new markets and additional hard currency. While gaining financially, the Soviets can watch the deleterious effects of oil deprivation on Western states without playing any direct role themselves. Maxwell Taylor, former chairman of the Joint Chiefs of Staff, has written: "For the USSR, the aggressive use of the oil weapon by the producer countries is a priceless asset, providing a peaceful and seemingly innocent means of undermining NATO and indeed the entire Western capitalist system without direct Soviet involvement. For the Kremlin, this must appear a thoroughly enjoyable economic war by proxy." [1] The Soviet Union encouraged the Arab embargo of 1973–74 and found satisfaction in the compounding of the Western energy crisis, but neither envisioned nor planned many of the consequences and side effects of this embargo, some of which even had a negative impact on Soviet interests.

As a reaction to the 1956 Suez War, the Arab states directed an oil embargo against Britain and France but it was not too successful since other Western states came to the aid of their allies. The Soviet Union did not become very active as an embargo breaker. It might possibly have been wary about an Arab reaction, but it also had a tanker shortage and only a small amount of additional oil for export. The British Minister of Fuel and Power, Aubrey Jones, said that Britain was interested in buying Soviet oil but none had been offered.[2] There were discussions between the Soviet Union and France on increasing Soviet oil deliveries, but

France said that these talks had begun before the war and the Soviets denied that they were offering extra oil to France.[3] Nevertheless, extra sales did take place.[4] The Soviets also supplied more oil to Egypt, partially replacing the British as marketers, and they delivered oil products to Syria, which had cut off its own oil supply by damaging the IPC pipeline from Iraq.[5]

Writing in 1958, a Soviet analyst claimed that Middle East states wanted to export as much oil as possible and would therefore not disrupt shipments to the West. Ignoring the 1956 embargo, he also asserted: "There is not a single instance on record of any Mid-East statesman or government suggesting the stoppage of oil exports to the West."[6] By June 1967, another Arab embargo was at hand and the Soviet Union was to lend strong encouragement.

The Arab Oil Embargo of 1967

The 1967 embargo lasted for almost three months and was directed primarily at the United States, Britain, and West Germany; it was largely unsuccessful because Iran increased sales and the Western states had emergency stocks.[7] Supertankers also transported large quantities of oil from those states willing to sell. The Soviets praised the embargo, calling it "a concrete and effective expression of Arab solidarity" against Israel and its supporters.[8] A commentator in *International Affairs* declared: "A powerful weapon in the hands of Arab countries is the oil boycott." He claimed that for the West to do without Arab oil would be "difficult, if not impossible."[9] An *Izvestiia* article lauded the use of oil as a "weapon" and charged that Western oil monopolies had spurred on Israeli aggression. It also indicated that half of the oil used in support of South Vietnam was coming from the Middle East and that while the United States was not very dependent on Arab oil, this oil was important to the U.S. war effort in Vietnam.[10]

By mid-August, it appeared as if the Arab states would call off the embargo, but the Soviets encouraged them to maintain it. On

August 15, Radio Moscow called the embargo "legitimate" and it supported the right of oil-producing states "to withhold sales from the countries whose policy is deemed hostile to them." [11] On August 25, just before the embargo ended, Radio Moscow asserted that "the Arabs assume rightly that a blow against the oil interests of the West will accelerate the elimination of the consequences of aggression." [12] However, when the Arab leaders meeting in Khartoum voted to terminate the embargo, the Soviets reluctantly approved of this decision. At first, the lifting of the embargo was mentioned without comment. *Pravda* stated: "The summit conference arrived at the conclusion that petroleum exports can be used as a positive weapon contributing to strengthening the economy of the Arab countries that suffered directly from the aggression. In this connection the conference adopted a decision to resume petroleum exports." [13] Thereafter, the Soviets lent stronger support, praising the Khartoum decision on the ground that money from oil sales would be used to assist Egypt and Jordan. Egypt was losing revenue as a result of the Canal closure and Jordan had lost its entire West Bank region. It was also pointed out that Iraq was losing revenue because of the embargo.[14] The Soviets acknowledged that the embargo had been a failure, indicating that the Arabs should have gone further by nationalizing Western oil properties. They also cited the large oil reserves built up by West European states and the loss of income on the part of the Arab oil producers.[15]

During the 1967 Arab-Israeli war, the Suez Canal again became closed to traffic and Soviet oil exports to India and Japan were disrupted. The Soviets therefore diverted some of the oil intended for Asian customers to Western Europe to take advantage of the Arab embargo.[16] Soviet crude oil exports went up by 7.6 percent in 1967 and their value by 8.5 percent but for sales to Western Europe the figures were 27.1 percent and 37.9 percent respectively.[17] The Soviets moved into West European markets with offers of additional oil and, recognizing the oil desperation of many states, they raised their prices as well. They claimed that the price rise was caused by increased transportation costs.[18] Extra oil supplies were offered to many states, but the main recipient of increased Soviet oil deliveries turned out to be Spain.[19] In

1966, Spain bought 163,000 tons of Soviet crude oil but the figure rose to 456,800 in 1967.[20]

The Soviets claimed that their increased sales to Western Europe represented no change in policy and were just part of an overall rise in oil exports. They averred that no new long-term contracts were initiated during the embargo, although they admitted that they sold an extra million tons of crude oil and oil products just after the 1967 war.[21] Soviet oil specialist Boris Rachkov maintained that the Soviet Union could not have benefited from the Arab embargo because Soviet oil exports increased less in 1967 than in the previous few years but his contention, although based on fact, is nevertheless invalid.[22] Soviet oil exports did not increase greatly in 1967 because the oil production growth rate was lower than in the preceding years. The key point is that the Soviets reduced their shipments to Asian states so that they could provide more oil to Western Europe, and thus profited from the Arab embargo.[23]

Although the Soviet Union had applauded the 1967 embargo and had not been anxious to see it lifted, Boris Rachkov continued to assert that the USSR did not favor Arab embargoes. In 1969 he claimed that Arab states owed outstanding debts to the USSR, which could be repaid only if the oil kept on flowing. The Soviets would therefore suffer financially if there was to be another embargo.[24] Rachkov wanted to assure the West of benign Soviet intentions in the Middle East and North Africa but, despite his comments, the Soviet Union seems to have decided that another embargo would serve its interests.

In 1971, Ruben Andreasyan wrote about the radicalization of Libya since the overthrow of the Idris monarchy and he indicated that rising demand for oil was helping the producing states. He charged that Libya was not receiving high enough prices for its oil and he sympathized with Libya's threat of an oil embargo as a means of securing better financial terms.[25] Such an embargo would have been more economic than political, but the USSR was signaling its support for such a move.

In 1972, another Soviet writer depicted the 1967 embargo as a "countermeasure," based upon Israeli occupation of Arab territory, and he asserted that any future embargo would also be a countermeasure.[26] He was thus implying that the Soviets might favor a politically motivated embargo aimed at securing an Israeli withdrawal. In February 1973, Radio Peace and Progress called upon the Arabs to use oil as a political weapon and it indicated that NATO, the U.S. Sixth Fleet, and U.S.-supported forces in Vietnam were dependent on Arab oil. It declared: "The Arab and other OPEC member countries have shown time and again how they can use oil as an effective political weapon in the defense of their vital interests. . . . In the opinion of a number of Arab economists oil as a weapon to protect the interests of the OPEC countries could be used on a much bigger scale."[27] The commentary also asked the Arab states to withdraw some of their funds from American and British banks, since Arab money was helping to support the value of the dollar and the pound.

In April 1973, Ruben Andreasyan wrote that the United States had benefited from the Arab embargoes of 1956 and 1967 by selling oil to West European states at high prices. The United States was not dependent on Arab oil during that period but it has since become dependent and fears the effects of a new embargo.[28] In August, an Arabic language broadcast on Radio Moscow commented favorably on the desire of many Arabs to use oil as a political weapon against the West and it claimed that money from Western oil companies was used to support Israeli aggression.[29] Shortly thereafter, a *Pravda* commentary maintained: "In light of the energy crisis, about which more and more is being said and written in capitalist countries, the importance of oil as an economic factor is constantly increasing. As a result, additional opportunities are being created for the Arab countries to use this important lever for political ends. Progressive Arab states are trying to use it to resolve such international problems as the Near East crisis."[30]

The Arab Oil Embargo of 1973–74

In October, just before the Arab embargo, an article in *New Times* stated that Arab unity could lead to effective use of the oil weapon against the West. It discerned a "more constructive approach" on the part of West European states as a result of "the oil factor."[31] Soviet analysts had therefore been rather explicit in advocating an Arab oil embargo against the West. C. L. Sulzberger, a columnist for *The New York Times,* maintains that Soviet diplomats suggested an embargo to Arab governments but, whether or not this actually occurred, the Soviet message was certainly clear.[32] With the advent of a new round of Arab–Israeli hostilities, Arab representatives, meeting in Kuwait, announced an oil embargo on October 17, 1973. Saudi Arabia, Libya, Algeria, Kuwait, Abu Dhabi, Iraq, Sudan, and Yemen participated in the decision and the embargo remained in effect until March 18, 1974. Arab states had their own reasons for imposing an embargo and it is unlikely that Soviet encouragement was in any way instrumental.

During the 1973–74 period, the Soviets stressed the West's reliance on Arab oil but noted that the West was attempting to find more politically reliable sources. The North Sea and Southeast Asia exploration programs fell into this category. The Soviets argued that great dependence on the Arabs would continue, thus strengthening the Arabs politically vis-à-vis the West.[33] Soviet assertions on this issue appear to be borne out by Western evidence indicating that three-quarters of the oil exploration money in recent years has been used outside of the Middle East but that two-thirds of the proven reserves are still located there.[34]

Soviet spokesmen extolled the political significance of the Arab embargo as a unifying force in the Arab world and a powerful weapon against Israel and its Western supporters. Soviet periodicals used terms such as "oil politics" and "political weapon." One writer maintained that the energy crisis was a political question as well as an economic one.[35] Another wrote that the Arabs could not be blamed for politicizing oil since the colonial powers and Western oil companies had exploited them for a long time and he thought it ironic that industrialized Western states had become dependent on their former colonies for oil.[36]

The Arab states did not impose the oil embargo equally on all Western states. They took the most severe measures against

Israel's strongest supporters. The Soviets approved of this action. There was praise for the "differentiated" embargo and an *Izvestiia* journalist wrote: "Special notice should be given to the fact that the Arab oil-producing states are legally exercising their right to dispose of their own natural resources and to pursue a carefully considered and, moreover, a differentiated policy in making oil deliveries to various countries." [37]

Soviet analysts asserted that the 1973–74 embargo had been successful because it occurred during a sellers' market for oil, the Arab states had larger financial reserves than ever before, and Western oil stockpiles were not very great.[38] In addition, most of the biggest oil producers participated in the embargo and even increased production by Iran could not make up for decreased Arab exports.[39] Higher oil prices also added to the embargo's success, since the Arab states were securing added revenue while exports were decreasing; this extra income helped protect the Arabs from inflation in Western states since a great amount of Arab money had been deposited in Western banks.[40] Another contributing factor was the leading role of Saudi Arabia. The Soviets emphasized that Saudi Arabia, which had always been closely aligned with the West, had surprised the West with its strong support for the embargo. The Saudis had large cash reserves, and they benefited from higher oil prices, so the embargo served their interests.[41]

Not only did the Soviets encourage the Arab embargo against the West but they also looked favorably upon other related actions and even advocated more far-reaching steps. They maintained that the Arab embargo against South Africa, Rhodesia, and Portugal helped unify Arabs and black Africans against colonialism and racism and they praised the actions of non-Arab states, such as Zaïre, which took control over foreign oil properties.[42] They also called upon the Arabs to nationalize Western oil properties—revolutionary and effective measure that would go beyond the scope of an embargo.[43] Furthermore, the Soviets implied that African states should use their raw materials and minerals as political weapons against colonialism and racism, mentioning Mauritania's iron ore, Sierra Leone's diamonds, Zambia and Zaïre's copper, and Niger's uranium.[44]

While Arab states were cutting down production and embargoing the West, the Soviet Union's closest friend in the Arab world, Iraq, was increasing production and breaking the embargo.[45] Iraq did not have large monetary reserves to ease its way through an embargo. It did, however, take an anti-Western action by nationalizing American and Dutch shares in the Basra Petroleum Company. Minister of Oil and Minerals, Saadum Hammadi, indicated that Iraq was increasing production but supplying oil only to "friendly" states.[46] Early in the embargo period, Leonid Brezhnev made a personal appeal to the Iraqis on the front page of *Pravda*, calling upon them to use their oil resources to increase the effectiveness of the Arab struggle against aggression and foreign monopolies; however, when Iraq failed to participate actively in the embargo, the Soviets did not criticize them publicly.[47] Boris Rachkov wrote that each state could choose its own tactic in the anti-imperialist struggle and that Iraq had chosen nationalization. He implied that nationalization was a stronger measure than an embargo.[48] However, Radio Moscow did attack Libya for breaking the embargo and called for Arab unity on the issue.[49] Iran, which increased its exports during the embargo, was exempted from criticism because of the Soviet Union's desire to maintain good relations. Boris Rachkov claimed that Iran was not trying to take over Arab markets and also asserted that anti-Arab press accounts in Iran were not representative of Iranian thinking and that Iran favored an Israeli withdrawal from occupied Arab territories.[50]

At the time the oil embargo was about to be terminated (March 1974) the Soviets were advocating its continuation and expressed their displeasure even after it had officially ended. In an Arabic-language broadcast one week before the embargo was lifted, a Soviet commentator declared: "If today some Arab leaders are ready to surrender in the face of American pressure and lift the ban on oil before those demands are fulfilled, they are taking a chance by challenging the whole Arab world and the progressive forces of the whole world, which insist on the continued use of the oil weapon." [51] On March 14, four days before the embargo ended, a *Pravda* article discussed a conference of Arab oil ministers in Tripoli, Libya, and emphasized the Syrian position that any termination of the embargo must be linked with an Israeli withdrawal from areas in the Golan Heights.[52] On March 17, *Pravda* implied that the Arab states should keep up the embargo because it had been effective in dividing the West and it had pressured the United States into making gestures toward the Arabs. It averred that American policy had become "utilitarian," since the U.S. wanted the embargo lifted.[53] On March 18, Arab oil ministers meeting in Vienna announced that the oil embargo against most states, including the United States, was to be ended. Syria and Libya did not support this decision and Algeria wanted the decision reviewed on June 1. The Soviets gave very little publicity to the termination of the embargo. Soviet television did not mention it at all, the radio touched upon it briefly, and the press paid only scant attention.[54] On March 24, *Pravda* discussed the ending of the embargo but the article seemed to sympathize with the Syrian position that a Golan Heights settlement should have been related to renewed oil deliveries to the West.[55]

The Soviet Union had wanted the embargo to continue because it was profiting from the high price of oil and it was also moving more strongly into West European oil markets.[56] In addition, the Soviet Union was trying to display its support for some of the more radical Arab states, such as Syria, which favored further use of the embargo tactic, and probably also desired to sow dissension in regard to Arab–Israeli peace negotiations. The Soviets felt left out of the diplomatic maneuvering, which was being dominated by the United States, and they also were unhappy about the growing American role in Egypt. Egyptian President Anwar al-Sadat supported the termination of the oil embargo and this represented a setback for Soviet interests in Egypt.[57]

The Arab decision to end the embargo may, to some extent, have been part of an effort to seek better relations with the West in order to reduce Soviet influence in the Middle East. Egypt probably had this in mind, and the prime mover behind the embargo termination, Saudi Arabia, distrusted Soviet intentions. The Saudis did not want a severe schism to develop between the Arab states and the West since this could lead to the furtherance of Soviet influence in the Persian Gulf. The Saudis also believed that the oil embargo was weakening the economies of Western Europe, the United States, and Japan, thus contributing to a relative increase in Soviet power.[58]

Perspectives on the International Oil Trade

The Organization of Petroleum Exporting Countries (OPEC) was responsible for the rising price of oil in 1973-74 while the Organization of Arab Petroleum Exporting Countries (OAPEC) was behind the Arab embargo.[59] The Soviets encouraged both organizations, since their actions generally hurt the West, but in past years the Soviets had many misgivings about OPEC and OAPEC. OPEC was founded in Baghdad on September 14, 1960, by Iran, Iraq, Kuwait, Saudi Arabia, and Venezuela. Except for Iraq, it was a basically pro-Western group of states and the Soviets did not have faith that this organization could accomplish much. Writing in 1964, Ruben Andreasyan called for unity among oil producers. He mildly praised OPEC, but he then turned to criticism: "The establishment of OPEC, a sort of oil 'anti-cartel' of the developing countries, is doubtlessly an important and positive development. But OPEC still lacks militancy and anti-imperialist orientation. Judging by all the evidence, some of its members are too hesitant, and the organization itself lacks adequate unity. That is why it has not been able to win a single one of its demands." [60] Andreasyan's remarks were rather typical of the Soviet attitude toward OPEC at that time. However, as OPEC's membership grew, it became bolder in dealing with the West, and the Soviet reactions became more favorable.

In January 1968, Libya, Kuwait, and Saudi Arabia created OAPEC (with Iraq refusing to join). The Soviets maintained that OAPEC was a group of "reactionary" Arab states which wanted to work against OPEC. They pointed out that "progressive" states were not members and that there was no need for OAPEC since OPEC was a satisfactory organization of oil producers. Furthermore, OAPEC had stipulated that only states whose main export was oil could become members and this effectively excluded the "progressive" states of Algeria, Egypt, and Syria. As a "reactionary" group, OAPEC would serve to divide the Arabs into competing camps.[61]

By the time of the 1973 energy crisis and oil embargo, the Soviets were praising the efforts of OPEC and OAPEC since these organizations were advocating greater control over Western oil concessions and higher oil prices.[62] The Soviets pointed out that the energy crisis was strengthening the hand of OPEC against the Western oil companies, and they encouraged anti-Western actions on the part of OPEC members. However, the Soviet Union had little influence within OPEC.[63] Among the major OPEC oil exporters were Saudi Arabia, Kuwait, Iran, Venezuela, and Nigeria, which all leaned toward the West politically, and a coincidence of Soviet and OPEC interests, rather than any directing role on the part of the Soviets, lay behind nationalization actions and oil price increases. The Soviet Union did possess some influence over OAPEC although that organization probably would have enacted the embargo anyway.

One of the trends in international oil relations that was particularly lauded by the Soviets was the growth of direct contacts between West European states and the oil producers, bypassing Western oil companies.[64] Such contacts had begun before the embargo, but became accentuated at that time as energy-hungry Western Europe sought long-term guaranteed supplies. Japan and some African states joined the bandwagon and the middleman role of Western oil marketers was greatly reduced.[65] Soviet analysts maintained that the Western oil companies were fighting to retain their position, even resorting to price-cutting in West European markets in order to keep states from dealing directly with the Arab producers.[66]

As oil importing states began to contract directly with the producers, they often reached barter agreements in which arms or technology were exchanged for oil. Britain, France, and West

Germany engaged in such transactions and a *New Times* commentary asserted that the oil producers preferred barter agreements since they did not want to rely on unstable Western currencies.[67] Although it failed to mention the issue, barter between Arab and Western states actually harms the interests of the Soviet Union. The Arabs become less dependent on Soviet arms and they no longer desire extensive barter arrangements with the Soviet Union since they can secure high-quality technology and machinery from the West on a barter basis.

The Energy Crisis

According to Soviet observers, the Western energy crisis had developed by early 1973 and was then compounded by the Arab embargo.[68] During the early stages of the embargo, Soviet press accounts did not directly link the energy crisis with the embargo, but the connection was made explicit as the embargo gathered momentum, and it was argued that a more pro-Arab political position could help solve the Western energy problem. Then, as it appeared that the embargo would end, the effects of the embargo on the energy crisis were deemphasized and the capitalist system and Western oil companies received most of the blame for the crisis.[69]

The Soviets consistently maintain that the Western energy crisis is not caused by a world oil shortage and they even predict that the quantity of oil should be sufficient to allow universal economic growth without disruption until at least the year 2000,[70] because better technology will facilitate the search for oil in remote locations, the utilization of small concentrations, and the extraction of oil from shale. Nevertheless, despite adequate world oil reserves, the Western states do have an energy problem because of their import policies, the structure of captitalism, the role of oil companies, and their political position on Middle East issues.

Soviet writers claim that capitalist states relied on cheap oil from the Third World instead of building up their own oil industries and the United States is accused of saving its own oil for a "rainy day." Oil exploitation in the Third World yielded greater profits than domestic production as the economic development of the West was financed by the oil-exporting states.[71] The West had placed itself in a position where it was dependent on oil imports. As the oil exporters asserted greater political and economic independence from Western control, the West decided to become more self-reliant, but was unable to do so because it had neglected its own oil development.[72]

A writer for *International Affairs* traced the "imperialist" exploitation of Third World oil resources to the capitalist system and claimed that the energy crisis has "socioeconomic and political" causes.[73] Soviet foreign minister Andrei Gromyko summed up the Soviet position on energy while addressing the United Nations in April, 1974: "Mankind—and all specialists seem to agree on this—is not threatened with an energy death. Science has not yet said its last word about new sources of energy. This crisis has not been brought about by nature, but by social and political causes. The fact that the socialist world has virtually not been affected by it is clear evidence of this." [74] It is certainly true that the communist-ruled states have been largely insulated from the world's energy problems but some conservation measures have been put into effect in the Soviet Union, Rumania, Bulgaria and Poland.[75]

The Soviets place part of the blame for the energy crisis on American oil companies. Their profits from oil extraction have been reduced as a result of actions by the oil-producing states so they have therefore raised the sale price of oil in order to make extra profits. They claim that the producing states are responsible for the high price of oil, but the oil companies have themselves raised the price in order to take advantage of an energy shortage.[76] The oil companies exaggerate this shortage and even hold back supplies to drive the price higher.[77] During the last quarter of 1973, American oil companies had record earnings.[78] American companies were also trying to raise oil prices in Western Europe and Japan and speculation and scandals in many capitalist states were also responsible for high prices and energy shortages.[79]

Furthermore, according to the Soviet analysis, some of the American oil profits were sent to Israel in the form of aid.[80]

The Soviets asserted that Western support for Israel had led to the Arab embargo, thus aggravating the energy crisis.[81] The well-known effects on Western societies, such as unemployment, a decline in production, and foreign trade deficits, were emphasized by Soviet observers as they saw a major crisis in the capitalist system.[82] In order to encourage the termination of the embargo, Western states cited the supposed "interdependence" between the Third World and themselves, claiming that a Western economic crisis would mean reduced machinery exports to the Third World, but the Soviets called such a Western argument an excuse to keep the Third World economically dependent by retarding its industrialization.[83]

Oil Diplomacy

The Soviets constantly pointed out that the United States was suffering less than other Western states because it was less dependent on oil imports. They charged that the United States was taking advantage of this situation to increase the value of the dollar at the expense of other Western currencies and they maintained that rising oil prices boosted the value of dollars, since most oil payments are made in dollars.[84] The Soviet analysis of the dollar's strengthened value was not too different from American critiques but it is more likely that the financial impetus came from the embargo rather than from any intentional machinations on the part of the United States.[85]

The Soviets rejoiced in the fact that the oil embargo had led to dissension among West European states and between the United States and Western Europe.[86] Common Market states had their differences over energy policies and the United States and France sharply clashed on the issue.[87] Such contradictions within the Western camp served Soviet interests, so the USSR was not anxious to see the formulation of any coordinated Western energy policy. Accordingly, the energy conference organized by the United States in February 1974 was attacked as an American effort to ensure West European dependence on U.S. oil companies.[88] The Soviets also complained that the Western states were colluding to prevent the Arabs from controlling their own oil resources and that the conference was clearly anti-Arab; Arab representatives had not even been invited.[89] Radio Moscow, in reference to the Washington energy conference, declared: "It was clear beforehand that the meeting would end in failure because the representatives of the oil-producing countries had not been invited. Without their participation, all discussions on the energy crisis are like a wedding without a bride." [90]

The Soviet solution for the world's energy problems was to convene a broad conference or producers and consumers, including the USSR. The Soviets maintained that Arab newspapers favored such a conference and that President Houari Boumedienne of Algeria had voiced his support.[91] Of course, the Soviets did not want the Arab oil weapon to be blunted by a coordinated bloc of Western oil importers so they criticized Western steps in that direction and tried to widen the forum for dealing with the energy problem. Despite Soviet efforts, and France's maverick role within the Western alliance, an International Energy Agency was formed by Austria, Belgium, Britain, Canada, Denmark, Ireland, Italy, Japan, Luxembourg, the Netherlands, New Zealand, Norway, Spain, Sweden, Switzerland, Turkey, the United States, and West Germany.

The Arab oil embargo seriously disrupted Western economies, but it was primarily a political weapon aimed at pressuring states into a pro-Arab position on the Arab–Israeli conflict. The Soviets stressed the political significance of the embargo and believed that the embargo was highly effective. Journalists rather accurately indicated that West European states were taking a more pro-Arab position as a result of the oil embargo, thereby dissociating themselves from American support for Israel.[92] There were Soviet comments on Italy's political shift and it was averred that many West Germans did not want their country to repeat its "mistake" regarding relations with the Arab states.[93] The Soviet press paid particular attention to Japan, explaining how the oil embargo influenced its pro-Arab pronouncements. Radio Moscow best expressed the Soviet view of the embargo by stating: "As you may well know, the Arabs' use of the oil weapon to defend their interests has demonstrated the extreme effectiveness of this weapon, since certain European countries and also Japan have reluctantly altered their attitude toward the Near East question, thereby condemning the aggressor." [94] The Soviets further maintained that even the United States had been motivated by the effects of the embargo to make an effort to arrive at a Middle East peace settlement. [95]

Soviet Oil Exports During the Embargo

The Soviet Union did not join the Arab oil embargo but instead benefited from the rising prices by selling oil to Western states. [96] First Deputy Minister of Foreign Trade, Ivan Semichastnov, stated that the USSR would fulfill its contractual obligations for oil deliveries but would not increase its oil exports to take advantage of the embargo. However, he indicated that the USSR would continue to negotiate long-term oil delivery contracts with states such as Japan. [97] The Soviets were trying to assure the Arab states that they were not destroying the effectiveness of the embargo by making additional sales to the embargoed states, and Radio Moscow broadcasts in Arabic stressed this theme, with one commentary asserting that not even one extra ton was being supplied to Western Europe. The Soviets pointed out that only 4 percent of the oil consumed in Western Europe came from the Soviet Union. [98]

It was basically true that the Soviet Union did not substantially increase oil exports during the embargo, largely because it just did not have extra oil available, but it nevertheless managed to advance its interests by undermining the embargo in other ways. [99] For example, the USSR had always resold some of the oil purchased from Arab states to West European customers; once the embargo came into effect, such sales became extremely lucrative. Many of the Soviet purchases were part of long-term agreements at fixed prices, but the Soviets resold this oil at the new high prices and often realized a 300 percent profit.[100] It also appears as if the Soviets rerouted some West European oil deliveries in order to secure a higher price. There were shortfalls on deliveries to West Germany during the last quarter of 1973 and the first few months of 1974, and this oil may have been sold to other West European states.[101] Oil intended for Norway may have been diverted as well.[102]

The Netherlands was a prime target of the Arab embargo and there are indications that the Soviet Union took advantage of the situation by increasing oil sales to the Netherlands during the embargo period. When a Swedish radio broadcast claimed that the Soviets were delivering oil to the Netherlands, the Soviets labeled the report a "canard." [103] Nevertheless, the Soviets were surely delivering oil as part of their normal contractual agreement with the Netherlands and the real question is whether deliveries increased or remained at their previous level. Frank Gardner, former editor of *Oil and Gas Journal,* maintains that the quantity increased during the embargo while Benjamin Shwadran does not believe such reports.[104] However, Soviet foreign trade statistics for 1973 do shed some light on the issue. Soviet oil sales to the Netherlands jumped from 2,433,400 tons of crude oil and products in 1972 to 3,219,900 tons in 1973. The ruble value of such sales was 40,226,000 in 1972 and 135,583,000 in 1973, reflecting rising world oil prices.[105] Whether total deliveries exceeded previously agreed upon levels is difficult to determine, as is the exact mix between crude oil and oil products. Nevertheless, some interesting hypotheses can still be drawn. Since the average price per unit of oil was so high and since world price increases were greatest toward the end of the year, it is likely that much of the Soviet oil received by the Netherlands was delivered late in the year during the embargo period. It is possible that there were previous agreements stipulating that Soviet deliveries would be concentrated toward the end of 1973, but this is not likely. Another contributing piece of evidence is that the price per unit charged to the Netherlands was higher than that for other West

European states, thus implying again that substantial deliveries were made at the end of the year when prices were raised. It is conceivable that the Netherlands receives a greater percentage of oil products from the Soviet Union than do other West European states, and this could explain the high unit price. But there is no reason to suppose that this is the case; the unit price to the Netherlands in 1972 was in line with that charged to other states. In addition, the Netherlands is a major oil refining center so there would be no reason to import large quantities of oil products. Soviet statistics for trade with Denmark show a pattern similar to that for the Netherlands, so perhaps oil was also diverted there during the embargo.[106]

Another principal target of the Arab embargo was the United States; the evidence is unmistakable that the USSR increased oil sales to the United States during the embargo. Shortly after the embargo began, a Radio Moscow English-language commentary suggested that the Soviets were willing to sell liquid fuel to the United States to help overcome the energy shortage.[107] Actually, the Soviet Union had already been supplying the United States with both crude oil and oil products. American purchases of fuel oil went back at least as far as 1969, crude oil purchases began in 1972, and gasoline purchases began earlier in 1973. However, Soviet sales in the American market were very small, with total value reaching only $7,464,000 in 1972.[108] Spurred on by the oil embargo, Soviet sales to the United States accelerated in late 1973 and early 1974 with the total value rising to $76,214,000 in 1973 and $33,283,000 for just the first two months of 1974. The value of gasoline sales for all of 1973 was $3,760,000, but it was $6,723,000 for the first two months of 1974. In 1973, 70 percent of American kerosene imports and 5 percent of home heating oil imports came from the USSR, but these figures rose to 80 percent and 8 percent during the first two months of 1974. In January and February 1974, the United States received 12 percent of its gasoline and motor fuel imports from the USSR, mostly for marketing by independent distributors on the East Coast.[109]

Soviet oil sales to the United States were aimed at obtaining hard currency. They did not accord with Soviet foreign policy in a political sense. The Soviets did not publicize these sales, and even failed to include them in their statistical yearbooks. The United States was not anxious to advertise the matter and generally kept it quiet. The Arabs would surely have reacted strongly if the Soviets had announced oil sales to the United States during the embargo, and public opinion in the United States would not have been very pleased. The Soviets did not want the Arab states to focus on this issue and tried to reassure them in an Arabic-language broadcast on Radio Moscow, but in so doing they really admitted that such oil sales were taking place. The radio commentator asserted: "And as to the United States, Soviet oil is being exported there only from time to time—rarely." [110] There were some American press accounts referring to the Soviet embargo-breaking and it was pointed out that the Soviet oil was delivered on the same ships used to transfer American wheat to the USSR. The wheat was left at Odessa and many of the ships then went on to Tuapse and Batumi to pick up oil. One-fifth of the ships delivering wheat returned with Soviet oil while all of the remaining ships came back with oil from other sources.[111]

The Soviet Union and United States had been discussing possible American participation in Siberian projects in return for oil and gas deliveries to the United States, and the Arab oil embargo could possibly have affected American attitudes toward such an economic relationship. Seeing the results of overreliance on Arab states, the U.S. could have sought to diversify its sources of supply by concluding energy agreements with the USSR. As Marshall Goldman observed even before the Arab embargo, the pressure the Soviet Union could exert through its control of oil resources is not really any worse than Arab pressure, and trade agreements with the Soviets may be more advantageous than those with the Arabs because the Soviets want to purchase so many American goods, thereby assisting the U.S. balance of trade.[112] On the other hand, the Arab embargo could have encouraged greater American self-reliance, so that the U.S. would not suffer from future embargoes. This does seem to have been one of its effects. Although "Project Independence" is certainly an overstatement of American resolve and capabilities, there is a growing conviction in the United States that self-sufficiency should be the eventual goal of American energy policy, and this would mean that the United States would probably not participate in Siberian projects. Shifting from the Arabs to the Soviets may be a case of going out of the frying pan into the fire. Harry Schwartz, writing in *The New York Times,* has warned against any oil or gas deals with the USSR, since they can be used as instruments of political pressure in the Arab manner.[113] The Soviets have shown a sensitivity to such reasoning and claim that U.S.–Soviet economic relations should not be affected by the Arab embargo since the Soviets were in no way responsible for Arab actions.[114]

Ramifications of the Embargo

Soviet oil shipments to the United States during the Arab embargo were not large enough to offset the effects of the embargo. Since American military might was weakened by the oil shortage, Soviet power interests stood to gain. The United States was less dependent on oil imports than were the West European states and Japan but was still the world's largest oil importer in terms of quantity, if not in percentage of dependency. Foreign oil was particularly crucial to the American military establishment. Much of the oil used for military purposes in South Vietnam and Cambodia had been cut off by the Arab embargo, so 23,500 barrels per day had to be diverted to these states from Pacific war reserves. In turn, these war reserves were replenished with oil from American civilian stocks.[115] It was also necessary to send oil from the United States to fuel both the Sixth and Seventh Fleets, which had previously relied on Arab oil supplied indirectly through third parties. Sixth Fleet oil had been provided by Italy and Seventh Fleet oil by Singapore and the Philippines.[116] In addition, the U.S. military had to resort to economy measures to save fuel, bringing about a 7 percent cut in fuel allocations, and the diversion of domestic oil supplies to overseas forces led to a reduction in military training within the United States. The Department of Defense invoked the Defense Production Act of 1950, taking 300,000 barrels per day out of civilian supplies in order to assist the military, and this further accentuated the domestic oil shortage.[117]

In another development, oil from Saudi Arabia was withheld from the U.S. military. The four American companies in Aramco (Mobil, Exxon, Texaco, and Standard Oil of California) were told by King Feisal on May 23, 1973, that their holdings would be nationalized if they did not work toward a reduction in American support for Israel. According to information released by the Senate Foreign Relations Subcommittee on Multinational Corporations, the companies complied with Feisal's dictate.[118] On November 4, while the Arab–Israeli war was still in progress, the Saudi foreign ministry ordered that Aramco could not permit products made from Saudi oil to be used by the American military. As a result, the New York headquarters of Exxon told its European divisions to withhold oil from the military during the course of the Middle East war.[119] Aramco reported the Saudi order to the U.S. Department of Defense and Aramco's nondelivery of oil was one of the reasons why 825 million gallons of oil were taken from the civilian supply and delivered to the military.[120] Furthermore, as reported in Soviet publications, Japan informed the United States that, beginning in mid-January 1974, it would no longer supply aircraft fuel for U.S. Air Force planes nor fuel for U.S. forces stationed in Japan. It indicated that the oil shortage was responsible for this step but it also pointed out that the Arab states would react negatively to a continuation of the fuel supplies.[121] The Philippines too took a cue from the Arab embargo, cutting off oil to American bases while it was in effect.[122]

The Arab oil embargo reduced American military capabilities and any future embargo could do the same thing. Thus, when viewed in a competitive strategic framework, embargoes serve the interests of the Soviet Union and the Soviets may therefore seek renewed applications of the Arab oil weapon. Without any direct participation, the Soviets can see the deleterious consequences of oil shortages on the United States.

The Chinese reaction to the Arab oil embargo was similar to the Soviets'. The Chinese verbally supported the Arabs, did not join the embargo themselves, and broke the embargo by selling diesel fuel to Thailand. The Chinese approved of the politicization of oil on behalf of the Arab cause and also praised the growing contacts between West European and Middle East states in the areas of oil, technology, machinery, and arms agreements since Soviet and American influence in the Middle East could be reduced in this manner.[123] However, the Chinese took advantage of the Arab embargo of Thailand by selling it 50,000 tons of diesel fuel which may possibly have come from the Middle East.[124] The Soviet Union's Radio Peace and Progress claimed that there was Thai confirmation of the fact that the diesel fuel originated in the Middle East and the Chinese were accused of betraying the Arabs.[125] *Pravda* noted that the Chinese were selling the diesel fuel to a state with a large American military base and Radio Peace and Progress asserted that China was delivering oil products to countries obligated to provide fuel for American bases.[126]

The Arab oil embargo revealed the economic and political vulnerability of Western states and the willingness of many of them to give in to Arab pressure tactics. It showed that the use of economic commodities for political purposes was effective and future actions of this type by raw material exporters may therefore be expected. The Soviet Union, which is largely self-sufficient in raw materials, cannot be easily victimized in this manner and thus has an advantage over Western states. Even the United States, which is not highly dependent on oil imports, is a fertile target for embargoes since, of thirteen basic raw materials, it imports a majority of its needs of six of them and an increasing percentage of six more.[127]

The Arab embargo hurt the West economically but it also led to a search for secure sources of oil supply and a major diplomatic effort to improve political and economic ties with the Arab states. The Western states want to make sure that they will have access to Arab oil and this has brought about a greater role for France, Britain, West Germany, the United States, and Japan in Middle East affairs. Machinery, technology, and arms agreements are multiplying at an astounding rate and the eventual result may be the undercutting of Soviet influence in the area. In addition, as the West attaches growing strategic importance to the Middle East, the likelihood of a direct confrontation between Soviet and Western forces is increased. Both sides are building up their strength in the oil lanes of the Indian Ocean and the reopening of the Suez Canal should accentuate this trend. Furthermore, the possibility of American intervention in an Arab state in order to seize oil installations cannot be ruled out if another embargo is imposed, and such an American action may evoke a Soviet response. Although the Soviet Union was elated about the West's economic distress which resulted from the Arab oil embargo, the repercussions of this embargo have opened up new strategic opportunities in the Middle East, which could tend to reduce Soviet influence and increase Soviet risks.

The embargo also had negative consequences for the Soviet Union. Some Arab states started to charge the Soviets high prices in hard currency for their oil and there was less of an Arab market for Soviet machinery and equipment thanks to increased Western offers to the Arabs. World oil prices soared, helping to fill Soviet coffers, but long-term agreements with East European states led to the maintenance of artificially low prices, and the Soviets could not shift these oil exports to more lucrative markets. Hostilities in the Middle East also showed that Soviet oil imports could be affected by the unstable political situation as the transport of oil purchased by the USSR was delayed at both Banias and Tartus in Syria.

The oil embargo had certain side-effects which were probably not part of Arab or Soviet designs. Third World states were seriously hurt by the rising price of oil, causing balance of payments deficits, a slower rate of industrialization, and fertilizer shortages. They could not conserve oil very easily because it was mostly used for essentials rather than luxuries, and the economic crisis in the West added to their woes as there was the possibility that both Western aid and purchases of Third World products would decrease.[128] The Soviets were embarrassed by these developments since they were loudly applauding the embargo but they did support the concept of having OPEC members contribute to a special fund to assist Third World states with their oil payments.[129] The problems of the Third World oil importers presented the Soviets with a golden opportunity to step in with oil at reduced prices in order to gain political prestige but this did not occur. The Soviets just did not have extra oil to spare and they preferred to continue directing most of their non-CMEA exports to states willing to pay with hard currency.

Overall, the Arab oil embargoes of 1956, 1967, and 1973–74 furthered Soviet interests, as economic and political warfare against the West was carried out by proxy. The supply effect of Western states had proved to be weak and fragile while the Soviet Union rejoiced in the knowledge that it was self-sufficient in oil production and greatly immune to the influence effect of oil-exporting states. Paradoxically, however, the increasing power of the Arab world which the Soviets have helped foster may lead to less Arab reliance on the Soviet Union, as the oil weapon has encouraged Arab self-assertion and independence.

9/Communist-Ruled States

The Soviet Union has used its control over the oil supply of most communist-ruled states to keep them within the Soviet sphere of influence, and in those situations where states have tried to break away from Soviet hegemony the oil weapon has been applied as a pressure tactic in order to retard such fissiparous tendencies. In the immediate post-World War II years, the USSR exploited the oil wealth of certain East European states, but by the mid-fifties oil was being used to help further the economic and political integration of a Soviet-dominated grouping of communist-ruled states. Exportation of oil replaced exploitation. As the energy needs of communist-ruled states grew enormously, greater demands were placed on the Soviet energy supply, which strongly affected Soviet oil export policies.

During the latter stages of the Second World War, the Red Army had occupied oil-rich Rumania and brought it under Soviet control. Oilfield equipment, much of it owned by American and British companies, was removed from Rumania and transported to the USSR. One of the main factors consolidating Soviet oil exploitation was the armistice agreement of September 12, 1944, under which Rumania was required to provide free oil for Soviet occupation forces and to pay war reparations for damages to the USSR. These reparations included the delivery of 1.7 million tons of oil per year for six years. Then, in 1945, the Soviet Union took over German oil assets in Rumania, in accordance with Allied agreements reached at the Potsdam Conference, and also entered into a commercial agreement, which included the Soviet purchase of some Rumanian oil. The USSR and Rumania also established a joint stock company for oil production named Sovrompetrol, on July 17, 1945. Ownership of shares was to be equal, but the USSR did not really contribute many assets of its own, since it provided the confiscated German oil properties. Sovrompetrol controlled one-third of Rumania's crude oil production before the nationalization of foreign oil properties in 1948, but it then gained control over virtually all of Rumania's production. During the late forties, Soviet acquisitions of Rumanian oil were so diversified and extensive that Rumania was left with less than 40 percent of her production for domestic use or export.

Rumanian reparations payments to the USSR were to be $300 million of goods delivered in equal installments over six years. Oil was to be a large part of the Rumanian payments, with the 1.7 million tons per year to be valued at $15 per ton. In 1946, the Soviets agreed to extend Rumanian payments over an eight-year period, but on July 7, 1948, the Soviets announced that Rumania would only have to pay half of its remaining reparations balance. The Soviets received about 9 million tons of crude oil and oil products from Rumania as reparations during the years 1944–48, but they may actually have received more oil than was called for in the reparations agreement, since they stole and confiscated additional oil from Rumanian supplies.[1] Although reparations payments stopped, the USSR continued to receive Rumanian oil as a result of Soviet ownership of shares in Sovrompetrol.

There was very little oil to exploit in Eastern Europe, except in Rumania, but the Soviets did manage to take advantage of their status as one of the occupying powers in Austria. They took control of an oil field within their occupation zone, northeast of Vienna, and transported the oil to the USSR. When their occupation status ended in 1955, they returned the oil field to Austria in return for compensation.[2] The Soviets also received oil deliveries from Austria as war reparations. These deliveries started in 1949 and rose to a million tons per year by 1956. Beginning in 1959 the Soviets decided to return half of the oil to Austria as a good-will gesture. The Soviets continued their policy of returning 500,000 tons per year until mid-1961, when they told Austria that it should only deliver 500,000 tons to the USSR per year, rather than one million tons. By July 1964, Austria had fulfilled its reparations obligation to the USSR and deliveries were terminated.[3]

The CMEA Oil Supply

The Soviet Union had been greatly devastated by the Second World War and it economically exploited the states under its postwar occupation in order to help rebuild its own economy. After Yugoslavia defected, the Soviet Union decided to organize an economic bloc which would bind communist-ruled states together into a cohesive unit under Soviet political control. The result was the formation of the Council for Mutual Economic Assistance, on January 21, 1949.[4] As the Soviets integrated the economies of CMEA states, they continued their exploitive economic role and their coercive political role, but under Khrushchev many authoritarian controls were relaxed and replaced with economic incentives.

The Soviet Union became the supplier of oil for most CMEA members, and while the Soviets charged a very high price, the CMEA states were assured of steady oil supplies. The Soviets used their control over the oil supply for political purposes. Gradually, as the oil needs of East European states increased tremendously, the ability of the Soviets to supply oil became somewhat restricted. Nevertheless, the flow was continued to help maintain the Soviet sphere of influence in the area.[5]

The CMEA states (Poland, Hungary, Czechoslovakia, East Germany, Rumania, Bulgaria, Cuba, Mongolia, and the USSR) collectively produce enough energy for their needs, chiefly because of the great energy production of the Soviet Union. Except for Poland and Rumania, all of the other states are energy deficient.[6] Poland is a major producer of coal and Rumania produces both oil and natural gas, but Rumania's needs are beginning to outstrip her production capacity and she is on her way toward becoming energy-deficient.

The Soviet Union is responsible for more than 95 percent of

the oil production of CMEA states, and there is little likelihood that this situation will change in the future. Eastern Europe produced only 17 million tons of crude oil in 1973, and the yearly production increase for 1971–73 was only about 2 percent. The proven oil reserves of Eastern Europe are only 200 million tons— with 165 million in Rumania and 20 million in Hungary. Exploration in the Black Sea by Rumania and Bulgaria, and in the Baltic Sea by Poland and East Germany, should lead to further oil finds but they will probably not be of any sizable quantity.[7] Furthermore, oil exploration in Eastern Europe is held back by a lack of capital, since scarce capital resources tend to be invested in industries that bring much greater financial returns.[8]

Rumania has 83 percent of Eastern Europe's crude oil reserves but its estimated reserves of 198 million tons are not very large.[9] Rumania's production has now leveled off at about 14 million tons per year, and during the period 1955–65, production rose by only 15 percent.[10] Consumption has been increasing steadily, so Rumania cannot contribute very much to the oil supply of CMEA. Rumania has been a net importer of crude oil since 1968 but still exports large quantities of oil products, some of which are exported to the USSR. Rumania's decline as an oil power really began during the thirties. In 1932, Rumania ranked fourth in world oil production, but it fell to fifth in 1937 (as few new reserves were found), to twelfth by 1963 and thirty-third by 1972.[11]

Outside of Rumania and the USSR, there is very little oil production within CMEA. Hungary and Poland are increasing their production, but are still far from self-sufficiency, while Czechoslovakia, Bulgaria, Mongolia, and Cuba produce small amounts. East Germany has only a little crude oil but it does have a large refinery capacity and therefore exports oil products. Among communist-ruled states which are not members of CMEA, North Korea and Vietnam have very small quantities of oil (but they rely primarily on other energy sources) while Yugoslavia produces fairly sizable amounts of oil but not enough for her needs. China and Albania are basically self-sufficient in oil.

Energy consumption in Eastern Europe is increasing more

rapidly than in Western Europe, and East Germany and Czecho-slovakia already consume more energy per capita than the USSR.[12] East European reliance on oil as an energy source is constantly growing. It was 7.5 percent in 1965, 20.7 percent by 1972. Projections for 1980 are in the range of 24.4 percent to 28.4 percent.[13] Eastern Europe will therefore have to import more oil from the USSR or turn to other sources of supply; the same holds true for Cuba.[14]

More than half of the Soviet Union's oil exports now go to East European states and most of the oil delivered there is crude oil. The USSR provides about 60 percent of Eastern Europe's oil needs and about 90 percent of her oil imports. During the period 1966–70, the USSR exported 138 million tons of oil to East European states and the plan for 1971–75 called for 243 million.[15] Thereafter, the Soviets may be supplying as much as 70 million tons per year but their ability to do so is questionable.[16] A study by the Economist Intelligence Unit estimates East European production in 1980 at under 25 million tons, which is similar to Polish economist Stanislaw Albinowski's projection of 23–33 million tons for all CMEA states other than the USSR. However, Albinowski estimates CMEA demand at 170 million tons, so huge imports will be necessary.[17] The most likely source is the USSR, since the other communist-ruled states are short of hard currency and will have difficulty buying oil from Middle East producers. Therefore, the Soviets will surely be faced with an energy squeeze and are now encouraging other CMEA states to look for additional sources of supply. Eastern Europe can attempt to develop atomic energy, or to rely more on coal, but its oil needs will still be great and Soviet oil minister Shashin was not particularly reassuring when he said that the USSR can fulfill CMEA's oil needs "almost fully." [18]

The Soviets informed the Czechs in late 1969 that they should try to import oil from the Middle East and North Africa.[19] However, there are indications that Soviet requests to East European states may have begun as early as 1965, since these states started to make oil deals with Arab producers and Iran at that time.[20] Later, at an Athens conference organized by the United Nations in November–December, 1967, Soviet economist L. Z. Zevin said that CMEA countries wanted to import more oil from Third World states.[21] Zevin probably would not have mentioned the issue had the Soviets disapproved of such an action. In 1968, an article in *International Affairs* pointed out that fuel requirements of CMEA states were growing but that extraction was behind schedule in all states except the USSR. It then hinted that the Soviets did not want to supply all of the needs of these states: "The Soviet Union's increasing deliveries of fuel and raw materials are a major contribution to solving the CMEA countries' acute problem of the fuel and power balance and provide the basis for developing a number of growth industries in these countries." [22] Soviet writers gradually became much more direct and explicit on this issue, with an article in *Foreign Trade* declaring in 1973: "The steadily growing demand of the CMEA member countries for oil and the desire of these countries to improve their total fuel and power supply above all through oil consumption can be met not only by deliveries of oil via the Friendship Oil Pipeline and expansion of their own oil production, but by supplies from the developing countries of the Middle East and the African continent." [23]

Since 1965, the East European members of CMEA have concluded numerous oil import agreements with Middle East and North African states.[24] Most of the oil imported by communist-ruled states was secured through barter agreements. Tankers, arms, and manufactured goods were exchanged for oil, and East European participation in oil development projects was also paid for with oil. In recent years, there have been many hard-currency transactions and, as previously mentioned, East European purchases of Middle East and North African oil are becoming highly problematic owing to the hard currency demands of the producing states. The producers no longer want to barter their oil for East European goods, which thus places East European states in a precarious position since they are short of hard currency and the USSR cannot meet all of their oil requirements.

Transporting oil from the Middle East to Eastern Europe is not a simple matter. For example, much of the oil imported from Iran is now shipped around Africa. The proposed Iran–Turkey oil pipeline would have facilitated the delivery of this oil to Eastern Europe, but the project now appears moribund. Iran was anxious to reduce its dependence on the Persian Gulf for exports, just in case it was ever sealed off, and Iran also did not want to rely on the undependable Suez Canal route. Discussions with Turkey have gone on for many years; a preliminary agreement was reached as far back as September 1957, but the project has floundered because many Western states, which consider it economically unviable, have been reluctant to provide funds for its construction or to commit themselves to using such a pipeline. Furthermore, since the initiation of Iranian oil exports to Eastern Europe, the Western states have had no interest in contributing to the growth of this oil trade. Gradually, Iran strengthened its military position in the Persian Gulf and also came to fear eventual instability in Turkey, so the impetus for the pipeline has largely been dissipated.[25]

Hungary and Czechoslovakia are landlocked—an obstacle to large oil imports from the Middle East and North Africa. However, a solution has now been found in the planned Adriatica pipeline, which will permit the delivery of oil via Yugoslavia. According to an agreement of February 12, 1974, supertankers will send crude oil through a pipeline at Rijeka, on the Yugoslav coast, and the oil will flow to Sisak, Yugoslavia. One branch of the pipeline will then go on to Belgrade while the other proceeds to Szaszhalombatta, Hungary. At Szaszhalombatta, some of the oil will enter the Druzhba I pipeline and the flow of that line will be reversed, enabling oil to be piped to Czechoslovakia. The capacity of the Adriatica pipeline will reach 34 million tons per year by 1979, of which 24 million will be used by Yugoslavia and 5 million each by Hungary and Czechoslovakia.[26] Libya and Kuwait may help with the financing, and Hungary has already made plans to increase its oil imports from Iraq and Libya once the pipeline opens.[27] The pipeline project makes Hungary and Czechoslovakia dependent upon oil transit across Yugoslavia, and this could have important geopolitical ramifications once Tito dies. These two states, and indirectly the USSR as well, will have a vested interest in making sure that any Yugoslav government (or perhaps there may be separatist governments) is favorably disposed toward their interests.

The USSR and East European states have not only turned toward the import of oil from the Middle East and North Africa but have also developed oil ties with Western capitalist states. Hungary, Czechoslovakia, and East Germany all purchase oil from the British Petroleum Company (BP) while Hungary also buys from the Italian company (ENI).[28] Both Hungary and Rumania receive oil from the British-Dutch company (Shell).[29] The largest import agreement was arranged in 1971 between BP and Poland. BP is to provide technical help for the building of a refinery at Gdansk. With its completion in 1975, Poland is to receive 3 million tons of crude oil per year for ten years.[30] Poland has also contracted with Snam Progetti, a subsidiary of ENI, for the building of another refinery at Gdansk and a preliminary agreement has been reached with Sweden on even another at the same location.[31] This latter deal would include 50 percent ownership of the refinery by Poland, 25 percent by Sweden and 25 percent by the Swedish company Beijerinvest, with 50 percent of the refinery's production to belong to Swedish interests.[32]

Western oil companies are active in Hungarian marketing operations, with both Shell and the Italian firm Agip, running service stations. They sell oil products which are refined in Hungary and accept Hungarian currency, although the first Shell station, opened in 1966, was permitted to accept only foreign currency.[33] Mobil provides lubricants for the Czechoslovak market and Western capitalist firms may even be invited to participate in oil exploration in Eastern Europe and the USSR.[34] Rumanian President Nicolae Ceausescu has said that he would welcome American oil companies' help in Rumania's search for oil under the Black Sea and he has indicated that these companies would share in the ownership of oil once it is produced.[35] The Soviet Union has discussed a search for offshore oil and gas deposits in the Barents, Black, and Caspian Seas with West German firms.[36] It has also discussed offshore exploration in the Arctic with an American firm, Global Marine Incorporated, and it has negotiated with Standard Oil of Indiana on developing oil fields in return for crude oil.[37] In addition, it has discussed numerous energy projects with

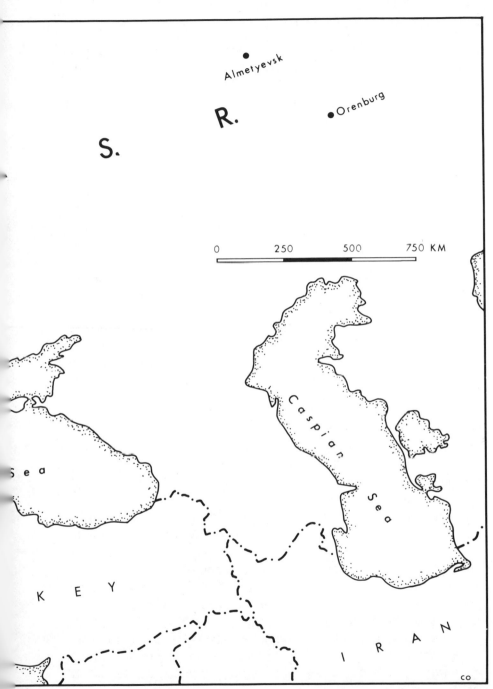

MAP 3. EASTERN EUROPE

American and Japanese companies, hoping to receive their assistance in the exploitation of Siberian resources.[38]

The economies of CMEA states are being opened up to include ventures by capitalist states and oil companies and it is no longer true that communist-ruled states have completely closed markets. The guidelines under which they have been opened have surely been set by the governments concerned, but the growing tendency among CMEA members is to be less autarkic and to collaborate more with outside firms and states. During the past few years, Soviet publications have emphasized that CMEA is not "an exclusive grouping of countries" and that "the strengthening of the CMEA countries' community does not lead to a closed economic grouping." [39]

Although CMEA members are increasing their economic ties with noncommunist states, they continue to receive the bulk of their oil from the Soviet Union.[40] Most of it flows through the Druzhba (Friendship) Pipeline, whose construction was approved by the Tenth Plenum of CMEA in December 1958. Each state was to build the section of the pipeline on its own territory and the USSR was to train technicians from other states.[41] Rumania may have opposed the pipeline project because Soviet crude oil was to be sent into traditional Rumanian markets. Eventually, this did work to Rumania's detriment in Czechoslovakia, but Rumania emerged with some profits by supplying pipe for the project.[42]

The Druzhba Pipeline begins at Almetyevsk in the Volga-Ural region and then proceeds to Mozyr in Byelorussia. At that point, it splits into a northern line which goes to Poland and East Germany and a southern line which goes to Hungary and Czechoslovakia. The northern line brings crude oil to the refineries at Plock, Poland, and Schwedt on Oder, East Germany, while the southern line delivers oil to refineries at Bratislava and Gnevice, Czechoslovakia, and Szaszhalombatta, Hungary.[43] The Druzhba Pipeline began to supply crude oil to Czechoslovakia on February 3, 1962; Hungary on September 17, 1962; Poland on November 7, 1963; and East Germany on December 18, 1963.[44] Many extensions have since been added to the original pipeline. The total length is now over 5000 kilometers (3100 miles) and about 60 percent of the pipeline is within the USSR.[45] A Friendship 2 Pipeline was completed in 1975, bringing the total capacity of the system to about 100 million tons per year.[46] According to the Soviet publication *International Affairs,* the Druzhba Pipeline can transport oil at 20 percent of the cost of railroad transport and 50 percent of the cost of sea transport, and the investment in the original sections of the pipeline was already recouped by 1966.[47]

The Druzhba Pipeline also serves a political function, since the USSR can easily cut off or reduce the flow of oil to a recipient state to apply pressure.[48] British economist Alec Nove points out that the route of the Druzhba Pipeline may have been based on political considerations. The Soviet Union had already been faced with a revolution in Hungary so a pipeline through that state was not deemed to be highly secure. Therefore, a large part of the pipeline was built through Czechoslovakia and a shorter length was extended into Hungary.[49] Czechoslovakia was possibly viewed as more politically reliable but, of course, this was before 1968.

While delivering large quantities of oil to Eastern Europe, the Soviet Union has nevertheless been complaining about the high cost of oil extraction and transportation and has been encouraging East European states to invest in Soviet oil development projects. Back in 1968, an article in *International Affairs* maintained that the fuel and raw material problem is "acute" and "complicated." It indicated that the USSR had sufficient fuel and raw materials but needed help in bearing the economic burden.[50] Later, a pair of *New Times* commentators averred that raw material production is costly because surveys must precede extraction and a long time passes before there is a return on the investment.[51] Minister of Foreign Trade Nikolai Patolichev joined the discussion by asserting that the Soviet Union was gearing its development of natural resources to the requirements of communist-ruled states but that investment by these states in Soviet fuel production was clearly needed.[52]

Czechoslovakia and East Germany responded to the Soviet plea many years ago but other states are unwilling to follow suit, possibly because the costs of such investment are high and the returns are low.[53] When new oil prices were negotiated for the 1976–80 Five-Year Plan, the Soviets applied pricing pressure to ensure greater East European oil investment but, with the energy situation becoming more problematic, East European states may have been prone to collaboration anyway. Investment does guarantee long-term, secure oil supplies and the Soviets have been warning East European states that larger Soviet deliveries are dependent upon investment in Soviet oil production. They indicate that Czechoslovakia and East Germany are "assured" of a sizable oil supply.[54]

Czechoslovakia made its investment agreement with the USSR in September 1966, and East Germany followed suit in April 1967. Czechoslovakia is to provide machinery and pipes on credit and is to receive repayment in crude oil. The credit amounts to 500 million rubles, and Czechoslovakia is to receive an extra 60 million tons of crude oil during the years 1971–84.[55] In addition, Czechoslovakia invested in Soviet metallurgy in 1960 and natural gas in 1968; Hungary invested in phosphorus, Rumania in iron ore, and Poland in potassium.[56]

The USSR also wants to attract East European laborers to work on Soviet projects and it has implied that it would like East European fuel importers to send laborers to work in Soviet fuel extraction industries.[57] In fact, Bulgaria has sent workers to Nebit-Dag, Turkmen, to participate in oil and gas extraction.[58] Bulgaria has also supplied labor for the Soviet timber industry in the Komi autonomous republic, and noncommunist Finland has provided 5000 workers for the Kostamus iron mines and other workers for the rebuilding of a pulp and paper mill in Svetogorsk.[59] The most extensive endeavor involving foreign labor is the construction of a gas pipeline from Orenburg, in the southern Urals, to Eastern Europe. East Germany, Poland, Czechoslovakia, Hungary, and Bulgaria are all providing workers. East Germany has agreed to supply as many as 5800.[60]

Yugoslavia and the Soviet Oil Weapon

In its relations with other communist-ruled states, the Soviet Union has often attempted to use oil as an instrument of political pressure, but it has had little success with such tactics. The first effort was directed against Tito's Yugoslavia, which was trying to break free from Soviet control. During the years 1945–48, Yugoslavia received 60 percent of its oil from the USSR and Rumania; when the Soviet–Yugoslav rift reached crisis proportions in 1948, the oil weapon was applied.[61] Apparently acting on Soviet orders, Rumania delayed the delivery of oil products to Yugoslavia in March and then threatened to cut off all oil in April.[62] When these tactics did not succeed in braking Yugoslavia's separatist momentum, the Cominform expelled Yugoslavia on June 28, and both the USSR and Rumania greatly reduced all oil shipments. The USSR had provided 39,100 tons of oil products in 1946, 175.300 in 1947, but only 78,600 tons in 1948. The total for 1949 fell to 15,200 tons and deliveries then ceased for four years.[63]

However, Yugoslavia was able to turn to Western sources of supply, and the Soviet embargo really amounted to retaliation rather than realistic political pressure. Soviet–Yugoslav relations remained in a state of great deterioration until late 1954, when the Malenkov government took some steps toward rapprochement, and oil was again offered to Yugoslavia.[64] A trade agreement of October 1 included Soviet oil, most of it crude, and 48,200 tons were supplied in 1954.[65] Deliveries have continued ever since, with the quantity rising to 3,891,000 tons in 1973, but there was a significant drop in 1961 which was possibly due to political causes.[66] Yugoslavia had initiated many reforms in the years 1958–60 which were considered too revisionist by the Soviets, and Soviet–Yugoslav relations were set back during that period: so perhaps the Soviets again resorted to oil pressure. In any case, the history of Soviet–Yugoslav political ties closely parallels the extent of Soviet oil deliveries to Yugoslavia, which fits in with the traditional Soviet policy of coupling diplomacy with trade. An element of pressure was surely present, particularly in the late forties and early fifties, but it appears that Yugoslavia's motive for improving relations with the USSR at certain times was not a desire for Soviet oil.

China and the Soviet Oil Weapon

During the more cordial years of the Soviet–Chinese alliance, the USSR supplied China with oil despite the logistical difficulty of shipping it all the way from the Black Sea. Both crude oil and oil products were provided, with the quantity gradually increasing, but Soviet–Chinese oil relations were seriously disrupted in 1960 as a result of political difficulties between the two states.[67] As part of the Soviet economic withdrawal from China, all Soviet oil assistance was terminated and Soviet oil equipment was removed. The Soviets also recalled the 1390 Soviet oil technicians who were in China at the time, although they did not actually stop delivering

Table 9.1. Soviet Oil Exports to China, 1955–1970 (in metric tons)

year	crude oil	oil products	total
1955	377,800	1,211,400	1,589,200
1956	397,300	1,335,000	1,732,300
1957	380,400	1,422,200	1,802,600
1958	672,000	1,835,300	2,507,300
1959	635,900	2,412,300	3,048,200
1960	567,600	2,395,200	2,962,800
1961	0	2,928,200	2,928,200
1962	0	1,856,400	1,856,400
1963	0	1,408,100	1,408,100
1964	0	504,900	504,900
1965	0	37,900	37,900
1966	0	40,000	40,000
1967	0	6,800	6,800
1968	0	7,600	7,600
1969	0	10,300	10,300
1970	0	0	0

SOURCES: *Vneshniaia torgovlia SSSR za 1956 god: statisticheskii obzor* (Foreign Trade of the USSR for 1956: Statistical Abstract) (Moscow: Vneshtorgizdat, 1958), p. 124; *ibid.,* 1958 (1959), p. 125; *ibid.,* 1960 (1961), p. 165; *ibid.,* 1962 (1963), p. 184; *ibid.,* 1964 (1965), p. 230; *ibid.,* 1966 (Moscow: Izdatel'stvo "Mezhdunarodnye otnosheniia," 1967), p. 259; *ibid.,* 1968 (1969), p. 232; *ibid.,* 1970 (1971), p. 233.

oil.[68] Crude oil deliveries continued until the end of 1960 and the supply of oil products did not begin to drop until 1962. Soviet provision of oil-drilling equipment had already begun to decline in 1959 and it was almost completely phased out by the end of 1962.[69]

The Soviet Union apparently decided to use economic warfare against China in stages so that a more severe political break would not occur. For example, they supplied food in 1961 when China was in need of assistance.[70] Only crude oil was cut off at

Table 9.2. China's Oil Supply (in metric tons)

year	China's approximate oil production	oil imports from the USSR	oil imports from sources other than the USSR	China's total oil supply	China's dependence on Soviet oil deliveries (%)
1960	5,200,000	2,962,800	927,000	9,089,800	32.5
1961	5,000,000	2,928,200	478,000	8,406,100	34.8
1962	6,000,000	1,856,400	1,201,000	9,057,400	20.5

first and then the supply of oil products was reduced gradually. In fact, 1961 marked the high point of oil-products deliveries.

Of total Soviet exports to China, oil made up 14.6 percent by value in 1958, 12.3 percent in 1959, and 13.8 percent in 1960. Since the delivery of oil products continued after 1960 while overall Soviet–Chinese trade volume was decreasing, oil made up 32.9 percent of Soviet exports to China in 1961 and the percentage was similar for the following two years.[71]

The impact of the Soviet Union's reduced oil deliveries can best be understood by determining China's oil dependence on the Soviet Union. To do so, China's oil production and her oil imports from sources other than the Soviet Union should be taken into account (see table 9.2).[72]

China had been dependent on the Soviet Union for about one-third of her oil supply, and did not have a large refining capacity. The withholding of oil products would therefore have caused more disruption than the withholding of crude oil, but the Soviets chose the more moderate tactic as their first step in economic warfare.[73] However, it appears that they intentionally decreased deliveries of particular oil products, such as jet and aviation fuel. China was completely dependent on the USSR for these products and military flights had to be reduced. The overall fuel shortage also led to cutbacks in bus and airline transportation, as well as in military activities.[74] Also contributing to the oil problem was the withdrawal of Soviet technicians and equipment, which was probably at least partially responsible for the slight decline in oil production in 1961.

China's reaction was to seek more oil from other states and make a concerted effort to achieve oil self-sufficiency. Rumania and Albania, which were both striving to assert their independence from the USSR at that time, increased their oil deliveries to China, and Rumania also provided drilling and processing equipment. China also began to import oil from Iran in 1960.[75] After 1961, Chinese oil production began to climb and in 1963 China claimed that it was "virtually self-sufficient." It appears, however, that China may not have achieved actual self-sufficiency until 1964.[76]

The Soviets supplied a dwindling quantity of oil products to China but, in 1966, they increased their deliveries of oil-drilling equipment to their highest total in five years and also provided spare parts for oil-operations machinery.[77] Politics may have been involved, since the Soviets showed restraint in their comments on China during 1965 and called for better ties. In February 1966, the Soviets sent a "secret" letter to a number of communist parties proposing steps for improving Sino–Soviet relations but the Chinese rejected the Soviet initiative and even failed to send representatives to the Twenty-third Congress of the Communist Party of the Soviet Union in March 1966.[78] Oil exports to China then decreased considerably in 1967, with politics again playing a probable role.

Soviet deliveries of oil products ceased after 1969, almost surely as a result of the battle at Ussuri and the bad political atmosphere. However, when the United States mined North Vietnamese ports in May 1972, the Soviet Union worked out an arrangement with China for supplying oil to North Vietnam. It had previously shipped oil directly to Haiphong but the American blockade led to a switch deal with China in which the Soviet Union delivered oil products to China and China supplied an equal amount of oil products to North Vietnam through two pipelines completed in July and August 1972.[79]

In 1973, Soviet analysts for the journal *International Affairs* claimed that China had unilaterally broken its economic ties with other communist-ruled states without prior consultation.[80] In truth, it was certainly the USSR, not China, which was responsible for the withdrawal of Soviet oil technicians and machinery and the termination of crudo oil deliveries in 1960. Many Chinese charges against the Soviets thus seem justified. In the "Letter of the Central Committee of the CPC of February 29, 1964, to the Central Committee of the CPSU," the Chinese maintained that the Soviets had refused to supply vital goods ever since 1960 and they asserted: "For several years you have used trade between our two countries as an instrument for bringing political pressure to bear on China." [81] In 1969, *Peking Review* exclaimed: "To strangle us economically, the U.S. imperialists tightened their economic blockade on China and the Soviet revisionist renegade clique put pressure on us on the question of petroleum just when China's economy met with temporary difficulties in 1960. Their political aim was to subvert socialist China." [82]

Albania and Czechoslovakia

As Albania drifted away from Soviet control in 1960–61, the Soviets applied the oil weapon, although Albania seemed to be an unlikely victim for oil pressure. It was self-sufficient, and even exported oil to the Soviet Union, but it did rely on the Soviets for investment capital, drilling equipment, and technicians. In December 1960, Albania requested that the USSR continue to supply oil technicians but the Soviets delayed the conclusion of any technical assistance agreement. Then, on January 20, 1961, the Soviet Union announced that all of its oil technicians would be leaving Albania within ten days. They did so and Albania accused them of sabotaging oil operations before their departure. In addition to withdrawing their technicians, the Soviets also reduced the export of oil equipment to Albania.[83]

Albania managed to get along without Soviet help, partially because of the assistance rendered by China. Among other projects, the Chinese designed and equipped an oil refinery at Cerrik but it was built by the Albanians.[84] Thus, the two states overcame their problems by cooperation; China provided technicians and equipment for Albania, and Albania supplied oil to China. In addition, no Albanian crude oil was delivered to the USSR after 1961.[85]

The Soviet use of oil politics against Yugoslavia, China, and Albania had proved to be ineffective (if one measures effectiveness by the ability to pressure a state into realigning with the Soviet Union) and this experience may have influenced Soviet thinking in regard to Czechoslovakia in 1968. In this instance, however, the Soviets had the option of using the military, and of course eventually did so. Furthermore, if the Soviets had stopped sending oil through the Druzhba Pipeline to Czechoslovakia, Hungary would also have been affected.

The Soviet Union did not withhold any oil from Czechoslovakia in 1968, although Soviet publications made some not too subtle threats by alluding to Czechoslovakia's oil dependence. An article in *International Affairs* pointed out that in 1967 Czechoslovakia had received 99.5 percent of its oil from the USSR. It was discussing overall Soviet fuel exports to Eastern Europe but it placed particular emphasis on Czechoslovakia. The article maintained that the Soviet Union was providing oil for Czechoslovakia on "advantageous terms" and that Czechoslovak economists had determined that importing oil from the Soviet Union was less expensive than importing it from Iran.[86] Although the flow of oil was not interrupted, the Czechoslovaks claimed that the Soviets held back shipments of natural gas, iron ore, and coking coals.[87]

Following the August invasion, Tass asserted that oil and gas deliveries had not been cut back during the Czechoslovak crisis period, and on September 10 the Soviets tried to accentuate the point by signing a new oil and gas agreement with Czechoslovakia. This signing was staged primarily for publicity, since the agreement had actually been reached in June.[88] Oil deliveries for 1969 were to exceed those for 1968 and the actual figures for 1967–1969 were 7,425,300 tons, 8,380,000 tons and 10,027,700 tons.[89] The Soviet invasion placed Czechoslovakia under strong military control, and the oil supply continued unabated, but the Soviets still warned Czechoslovakia that the flow of oil could be cut off if the Czechs complained too much about the price. It was asserted that the oil sent to Czechoslovakia could be sold to capitalist states for hard currency.[90]

Czechoslovakia was of vital importance to the USSR since it was being developed as the major transit route for Soviet gas exports to Western Europe. From the Soviet point of view, firm control of Czechoslovakia was economically essential, but any attempt to use economic pressure against the Dubcek government could have pushed Czechoslovakia closer to the West. Czechoslovakia was highly industrialized and was better equipped than any other East European state to redirect its trade toward the West.[91] It could also have found alternative sources of oil but it would have had difficulty in accumulating sufficient hard currency to pay for it.[92] As political scientist Robert Freedman has persuasively argued, the Soviet Union has reduced its use of economic warfare against other communist-ruled states since it is fearful of encouraging moves toward the West, it does not want to foster even more stubborn resistance to Soviet efforts at control, and it prefers to leave open the option of eventual rapprochement.[93] Freedman's observations are relevant in the case of Czechoslovakia in 1968, as past Soviet failures in Yugoslavia, China, and Albania most likely influenced later Soviet perspectives on the efficacy of economic warfare against communist-ruled states.

Cuba and the Soviet Oil Weapon

Soviet oil relations with Cuba have been multifaceted and have often shifted with the prevailing political winds. At first, the Soviet

Union used oil as its prime means of political entree since Cuba was engaged in a dispute with Western oil companies. Once Cuba became almost completely dependent on Soviet oil, the Soviets used oil as a weapon aimed at influencing Cuban internal and foreign policies. Now, the Soviets have found Cuba to be an economic burden, while at the same time the Cubans have been attempting to improve their economic and political ties with other Latin American states. This has led to negotiations concerning oil imports from Venezuela and Mexico, with the aim of reducing Cuban reliance on Soviet oil, and Cuba apparently has the Soviet Union's blessing in this search for alternative sources of supply.

When Castro came to power on January 1, 1959, Cuba produced almost no oil; most of the refining, and all of the distribution, was controlled by three Western companies, Esso, Texaco, and Shell. Each of these companies operated a refinery and there was also another refinery owned by private Cuban interests. The oil was imported from Venezuela and the prices were rather high. In 1959, Castro moved to establish greater state control over oil operations but he did not take any strong action against the Western companies. He seized their oil exploration records, mistakenly believing that they had concealed oil discoveries in order to retain their grip over imports, but he did not attempt to seize their properties. When the Cuban Institute of Petroleum was established, the Cuban-owned refinery was nationalized and put under its control and service stations were encouraged to sell oil supplied by the Institute in addition to their brand-name product. It was also announced that the Cuban government would own 60 percent of any oil discovered in Cuba as opposed to the previous 10 percent.[94]

In order to reduce its dependence on Western oil companies, as well as to secure oil at a lower price, Cuba reached an oil agreement with the Soviet Union on February 13, 1960. It was arranged during the visit to Cuba of the Soviet Union's First Deputy Prime Minister, Anastas Mikoyan. Cuba was to receive 6 million barrels (about 820,000 tons) of oil per year for five years, as well as other Soviet goods and a $100 million credit at 2½ percent interest. The Soviet goods were to include wheat, pig iron, rolled steel products, fertilizer, rolled aluminum, aluminum ingots, and some machinery. In return, Cuba was to provide one million tons of sugar per year over the five-year period.[95] Not only did Cuba manage to acquire oil at a price lower than that previously paid to Venezuela but it also helped its balance of payments by contracting for oil on a barter basis. It had traditionally paid hard currency for Venezuelan oil.[96] Cuba also found a long-term market for some of its sugar, which made up 80 percent of Cuba's exports. The Soviet–Cuban trade agreement led to a strengthening of ties between the two states, and diplomatic relations were established on May 7, 1960.[97] In June, Khrushchev was invited to visit Cuba.[98]

By importing Soviet oil, Cuba was setting the stage for a showdown with the Western companies over importing and refining operations. The Soviet oil represented only half of Cuba's imports but the Western companies did not want to lose their right to acquire oil from their own marketing networks. The refinery issue was also important, since the refinery operated by the Cuban Institute of Petroleum was not capable of processing more than a small amount of the Soviet imports. Therefore, the first Soviet tankers, which began to deliver oil on April 19, 1960, carried oil products rather than crude oil.[99] However, the Cubans soon started to receive Soviet crude oil and they requested that some of it be processed in the Western-owned refineries.

Cuba owed money to the three Western companies for oil they had provided for Cuba, and in May 1960 Ché Guevara asked these companies to accept Soviet crude oil as part of their payment. The oil was to be refined by the Western companies, but they were opposed to the importing of Soviet oil and they did not want to refine it. They claimed that Soviet oil would damage their refinery equipment (although the equipment could have been adapted), and on June 7 they informed the Cuban government that they would not refine the Soviet oil. Esso and Texaco, which were American-owned, had received previous support from the U.S. Department of the Treasury and Shell, which was owned by British and Dutch interests, went along with them.[100] Cuba, which was having its share of political differences with the United States, believed that the oil companies were colluding with the U.S. government in an effort to subvert the Cuban revolution.[101]

At first, Cuba reacted mildly to the refusal of Western companies to refine Soviet crude oil. Alfonso Gutierrez, Director of the Cuban Institute of Petroleum, said that Cuba would have to increase the capacity of the government-owned refinery and then either import a higher percentage of oil products from the USSR or send Soviet crude oil to Mexico or Brazil for refining.[102] Three days later, however, Castro asserted that the Western refineries would have to process Soviet crude oil or face the "consequences." [103] On June 29, Cuba sent two barges loaded with Soviet crude oil to the Texaco refinery, and when the refinery refused to accept the oil it was seized by the militia and "intervened," thereby placing it under temporary government

Table 9.3. Soviet Oil Exports to Cuba, 1960–1973 (in metric tons)

year	crude oil	oil products	total
1960	1,648,500	516,300	2,164,800
1961	2,979,800	1,048,800	4,028,600
1962	3,629,300	755,100	4,384,400
1963	3,765,600	454,300	4,219,900
1964	3,426,600	1,132,700	4,559,300
1965	3,512,600	1,214,000	4,726,600
1966	3,840,200	1,250,200	5,090,400
1967	3,837,700	1,448,500	5,286,200
1968	3,851,000	1,452,200	5,303,200
1969	4,300,000	1,459,500	5,759,500
1970	4,500,000	1,487,000	5,987,000
1971	——	——	6,444,000
1972	——	——	7,025,000
1973	——	——	7,435,000

SOURCES: *Vneshniaia torgovlia SSSR: statisticheskii sbornik, 1918–1966* (Foreign Trade of the USSR: Statistical Compendium, 1918–1966) (Moscow: Izdatel'stvo "Mezhdunarodnye otnosheniia," 1967), p. 225; *Vneshniaia torgovlia SSSR za 1967 god*, p. 304; *ibid.*, 1969, p. 285; *ibid.*, 1971 *god*, p. 307; *ibid.*, 1972, (Moscow: Izdatel'stvo "Mezhdunarodnye otnosheniia" (1973), p. 304; *ibid.*, 1973, p. 304; United Nations, Statistical Office, *World Energy Supplies, 1961–70*, Statistical Papers, series J, no. 15 (New York: United Nations, 1972), p. 102; *Petroleum Press Service* 39, no. 8 (August 1972): 289; and *Petroleum Press Service* 40, no. 7 (July 1973): 269.

control.[104] The Shell and Esso refineries were "intervened" on July 1.[105] An American-owned electric company was also taken over for refusing to use Soviet oil.[106]

Cuba's actions against American-owned companies brought a quick response. On July 6, President Eisenhower announced that the United States would cut back its purchases of Cuban sugar by 700,000 tons. On July 10, the Soviet Union agreed to buy whatever sugar the United States refused. On August 7, Cuba's "intervening" became permanent, as the Western-owned refineries were nationalized.[107] No compensation agreement was ever reached and the companies never received the $50 million which had previously been owed to them for supplying oil to Cuba.[108]

Once Cuba had control over the Western-owned refineries, it was in a position to refine large quantities of Soviet crude oil. The groundwork for closer Cuban–Soviet oil ties had been laid in June, when Cuban oil specialist Admundo Cintra Mata toured Soviet oil facilities. Once the refineries were taken over, the USSR agreed to provide virtually all of Cuba's oil needs. The Soviets also began prospecting operations in Cuba in November 1960, and they adapted the equipment in the "intervened" refineries to handle Soviet crude oil.[109] With Soviet help, Cuba won its confrontation with the Western companies. One Cuban writer declared: "This was the first dramatic battle of the Cuban Revolution against Yankee imperialism in the economic and commercial field." [110]

Cuba was anxious to reduce its economic dependence on the United States but it probably would not have succeeded so thoroughly had it not been for Soviet assistance. The Soviet Union guaranteed a market for a large quantity of Cuba's major export, sugar, but it was essentially the provision of oil which broke the financial hold of American companies over the Cuban economy. Once Cuba was free of U.S. economic control, its foreign policy was radically realigned. Thus, by early 1962 Castro had declared himself a "Marxist-Leninist" and Cuba was accepted as a member of the Soviet-led group of communist-ruled states. In the same year, Cuba also had its most favored nation trading status take away by the United States.[111] Cuba had ended its economic subservience to the United States but it had become dependent on the Soviet Union, thus strengthening the Soviet hand for future use of oil politics against the Castro government.

Castro's support for Third World revolutionary activities and his sympathy for many of China's ideological positions and programs led to friction between the Soviet Union and Cuba in 1964 but the Soviets did not hold back on the oil supply. Nevertheless, Castro anticipated a possible Soviet action of this type since, in a January 1965 speech, he declared that if oil deliveries to Cuba were cut, the last oil would be used by the army and the urban population would be moved to rural areas.[112] He was obviously referring to the USSR, since almost all Cuban oil imports came from there. There was a popular adage that Castro's heart lay in Peking and his stomach in Moscow, and it bore a great amount of truth—especially in the area of oil. Cuba was almost completely dependent on Soviet deliveries and China was in no position to replace the USSR as an oil supplier.[113] This dependence on the USSR probably kept Castro within somewhat restricted bounds when he commented on issues related to the Sino–Soviet dispute.

The flow of Soviet oil to Cuba was slowed down during the latter half of 1967, apparently owing to political pressure.[114] The Soviets claimed that they were fulfilling all oil delivery contracts with Cuba but Castro maintained that shipments were delayed.[115] Cuba had asked the Soviets for a 10 percent increase in oil deliveries for 1968 but was told that the increase would be no more than 2 percent. The average yearly increase during the previous years had been 5.5 percent.[116] On January 2, 1968, Castro announced that the rationing of gasoline was necessary since the Soviet Union could not meet Cuba's expanding oil needs and the leading Cuban newspaper, Granma, asserted that the Soviet Union had no oil shortage. The Cubans were clearly implying that oil was being withheld intentionally.[117] As a result of the oil shortage, the Cuban armed forces contributed some of their fuel for use in agriculture.[118] In April, Castro called for an intensified search for oil in Cuba since he was not sure if the Soviets could provide a sufficient quantity.[119]

The Soviet Union's reluctance to supply Cuba with more oil

was related to the poor political relations between the states during late 1967 and early 1968. The Soviets were holding back on other products as well. The conclusion of the Soviet–Cuban trade agreement for 1968 was delayed by the Soviets until March 22, 1968, and the agreement provided for only a 10 percent rise in trade. In contrast, trade in 1967 had been 23 percent greater than in 1966.[120]

Politically, the Soviets were especially disturbed by the fact that some Cuban communists had been purged from the party and put on trial for conspiring with the USSR against Cuba.[121] They also did not appreciate Cuba's snub on the occasion of the fiftieth anniversary of the Bolshevik revolution in November 1967. High Cuban officials had not appeared at the Moscow celebration or at the festivities held at the Soviet embassy in Havana. Then, in February 1968, the Cubans did not send a delegation to the Bucharest meeting of communist parties, at which the Chinese were attacked.[122] When Castro supported the Soviet invasion of Czechoslovakia in August 1968, political relations between the USSR and Cuba began to improve and Cuba received a sizable increase in oil supplies for 1969.[123]

The Soviet Union had to overcome some significant obstacles in order to deliver large quantities of oil to Cuba. Western oil companies blacklisted any firm willing to charter tankers to the Soviet Union for use in the Cuban oil trade, and in October 1962 the United States enacted a law which permitted the discontinuation of foreign aid to any state whose ships transported oil to Cuba.[124] The Soviets did not have sufficient tankers of their own, but they were able to break through the Western economic wall to charter tankers since 10 percent of the world tanker fleet was idle at the time.[125] British companies were among those willing to charter tankers for oil deliveries to Cuba.[126]

The great distance between the Soviet Union and Cuba also presented problems since a large number of tankers had to be at sea in order to supply Cuba. As of 1966, approximately 10 percent of the Soviet tanker fleet.[127] Shipping Algerian oil to Cuba cut down on some of the distance and it was also reported that the Soviets delivered to Cuba some of the oil they had bought in

Egypt.[128] After unloading their cargo in Cuba, many Soviet tankers returned empty, so the Soviets arranged for some tankers to transport Venezuelan crude oil to Italy and Finland on the return trip.[129] The Soviets would have preferred to be less tied down as Cuba's oil supplier so they built small tankers for the Cubans and engaged in extensive oil exploration in the hope of making Cuba more self-sufficient, but only insignificant quantities of oil were ever found.[130]

Cuba has been almost 100 percent dependent on Soviet oil ever since 1960, but it has been able to refine about 75 percent of its own oil products. Cuban oil imports from the USSR have not risen too dramatically and Cuba's per capita energy consumption has increased very slowly, implying a slow rate of industrialization.[131] This is partially explainable by the fact that the Soviets have not always supplied as much oil as Cuba has wanted, leading some Western analysts to believe that the USSR has intentionally held back Cuba's industrialization by pressuring it to concentrate on sugar production. They assert that the Soviets have wanted to make sure that Cuba has a commodity, such as sugar, to use as repayment for Soviet aid.[132] Of course, sugar has also been used to pay for Soviet oil.

When the Soviets first began to sell oil to Cuba, they used the attraction of a low price in order to replace the Western oil marketers, but as Cuba became aligned economically and politically with the USSR, the price rose to a level similar to that of other communist-ruled states. In June 1963, the price was raised, forcing Cuba to reduce its oil imports to help overcome its trade deficit with the USSR, and the import of Soviet oil in 1963 was actually lower than in 1962.[133] High prices have continued ever since and a *New York Times* correspondent has argued that, even before 1963, the Cubans were paying a high price for Soviet oil. He maintained that the nominal price was low, but that since the oil was being bartered for Cuban sugar, the price of this sugar had to be taken into account. He found that the Soviets were paying such a low price for the sugar that it outweighed the low price paid by the Cubans for Soviet oil, resulting in an actual oil price which was higher than that previously paid to Venezuela.[134]

The logistical difficulty involved in exporting so much oil to

Cuba has led the Soviets into an attempt to extricate themselves economically. During Brezhnev's visit to Cuba in late January 1974, he asked the Cubans to reduce their oil imports from the USSR by importing oil from Latin American countries; Brezhnev also promised continued Soviet assistance for Cuba's oil exploration program.[135] Acting on Brezhnev's cue, Cuba began oil negotiations with Venezuela; the Cuban Minister of Mining, Fuels, and Metallurgy, Manuel Cespedes, said that it would be preferable to import Venezuelan rather than Soviet oil because the shipping costs for Soviet oil are so high.[136] In order to cut such costs, it was decided to set up a switch deal according to which Venezuela would deliver oil to Cuba and the Soviet Union would in turn supply some of Venezuela's regular customers in Western Europe. This plan was not activated because of Western Europe's oil glut in 1975, but the Soviet Union may simply pay Venezuela for shipping its oil to Cuba.[137] Cuba's oil negotiations with Mexico were announced by Horacio de la Pena, Mexico's Minister of National Property, and they led to deliveries which may have been paid for by the Soviet Union.[138] Closer Cuban oil relations with Venezuela and Mexico are to be expected, as the United States has softened its objections to Latin American trade ties with Cuba. In addition, the world demand for sugar has risen to high levels in recent years, thereby providing Cuba with a marketable commodity which it can possibly exchange for oil.

Soviet Provision of Gas

CMEA states, excluding the USSR, not only have an overall deficiency in oil but in natural gas as well. Only Rumania produces enough for her needs, and Hungary is the only other sizable producer.[139] East European production during 1966–73 rose at a rate of 11 percent per year, but large imports from the USSR were still necessary.[140] Soviet deliveries from 1960 through 1970 were 8 billion cubic meters but the plan for 1971–75 called for deliveries of 33 billion cubic meters. In 1975, the USSR provided about 20 percent of Eastern Europe's natural gas needs.[141]

Poland has been importing Soviet gas for at least twenty

years and Czechoslovakia began to receive Soviet gas in 1967. In 1973, Poland imported nearly 1.710 billion cubic meters and Czechoslovakia nearly 2.363 billion cubic meters.[142] The Bratsvo (Brotherhood) Pipeline to Bratislava, Czechoslovakia, was completed in 1967 and it was then extended into Austria in 1968. It was later extended into Italy and may eventually branch into Yugoslavia. Czechoslovakia is the focal point for Soviet gas exports, since another pipeline from the USSR crosses through Czechoslovakia on its way to East Germany and West Germany. Soviet gas began flowing to East Germany in April 1973 and to Bulgaria in September 1974. The pipeline to Bulgaria cuts across Rumania, but Rumania does not receive any gas from it.[143] Hungary started to receive Soviet gas in 1975 and deliveries to Yugoslavia have also been initiated.[144] Much of the gas exported to Eastern Europe comes from Tiumen in Western Siberia, but the Soviets are now placing greater emphasis on the Orenburg gas fields in the Volga-Ural region, since they are closer to East European markets.[145]

Among communist-ruled states, Yugoslavia, China and Albania had serious splits with the Soviet Union and Rumania has exercised a great degree of independence from Soviet control. Other factors are certainly relevant but it appears that oil self-sufficiency or near self-sufficiency (as in the cases of China, Albania and Rumania), or the ability to add to one's oil supply by importing from other sources (as in the case of Yugoslavia), is an important element acting in support of separatist behavior. It is probably no accident that Rumania has been able to follow a fairly independent course in foreign affairs and that Rumania also happens to be the only CMEA state not reliant on the Soviet Union for its oil supply.[146]

Despite difficulties in meeting the rising oil demand in Eastern Europe, the Soviet Union will continue to supply a large percentage of the oil needs of this area and will maintain extensive influence because of its control of the oil tap. The problem is more economic than political, since the Soviets have already decided to give top priority to Eastern Europe, and in order to overcome the economic obstacle, conservation measures can possibly be used to hold down East European oil consumption. An American government analyst has estimated that the conservation program drawn up by Bulgaria is capable of reducing yearly consumption by 10 to 15 percent.[147] Greater East European reliance on Soviet gas is likely; many pipelines have been built and the Soviets should be able to export gas more readily than oil. East European states have been shifting away from their heavy dependence on coal toward greater usage of oil and gas but reversion to energy systems based more heavily on coal could help alleviate the growing oil squeeze.

10/Western Europe

Western Europe produces barely 3 percent of its oil needs and even the booming exploitation of the North Sea can provide only 20 percent of its oil requirements by 1985.[1] It is geographically convenient for the Soviets to export oil to Western Europe (there were large sales as far back as the late twenties) and by doing so they can acquire hard currency. Extension of their political influence is only a secondary motivation.

The Soviets' oil relations with West European states tend to be on a purely commercial basis; their use of oil politics is rare (as in the previously discussed cases of Iceland and Finland). In fact, it is the West European states that have more often introduced the political element, citing the containment of communism as their motive for attempting to restrict the Soviet Union's oil role on the Continent. The most important contemporary issue in Soviet–West European oil relations, which concerns Norway, is not related to the political manipulation of Soviet oil exports.[2]

The Soviet–Norwegian Controversy

The Treaty of Paris in 1920 gave equal commercial and mineral rights on Spitsbergen (Svalbard), an archipelago north of Norway, to all of its signatories, but sovereignty was granted to Norway. At that time, the Russian civil war was still in progress and the signatories of the treaty were unwilling to recognize the Bolshevik government. Russia was therefore not a party to the treaty but it was nevertheless given the same privileges as the signatory states, pending the establishment of a permanent Russian government. The Bolsheviks emerged victorious from the civil war, the USSR was established, and the Soviet government eventually ratified the Treaty of Paris in May 1935.[3]

The Soviet Union enjoys the right to exploit minerals on Spitsbergen and it has been extracting coal. Now it plans to prospect for oil and sample drilling for a geological survey took place during the winter of 1974–75. The Soviet Union is operating in a 963-square-kilometer area on Spitsbergen, and is the only state other than Norway to have established a permanent commercial presence on the island.[4] However, the key issue in oil politics is not Spitsbergen itself but the surrounding continental shelf. The Treaty of Paris made no stipulations regarding the continental shelf in the area of Spitsbergen, and because of the prospect that offshore oil may be found there, an international controversy is developing. Norway claims that Spitsbergen has no continental shelf of its own and that Norway's own continental shelf includes the area around Spitsbergen. Of course, Norway would have exclusive rights to offshore oil if its contention is accepted by other powers. On the other hand, some states maintain that Spitsbergen has its own continental shelf and that mineral rights granted in the Treaty of Paris should be extended to this shelf as well. This would mean that the states ratifying the treaty, including the USSR, would share in offshore oil exploitation. The United States and Britain are leaning toward this interpretation, since they would like a share of the oil. Just before the Soviet–Norwegian negotiations of November 1974, the British ambassador to Norway informed the Norwegian Foreign Ministry that Britain was not taking any position on the Spitsbergen continental shelf dispute—a diplomatic way of saying that Britain would not support Norway in its controversy with the USSR.[5]

The USSR, also wants to share in the offshore oil wealth, and therefore advocates the separate shelf argument. However, the Soviets may reconsider their stance, since they are faced with a serious dilemma regarding this issue. If they continue to support the position that Spitsbergen has its own shelf, Western oil companies will start operating in an area the Soviets view as strategic to their own interests.[6] Further complicating the matter is the Soviet–Norwegian dispute over oil rights in the Barents Sea. The

Soviets want a sea boundary to be drawn in accordance with the sector principle, which would place the line slightly east of Spitsbergen, while the Norwegians want to apply the equidistance principle, which would give Norway a larger chunk of the Barents Sea by placing the line farther to the east. The sector principle is based on the proposition that Arctic states should own all territory included in the zone created when lines are drawn to the North Pole from the easternmost and westernmost Arctic points of a state. Canada also advocates the sector principle.

This principle has not been completely clarified; it originally referred to land and islands, not water and ice, and a rigid interpretation could exclude rights for offshore oil drilling. The equidistance principle, advanced by Norway, calls for a median line to be drawn between the land and islands owned by the two states.[7] Norway has decided not to drill in the disputed area until some agreement is reached with the USSR but it is engaged in exploration.[8] The Soviets may be willing to collaborate with the Norwegians in joint exploration and drilling in the disputed part of the Barents Sea but the Norwegians seem to be cool to such suggestions.

The Soviet Union and Norway held talks in Moscow in late November 1974, and future discussions are planned to help resolve the contentious issues. Looking beyond the Spitsbergen continental shelf and Barents Sea boundary problems, the Soviets may also be pressuring the Norwegians for a larger voice in the use of Spitsbergen, since the Soviets are fearful of a possible NATO role there.[9] They see the whole Barents Sea area as vital to their security, since 70 percent of the Soviet submarines equipped with nuclear missiles are based in the nearby Murmansk area and must pass through the Barents Sea on their way to or from the Atlantic Ocean.[10] These submarines are part of the Northern Fleet, the largest of the Soviet Union's four fleets. Norway, a NATO member, regularly monitors the movements of Soviet submarines, as they pass between Spitsbergen and the Norwegian mainland. Planes now perform the monitoring, but the Soviets are concerned that more efficient observations will be made from atop Norwegian oil rigs when drilling begins in the

Barents Sea. The Soviets would like to exclude NATO from the area and are asking for the cessation of submarine monitoring, the demilitarization of Norway's North Cape, and the exclusion of NATO activities from Spitsbergen.[11] According to the Treaty of Paris, Spitsbergen is to be completely demilitarized; up to the present, neither Norway nor NATO has violated this provision.

The coast from the Norwegian border to Murmansk is the only ice-free zone on the entire northern coast of the USSR and it includes the ports of Petsamo and Murmansk. This enhances the strategic value of the region, and explains why Murmansk is such

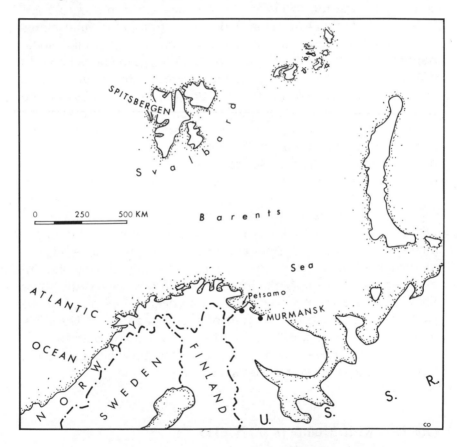

MAP 4. BARENTS SEA

an important naval base. The Soviets have been building other facilities along the entire ice-free coastline and if the Soviet Union
and the United States reach an agreement on the "North Star"
gas project, the gas will be exported from Petsamo.[12]

Norway wants to avoid any Arctic confrontation with the
USSR and a specialist on Scandinavian international relations,
Finn Sollie, has cited the steps Norway has taken to reduce ten-
sion in the area. He points to Norway's demilitarization of the Arctic, its rejection of foreign NATO troops on its soil, its policy of
not staging military exercises in northern Norway, and its decision not to drill for oil in the Barents Sea at the present time.[13]
Sollie contends that the area can remain tranquil if other states
accept the Norwegian claim to the continental shelf around Spitsbergen but he foresees possible trouble if outside states begin to
drill for oil and get involved in the politics of the region. Sollie
calls for cooperation in the Barents Sea between Norway and the
Soviet Union but he does not advocate joint oil projects. He
thinks Norway should exploit the oil resources on its side of a
negotiated boundary but he warns against introducing a NATO
presence into the Barents Sea to protect Norwegian oil interests.
Norway should rely instead on some peaceful accommodation
with the USSR.[14]

Growing oil wealth is making Norway more strategically important than ever before. As Sollie observes, Norway is no longer
a NATO backwater but rather a country whose defense is becoming vital because of its energy resources. Norway is playing an increasingly significant role in international affairs, but at the same
time it is a greater strategic object than ever before and is more
likely to be attacked in the event of a European war.[15] Norway's
major zone of oil exploration is in the North Sea and both Norway
and Britain have been taking steps to protect their oil rigs against
the distant possibility of Soviet sabotage.[16]

Oil Ties with Members of NATO

The Soviet Union has rarely engaged in oil politics with West European states since it has not wanted to jeopardize its lucrative

commercial relationships, but politics has clearly motivated West European states in their actions concerning Soviet oil. Reacting both to the construction of the Berlin Wall and to American pressure, the Executive Commission of the Common Market recommended in July 1961 that each member restrict its purchases of Soviet oil so that the percentage of Soviet oil in the total imports of each state would not rise in the future. Italy objected to such a proposal and it was not instituted as policy. In March 1962, the Assembly of the Common Market called for restrictions on fuel imports from states which could not guarantee "long-term stability of supply" and this measure was again opposed by Italy.[17] However, it was in connection with NATO that anti-Soviet oil policies were implemented as COCOM, the NATO-organized Coordinating Committee for Export Control, worked to limit Soviet oil exports to Western Europe, to blacklist shipping companies that transported Soviet oil, and to prevent the sale of large-diameter steel pipe to the USSR.

NATO did not want its member states to become reliant on Soviet oil deliveries for fear that the oil would be cut off at a time of crisis. It also wanted to delay the construction of the Druzhba Pipeline from the Soviet Union to East European states because the pipeline would assist the Soviet strategic position by providing large quantities of oil for troops stationed in Eastern Europe.[18] This was the rationale behind the embargo on steel pipe, as 40 percent of the pipe used in the construction of the Druzhba Pipeline between 1959 and 1962 had come from West Germany, Italy, and Sweden and pipe had also come from Japan.[19] Sweden, which was not a member of NATO, did not go along with the steel pipe embargo but Japan, the only non-NATO member of COCOM, did. Japan was strongly pressured by the United States and it turned down Soviet offers of increased oil deliveries in return for pipe.[20] The Soviets encouraged Japan to continue its provision of pipe, claiming that Japan's place in the Soviet pipe market would be taken by another supplier, and the Soviets additionally asserted that Japan's temporary recession and unemployment would become worse if pipe production were reduced.[21]

The United States played a large role in organizing Western

Table 10.1. Soviet Crude Oil Exports to Western Europe, 1961–1969 [a] (in millions of metric tons)

| year | Crude Oil | | West European import dependence on Soviet crude oil |
	Soviet exports to Western Europe	total West European oil imports	
1961	8.7	201.4	4.3%
1962	10.3	217.2	4.7%
1963	11.4	236.8	4.8%
1964	13.7	284.8	4.8%
1965	13.9	332.2	4.2%
1966	17.8	369.8	4.8%
1967	22.2	415.7	5.3%
1968	24.9	461.0	5.4%
1969	22.1	525.2	4.2%

[a] Western Europe is defined as including Finland, Austria and Yugoslavia. Sources for this table, and Table 10.2, accompany Table 10.2.

Table 10.2. Soviet Oil-Products Exports to Western Europe, 1961–1969 (in millions of metric tons)

| year | Oil Products | | West European import dependence on Soviet oil products | overall West European import dependence on Soviet oil |
	Soviet exports to Western Europe	total West European oil imports		
1961	7.3	63.0	11.6%	6.1%
1962	8.4	79.5	10.6%	5.4%
1963	9.2	86.6	10.6%	6.4%
1964	9.1	89.8	10.1%	6.1%
1965	9.9	98.1	10.1%	5.5%
1966	11.9	109.5	10.9%	6.2%
1967	13.4	110.1	12.2%	6.8%
1968	13.9	112.4	12.0%	6.8%
1969	12.8	118.4	10.8%	5.4%

SOURCES: United Nations, Economic Commission for Europe, "Trade Between Eastern and Western European Countries," *Economic Bulletin for Europe* 16, no. 1 (September, 1964): 52; *ibid.,* 17, no. 1 (1965): 54; United Nations, Economic Commission for Europe, "Recent Developments in Trade Between Eastern and Western European Countries," *Economic Bulletin for Europe* 20, no. 1 (November, 1968): 37; United Nations, Economic Commission for Europe, "Recent Changes in Europe's Trade, *Economic Bulletin for Europe* 21, no. 1 (1970): 40; *ibid.,* 22, no. 1 (1971): 39; and United Nations, Statistical Office, *World Energy Supplies, 1961–1964* (New York: United Nations, 1966), pp. 51 and 60.

actions against the Soviet oil export program, partially because of strategic considerations related to the Cold War, but the protection of American oil interests was probably involved as well. American oil companies did not want to be challenged by Soviet competition in West European markets and they also wanted to keep oil prices high by excluding large-scale Soviet sales of oil at reduced prices. Soviet oil specialist Boris Rachkov perceived oil company influence on U.S. policy, since the government was striving to hold back Soviet oil sales in Western Europe.[22]

Table 10.3. Soviet Oil Exports to Western Europe, 1970–1972 [a] (in millions of metric tons)

year	Soviet exports of crude oil and oil products to Western Europe	total West European imports of crude oil and oil products	West European import dependence on Soviet oil
1970	41.125	718.540	5.7%
1971	44.679	746.419	6.0%
1972	44.635	783.630	5.7%

SOURCES: *Vneshniaia torgovlia SSSR za 1971 god: statisticheskii obzor* (Moscow: Izdatel'stvo "Mezhdunarodnye otnosheniia," 1972), pp. 68–69; *ibid.*, 1973 (1974), pp. 70–71; and United Nations, Statistical Office, *World Energy Supplies, 1969–1972* (New York: United Nations, 1974) pp. 55 and 85.

[a] Western Europe is defined as including Finland, Austria and Yugoslavia.

NATO's embargo on all steel pipe with a diameter of at least 19 inches was imposed in 1962 and followed by all members. Italy continued to supply pipe under a previous contract but it made no new commitments to the USSR. West Germany canceled its contracts with the USSR, bringing about a Soviet protest, but the West Germans claimed that it was in the interest of the country's security.[23] By 1966, West Germany and France were leading the fight to end the embargo, arguing that the Druzhba Pipeline had already been completed and that the Soviets were capable of producing their own pipe.[24] The embargo did affect the construction of the Pipeline, since it was finished more than a year behind schedule and its capacity was less than originally planned.[25] The United States agreed that the embargo could be lifted and it was declared terminated in November, 1966.[26] As British oil analyst

Peter Odell viewed the situation, the economic interests of NATO states took precedence over their strategic interests.[27]

NATO's measures against the USSR did not affect Soviet oil exports to Western Europe.[28] Commercial relations continued, as the West European states were anxious to buy low-priced oil, despite its communist source. However, a bias against importing Soviet oil did exist in Britain, but it predated the 1962 NATO sanctions. Britain had enacted a ban against Soviet crude oil in 1941 and it was not until 1961 that one import license was granted. (Britain consistently imported small quantities of Soviet oil products.)[29] In 1963, the Soviets offered additional fuel oil which would be paid for by British construction of ships for the USSR. This proposal sounded attractive to the Labour Party because it would have provided work for many unemployed shipbuilders but the Conservative government of Harold Macmillan was reluctant to import additional Soviet oil products.[30] In 1971, Britain granted its first license in ten years for the import of Soviet crude oil and other licenses have followed. This oil is imported by Nafta, a Soviet-owned marketer of oil in Britain, not by British companies.[31] In 1973, Britain permanently rescinded the import ban and oil deliveries from the Soviet Union increased.[32] Peter Odell has written that past British opposition to Soviet crude oil was not based solely on anticommunism but was actually directed at the retention of domestic markets by British companies. BP is British-owned and Royal Dutch Shell is partially owned by British interests.[33] When oil was in short supply in 1974, BP actually looked into the possibility of importing Soviet oil into Britain for use by its own marketing network. V. A. Kirilin, a Soviet Deputy Prime Minister, announced at a press conference in London on May 22, 1974, that BP officials were engaged in such negotiations in Moscow.[34]

Soviet oil sales to the Italian company Ente Nazionali Idrocarburi (ENI), which began in 1957, were possibly aimed at extending Soviet influence in Italy and undermining the southern flank of the NATO alliance (it should also be kept in mind that the Italian communists were an important force in domestic politics). Nevertheless, the prime Soviet motivation was to weaken the hold of the major Western oil companies over the Italian market, as ENI was an active foe of the "Seven Sisters." [35] The Soviets generally praised the role of ENI; Boris Rachkov, writing in 1967, drew distinctions between ENI and members of the Western oil cartel. For example, he asserted that ENI permitted host states to share in ENI's oil investments overseas, with ENI retaining only 25 percent of the profits.[36]

ENI began to purchase Soviet oil in 1957 but the first major agreement was in 1960.[37] ENI paid less than any other Soviet customer in Western Europe; the price in 1960 was only $1.40 per barrel delivered in Italy or about $1 per barrel at Black Sea ports.[38] In 1961, ENI received 72 percent of its total oil supply from the USSR,[39] and Italy as a whole received 22.9 percent of its oil from the USSR in that year. By 1967, the figure had fallen to 11 percent, as Italy's purchases from other sources increased.[40] A study prepared for the U.S. government by Halford Hoskins and Leon Herman expressed the fear that Italy would refine Soviet oil and then reexport some of it as Italian oil. This indeed proved to be the case.[41]

In 1973, the Soviet Union exported 45,022,000 tons of crude oil and oil products to Western Europe, including Yugoslavia, which represented 38.1 percent of total Soviet oil exports; if Yugoslavia is excluded, the figures are 41,131,000 tons or 34.8 percent. The largest recipients (in descending order) were Finland, Italy, West Germany, France, Yugoslavia, the Netherlands, and Sweden; smaller amounts went to Austria, Belgium, Britain, Denmark, Greece, Iceland, Ireland, Norway, Spain, and Switzerland.[42]

In addition to their oil export program, the Soviets are also engaged in marketing and refining. As Marshall Goldman indicates, they try to avoid political controversy by forming a partnership with local interests. In Finland, for example, joint stock companies were created in 1946 (Suomen Petrool) and 1948 (Teboil).[43] The Soviet Union, through Soiuznefteeksport, holds a majority of the shares in each company. Suomen Petrool and Teboil operate service stations, own fuel depots and gasoline trucks, sell spare parts and accessories for motor vehicles, and maintain a tanker fleet for use in the Soviet–Finnish oil trade.[44]

On June 1, 1971, Soviet Minister of Foreign Trade Nikolai Patolichev and French Minister of Finance Valéry Giscard d'Estaing reached an agreement on the joint construction of an oil refinery, probably to be located at Le Havre. The Soviets were to collaborate with ERAP, a state-run company, and the refinery was to serve France and other West European markets.[45] This project has lain dormant for several years and it now appears that instead of the original arrangement, the Soviets will supply oil and equipment for an already existing refinery whose production capacity will be expanded. The Soviets also had an agreement with Raffineries du Rhône in Switzerland according to which 20,000 barrels per day of Soviet crude oil was refined over a seven-year period beginning in 1965. The oil was shipped from Black Sea ports to Genoa, where it was sent through a pipeline to Switzerland. The Soviets received hard currency in return, minus a refining fee and transportation costs.[46]

On December 1, 1967, Soiuznefteeksport and two Belgian firms created Nafta in Antwerp, Belgium, with the Soviets having 40 percent of the shares. By 1971, the Soviets had 90 percent.[47] Nafta imports, stores, and markets Soviet oil and it has also become involved in refining operations. Nafta receives oil from Baltic ports of the USSR, but it imports non-Soviet oil as well. It has facilities for storing both crude oil and oil products and it maintains service stations to market its products.[48] Nafta wanted to refine oil for the Belgian market, but one of its primary functions was to refine Soviet crude oil for sale to Nafta's affiliate in Britain.[49] Until 1971, Britain banned the import of Soviet crude oil, but allowed products refined from Soviet crude. Nafta was unable to acquire its own refinery because the major Western oil companies, which did not want marketing competition, pressured Belgium to keep out a Soviet-owned refinery.[50] However, Nafta did manage to process Soviet crude at the Albatros refinery in Antwerp.[51]

The Soviet-owned Nafta company in Britain began operations

in 1959. It imports oil and runs a network of service stations. Until it was given a license to import Soviet crude oil in 1971, it imported some of its oil from the Middle East and some from Finland.[52] Finland was really engaged in a switch arrangement, since it imported most of its oil from the USSR but exported part of its own supply to Nafta in Britain. Nafta does not have its own refineries in Britain so refining is done at the BP refinery on the Isle of Grain in Kent and at the BP refinery in Belfast.[53] When Britain permitted the import of Soviet crude in 1971, Nafta was able to bring in 150,000 tons that year, a figure that subsequently rose to 300,000 tons per year.[54] Nafta operates about 400 service stations in Britain, and it charges somewhat less than other gasoline marketers. Its percentage of the British market is tiny, perhaps only 1 percent, but Nafta earns hard currency for the USSR and serves as an experimental marketing operation which can serve as a guide for future Soviet endeavors.[55]

Soviet Gas Sales

The USSR is in a position to increase the export of natural gas more rapidly than the export of oil, since Western Siberian gas production is starting to boom and the domestic oil industry is beset with numerous problems. Western Europe provides an attractive market for Soviet gas. Its geographical location is convenient, it pays with hard currency or pipe, and its need for gas is growing. By 1985, Western Europe may be importing about one-third of its natural gas requirements.[56]

The first West European state to start receiving Soviet gas was Austria in September 1968. The gas comes through a pipeline via Czechoslovakia and is largely paid for with pipe.[57] In 1968, the Soviets agreed to send Austria approximately 1.4 billion cubic meters per year for twenty years beginning in 1971, and smaller quantities were to be provided during the period 1968–70.[58] Then, in November 1974, the Soviets promised an additional 500 million cubic meters per year from 1975 through 1977 and one billion cubic meters per year thereafter through the year 2000.[59] The Soviet decision to furnish this extra quantity will probably preclude an agreement between Austria and Algeria. The Austrians have been reluctant to provide the large credits desired by the Algerians in order to build a pipeline to Europe. In 1973, the USSR supplied Austria with 1621.8 million cubic meters of gas.[60]

Deliveries to West Germany began in October 1973, coming through a pipeline across Czechoslovakia. The East Germans were not happy with this arrangement; they had opposed Soviet gas sales to West Germany, but if such sales were to take place they wanted the pipeline to pass through their territory so that they could receive some transit revenue.[61] The original agreement between the Soviet Union and West Germany, signed on November 30, 1969, provided for 120 billion cubic meters of gas over 20 years. West Germany was to pay with steel pipe.[62] Later agreements increased the quantity of gas to be delivered and it is possible that deliveries will reach 7 billion cubic meters per year.[63] The Soviet Union will be receiving 2.4 million tons of steel pipe, which will constitute more than half of West Germany's pipe exports.[64] There were conflicting reports on whether Soviet gas exports to West Germany in 1973 were as high as the contracted quantity but it appears that the shortfall—if any—was very small and deliveries have proceeded as scheduled ever since.[65]

The gas pipeline from the Soviet Union to Finland opened on January 9, 1974.[66] Agreement had been reached in December 1971 for gas deliveries over a 20-year period, but the quantity is still subject to negotiation.[67] Finland hopes to receive as much as 3 billion cubic meters per year, but to obtain such a large volume, Finland will have to aid in the construction of a gas pipeline from the Soviet Union to Sweden.[68] In the meantime, Finland was supplied with 500 million cubic meters in 1974 and 1 billion in 1975. The rate is to increase by 100 million cubic meters per year through 1979, and then remain constant at 1.4 billion cubic meters.[69] Soviet deliveries to Italy also began in 1974 through a pipeline that crosses Czechoslovakia and Austria on its way to Vicenza, Italy. The Soviet–Italian gas agreement was signed on December 10, 1969, and under its terms Italy will be supplied with 6 billion cubic meters per year over 20 years. The pipeline opened in June 1974.[70]

The Soviet Union and France reached a gas agreement on August 6, 1971. Deliveries started in 1976. France will receive 2.5 billion cubic meters of gas per year until 1981 when, as arranged during Brezhnev's visit to France in December 1974, the quantity will be raised to 4 billion cubic meters per year and remain at that level for 15 years.[71] The import of Soviet gas will lessen France's dependence on Algeria, and it really places the USSR in competition with Algeria for the French market. At one time, the Soviets thought about building a gas pipeline through Italy to France but a switch deal has now solved the transport problem.[72] France and Italy agreed in July 1972 that Italy is to receive the gas sold to France by the USSR, since the Soviet pipeline to Austria now extends into Italy. In return, France will receive the same quantity of gas from the Groningen field in the Netherlands, the quantity to be deducted from Italy's import contract with that state.[73]

The Soviet Union may export gas to Sweden, and Prime Minister Kosygin indicated that deliveries could start in 1978.[74] Of course, any pipeline will have to cross Finland, and the present Soviet–Finnish pipeline does not have the capacity to serve Sweden as well. A new pipeline will therefore have to be built through Finland and then under the Baltic Sea. Studies have shown that the envisioned pipeline would be capable of transporting 6 billion cubic meters per year, but perhaps part of the quantity actually transported will be sold to Finland rather than Sweden.[75] The Swedes would like to receive 6 billion cubic meters for themselves, and negotiations with the USSR are in abeyance since the Soviets, claiming an insufficient gas supply, are presently offering only 1 billion cubic meters per year.[76]

Soviet sales of oil and gas to West European states are rarely manipulated for political ends, since any such actions would be self-defeating. The Soviets want hard currency, pipe, and technology from Western Europe and the politicization of the energy trade would lead West European states to lessen their dependence on Soviet supplies. At this stage, the Soviets prefer the benefits of commerce to those of political leverage, but they are in a good position to change their tactics should the need ever arise.

11/The Third World

Outside of the Middle East and North Africa, most states in the Third World * are oil importers (Venezuela, Nigeria, and Indonesia are obvious exceptions). Until the Soviet Union began its oil offensive in the mid-fifties, Third World states were greatly reliant on the major Western oil companies, but the Soviet provision of oil and assistance in domestic oil industry development have since contributed to the Western oil interests' decreasing control and influence.[1]

The Soviet Union's main aim in offering oil and technical assistance is political. While it certainly hopes to generate good will, more significantly it seeks to undermine the power of Western oil companies, which it views as bastions of Western political influence in the Third World. The Soviets do derive some economic dividends (they expand trade ties and secure some needed raw materials), but oil sales to Third World states are not especially profitable and the provision of equipment and technicians deprives the Soviet Union's own oil industry of some valuable resources.[2]

The Soviets help states to become more self-sufficient in oil and often serve in an advisory capacity and attempt to steer the states in a socialist direction as oil industries are developed. Third World states have less of a need for Soviet oil once their own oil independence is strengthened, but they become increasingly dependent on Soviet oil equipment. The USSR, which does not have large quantities of oil available for export to the Third World, is satisfied with this arrangement. Less than three million tons was sold to Third World states in 1973, while total oil exports were more than 118 million tons.

* The "Third World" refers to all states in Asia, Africa, and Latin America—except Japan, states in the Middle East and North Africa, and states under communist rule.

From the viewpoint of Third World states, Soviet involvement in their oil programs is beneficial because the Soviets construct refineries, aid in oil prospecting, and they provide oilfield equipment. The Soviets do not share in the ownership of any facilities, and they derive no profit; they offer low-interest credits, which need not be repaid until after a project is completed.[3] Repayment can often be made out of the profits which are derived once a facility is operating.[4] The Soviets accept local currency or goods as payment and they train local people as oil technicians. Most importantly, however, the Soviets offer an alternative to Western oil companies, thereby reducing the dependence of Third World states on the latter. The offer of Soviet oil has contributed to a lowering of oil prices (as in India) and to the nationalization of a Western-owned marketing network (as in Ceylon), and Soviet assistance in building refineries has cut oil import costs since crude oil is considerably cheaper than oil products. Soviet aid in prospecting and production has also made states more self-reliant, thus lessening their need to import large quantities of oil from Western firms.

South and Southeast Asia

On December 2, 1953, the Soviet Union and India concluded a trade agreement which listed crude oil and oil products as possible Soviet exports to India. However, deliveries never took place since India did not have its own refineries or marketing system and the Western companies which controlled the Indian oil industry had no interest in refining or marketing oil from the USSR.[5] Then, in June 1955, Prime Minister Nehru paid a visit to Moscow and the warming political ties were accompanied by Soviet aid for India's oil industry. In November, the Soviets offered assistance in prospecting and refinery construction, and in December they agreed to supply oil-drilling equipment.[6] Soviet experts arrived in India in late 1955 to begin their search for oil. They made discoveries in the Cambay area in 1958 and at Ankleshwar in 1960.[7] Western states had been reluctant to assist India with oil exploration because Western companies had firm control over the Indian oil market and did not want their sales to be challenged by domestically produced oil. The largest Western oil companies in India were Burmah Shell, Caltex, and Esso.

The Soviets provided significant aid for India's oil industry, attempting to reduce India's dependence on Western companies. In May 1956, they agreed to provide drilling rigs and technicians; [8] in May 1957, they extended a gift of oil equipment; [9] in September 1959 they offered to prospect further; and, in October 1959 they arranged to build an oil refinery at Barauni.[10] In both February and June 1960, they made agreements to assist with oil production, and in July they contracted to do an oil survey.[11] The Soviets also helped India develop a state-operated oil distribution system; by 1960 India was producing one-third of its oil needs.[12]

The most important Soviet oil initiative came early in 1960, when it offered crude oil at low prices.[13] Western oil companies, which controlled all of India's refineries, had been importing their own oil and had been giving no discount off world market prices. The Soviets were willing to provide about half of India's import needs at a 20 to 25 percent discount.[14] Furthermore, the Soviets were offering the oil on a barter basis, thus creating a market for Indian exports and helping India conserve its hard-currency reserves. The Soviets made their overture to India at the same time that they were making a similar proposal to Cuba. As in Cuba, the Western owned refineries would not process Soviet crude oil, since they wanted to retain their control over imports and to keep prices high. In July, they informed the Indian government that they would not refine the Soviet oil. India therefore had to turn down the Soviet offer; government-owned refineries were not yet in operation. Perhaps India could have nationalized the Western refineries, as Cuba had done, but it did not want such a serious confrontation with the West over the issue. India's state sector in the oil industry was as yet very undeveloped, so the Indians wanted continued assistance from Western oil companies—particularly in prospecting.[15] In addition, the Soviets were not offering to supply India with all of her oil needs and some reliance on Western companies would still be necessary.

Although the Western companies would not refine Soviet oil,

the threat of cheap Soviet oil exports to India led them to lower their prices. After an initial reduction of about 10 percent, discounts off the Persian Gulf list price were even greater during the following four years.[16] The companies may easily have been influenced by the "interventions" and subsequent nationalizations in Cuba. The companies therefore reached an accommodation with India on the price of oil imports in order to help preserve their position in the Indian oil industry.

World Petroleum asserted that Western oil companies in India were planning to lower their prices even before the Soviet oil offer and Harold Lubell, an American specialist on the international oil trade, took the same position.[17] Lubell argued that there was a world oil surplus at the time and that the Western companies had wanted to lower prices but were afraid that the oil producing states would react strongly and therefore used the Soviet offer to India as an excuse to force the lowering of prices. The oil companies passed on their revenue loss to the producing states by paying them less for their oil. Lubell's contention that there was an oil surplus is correct, but this surplus was due in part to the Soviet Union's oil offensive during that period. Western companies wanted to keep prices as high as possible and it was only the threat of cheap Soviet oil in West European and other markets that compelled them to compete by lowering their prices.

India was unable to import Soviet crude oil, but in July 1960 it arranged to import Soviet kerosene and diesel fuel. The first shipment arrived in August.[18] The USSR supplied almost one-fourth of India's oil-product imports during the years 1961–65, and it provided virtually all of the kerosene and diesel fuel.[19] The Soviets raised the price of their oil in 1962, citing higher freight costs, and increased it again in 1965.[20] However, they were still underselling the Western companies. The major companies in India—Esso, Caltex, and Burmah Shell—were disturbed by the Soviet oil sales to India, because their refining profits were reduced. As India imported Soviet oil products, its requirements for crude-oil imports and the refining of this crude by the Western companies were obviously lessened. The companies therefore resorted to pressure tactics in order to have restrictions placed on the import of Soviet oil. They intentionally held back deliveries of their own oil and disrupted the distribution of Soviet oil products, causing an artificial oil shortage.[21] Nevertheless, India continued to import Soviet oil products, and the government, through the Indian Oil Corporation, gradually extended its control over the import, refining, and marketing of oil.

The Soviet Union has been active in prospecting for oil in India. Prospecting agreements were signed in October 1963, March 1965, and January 1974. The focal point of the explorations has been the Gulf of Cambay off the Bombay coast.[22] J. A. Naik, an Indian analyst of Soviet foreign policy, maintains that the Soviets have found oil or gas in 75 percent of the test wells drilled in India and a Soviet journalist claims that the USSR has aided in oil-field development to the point where 50 percent of all oil extracted in India comes from projects built with Soviet assistance.[23]

In accordance with an October 1959 agreement, the Soviets constructed a refinery at Barauni in Bihar, and later, fulfilling a February 1961 agreement, they built another refinery at Koyali in Gujerat.[24] In July 1973, they agreed to construct a refinery at Mathura in Uttar Pradesh, to be operational in 1977, with an eventual capacity of 6 million tons per year.[25] The two refineries built with Soviet assistance are part of the government sector of the oil industry and they produce about one-third of the oil refined in India.[26] All of the oil they refine is Indian crude.[27] The Soviet-built refineries turned out to be rather expensive, as Phillips constructed a refinery at Cochin for less than the cost of the Soviet refineries, but the Soviets have been helpful to India in developing a state-controlled oil industry. They have trained Indian specialists and have provided the first of three tankers to be delivered to India. The Soviets constantly praise India for its socialistic steps in the oil industry and its policy of nationalizing foreign holdings.[28]

The USSR exported 378,500 tons of oil products in 1972, 476,700 tons in 1973.[29] By the end of 1973, India was reeling under the impact of the energy crisis and its hard-currency reserves were dwindling.[30] It hoped to acquire more oil from the Soviet Union, especially because hard currency would not be needed for such purchases. When General Secretary Brezhnev visited India in November 1973, he promised to increase oil exports, and there was speculation that the USSR would deliver 3 million tons of crude in 1974, in addition to an increased quantity of oil products.[31] If so, it would have marked the first delivery of Soviet crude to India since its independence. However, when an oil contract between Soiuznefteksport and the Indian Oil Corporation was eventually signed on April 4, 1974, it provided for one million tons of kerosene and 100,000 tons of diesel fuel.[32] This was a substantial increase over 1973, but no crude oil was to be provided. In 1975, the Soviets slightly increased the supply to 200,000 tons of diesel fuel and held the quantity of kerosene constant.[33]

When Soviet oil minister Shashin was in India in early January 1974, he said that India would achieve oil self-sufficiency in two years and he emphasized Soviet assistance for India's oil exploration program.[34] Shashin was really indicating that the Soviet Union did not want to supply India with crude oil; it so informed India shortly thereafter, claiming that it did not have enough crude oil to deliver.[35] This was apparently true. The East European states were biting into the Soviet oil supply and the Soviets were also diverting some oil to hard-currency markets in Western Europe and the United States in order to take advantage of the Arab embargo. Furthermore, with the oil available for export to noncommunist states becoming very limited, the Soviets are not anxious to begin large deliveries to a state like India, which does not pay with hard currency and whose oil needs are quickly rising. Despite close political ties with India, and a desire to secure India's support for the containment of Chinese influence, the Soviet Union must be economically circumspect as it tries to cope with the growing restraints placed on its oil export program.

In order not to offend it and to keep some semblance of balance, the Soviet Union has also made limited oil commitments to Pakistan. In 1958, the Soviets offered a credit for oil exploration, but the Pakistanis, who were closely tied into the Western defense system, rejected it.[36] In March 1961 the Soviets renewed the offer; it was accepted. The Soviets provided a credit of $30 million for oil exploration by Soviet specialists and oil drilling equipment, hoping to make a political impact by finding oil where Western companies had already been unsuccessful.[37] They found oil in the Kotarange and Kutch regions in 1958 and in the Karachi and Chittagong regions in 1971 (Chittagong later became part of Bangladesh). The Soviets then agreed to extend their stay in Pakistan.[38] As Pakistan developed close relations with China during the late sixties, some elements of Sino-Soviet competition crept into the Pakistani oil program. For example, the Soviets offered a credit for oil equipment, to be paid over 12½ years, and the Chinese countered with an interest-free loan payable in 20 years. The Soviets then increased the size of their credit, but Pakistan still opted for the Chinese offer.[39]

In Ceylon (now Sri Lanka), Prime Minister Bandaranaike wanted to establish government control over the distribution of oil products but she was afraid that Western oil companies would react by withholding their oil. She therefore sought to protect Ceylon's interests in advance, and in March 1961 Ceylon arranged to import 40,000 tons of oil products from the USSR and smaller amounts from Egypt and Iraq. In May, the Ceylonese legislature decided to create a government oil corporation which would handle 25 percent of the oil marketing. Compensation was to be paid to the Western oil companies for the nationalization of some of their facilities. On June 1, the Ceylon Petroleum Corporation was established, largely to distribute Soviet oil products once they were received. On December 26, the USSR agreed to provide 1.25 million tons over a five-year period, which represented 20 percent of Ceylon's needs. On February 7, 1962, Ceylon contracted with Rumania for 30,000 tons, and on March 20 with Egypt for 40,000 tons. The first Soviet shipment arrived in March 1962.[40]

Having secured an oil supply from non-Western sources, Ceylon accelerated its campaign against the major oil companies active in Ceylon—Shell, Esso, and Caltex. It set a ceiling on the price they could charge for their imported oil (slightly higher than the price Ceylon paid for USSR), but the companies refused to adhere to such guidelines.[41] In June 1962, Ceylon nationalized Western-owned service stations so that they could be used to distribute Soviet oil products and a controversy developed over compensation. Since most of the nationalized property belonged to American companies, the United States resorted to pressure tactics and suspended all aid as of February 6, 1963. It was not resumed until July 1965, when a compensation agreement was reached.[42] Ceylon continued to receive some of its oil from Western companies, especially after the Suez Canal was closed in 1967, since transportation problems caused some irregularities in Soviet deliveries.[43] In addition to their provision of oil products, the Soviets have consistently prospected for oil in Ceylon and did find some deposits in 1971.[44]

The Soviet Union has been prospecting and supplying oil products to Bangladesh since its independence in 1971 (test wells were drilled in the Barisal region in 1974);[45] it has also delivered oil to Burma, prospected there, and offered to construct a refinery; it has prospected in the Philippines; and it built a refinery and supplied oil equipment to Indonesia while Sukarno was still in power.[46]

With the overthrow of Sukarno in October 1965, the USSR no longer gave assistance. Singapore had been part of Malaysia until August 1965, and Sukarno had conducted his "confrontation" with Malaysia up to the time of his removal. The Soviet Union had been reluctant to offend Sukarno by seeking better relations with Malaysia or Singapore, but quickly sought warmer ties with both Malaysia and Singapore after his ouster.[47] The Soviets had a strategic interest in the area since their merchant shipping and elements of their Pacific fleet frequently passed through the Straits of Malacca—important as a supply route to North Vietnam.[48] On April 2, 1966, the Soviets agreed to export oil products to Singapore and they eventually acquired the use of docking and ship-repair facilities there.[49]

Afghanistan

The Soviet Union has always regarded Afghanistan as a buffer to be protected against encroachments by any outside powers. In the fifties, as Iran and Pakistan became affiliated with the anticommunist CENTO alliance, its strategic importance increased. The Soviet Union has traditionally enjoyed close economic ties with Afghanistan, and the economic interaction between the two states has been reinforced by geographical considerations, since Afghanistan's route to the sea has often been obstructed by Pakistan.

Afghanistan and Pakistan have always been at odds over the Pushtunistan and Baluchistan issues. In 1950 Pakistan closed Afghanistan's trade route to the sea, which ran to Karachi. Until then, Afghanistan, which had received most of its oil from the West, arranged (in July) to import Soviet oil. The Soviets also offered to prospect for oil—measures clearly dictated by the fact that oil deliveries via Karachi had been cut off for three months. Soviet-Afghan trade was also bolstered in 1955 when Pakistan again closed the trade route, this time for five months, and the Soviets agreed to the duty-free transit of Afghan exports through the USSR.[50] On September 6, 1961, Afghanistan and Pakistan severed diplomatic relations and the route to Karachi was then closed to Afghan goods until September 15, 1963. Pakistan did not permit any products to pass through its territory on their way to Afghanistan except for those coming from the United States. After a slight drop in 1962, American exports to Afghanistan increased substantially in 1963 but still fell far short of Soviet exports.[51]

Geographical, strategic, and economic considerations have led to close Soviet–Afghan cooperation in the use and control of energy resources. The Soviets have regularly supplied Afghanistan with about half of its oil needs and, in an unusual gesture of generosity, they have frozen prices at the 1973 pre-embargo level.[52] In 1954 and 1956, they provided credits for oil storage tanks, and on July 30, 1957, they extended a $15 million credit for oil and gas exploration.[53] At the same time, the Soviets warned Afghanistan not to allow American oil experts in northern Afghanistan, an action similar to their effort to keep Western oil interests out of northern Iran.[54] Soviet oil prospectors met with success in 1960 when they found oil at Aq Shah and the Soviets also trained hundreds of Afghan oil technicians.[55] They additionally helped to create a petroleum technology college at Mazar.[56] In 1972, they agreed to build an oil refinery and pipeline.[57]

Acting upon the 1957 gas prospecting agreement, the Soviets made their first finds near Shibarghan in April 1961. In October 1963, the Afghans promised future deliveries of natural gas to the USSR through a pipeline, the construction of which began in 1965. The pipeline links the Shibarghan gas fields with the Soviet gas pipeline network.[58] In June 1964, the Soviets provided a credit of $39 million to assist with gas exploitation, the credit to be repaid with gas deliveries.[59] An agreement of May 10, 1967, provided for 58 billion cubic meters of gas to be delivered between 1967 and 1985. The gas was to repay all of the credits Afghanistan had received from the USSR and was also to cover continued Soviet technical assistance and the import of Soviet goods.[60] Some of the gas produced at Shibarghan was to be used domestically by Afghanistan.[61] The Soviets were pleased that Afghanistan had a large quantity of gas available for export, since this meant that Afghanistan's debts to the USSR would be paid.[62] One Soviet journalist called upon Third World states to emulate Afghanistan and Iran by repaying Soviet credits with reliable exports such as fuel.[63]

The Soviet decisions to help exploit and import Afghan natural gas made sense politically and economically: the Soviets were sure to create a reservoir of good will in Afghanistan by developing such a valuable export industry and then serving as a market for its production; in addition, past Afghan debts would be repaid, the Soviets' temporary gas shortage would be alleviated, and more of their own gas would eventually be freed for export to the hard-currency markets of Western Europe. Finally, while the adjoining Central Asian republics required no Afghan gas themselves, its import was still economically useful, since it entered a pipeline to gas-deficient areas of the Russian republic.[64]

The Afghans benefited from the gas export agreements in many ways: Afghanistan could redress its persistent trade deficit with the USSR and pay off its debts; [65] it would have a nearby market for gas that it had little ability to consume domestically; and it would be able to use gas as payment for needed imports from the USSR. Furthermore, Shibarghan is in a remote area, separated from southern Afghanistan by the Hindu Kush mountains, and it would not be feasible to transport the gas southward.[66]

Afghan gas deliveries to the USSR began in September, 1967 and reached approximately 2.8 billion cubic meters in 1974.[67] The yearly quantity will probably rise to 3.5 billion cubic meters by 1980.[68] As of 1974, the Soviets were paying 19.7 cents per thousand cubic feet, but they agreed to begin paying 34 cents as of October 1, 1974.[69] This new price was decided upon during Prime Minister Daud's visit to the USSR in June 1974. The Soviets are paying Afghanistan much less than they are paying Iran, and a huge amount less than they are charging their East and West European customers, so they are obviously deriving some economic advantage.

Africa

The Soviet Union developed very close ties with Ghana shortly after its independence in 1957. Its president, Kwame Nkrumah, was even honored with a Lenin Peace Prize in 1962. The Soviets supplied oil products and conducted a geological survey for oil, but deep involvement began in 1965 with the provision of 595,300 tons of crude oil for Ghana's sole refinery at Tema.[70] Nkrumah's government was overthrown in January 1966, but the Soviets continued to deliver oil. In fact, total exports of crude oil to Ghana rose to 603,500 tons in 1966.[71] At the same time, however, there was a decline in Soviet–Ghanaian trade, which one Soviet analyst attributed to "the change of course of the new Ghanaian government in the area of trade and economic relations." [72] This was probably close to the truth since Nkrumah's successors wanted to reduce Ghana's economic dependence on the USSR. Soviet exports to Ghana fell from 31.1 million rubles in 1965 to 12.6 million rubles in 1966 while Ghana's exports to the USSR stayed fairly constant.[73] Interestingly, the reduction in trade did not affect Soviet oil exports and the Soviets did not withhold oil to protest Nkrumah's removal.

Soviet oil exports to Ghana fell to 452,600 tons in 1967, but not because of political pressure.[74] Ghana had decided to import very little Soviet oil after September 1, 1967, and to rely instead on Western suppliers. However, Ghana switched back to large Soviet deliveries a year later, after the USSR offered lower prices.[75] This renewed Soviet–Ghanaian oil relationship was quickly disrupted; on October 10, 1968, two Soviet trawlers were seized in Ghanaian waters and taken to Takoradi. Ghana suspected that the ships had been engaged in transporting arms to pro-Nkrumah forces.[76] Soviet–Ghanaian relations were somewhat strained at the time: Ghana had criticized the Soviet intervention in Czechoslovakia, and on September 12 Radio Moscow had accused Ghana of conducting an anti-Soviet campaign.[77] Once the trawlers were seized, the Soviets reacted strongly. On October 17, the Soviet news agency Tass admitted that the trawlers had been within Ghana's territorial waters but claimed that wind and the current had forced them in once their engines had been damaged. Tass asserted that "certain circles in Ghana" were trying to dampen Soviet–Ghanaian relations and that the seizure of the vessels was "not simply an unfortunate incident." Hinting at economic retaliation, Tass maintained that the worsening of relations between the two states was "most harmful to Ghana's own interests, especially as the Soviet Union is a very good trading partner." [78]

The Soviets failed to deliver the first four oil shipments expected in early 1969, and in February they announced that no oil would be delivered in March, nor could they guarantee supplies thereafter. They were particularly incensed because the crew members of the two trawlers had been arrested on February 5. Soviet actions were not constrained by the fact that the USSR and Ghana had a contract for 700,000 tons of crude oil in 1969, and that Ghana had already sent some cocoa beans to the USSR in exchange for the oil.[79] The Soviets may have believed that Ghana would experience difficulties in securing Western oil as a replacement. After all, Ghana had forsaken its Western suppliers by shifting to the Soviets the previous September and still owed to Western states the huge debt that had accrued during the Nkrumah period. Western companies, however, quickly agreed to supply crude oil for the Tema refinery, and Ghana arranged for shipments on a cargo-to-cargo basis for the months of March through June, and negotiations to extend deliveries beyond June continued. The Western companies were to provide somewhat less than what the Soviets had promised, but they agreed to increase deliveries if necessary. For its part, Ghana indicated that it would repay part of its debt to Western states.[80]

These arrangements proved to be academic; Soviet oil deliveries were renewed in March, and the USSR provided 540,400 tons during the course of 1969.[81] The Soviets have continued to supply oil on a regular basis ever since, with the quantity fluctuating in the general area of 600,000 tons per year.[82] The resumption of Soviet oil deliveries was surely due to the release of the two trawlers and their crews. On February 26, the captains of the two vessels were fined 200 cedis (somewhat over $200) each and the trawlers and crews were released on February 28. The two captains, who had been asked to testify before an investigatory commission, remained in Ghana until March 19.[83] Whether Ghana's relative leniency was influenced by Soviet oil pressure is difficult to determine, but the timing of events makes such a connection likely. On March 3, Accra radio called for good relations with the USSR and blamed past difficulties on the uncooperative behavior of the trawler captains and their crews.[84]

Nigeria, itself one of world's largest oil exporters, is a special case. Nigeria's oil wealth is concentrated in the former Eastern Region, which attempted to secede as the state of Biafra in 1967, and Western companies have traditionally played a large role in Nigerian oil development. The Soviet Union had very little contact with Nigeria before the civil war, considering it to be under Western neocolonialist control, but the Soviets supported the Nigerian war effort against Biafra and have become active in oil development since that time.[85] They hope to reduce Western oil influence and have been assisting Nigeria with the organization of a state oil corporation.

According to the Soviet analysis, Western oil companies encouraged Biafran separatism so that they could set up a puppet, capitalist state which would protect their oil interests and not tax them very highly. Soviet commentators frequently compared the Biafran secession with that of Katanga's from the Congo. In the latter instance, Belgian copper interests had been instrumental.[86] As the Nigerian war dragged on, the Soviets maintained that oil, not tribalism, was the key to the conflict. Radio Moscow declared on August 26, 1968: "The rivalry between the foreign oil monopolies is the real reason for the prolonged Nigerian crisis. Alien interests are preventing the conflicting sides from coming together."[87] In April 1969, a Soviet commentator summed up events by writing: "The Marxist, class view of the proclamation of Biafra shows that behind the slogan of self-determination for the Eastern Region are extreme bourgeois nationalists from among the compradors, who would like to set up a full-fledged capitalist state as an ally and watchdog of foreign monopoly interests."[88]

Once the Nigeria–Biafra war ended in 1970, and the Eastern Region was reincorporated into Nigeria, the Soviet Union began to lend oil assistance to the Nigerian government. Soviet advisers helped run the Nigerian National Oil Corporation, Soviet instructors served at the oil training center in Warri, Soviet technicians aided in oilfield development, and Soviet prospectors searched for offshore oil.[89] Nevertheless, Nigeria has maintained its close oil ties with the West and even increased exports to Western states during the Arab embargo of 1973–74.[90]

Although Nigeria is a major oil exporter, it has a refinery shortage and must import some gasoline and other oil products.[91] The Soviet Union provides some of these needed products but, in a curious twist, the Soviets have indicated that they would like to buy Nigerian crude oil.[92] An article appearing in the Soviet journal *Foreign Trade* in June 1974 stated: "Although the Soviet Union is itself a major oil producer, it might, under certain circumstances, buy Nigerian oil."[93] Perhaps the Soviets could take advantage of Nigeria's geographical location by reexporting Nigerian oil to Cuba or to Soviet customers in West Africa.

In Ethiopia, the Soviets have searched for oil and have built the Assab refinery in the province of Eritrea on the Red Sea coast.[94] They first extended a credit for the refinery on July 11,

1959, but a controversy ensued because British oil companies were afraid that they would be shut out of the Ethiopian market. These companies had provided much of Ethiopia's oil and were fearful that only Soviet oil would be processed in the envisioned refinery. They therefore made a counterproposal, offering to build a refinery for less than the Soviet estimated cost, but the Soviets lowered their price and reached final agreement with Ethiopia in 1962. The Soviets promised that oil from Western companies could be refined at Assab.[95] Construction did not begin until 1965 and the refinery opened in 1967. Soviet advisers are still present at Assab; in July 1974, the Soviets announced a plan to increase the refinery capacity from 500,000 to 820,000 tons per year, with eventual capacity reaching one million tons.[96]

The Soviet presence at Assab could cause political problems, so the USSR has been trying to adopt a very low profile in the area. Both the Ethiopian revolution against the late Emperor Haile Selassie and the Eritrean secession issue are highly relevant to continued Soviet activities at Assab. Therefore the Soviets have been very careful not to offend the new ruling Dirgue, despite some Chinese inroads into Ethiopia, and they have avoided taking sides in the Ethiopian–Eritrean dispute.

In a show of political support for President Sékou Touré's government upon its achievement of independence in September 1958, the Soviets immediately agreed to deliver oil products to Guinea. At the time, there was strong Western economic retaliation against Guinea because of its vote to become independent rather than join the new French Community. The Soviets have supplied Guinea ever since early 1959. They have also sold oil to Somalia, Senegal, and Sierra Leone and have discovered oil and gas reserves in Mali. In Tanzania, they have assisted in setting up a state oil corporation and have prospected for oil.[97]

South America

Soviet oil activities in South America have been minimal as this geographically remote area is rather peripheral to Soviet foreign policy interests. During the late fifties and early sixties, at the height of their oil offensive, the Soviets supplied oil to Argentina, Brazil, and Uruguay. They wanted to import coffee, wool, meat, and hides (also wheat, since 1962) and oil served as a useful barter item. The Soviets did not want to pay with hard currency or to develop a trade deficit with these states.[98] In addition to their deliveries of oil, the Soviets explored for oil in both Argentina and Brazil and extended a credit to Argentina for oil drilling equipment.[99] They also provided oil advisers for Cheddi Jagan's Marxist-oriented government in British Guiana (later Guyana) and discovered oil there as well.[100] Much more recently, in conjunction with the Soviet Union's rapprochement with Peronism, another credit was extended to Argentina for the purchase of Soviet oilfield equipment.[101]

Except for good will, the Soviet Union has rarely used its oil assistance to Third World states to derive direct political benefits for itself. However, by helping Third World states to become less economically reliant on the West, overall Soviet political interests are clearly furthered. Twenty years ago, most of Asia, Africa, and Latin America was under Western tutelage, either *de jure* or *de facto,* and Soviet economic policies since that time have played a small role in contributing to the growing schism between the major Western powers and Third World states.

12 / The Pacific Connection: Japan, the United States, and China

The Soviets have been encouraging Japanese participation in Siberian development projects, including the exploitation of oil and gas resources, since the early sixties. They have sought to secure financial and technological assistance from the Japanese and they intentionally fostered a Japanese economic stake in Siberia in hopes that Japan will favor the existing boundaries along the Sino-Soviet border.

The thaw in Sino-American relations precipitated by President Nixon's visit to China in February 1972 made the Soviets even more anxious to further their economic collaboration with the Japanese to help forestall a political rapprochement between Japan and China. Accordingly, the Minister of Foreign Affairs, Andrei Gromyko, was dispatched to Tokyo in January 1972, just before Nixon's China visit. Despite Soviet entreaties, Japan delayed decision on projects within the USSR and followed the American lead by seeking improved ties with China. Prime Minister Kakuei Tanaka traveled to Peking in September and diplomatic relations between the two states were established. Japan had previously offended Chinese political sensitivities by sending a military delegation to tour Soviet installations in Siberia in 1971 and agreeing to establish diplomatic relations with Mongolia as late as February 24, 1972.[1] This latter action even took place in Moscow, where it was worked out by Japanese and Mongolian diplomats stationed in the USSR.

Once the United States made its opening toward China, it began to show a greater interest in Siberian energy projects. It tried to balance its relationships with the Soviet Union and China so as to affront neither state and Nixon pointedly went to Moscow three months after his call upon the Chinese leaders. Japan and China, for different reasons, felt that joint Japanese–American participation in Siberian endeavors was preferable to involvement by Japan alone and the Soviets, in accordance with their policy of détente, showed a willingness to include the United States. Three-way energy negotiations have taken place even since, but the obstacles standing in the way of major agreements have proliferated since 1972.

The Soviet Union has assigned a high priority to Siberian economic development and great publicity has been attached to the new trans-Siberian railroad project. Whereas 1.5 billion rubles for Siberian development were allocated for the 1966–70 Five-Year Plan, 5 billion rubles were provided for the years 1971–75 and the amount is expected to increase. Siberia contains the largest oil and gas reserves in the USSR and most of the energy growth during the years 1975–80 should be provided by expanded Siberian production. Transportation, technology and finance problems are obstacles to the rapid development of Siberian energy resources; it has been estimated that the Soviets must spend $36,000 to create each new Siberian job.[2] Technological and financial assistance from Japan and the United States has therefore been given serious consideration and there are also geographical and economic advantages in exporting oil and gas to these two states rather than transporting these fuels to the populated western regions of the USSR for domestic use.

Soviet–Japanese Energy Collaboration

Japan has historically been deficient in fuel and some basic raw materials and has always coveted the abundant resources of Siberia. Since the USSR is anxious to exploit these resources in co-operation with Japan, there appears to be a natural economic fit and this point has frequently been cited by Soviet analysts.[3] They have written about Japan's "acute need" for "stable sources of raw materials" and have stressed Japan's geographical proximity to the USSR and the low transportation costs involved in Soviet–Japanese trade.[4] They have also claimed that Japan can import fuel and other goods from the USSR more cheaply than from her traditional trading partners.[5] The Arab oil embargo of 1973–74 had a devastating effect on the Japanese economy and the Soviets were quick to point out that it was in Japan's interest to reach agreement with the USSR to ensure an adequate energy supply.[6] By this time, however, the Soviets were thinking more in terms of gas deliveries to Japan than of large shipments of oil.

The United States, looking at the strategic implications of Siberian development, constantly put pressure on Japan to avoid major energy deals with the Soviet Union, but détente has created an atmosphere more conducive to the furtherance of Soviet–Japanese energy relations. On the other hand, Japan too is concerned about the Soviet Union's strategic position in the Far East and in particular realizes that any contribution to Siberian oil exploitation and transportation will facilitate the fueling of the Soviet Pacific fleet. In addition, Japan is not anxious to become dependent on Soviet energy and it therefore seeks American participation in any joint Siberian oil and gas ventures as insurance against a possible Soviet embargo. Energy collaboration with the USSR is not viewed favorably by China, so the Japanese are careful to inform the Chinese about their economic negotiations with the Soviets. The Americans are also kept abreast of developments.[7] Paradoxically, Japan's dependence on Middle East oil provides the impetus for seeking an alternative source of supply in Siberia, but the escalating price of Middle East oil imports has created a serious balance of payments problem for Japan, making investment in Siberia more difficult.[8]

Soviet oil sales to Japan, which began in 1958, represented 30 percent of Japan's imports from the USSR during the period 1958–63.[9] This high percentage was the result of limited trade between the two states; Soviet oil has always made up an insignificant percentage of total Japanese oil imports. To some extent, the Soviets wanted to sell oil to Japan during the early sixties because shipments to China were being reduced but, more importantly, they were trying to reduce Japan's dependence on American oil middlemen. At the time, the United States, engaged in economic warfare to combat the Soviet oil offensive, was attempting to limit Soviet oil sales to Japan. In December 1961, the Department of Defense announced that it would no longer pur-

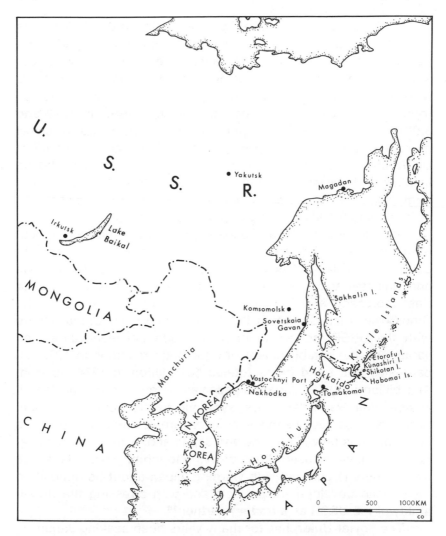

MAP 5. EASTERN SIBERIA AND JAPAN

chase jet fuel from Idemitsu Kosan, Japan's largest importer of Soviet oil.[10] Such a tactic was attuned to the anti-communism prevalent at the time, but the protection of American oil interests in Japan was also pertinent since many refineries were American-owned and U.S. oil companies were instrumental in the delivery of Middle East oil to Japan.

Most Soviet oil exports to Japan originated in Black Sea ports since export facilities had not been sufficiently developed in Siberia. The closure of the Suez Canal therefore served as an obstacle to the Soviet–Japanese oil trade but some switch deals were arranged and deliveries continued. Japan received 2,010,600 tons of crude oil and oil products from the USSR in 1972 and 3,022,500 tons in 1973.[11] Preparations are being made to export more than token quantities of oil from Siberia and an office of Soiuznefteeksport opened in the Soviet Pacific port of Nakhodka in 1968.[12] However, Soviet oil exports to Japan are still rather negligible when one realizes that the Japanese were once seeking an eventual 50 million tons per year of Tiumen oil.

Although the USSR and Japan appear to have a natural economic fit, China and Japan also have many reasons to cooperate economically. Japan's technology is coveted by both the Soviets and Chinese, and Japan, as the largest trading power in the Far East, represents an excellent potential market for both states. The Sino-Soviet dispute, which led to a reduction in China's trade with the USSR, served to increase trade between China and Japan and the establishment of diplomatic relations in 1972 accentuated this trend (trade totaled $3.3 billion in 1974, up from $1.1 billion in 1972). Japan is especially interested in Chinese oil while China wants fertilizers, synthetic textile plants, and steel products.[13] Soviet observers are concerned about the growing economic ties between China and Japan and, with some justification, they have accused China of trying to inhibit Soviet-Japanese trade. China is charged with warning Japan about its opposition to Siberian development projects and with stressing the unreliability of the USSR as a trading partner.[14]

The Soviet Union has for many years been seeking Japanese credits and equipment in return for Siberian raw materials and negotiations took place as early as 1962.[15] In 1964, Anastas Mikoyan proposed that a Japanese–Soviet committee be established to deal with the development of trade relations and an agreement of June 1965 established the Japan–Soviet Economic Cooperation Committee.[16] The first meeting took place in March 1966.

The Soviet Union and Japan have reached numerous agreements on Siberian development. In July 1968, Japan extended credits to cover the purchase of Japanese forestry machinery, and in return the Soviets were to deliver lumber to Japan.[17] A further agreement, of December 1971, dealt with wood chip and pulp production. In December 1970, Japan provided $80 million in credits to finance the construction of a port on Wrangel Bay, 30 kilometers (18.6 miles) north of Nakhodka. Temporarily called Vostochnyi Port, it will eventually be the Soviet Union's largest commercial port on the Pacific. Japan is to be repaid with Siberian raw materials and this new port should facilitate Soviet exports.[18] In March 1974, the USSR and Japan agreed in principle that Japan would import coal from the Chulman area, south of Yakutsk.[19] Deliveries may not begin until 1983 and they should then be at the rate of about six million tons per year.[20]

The USSR and Japan have encountered many difficulties while trying to arrive at major agreements on Siberian oil and gas. Japan has been highly reticent because it considers Soviet credit and investment demands excessive, particularly the Soviet insistence on receiving credit on terms usually reserved only for poor Third World states. Japan also wants the USSR to buy more Japanese products as part of any agreement and it is wary about having all of its credits returned in the form of deferred fuel payments. Disagreements on the transport of fuel are also basic, as is Japanese uneasiness over the fact that the Soviets do not provide sufficient technical information to warrant such large Japanese expenditures. In addition, many members of the ruling Liberal Democratic Party have an aversion to dealing with a communist-ruled state and there is also the crucial issue of Japanese territorial claims on islands presently controlled by the Soviets.[21] Japan's fears about partial energy dependence on the USSR and about offending China are of utmost importance, as is American indecision on possible participation along with the Japanese. Japan wants American political support and the inclusion of American investment capital and is reluctant to enter Siberian energy deals on its own. As the U.S. ponders its future energy policies and grapples with Congressional restrictions on trade with the USSR, Japan is forced to bide its time. It even postponed negotiations with the USSR from July to October 1974 to seek clarification of the American position.[22]

In general, the Soviets have been more anxious than the Japanese to conclude Siberian energy agreements, especially in regard to natural gas. However, they have not been pleased with the Japanese credit offers, they have not wanted to supply the quantity of oil desired by the Japanese, and they have been distressed by Japan's hesitation over the Yakutsk gas project. As David Hitchcock Jr. of the United States Information Agency perceptively argues, the Soviet Union and Japan each sees itself as having the more solid bargaining position. The Soviets believe that their fuel resources are essential to Japan while the Japanese think that their market, capital and technology are critical to the USSR.[23]

In their economic negotiations, the Soviets are able to present a consistent line indicative of state policy, but the Japanese delegates usually represent conflicting business interests.[24] Japanese participation in Siberian energy projects would be carried out by private capitalist firms, although credits from Japan's Export-Import Bank would be provided. The Soviets can therefore take advantage of splits within the Japanese ranks and *The Economist* has suggested that they have attempted to play off competing groups interested in Tiumen oil and Yakutsk gas.[25]

The Soviets and Japanese have made modest progress in their energy negotiations regarding Sakhalin and there is now a cooperative search for offshore oil and gas. Sakhalin is a Soviet-owned island just north of Japan, and the proximity has made the Japanese particularly interested in Sakhalin energy projects. Sakhalin produces less than 1 percent of the Soviet Union's crude oil but there may be ample offshore reserves.[26] It provides 30 to 40 percent of the needs of the Soviet Far East and strategic considerations related to the Sino-Soviet dispute (such as providing fuel for the Pacific fleet) have led the Soviets to emphasize Sakhalin oil development, despite the costs involved.[27] The oil industry on Sakhalin is faced with high operational costs, owing to inclement weather and geographical remoteness, and worker productivity is low. Well output is lower than the national average, and during the period 1966–70, exploration costs were 4.3 times the national average when one relates expenses to the quantity of oil found.[28] Also problematic is the fact that there is no refinery on Sakhalin and crude oil is sent by underwater pipeline to Komsomolsk on the mainland for refining. This may facilitate the distribution of refined products in the Far East, but the oil to be used on Sakhalin must be piped back from the Komsomolsk refinery.[29] The Far East must partially rely on Sakhalin oil because the pipeline extending eastward from the Western Siberian oil fields goes only as far as Irkutsk and it is expensive to transport the oil to the Far East by train or truck.

Sakhalin is basically used to provide oil for the Far East, and its ports are frozen in winter. Therefore perhaps as little as 10 percent of Soviet oil exports to Japan, originate in Sakhalin, the remainder coming from Black Sea ports, the Trans-Siberian Railroad, or Middle East switch deals.[30] If the Siberian oil pipeline is eventually extended to Nakhodka, thus furnishing Western Siberian oil for the Soviet Far East, there is a strong likelihood that more Sakhalin oil will be exported to Japan through a new pipeline built exclusively for that purpose, but it now appears that the construction of a Siberian pipeline east of Irkutsk is still far in the future. Perhaps the completion of the Baikal–Amur Mainline railroad will serve the same purpose, but that too will take many more years.

Japan had a strong interest in importing northern Sakhalin natural gas, which was to flow through a projected pipeline from Sakhalin to the northernmost Japanese island of Hokkaido. An agreement with the USSR was almost reached in 1969. The Soviets, who were anxious to secure Japanese assistance in the exploitation of Yakutsk's huge reserves, then indicated that a Japanese commitment to collaborate on Yakutsk gas development would have to be linked with any Sakhalin deal. The Japanese balked at any such linkage, and were hesitant about extending extensive credits for the Yakutsk project since they had not been supplied with sufficient technical data and they had not had the opportunity to examine the area firsthand.[31] The Japanese therefore preferred to conclude a Sakhalin gas deal and to delay a decision on Yakutsk until later.

The Soviets claimed that they had overestimated the gas reserves in northern Sakhalin and they continued to push for a Yakutsk agreement.[32] At a meeting of the Japan–Soviet Economic Cooperation Committee in Moscow in February 1970, Prime Minister Alexei Kosygin proposed that a pipeline be built from Yakutsk to the port of Magadan, where the gas would then be liquefied for shipment to Japan. He claimed that Japan could receive greater quantities of gas than it would from a Sakhalin–Hokkaido pipeline and he indicated that the unit cost could possibly be lower. He also pointed out that by shipping the gas from Magadan, deliveries could be made to any part of Japan, whereas a pipeline from Sakhalin would serve only Hokkaido.[33] Despite Kosygin's arguments, the Japanese refused to enter into a Yakutsk deal at that time and the Sakhalin project was therefore held in abeyance as well.

Although no agreement has been reached on northern Sakhalin natural gas, there is cooperative exploitation of Sakhalin's offshore oil and gas deposits. An agreement in principle was reached on November 24, 1972, and a formal agreement was signed in January 1975.[34] Japan is to provide $100 million for a five-year oil and gas search off the northeastern and southwestern shores of Sakhalin and an additional $52.5 million for procurement costs and computer analyses. The money is to be supplied by a combination of government and private interests and, if the search is successful, Japan will be repaid with crude oil or natural gas deliveries over a ten-year period. Japan will also have the option to purchase as much as 50 percent of the oil and gas found, at prevailing world prices. If no oil or gas is found, Japan will not be repaid but it may provide $100 million for a further five years of exploration.[35] Four Japanese companies have joined to form the Sakhalin Oil Development Cooperation Company and test drilling is to begin in the spring of 1977. American companies may possibly participate by selling equipment and computers. Gulf Oil is likely to be involved, and Atlantic Richfield may also enter the project, since it has negotiated with both the Soviets and Japanese on this subject.[36] The Soviets are stressing Sakhalin oil development partly because of their concern about Chinese oil exports to Japan. They do not want Japan to become too dependent on Chinese energy and they therefore hope to increase their own oil exports to Japan from the most convenient geographical location, Sakhalin.

The Yakutsk Gas Project

The Yakutsk area of Eastern Siberia has an estimated 450 trillion cubic feet of gas reserves, 8 trillion in proven reserves, but its gas resources are now exploited only to a very limited extent to supply energy for local needs.[37] The Soviets would like to expand Yakutsk gas production and have tried to encourage both Japanese and American participation. Japan and the United States would have to provide $3.4 billion between them, some of this financing to be in the form of government credits and the remainder to be raised by private interests.[38] In addition, funds must also be supplied for a preliminary survey of the area. Japan and the U.S. would each receive 10 billion cubic meters of gas annually for 20 to 25 years and the USSR would derive an equal amount of gas from the joint project.[39]

There are three possible routes for Yakutsk gas exports. One is by pipeline to Magadan, where the gas would then be liquefied for shipment by sea; another is by a longer pipeline to Nakhodka for liquefication and shipment; a third alternative would have the gas piped all the way to Tomakomai, Hokkaido, via Sakhalin. The Japanese, if they are to participate in the project at all, seem to prefer the pipeline to Tomakomai since it would bring the gas directly to Japan. Furthermore, Tomakomai is not far from the industrial center of Muroran and energy could be supplied efficiently. Tomakomai is also a major port and some of the gas could be liquefied for delivery to other Japanese islands. The United States leans toward the first two options since a pipeline to Tomakomai adds to the cost of the project and provides no direct benefits to the United States.[40]

Before the Arab oil embargo, American companies had displayed a serious interest in the Yakutsk project while Japan was rather hesitant. Since then, Japan has become more enthusiastic while the U.S. Congress has disrupted the plans of American companies by stressing eventual energy self-sufficiency and by withholding any Export-Import Bank credits.

In June 1973, three U.S. firms and the USSR signed a letter of intent to develop Yakutsk gas resources.[41] Japan was proceeding cautiously, but the following month it did agree to send a joint Japanese–American technical delegation to Yakutsk to look into the feasibility of large-scale gas production (the delegation arrived in Eastern Siberia in December) and it also signed a letter of intent with the USSR to help develop Yakutsk gas resources.[42] Nevertheless, when Soviet–Japanese economic negotiations were held in Tokyo in August 1973, the Japanese were unenthusiastic about supplying credits for the Yakutsk project; after the sessions, the Soviet First Deputy Minister of Foreign Trade, Ivan Semichastnov, pointedly failed to mention Yakutsk while discussing Soviet–Japanese economic collaboration.[43] At the same time, Japanese Prime Minister Tanaka was telling his *Pravda* interviewer that it would be more difficult to reach agreement on Yakutsk gas than on Tiumen oil.[44]

By April 1974, Japan was anxious to look into new sources of energy and its Export-Import Bank combined with private firms to provide $99 million for a survey of Yakutsk gas reserves. However, Japan did not want to act without U.S. participation and it decided to postpone any survey until such time as the U.S. would contribute matching funds. By agreeing to conduct a survey, Japan was not signifying its willingness to enter the Yakutsk project. It was only delaying decision until it acquired a better knowledge of the prospects for Yakutsk gas exploitation.

Meanwhile, the United States Congress was reluctant to support the import of energy from the USSR, and the appropriation of $49.5 million in Export-Import Bank credits was stalled. Private companies were to have provided the other half of the credit.[45] The Soviets wanted Japan to proceed with the survey, even without U.S. participation, but at a November meeting of Soviet, American, and Japanese trade specialists in Paris, the Japanese made it clear that their credits for a gas survey would be released only if the Americans extended matching credits.[46] The Japanese do not want to bear the entire financial burden of the Yakutsk project and they would like an American contribution of pipeline, compressors, and ships capable of transporting liquefied natural gas. The American companies interested in joining with the Japanese are the El Paso Natural Gas Company, Occidental Petroleum Company, and Bechtel Incorporated.

For their part, the Chinese prefer American inclusion in any Yakutsk deal so that the Soviets would have more difficulty in pushing the Japanese into an anti-Chinese position by economic pressure. It should be pointed out that the Chinese have fewer objections to Yakutsk gas development than they do to Tiumen oil development. Gas is less important militarily and it cannot fuel the Soviet Pacific fleet.[47]

The Tiumen Oil Project

The possibility of building an oil pipeline extending from Tiumen in Western Siberia to Nakhodka on the Pacific coast has been discussed by the Soviets and Japanese for almost twenty years but it seems unlikely that such a venture will reach fruition in the near future. The USSR has benefited economically from the rise in world oil prices and is more capable than ever before of developing Siberian oil resources without Japanese financial assistance. It has therefore reduced the quantity of oil offered to Japan as repayment for Japanese credits, preferring to retain large stocks of oil for eventual use in the USSR and Eastern Europe; it has also decided to build a new railroad across Siberia which will transport oil as well as raw materials. The construction of an oil pipeline has thus been postponed. Japan has suffered as a result of high oil prices and is reluctant to invest a substantial sum in the Tiumen project. American indecision has also forced Japan to bide its time. Furthermore, its prospects for importing significant quantities of Chinese oil without having to invest any capital have helped cool its interest in a Tiumen deal.

Soviet-Japanese discussions about Tiumen oil began during the late fifties and the subject was on the agenda at the first meeting of the Japan–Soviet Economic Cooperation Committee in March, 1966.[48] An oil pipeline from Tiumen to Nakhodka would cover 7000 kilometers (4340 miles) but only 4700 kilometers (2914 miles) of new construction would be necessary since an existing pipeline already extends from Tiumen as far east as Irkutsk.[49] Japan's share of the cost for oilfield exploitation and pipeline construction was to have been about $1.5 billion, plus the provision of pipe, but the figure could rise to $3 billion.[50] Japan has generally imported a few million tons of crude oil per year from the USSR, a small part being transported from Tiumen to Nakhodka by pipeline and railroad, but an agreement on the Tiumen project would greatly increase Soviet oil exports to Japan. The Soviets were at first offering the Japanese 10–12 million tons per year but the Japanese, unwilling to accept so little oil in return for their investment, asked for 50 million tons. By 1972, both sides were thinking in the neighborhood of 40 million tons, but in August 1973 the Soviets indicated that they could supply only 25 million tons.[51] The quantities of oil cited refer to annual deliveries under a twenty-year contract and any agreement would take at least four years to become operational because of the need to build a new pipeline.

If Japan were to participate in the Tiumen project, it would receive a very small percentage of its oil requirements from the Soviet Union, perhaps 5 to 8 percent. However, it would be diversifying its sources of supply to become less dependent on unreliable shipments from the Middle East. In addition, it could conceivably arrange some switch deals with Middle East states to cut down on transportation costs. Middle East states that regularly ship oil to Japan could send it to the Soviet Union instead, and in return the

Soviets could export an equivalent amount of Tiumen oil to Japan.[52]

Before 1972, technical considerations, costs, and the possible political side effects of participation combined to discourage Japanese investment in the Tiumen project but a new enthusiasm was kindled in early 1972. Japan had previously been given very little technical data about Tiumen oil reserves and the prospects for drilling but, in February, the Soviets finally agreed to permit Japanese examination of the Tiumen area and the Japanese surveying team arrived in May.[53] Its appraisal was favorable and Prime Minister Tanaka began to lean toward concluding a deal with the Soviets.[54] At the same time, the United States was seriously considering participation, which could have helped the Japanese in two ways: The U.S. would share some of the costs and U.S. involvement would eliminate the likelihood of Japanese–American, as well as Japanese–Chinese, political friction over a bilateral Japanese–Soviet agreement.

U.S. Secretary of Commerce, Maurice Stans, went to the USSR in November 1971, and he indicated that the U.S. was interested in joint Siberian projects with the USSR.[55] In May 1972, he stated that harmonious Soviet–American relations could assure the U.S. of a "safe supply" of oil and gas and Nixon's summit meeting with Brezhnev that same month, with its spirit of détente, served to increase the prospects for energy cooperation.[56] Gulf, Exxon, and Occidental all displayed interest in the Tiumen project.[57]

Japan had mixed feelings about the new American stance on Tiumen. Collaboration with the United States would bring many advantages, but Japan could not forget that the United States had constantly pressured her not to participate in the Tiumen project. Now, all of a sudden, the U.S. had changed course and Japan had to consider the possibility that the U.S. would try to push her aside by concluding bilateral energy agreements with the USSR. Although Japan was not pleased with the American methods, it decided that cooperation with the U.S. was the wisest course. It would be economically and politically beneficial and would help shortcircuit any Soviet–American deals at the expense of Japan.[58]

In August 1972, the Japanese Minister of International Trade and Industry, Yashuhiro Nakasone, declared that his country would welcome American participation in the Tiumen project and Nixon told Tanaka at their Honolulu summit of August 31–September 1 that the U.S. was considering cooperation with Japan on Tiumen.[59]

The Soviet Union could have attempted to drive a wedge between Japan and the United States by reaching a bilateral agreement with Japan but including the United States was seen as more advantageous.[60] The U.S., in order to protect any Tiumen investment, would tend to support Soviet Siberian interests in case the Chinese challenge ever becomes more serious and the U.S. could certainly provide highly sophisticated technology for the Tiumen project. In addition, Japan was reluctant to enter without the U.S. The Soviets therefore showed a willingness to work out a trilateral agreement on Tiumen but they left the decision on American inclusion up to the Japanese.

Both Japan and the United States were trying to improve relations with China in 1972 and this caused them to go slow on Siberian energy deals with the Soviet Union. Then, in January 1973, a new ingredient was added when China agreed to export crude oil to Japan. The quantity was very small but there was speculation that the Chinese could eventually match the 40 million tons per year offered by the USSR. Once Japan was assured of Chinese oil deliveries, it hardened its position in the Tiumen negotiations with the USSR. On March 6, Tanaka sent a letter to Brezhnev in which he linked the Tiumen project with the return to Japan of some islands occupied by the Soviet Union since the end of the Second World War.[61] In his response of March 28, Brezhnev invited Tanaka to come to Moscow and an August date was arranged for the visit. However, the Soviets were irritated by Tanaka's linkage of the territorial issue with economic negotiations and they also realized that it was too late to forestall a Japanese rapprochement with China by encouraging Japanese involvement in Siberian projects. In addition, the world energy crisis was becoming more severe, the price of oil was rising, and the Soviets wanted to reconsider their long-range energy policies.

Accordingly, they announced in June that Tanaka's August visit would have to be delayed until a later date and they also postponed the Tiumen oil talks scheduled for June and a meeting of the Japan–Soviet Economic Cooperation Committee which was to have met in July.[62]

The Soviets tried to keep the Tiumen project alive as a possibility while they pondered their future energy plans. Soviet periodicals stressed the impact Tiumen oil would have on the western part of the Japanese island of Honshu and claimed that the Tiumen negotiations, "after a comprehensive and painstaking study, are now entering a practical phase."[63] Nevertheless, the Soviets had lost some of their interest in such a large-scale project with the Japanese, partially because they were becoming more capable of funding Tiumen development without outside assistance. Their earnings from oil sales would enable them to buy significant quantities of Western oilfield equipment, whereas their shortage of hard currency in 1972 and early 1973 had led to a decline in purchases of such equipment.[64] In August 1973, the Soviet Union informed Japan that it was willing to provide only 25 million tons per year of Tiumen oil since it needed most of the Tiumen production for domestic energy requirements.[65] This Soviet position greatly reduced the possibility that an agreement could be reached with Japan, since the Japanese wanted much larger deliveries of Tiumen oil.

When Tanaka came to the Soviet Union in early October, the Soviets repeated their offer of 25 million tons and they also mentioned that they were considering a new railroad as an alternative to an oil pipeline.[66] They were no longer anxious to have Japanese assistance with the Tiumen project and therefore adopted a very hard line. Brezhnev implied that no agreements would be reached during Tanaka's visit when he stated that good relations "can scarcely be accomplished at a single stroke" and that "we may encounter still more difficulties." Adding to Soviet apprehension was the Middle East war, which erupted the day before Tanaka arrived in Moscow. The threat of an Arab oil embargo was in the air and the Soviets could not risk offending the Arabs by making an oil deal with Japan at that time. The Japanese were not especially interested in a Tiumen agreement and Tanaka again indicated that a settlement of the territorial issue was fundamental to Siberian cooperation.[67] Despite the possibility of an Arab embargo, Japan did not soften its position in order to receive Tiumen oil on Soviet terms, although the Soviets may have thought that an energy shortage would push Japan in that direction.[68]

By early 1974, the Soviets realized that Japan would not settle for a reduced flow of Tiumen oil, that it was reluctant to provide large credits to the USSR, and that it would not enter the project without the participation of an indecisive United States. The Soviets were in the process of formulating a new Five-Year Plan for 1976–80, and it was necessary to take Siberian oil development into account, so they made one final attempt to sound out the Japanese before drawing up their own future economic programs. In February 1974, Brezhnev sent a letter to Tanaka in which he pointed out that agreements on Siberian projects would have to be reached quickly if they were to be included in the next Five-Year Plan.[69] The Soviets were not optimistic about a Tiumen agreement on their terms and, on March 15, in a nationally televised speech from Alma Ata, Brezhnev announced plans for a new Siberian railroad.[70] The building of a railroad would not exclude the construction of a Tiumen oil pipeline but it would certainly make it less likely. Brezhnev's announcement, which came just before the Japanese trade delegations' arrival in Moscow, did not create an auspicious atmosphere for an oil agreement.

Japanese members of the Japan–Soviet Economic Cooperation Committee were in Moscow in late March, and they were received by both Brezhnev and Kosygin. This marked the first time that Brezhnev had ever appeared before a Japanese trade group and it signified the importance of the discussions.[71] The Soviets were probably willing to go through with the Tiumen project if the Japanese were ready to accept a modest flow of oil and they offered deliveries over a twenty-year period, starting with 5 million tons in 1981. Deliveries were to increase gradually to a level of 25 million tons per year beginning in 1985.[72] No agreement was reached while the Japanese were in Moscow, and in

April the Soviets dispatched to Tokyo a delegation headed by Vladimir Alkhimov, Deputy Minister of Foreign Trade. Again Tiumen was discussed; again the Japanese did not accept the Soviet offer because the quantity of oil was negligible and the economic risks great. They also expected to receive at least that much oil per year from China by 1985. Instead, the Japanese opted for cooperation on Yakutsk gas development and the Export-Import Bank of Japan expressed its willingness to provide the credits necessary for a Yakutsk gas survey.

On May 27, Soviet oil minister Shashin declared that the newly planned Siberian railroad, the Baikal–Amur Mainline (BAM), would transport Tiumen oil to the Pacific coast and that the proposed joint oil pipeline project with Japan was off. He indicated that Japan would have to wait seven or eight years if it wanted to buy oil transported by the railroad. He also emphasized that the Soviet Union had decided to stress energy self-sufficiency and he hinted that there would not be cooperative projects on oil and gas development.[73] On the other hand, Shashin did indicate that an oil pipeline project could again be discussed with Japan once the railroad was completed.[74] Tass charged that the Western press had distorted Shashin's remarks and it reassured Japan that it would continue to receive oil from the USSR.[75] This was certainly true but the quantity was to remain minimal throughout the seventies.

The BAM is to start northwest of Lake Baikal and extend 3145 kilometers (1950 miles) to Komsomolsk, where it will link up with an existing railroad to reach the coast at Sovetskaia Gavan. It is to be completed in 1982 but trains will run on western portions of the line before construction is finished in the east.[76] BAM is to be built from 250 to 500 kilometers (155–310 miles) north of the Trans-Siberian Railroad,which should make it fairly secure in case of a border conflict with China.[77]

BAM will encourage Siberian economic development and there are plans to construct settlements, which will eventually become cities, around the large stations. Because of the difficulties in attracting labor to such an inhospitable area, at least

20,000 Komsomols (members of the Communist Youth League) were sent to work on BAM in 1975 and truck drivers and machine operators were recruited among demobilized soldiers.[78]

BAM is to transport Tiumen oil, Udokan copper, Chulman coal (there is a 217 kilometer [124.5 mile] spur line linking it with Chulman), and timber and it will be important in opening up Siberia to settlement and industrialization. It will also have great strategic value in the event of a Soviet military buildup along the Chinese frontier. A Tiumen oil pipeline would not have so many diversified uses, although it would be able to transport more oil than BAM. In addition, a Tiumen pipeline would be less costly and the economic burden would possibly be shared by Japan and the United States. The Soviets must finance BAM by themselves since the railroad is only of minor economic benefit to either Japan or the United States. Furthermore, its military significance would discourage any Japanese or American investment, since these two states would not want to aggravate their relations with China.[79]

During the summer of 1974, the Soviets played down the issue of Tiumen oil agreements with either the United States or Japan. In an article on Soviet–American economic relations, the Soviet Journal *International Affairs* covered a broad range of topics—but not Tiumen oil.[80] In a printed conversation between Deputy Minister of Foreign Trade Vladimir Alkhimov and President of the Export-Import Bank of Japan Satoshi Sumita, the former did not comment on Tiumen oil and the latter mentioned it only in passing.[81] However, the issue was revived when the Japan–Soviet Economic Cooperation Committee met in Moscow in late October and early November. Despite Shashin's May assertion that there would not be joint energy agreements with Japan, Kosygin asked for Japanese assistance in Tiumen oil development, indicating that the oil could be exported to Japan via the Baikal–Amur Mainline. He offered deliveries of 5 million tons in 1981, 10 million in 1982, 15 million in 1983, 20 million in 1984 and 25 million per year beginning in 1985.[82] These were the same quantities which the Soviets had originally wanted to deliver through a pipeline. Kosygin is reported to have told the Japanese: "Japan will regret it later if it doesn't come to a decision now to participate in the development of the Tiumen oil fields." [83] Japan was asked to invest $3 billion in the project.

The Japanese were still reticent because of high costs, probable American nonparticipation, and an expected hostile reaction from China but they also preferred a pipeline to a railroad and were not convinced that the Soviets could supply the promised quantities. They therefore informed the Soviets that their participation in Tiumen oil development was very unlikely.[84]

Chinese opposition to a Tiumen oil pipeline (and now to BAM) has had a considerable effect on the negotiations between the USSR, Japan, and the U.S.—particularly since Japan and the U.S. effected rapprochements with China in 1972. The Chinese were concerned about the fact that the pipeline was to run close to its border and was to be covered by a paved road. Both the road and the ability to transport oil into border areas were seen as security threats. In a similar vein, the pipeline was to have provided fuel for Siberian industrialization, thus adding to Soviet military potential, and it was to have transported oil to the Far East for use by the Soviet Pacific fleet. Both the Chinese and Japanese were worried about this latter problem and Japan was not willing to finance a refinery which the Soviets wanted to build on the coast at Nakhodka.[85]

In January 1973, Chou En-lai told Japan's Minister of International Trade and Industry, Yasuhiro Nakasone, that China was somewhat alarmed about joint Japanese–Soviet development of Siberia. For example, Chou pointed out that the proposed Tiumen pipeline was capable of transporting much more oil than Japan was to import from the USSR.[86] Shortly afterward, the Chairman of the Sino-Japanese Friendship Society, Liao Cheng-chih, headed a delegation to Japan. He indicated in an interview with the Yomiuri Shimbun on March 12 that he understood Japan's interest in Tiumen oil but that this oil could be used by the Soviet military against China. He warned Japan about extending credits for a Tiumen pipeline and said that China would take "appropriate measures" if there was a Japanese–Soviet agreement. Liao asserted that China would be like a "divorced person" and would "harbor a bitter feeling." [87] The Soviets accused Liao of interfering in Soviet–Japanese relations and of trying to "sabotage the reaching of an accord." [88]

There seemed to have been some momentum in the Tiumen negotiations by 1972 but anticipated Chinese objections to the project probably cooled Japanese and American enthusiasm and helped prevent progress toward an agreement. Japan and the U.S. were trying to improve relations with China and the Tiumen issue was sure to cause offense. In 1973, the Chinese strongly set forth their position on Tiumen but, more significantly, they began to supply Japan with crude oil. These deliveries served their intended purpose of reducing Japanese interest in Tiumen oil.

Northern Territories and Collective Security

Toward the end of the Second World War, the Soviet Union occupied four islands that had previously belonged to Japan: Kunashiri, Etorofu, Shikotan, and Habomai (the latter is actually a grouping of small islands) and they are still under Soviet control. They are located just north of the Japanese island of Hokkaido and whether or not they constitute part of the Kurile Islands is a matter in dispute. Japan obviously would like to see these four islands returned to her sovereignty and this territorial controversy is closely tied in with the fact that no Soviet–Japanese peace treaty officially ending the Second World War has yet been concluded. These twin issues of the "northern territories" and a peace treaty have consistently interfered with Soviet–Japanese negotiations on joint Siberian economic development, and since 1969 the related Soviet call for "collective security" in Asia has also been fundamental to these negotiations.

Basically, Japan wants to link the territorial and peace treaty issues with possible Siberian agreements, hoping to reacquire the islands in return for the provision of large credits. Some Japanese businessmen, anxious to invest in Siberia, have wanted to further their own economic welfare by divorcing the former issues from Siberian development programs, but they have not been successful in trying to influence their government's position.[89] The Soviet Union does not want to return all of the islands to Japan and insists that there should be no connection between territorial and economic questions. It also charges that China is encouraging Japan to make territorial claims against the USSR.[90] The four islands are not of great importance to the Soviets but they fear that the return of these islands would set a precedent leading to renewed Chinese claims on Soviet territory.

On August 9, 1955, Soviet diplomat Jacob Malik informed a Japanese counterpart, Shunichi Matsumoto, that the USSR was willing to return Habomai and Shikotan and Soviet Foreign Minister Dmitrii Shepilov indicated the same thing in August 1956.[91] Shepilov maintained that the USSR would return the islands after the conclusion of a peace treaty, but Japan refused the offers of Malik and Shepilov, insisting on the reversion of all four islands.[92] Japan was evidently ready to renounce its claims to southern Sakhalin and the Kuriles if the Soviets agreed to return Kunashiri and Etorofu, in addition to Habomai and Shikotan.[93] Japan and the Soviet Union established diplomatic relations on October 19, 1956, but the territorial issue was not resolved.

An extra ingredient was added to the controversy on June 8, 1969, when Brezhnev proposed a "collective security" system in Asia. Despite Soviet denials, collective security was generally aimed at the containment of Chinese influence (it should be pointed out that Brezhnev's proposal came shortly after the March battle at Ussuri).[94] Although somewhat vague, the collective security system implied recognition of the existing territorial status quo in Asia and it was therefore pertinent to the northern territories dispute. The Soviet Union wanted Japan to endorse the concept of collective security but Japan continued to demand the return of the four islands. Japan has continued to resist Soviet calls for collective security but may make some gesture toward the Soviets if it is given all four islands. Of course, the Japanese would not join any concrete collective security network or alliance, since it would be directed against China, but Japan could conceivably endorse some general principles of peace and noninterference in the affairs of other states.

In January 1972, Soviet Foreign Minister Gromyko rushed to Japan just before Nixon's visit to China. He wanted to prevent the establishment of close relations between Japan and China and proposed that the Soviet Union and Japan should hold talks on a peace treaty within the coming year. Gromyko was therefore implying that the territorial issue was subject to discussion.[95] Nevertheless, Japan established diplomatic relations with China in September. In order to display their anger, the Soviets reverted to a hard line on the "northern territories," and Brezhnev did not receive Japanese Foreign Minister Ohira when he journeyed to Moscow in October 1972.[96]

As far as Japan was concerned, progress on Siberian economic projects was closely related to the northern territories dispute, as Tanaka indicated in his March 1973 letter to Brezhnev. The USSR still wanted to conclude a peace treaty with Japan, but it would not return all four islands or link the territorial and economic issues. While advocating a peace treaty, the Soviets asked the Japanese to be "realistic and businesslike"—in other words, to accept Soviet control over Kunashiri and Etorofu and proceed with Siberian negotiations nevertheless.[97] When Tanaka made his delayed visit to Moscow in October 1973, he again raised the territorial issue. The Soviets probably offered to return Habomai and Shikotan but the Japanese held out for all four islands.[98] No agreement was reached on either territorial or economic questions and the Soviet journal New Times declared: "It is also natural that the results of the talks should have displeased the quarters in Japan that make unjustified territorial claims upon the Soviet Union." [99] The journal was expressing the official line that no territory would be conceded, although in private the Soviets have shown greater flexibility, indicating a willingness to give up two islands for Japanese concessions on credits or collective security.

Soviet reticence to return all four islands has encouraged Japan to look more favorably upon peace treaty negotiations with China. Japan did sign a peace treaty with the Chiang Kai-shek government in 1952, but there has never been a peace treaty between Japan and the Peking government. There are no significant territorial obstacles, as Japan relinquished its claim to Taiwan in the 1951 peace treaty with the United States, but a controversy has developed over the inclusion of an anti-hegemony clause. China has wanted to make an oblique criticism of the Soviet Union by inserting a clause condemning any state that attempts to assert its hegemony over Asia; Japan, for fear of offending the Soviets, has shied away from concluding a treaty that includes this clause.[100] However, Japan indicated a major policy shift in January 1976, following Gromyko's visit to Tokyo. Gromyko apparently turned down Japanese demands for the four contested islands and he strongly warned Japan about concluding a peace treaty with China. Piqued by Gromyko's attitude, Prime Minister Takeo Miki announced just hours after the Soviet foreign minister's departure that Japan was willing to accept the Chinese-sponsored anti-hegemony clause as part of a Sino-Japanese peace treaty. Miki also took the occasion to label Japan's "equidistance" policy regarding relations with the Soviet Union and China a "myth." [101]

The American Stance

Ever since 1972, Japan has favored American participation in the Tiumen, Yakutsk, and Sakhalin projects but the leisurely American pace has often caused Japan to go slow in its negotiations with the USSR. Speaking in Japan on July 16, 1973, U.S. Secretary of State William Rogers, in discussing "sound international energy policy," advocated "multinational efforts to expand oil and gas production in the Soviet Union and elsewhere. If the Japanese Government wishes, we will encourage our firms to consider joint ventures with Japanese companies, though final investment decisions will of course be made by the investors." [102] Despite such encouragement from the U.S. executive branch, snags developed in Congress over the provision of Export-Import Bank credits and the only progress made so far has been on the small Sakhalin offshore exploration project. The concept of tripartite economic cooperation is not problematic, since it has been endorsed by all three parties, but the Soviets are unwilling to let the Americans attach "strings," such as the "Jackson amendment." [103]

Although American firms have failed to reach final contracts with the USSR on Tiumen oil or Yakutsk gas, they have been active in selling equipment to the Soviets. In December 1969, Congress liberalized the Export Control Act, thus permitting the sale of oil equipment to communist-ruled states.[104] Then, in July–August 1970, Soviet oil minister Shashin headed a delegation to the U.S. whose purpose was to buy American equipment, and numerous sales to the USSR followed.[105] From October 23 to 31, 1973, during the Arab oil embargo, 189 American firms were showing their oil wares at a Moscow exhibition.[106] Furthermore, the Soviets have been negotiating with a number of American companies, hoping to receive equipment in return for a percentage of the oil extracted. They believe that American technology can help them exploit wells more completely, particularly those which are nearly depleted.[107] The Soviets are somewhat sensitive about the fact that their technologically oriented society must seek equipment from a capitalist state, so they contend that the USSR has sophisticated technology to offer the U.S. They point to electric generators and equipment for electric transmission lines and also cite Soviet know-how regarding dams, hydroelectric stations, thermal electric poser, atomic energy, underground heat, and solar energy.[108]

On July 14, 1972, Occidental Petroleum reached a multifaceted agreement with the USSR. According to its provisions, Occidental was to contribute technology and patents and was to receive some oil and gas in return. Occidental was also to construct a fertilizer plant near Kuibyshev and an international trade center in Moscow and one Soviet journalist described the deal as the largest in the history of international trade, totaling $8 billion over a twenty-year period.[109] The Soviets had particular interest in cooperating with Occidental because its chairman, Armand Hammer, has had economic dealings with the USSR since the days of Lenin. However, there does not yet appear to be any implementation of the agreements regarding oil and gas, partially because they are bound up with the continuing discussions about Yakutsk and Tiumen.

An extra ingredient was added to Soviet–American oil negotiations in the fall of 1975, when the disastrous Soviet failure in grain production led to a large grain deal between the two states. The grain negotiations also dealt with the oil issue as the United States was anxious to link the two commodities on a long-term basis. The Soviets wanted to separate the trade transactions—probably so they would not appear to be entering into the grain agreement from a position of weakness which forced them to supply oil in return—but some linkage is practically automatic because the tankers carrying American grain to the USSR frequently return with Soviet oil. Another problem regarding the trade negotiations was price. The Soviets were willing to buy American grain at the prevailing market prices but the Americans were asking for an oil price discount of about 15 percent. The U.S. wanted to provide a signal to OPEC which could possibly have led to a reduction in world prices. Domestic political considerations were also evident; the government wanted to make additional oil reliance on the USSR more palatable to the public by pointing to a low price tag. The Soviets obviously wanted to be paid at the world price level and they did not want to offend their Arab allies by undercutting them with discounted oil. In October 1975, a five-year grain pact was signed and the Soviets had their way by separating the grain and oil agreements. An oil pact was held in abeyance, subject to later negotiations, but the grain pact did indicate that the United States would have an option to buy 10 million tons of Soviet oil per year, about ten times the present level of American imports. The price issue was left unresolved.[110]

A major concern in energy negotiations between the Soviet Union and United States is the "North Star" gas project. Japan is in no way involved with North Star, which would bring Western Siberian natural gas to the East Coast of the United States. A letter of intent was signed in June 1973, but no final agreement has been reached.[111] The American companies participating in the negotiations are Tenneco, Texas Eastern Transmission, and Brown and Root.[112] According to the North Star plan, natural gas from the Urengoi fields would be piped to the Barents Sea port of Pet-samo, just west of Murmansk. It would then be liquefied to 1/600 of its volume and sent by special LNG tankers to West Deptford, New Jersey, a Delaware River port near Philadelphia.[113] Even though the Soviets have a gas pipeline network extending to the Baltic Sea, the North Star would have to be exported via the Arctic, since the Baltic is too shallow to handle the large LNG super-tankers which would be required for the project.[114] In contrast with the Yakutsk gas project, large reserves of gas have already been proven to exist at Urengoi and the Soviets began working these gas fields in January 1974.

The North Star contract would cover gas deliveries for 25 years. American credits would be repaid in 12 years by 75 percent of the gas and the remaining 25 percent would be used to buy American goods. During the last 13 years of the contract, all of the gas would be used for this latter purpose.[115] About $20 billion of gas would be delivered over the 25 years, but the value of the gas is certainly subject to change—especially if gas and oil prices are linked as Minister of Foreign Trade Patolichev has suggested.[116] There are various estimates of North Star's cost but it appears that American firms and the Export-Import Bank will have to come up with $6 billion while the Soviets will provide $1.5 billion. In fact, the Deputy Chairman of the State Committee for Science and Technology, Dzherman Gvishiani, has indicated that there will be no joint project unless the U.S. supplies approximately $6 billion.[117] About $2.3 billion of the American cost will be for the construction of liquefied natural gas tankers and the U.S. would also furnish pipelines and compressors.[118]

It is estimated that North Star could provide 2.5 percent of American gas needs in 1980 and .6 percent of total national energy requirements. However, it would supply 11.5 percent of the gas used in the area served by the project—an area extending from Maine to Tennessee.[119] The American companies participating in the North Star negotiations claim that they will proceed even without Export-Import Bank credits since they are capable of raising funds in Western Europe.[120] On the other hand, the Soviets have become impatient about American delays and have already started to exploit Urengoi natural gas by themselves.[121] However, large-scale shipments of gas to the U.S. would require American inclusion in the project and Gvishiani has said that if the U.S. wants North Star, it must pay for it.[122]

U.S. energy relations with the Soviet Union must be viewed in the broader context of U.S.–Soviet trade to analyze their development adequately. During the period 1966–73, Soviet exports to the U.S. rose from $49.4 million to $213.7 million while American exports to the USSR rose from $41.7 million to $1.19 billion.[123] As trade grew, the United States built up a large positive balance since the USSR purchased significant quantities of grain and industrial equipment, although the USSR did manage to export more than it imported in 1966 and 1968. In 1972, total trade amounted to $642.1 million ($546.7 million in U.S. exports and $95.4 million in Soviet exports) and, in 1973, approximately $1.4 billion ($1.19 billion in U.S. exports and $213.7 million in Soviet exports).[124] This trade helps the U.S. balance of payments, and probably keeps more Americans employed, while the Soviets benefit by securing sophisticated technology. Although the Soviets are running up a trade deficit with the United States, it is possible that present purchases from the U.S. will assist the USSR in developing Siberia, thus creating the potential for an eventual expansion of exports. This is certainly the Soviet plan regarding energy exploitation in Yakutsk and Urengoi.

Both the United States and the Soviet Union claim that trade promotes the political atmosphere of détente and they therefore seek a long-term economic relationship. The Soviets even cite Lenin's support for U.S.–Soviet trade and his willingness to let Americans invest in the Soviet Union.[125] However, they are quick to point out that any American investment will be in a project owned by the Soviet state and laid out in accordance with Soviet state plans. Americans will not be allowed to participate in the direction of joint enterprises, although ways can be found for U.S. companies to "obtain definite benefits." [126] From the American point of view, investments in the Soviet Union may bring profits and an adequate supply of energy. In addition, encouraging growth efforts in Siberia could possibly turn Soviet priorities away from defense-oriented industries and U.S. sharing in the enterprises could help undermine the centralized system of economic decision-making.[127]

Soviet–American trade was long obstructed by the problems of the Soviet Union's Second World War Lend Lease debt to the United States. The United States was unwilling to extend "most favored nation" (MFN) status or Export-Import Bank credits to the USSR unless the Soviets agreed to repay the debt and progress was not made on this issue until the Nixon-Brezhnev summit in May 1972. At that time, the Soviets promised to pay $722 million if the U.S. relaxed its restrictions and formal agreements were signed on October 18, 1972.[128] U.S. Secretary of State William Rogers and Soviet Minister of Foreign Trade Nikolai Patolichev signed the Lend Lease accord, and President Nixon made the USSR eligible for Export-Import Bank credits, maintaining that it was "in the national interest." A trade agreement was signed the same day by Patolichev and U.S. Secretary of Commerce Peter Peterson and Soviet–American trade started to grow substantially.[129] However, the question of MFN status for the USSR ran into considerable difficulty in Congress.

The Soviet Union enjoyed MFN status from 1935 to 1951, when it was revoked because of the Korean War. Soviet natural gas and oil exports to the U.S. would be affected very little by the absence of MFN, since the U.S. levies no tariff on liquefied natural gas and only minimal tariffs on some oil products. In fact, only 10 percent of Soviet exports to the United States are treated in a discriminatory manner due to the lack of MFN but, as explained by Soviet spokesman Ivan Ivanov, the USSR refrains from exporting certain goods to the U.S. because they would be heavily tariffed.[130]

On October 4, 1972, Senator Henry Jackson of Washington introduced an amendment to the "East-West Trade Relations Bill" which denied MFN status to the USSR unless it made concessions on its emigration policies. In regard to MFN, the Jackson amendment did not really interfere with possible Soviet–American energy cooperation, since fuels were scarcely tariffed anyway, but this amendment also linked Export-Import Bank credits to freer

Soviet emigration and this was indeed crucial. Without such credits, American participation in the Tiumen, Yakutsk, and "North Star" projects would be rather unlikely.

The Soviets vehemently attacked the Jackson amendment, asserting that politics and foreign trade should not be mixed. They claimed that no concessions should be called for in return for MFN since MFN was the natural status for international trade and its absence was inherently discriminatory. The Soviets were especially concerned about the American attempt to influence Soviet emigration laws and Ivan Ivanov declared: "In fact, we find ourselves pressed to pay a political price, even in the form of intervention into our domestic affairs, for trade normalization. We cannot afford such a linkage." [131]

Despite public Soviet opposition to the Jackson amendment, it appears that the Soviets did privately assure the American government that they would permit an increase in emigration in exchange for MFN status and Export-Import (Ex-Im) credits. Because of this apparent assurance, Jackson and his supporters reached a compromise with the executive branch in October 1974, according to which the President was authorized to extend trade privileges to the USSR for a trial period of 18 months. Renewal or suspension of such privileges would then depend on Soviet adherence to its promise regarding increased emigration. On December 20, Congress enacted legislation activating this compromise solution but it also placed severe restrictions on the Ex-Im credits which could be given to the USSR. It limited credits to $300 million over a four-year period, placed a ceiling of $40 million on credits for oil and gas exploration, and refused any credits for oil and gas production. [132]

The Congressional hard line on the extension of credits was attuned to a new American attitude toward energy agreements with the Soviet Union. First of all, détente had somewhat soured since the Soviets had encouraged the Arab oil embargo and obstructed American peace efforts in the Middle East by sending large quantities of arms to Syria. The embargo also raised fears that the Soviets could eventually embargo energy exports to the United States or threaten to raise fuel prices to apply political pressure in the Arab manner.[133] Among the concerned voices was Harry Schwartz, a member of the editorial board of *The New York Times.* While the Arab embargo was still in its infancy, he warned against oil or gas deals with the USSR because the result could be an attempt by the Soviets to secure political leverage.[134] *The Washington Post* editorially opposed energy agreements with the USSR because it had shown its unreliability by supporting the Arab embargo and the *Post* suggested that the Soviets could use the embargo tactic against the United States. It went on to assert: "Given the uncertainties of both trade and détente, both countries might do better at this point to steer their economic relations into less politically roiled waters." [135] One Western oil expert quipped that investing in Siberian oil would be "a way of diversifying the West's insecurity." [136]

In addition to the lesson of the Arab embargo, doubts were raised about the economic feasibility of investing in Siberian energy projects in return for deliveries of oil and gas. Senator Frank Church (Democrat of Idaho), Chairman of the Subcommittee on Multinational Corporations of the Senate Foreign Relations Committee, said that he saw "no justification" for gas deals with the USSR and that he was against extending large energy credits.[137] Other members of Congress were reluctant to assist in the economic development of a communist-ruled state or to supply technology that could contribute to Soviet military capabilities.[138] *The Washington Post* raised questions about the cost of Soviet gas in comparison with fuel from alternative sources and it stated that there was no practical economic reason for importing Soviet gas, although a U.S.–Soviet deal could make political sense.[139] *The New York Times* maintained that the U.S. should invest its money in internal energy development rather than in Soviet projects, and it declared: "However valuable a mood of reduced tensions between the two superpowers, political atmosphere is not something to be bought by economic transactions that cannot be justified on their own merits." [140]

Another objection to importing Soviet LNG was raised by Nicholas Fedoruk and Barry Smernoff. Writing just before the Arab embargo, they argued that highly inflammable liquefied natural gas is unsafe. They presented a scenario in which imported LNG creates a fire in Boston harbor and public pressure then leads to a cessation of imports of LNG from the USSR. However, the Soviets then refuse to repay American credits with anything but LNG. Fedoruk and Smernoff contended that converting natural gas into methanol for the purpose of shipping is safer and cheaper than transforming it into LNG.[141]

The credit terms for Soviet energy projects proved to be controversial. Not only was the U.S. thinking about offering credits to a fairly rich and communist-ruled state but it was possibly going to extend credits on terms more favorable than those received by other borrowers from the Export-Import Bank. The U.S. was considering an extended repayment period and the deferral of any repayment until a project was completed.[142] *The Washington Post* complained that the American taxpayer would really be subsidizing any gas deal with the Soviet Union since Ex-Im credits bear lower interest than loans from commercial banks.[143]

The most important reason for growing American disenchantment with Soviet energy deals was that there was increasing support for a policy of energy self-sufficiency by 1980 or 1985. The advocacy of such a policy was clearly influenced by the Arab embargo and it was strengthened by Nixon's call for Project Independence. Curiously, American energy self-sufficiency could not possibly be approached until the early 1980s, but that is the same time that the deliveries of Soviet oil and gas would be scheduled to begin. Obviously a contradiction existed between attempts at energy independence and negotiations with the Soviet Union on the import of energy. If the Yakutsk and North Star projects were to be activated, the United States would be dependent on the Soviet Union for 10 to 15 percent of the gas used on both the East and West Coasts as of 1982, and the U.S. as a whole would be about 4 percent dependent on Soviet gas.[144]

In December 1974, Congress imposed credit limitations on Soviet energy deals but it approved MFN status for a trial period in exchange for what it considered to be Soviet assurances on the emigration question. In January, however, the Soviets denied that they had made any assurances to the United States and they refused to accept the conditions of trade as laid down by Congress. They also indicated that they would not pay their Lend Lease debt, since the agreement of 1972 linked the debt with the resumption of unconditional trade. The Soviet Union's improved financial situation in 1973 and 1974 probably influenced the decision not to make concessions on emigration in return for MFN or Ex-Im credits. As Marshall Goldman had warned, American efforts to use MFN and credits as political weapons in regard to Soviet emigration policies could have had only limited success once the USSR was in a secure financial position and capable of developing its energy resources without U.S. assistance.[145] Some new compromise may yet be reached between the two states, or private credits may be made available, but the prospects for major Siberian energy agreements are dim. They had already been diminishing before the American and Soviet actions of December, 1974–January, 1975 but now appear even more unlikely.

The China Factor

China's ability to supply crude oil to Japan has become a significant part of the Pacific energy equation. United Nations statistics for 1973 place China's proven oil reserves at 1.709 billion tons, but Chang Chun, a Nationalist Chinese observer of the mainland economy, discusses estimates of China's reserves ranging from 2.7 to 50 billion tons and indicates that 20 billion is probably the most realistic estimate.[146] China's crude oil production figures are shrouded in mystery, since many outside analysts do not accept recent Chinese claims at face value. Chang Chun presents the estimates of six different observers for the years 1957–72 and great disparities are obvious. For 1972, China claimed production of 29.5 million tons but an estimate from Taiwan was only 21.5 million tons.[147] More curiously, a Japanese analyst estimates that the Chinese actually produced 42.3 million tons, much more than they themselves claimed.[148] China produced approximately 50 million tons of oil in 1973 and 70 million tons in 1974 but these figures too are subject to controversy.[149] In August 1974, a Japanese oil negotiator, Ryutaro Hasegawa, indicated after a visit to Peking that the Chinese expected to produce 70 million tons in 1974, 100 million in 1975, and 400 million in 1980.[150] Chinese energy consumption per capita in 1972 was only 567 kilograms as compared with 4767 for the USSR and 11,611 for the U.S.[151] Approximately 85 percent of Chinese energy is derived from coal and 10 percent from oil, since agriculture and industry emphasize coal usage. There is little civilian consumption of oil products but the military is dependent on them.[152]

Until the sixties, most of China's oil production was concentrated in the remote western province of Sinkiang, but the focus then shifted to northeast China. The Karamai, Tushantzu, Kashgar, Urumchi, and Turfan oil fields are still active but the Taching field in northern Manchuria now provides about 40 percent of China's oil production.[153] Production is also increasing in the Gulf of Po Hai, which is an arm of the Yellow Sea, and at the adjacent onshore fields at Takang and Shengli. To some extent, Chinese oil fields are militarily vulnerable in case of war with the USSR, particularly Taching and those in Sinkiang.

China has been largely self-sufficient in oil production since 1964 but it has continued to import oil nevertheless. Among the states supplying China with oil have been Albania, Rumania, Egypt, and Iran (1960–66).[154] One reason for importing oil is that China has poor facilities for transporting its own oil from northern oil fields to southern population centers. Oil can therefore be imported and docked at southern Chinese ports.[155] China also has a refinery shortage and this causes it to be a net importer of oil products.[156] In addition, China may possibly import low-quality crude oil for its own use and thereby free some of its own higher quality crude for export. It can thus increase its foreign exchange earnings.[157]

China must purchase ships and equipment abroad in order to develop its oil industry and these purchases are largely funded through oil exports. China has bought eight Danish ships for offshore exploration and five tankers from Norway for use in the China–Japan oil trade.[158] It has also acquired oil refineries from West Germany, Italy, and France, and it is using Japanese equipment to develop its petrochemical industry.[159] China is negotiating the purchase of oilfield equipment from both Japan and the United States but it will not permit either state to share in prospecting and production.[160] However, it may permit Iran to conduct explorations for oil.[161]

China has been exporting oil to Asian states as it does not need all of its production for domestic consumption and it also hopes to spread some political good will. It additionally wants to earn foreign exchange in order to pay for machinery imports, as oil sales can help redress the trade deficits that have developed in recent years. These deficits are the result of the rising price of fertilizer and of China's purchases of wheat and technology. China is therefore trying to benefit from high world oil prices and it has even offered to sell crude oil to distant Brazil.[162]

China has built oil loading facilities at Canton to handle its exports to Southeast Asia. Agreements have already been reached with Thailand and the Philippines and exports to Sri Lanka (formerly Ceylon) and Malaysia are also possible. Sri Lanka has indicated its interest in buying Chinese crude oil, and the Chinese have already held talks with the Malaysians.[163] China's sale of diesel fuel to Thailand has been discussed previously and a Chinese-Filipino oil accord was reached in September, 1974 (see chapter 8).

China and the Philippines began indirect contacts regarding oil during the Arab embargo, and the Philippines apparently requested oil from the USSR at the same time.[164] A Filipino oil mission, headed by the President of the Philippine Oil Company, traveled to China in July 1974, and a deal was eventually concluded in September during the Peking visit of Imelda Marcos, wife of the Philippine president.[165] China agreed to deliver 250,000 tons of crude oil over the last three months of 1974 and 750,000 tons in 1975.[166]

China sells oil to the communist-ruled states of North Korea, Vietnam, and Laos but it also is an important supplier of the British colony of Hong Kong.[167] According to Yoshio Koide, Hong Kong receives ¼ of its kerosene, $1/7$ of its gasoline, and $1/9$ of its diesel fuel from China.[168] Deliveries were small in 1973 but they then increased substantially as China took advantage of the Arab embargo.[169] In one deal, China supplied 100,000 tons of diesel fuel through a middleman and it was to be marked in Hong Kong by Exxon, Mobil, and Shell.[170]

The largest recipient of Chinese oil is Japan and deliveries are clearly part of an effort to persuade Japan not to enter into a Tiumen agreement with the USSR. In late 1972, the Chinese offered to sell 200,000 tons of crude oil per year and an agreement was then reached in January 1973. However, the quantity was raised to one million tons in April. There is some disagreement as to when deliveries began, but it is apparent that the entire one million tons was indeed supplied.[171]

Chou En-lai and Japanese Minister of Foreign Affairs Ohira discussed oil for three hours on January 4, 1974, and a series of agreements was worked out gradually during the course of the year.[172] Eventually, the Chinese furnished 4.5 million tons of oil, even though they had offered only 1.5 million earlier in 1974.[173] Uncertainty about their delivery capabilities probably prevented the Chinese from making one definitive oil deal for the entire year. The oil exported to Japan comes from the Taching fields in northern Manchuria, but the pipeline from Taching to the port of Dairen was not yet completed and loading facilities at Dairen were still not fully constructed.[174]

The price charged by the Chinese became somewhat controversial, since it rose from the 1973 pre-embargo level of $3.94 per barrel to an early 1974 figure of $14.80.[175] The Chinese gradually lowered the price during the course of the year but there were indications as late as December that the Japanese were thinking about reducing their purchases from China and turning more toward Indonesia for lower-price crude.[176] It appears, however, that the Japanese were just exerting some pressure on the Chinese in order to gain further price reductions, since they bought 8.3 million tons of Chinese crude in 1975. The figure for 1976 should be somewhat lower, because Japan has an oil glut and it also has to adjust its refining operations to handle the byproducts found in the Chinese oil; but the Sino-Japanese oil trade should again expand in 1977 and continue to grow thereafter.

Pacific Options

Both China and the Soviet Union, which see Japan as an obvious customer for their oil exports are now engaging in economic competition. They are accelerating their offshore oil exploration programs with an eye on the Japanese market, and their efforts are highly political as well. China does not want Japan to join with the Soviet Union in Siberian energy development, because of the strategic advantages the Soviets would derive, and it is using oil to prevent such cooperation. On the other hand, the Soviet Union wants to prevent close political collaboration between Japan and China and it hopes to strengthen its energy ties with Japan in order to solidify Soviet–Japanese relations and reduce Japanese interest in further ties with China. It is conceivable that China and the Soviet Union may eventually compete in the same manner, and with the same political overtones, for the American energy market.[177]

Soviet efforts to develop the Tiumen oil fields are becoming more essential since East European oil requirements are soaring and import prices paid by the USSR for Middle East and North African oil are rising. However, the Soviets' interest in exporting Tiumen oil to Japan or the United States is now reduced, because much of it must be retained for domestic and East European needs. Provided that the Soviets wish to continue their large exports to the hard-currency markets of Western Europe, they are faced with a growing oil squeeze, and the export of large quantities of Tiumen oil to the United States and Japan would aggravate the problem. Furthermore, the Soviets were counting on imports from the Middle East and North Africa to offset the amount exported from Tiumen, but it now appears that the Soviets will not increase these imports substantially owing to the high price and hard-currency demands of the exporting states. Fortunately for the Soviets, they are presently in an advantageous economic position as a result of windfall oil profits so they are capable of developing the Tiumen oil fields without outside financing (and therefore do not have to repay any credits with oil.) In the absence of Japanese or American assistance, Tiumen oil production may not be expanded so rapidly, and this may necessitate continued reliance on imports from Arab states and no significant increase in exports to Western Europe and the Third World. At the same time, Japan and the United States may seek closer oil collaboration with China.

The situation regarding Siberian gas is somewhat different from oil. Reserves are huge and plenty of gas should be available for export. This means that the Soviets still favor agreements with Japan and the United States on Yakutsk and North Star since they will not be squeezed by the ensuing gas exports. Pricing is also an important consideration as the Soviets charge much more for gas exports than they pay for their Iranian and Afghan imports. It therefore pays to import gas to help compensate for large exports but, of course, the pricing policies of Iran and Afghanistan could change in the future and thereby bring about a reassessment of the Soviet gas trade.

13/The Future of Soviet Energy Policies

The Soviet Union has ample fuel reserves but it is still faced with an oil problem since the growth rate of production will probably not keep up with increasing consumption during the remainder of the decade. Production is leveling off in the Volga-Ural region and the Caucasus and only modest gains are expected in Central Asia and the Far East.[1] The key, of course, will be Western Siberia, as almost all future growth will be concentrated in the Tiumen region. The outlook has improved somewhat in recent years and oil minister Shashin has now raised his 1980 projection for Western Siberian production from 230–260 million tons to 300 million tons.[2] This certainly represents a substantial increase over the 116 million tons produced in 1974 and the 148 million tons produced in 1975, but it may not offset the rise in oil consumption, which will probably be at least 8 percent per year. Oil consumption as a percentage of total energy usage may start to decline somewhat by 1980, as the Soviets emphasize natural gas and atomic energy development, but overall energy consumption will increase so rapidly that the demand for oil will be greater than ever before.[3] One Soviet energy specialist even predicts that the USSR will consume more energy per capita than the U.S. by 1990, though it was using less than half of the American figure as of 1974.[4]

Some Western analysts have maintained that the USSR will be a net importer of oil by 1980, but this now appears unlikely.[5] If one takes the 1973 production of 421 million tons as a base and then projects a yearly growth rate of 5 percent, the USSR will produce approximately 592 million tons in 1980. If the growth rate is as high as 10 percent, approximately 820 million tons will be

Table 13.1. Estimates of Soviet Oil Resources in 1980 (in millions of metric tons)

source	year estimate was made	estimated production	estimated consumption	estimated net exports
(1)	1966	630	560	70
(2)	1967	630	560	70
(3)	1968	600–620	560	40–60
(4)	1969	770	700	70
(5)	1970	—	—	135
(6)	1970	630	613	17
(7)	1971	625–45	—	—
(8)	1972	—	600	—
(9)	1972	600–620	—	—
(10)	1972	607	613	−6
(11)	1973	620	—	—
(12)	1973	611	500	111
(13)	1973	640	530	110
(14)	1973	625–45	480–613	12–165
(15)	1974	600–640	500–600	0–140
(16)	1974	638	550	88
(17)	1974	600–620	—	—
(18)	1976	620–40	—	—

SOURCES: (1) Stanislaw Albinowski, "Where is the Oil to Come From?," *Polityka,* September 24, 1966 (translated in Robert Ebel, *Communist Trade in Oil and Gas.* New York: Praeger, 1970, p. 251); (2) "The Communist Oil Conundrum," *The Economist* 222, no. 6437 (January 7, 1967): 46; (3) Valentin Shashin, Soviet Minister of Oil Extraction, cited in *Petroleum Intelligence Weekly,* February 26, 1968, p. 2; (4) Stanislaw Wasowski, "The Fuel Situation in Eastern Europe," *Soviet Studies* 21, no. 1 (July 1969): 36, 43–44; (5) Robert Ebel, *Communist Trade in Oil and Gas* (New York: Praeger, 1970), pp. 89–91; (6) "When Oil Flows East," *The Economist* 234, no. 6594 (January 10, 1970): 51; (7) Rafkhat Mingareev, Soviet Deputy Minister of Oil Extraction, cited in *Petroleum Press Service,* February, 1971, p. 64; (8) R. M. Burrell, "Opportunity Knocks for the Kremlin's Drive East," *New Middle East,* no. 46 (July 1972): 11; (9) John Berry, "Oil and Soviet Policy in the Middle East," *Middle East Journal* 26, no. 2 (Spring 1972): 150; (10) Werner Gumpel, cited in John Hardt, "West Siberia: The Quest for Energy," *Problems of Communism* 22, no. 3 (May–June 1973): 35; (11) "Russian Headaches," *Petroleum Press Service* 40, no. 3 (March 1973): 88; (12) "Russian Oil: Where Will They Get it From?," *The Economist* 249 no. 6797 (December 1, 1973): 40 (13) *Soviet Oil to 1980,* QER Special, no. 14, June 1973 (London: The Economist Intelligence Unit), pp. 18 and 33; (14) Abraham Becker, "Oil and the Persian Gulf in Soviet Policy in the 1970s," in Michael Confino and Shimon Shamir, eds., *The U.S.S.R. and the Middle East* (New York: John Wiley; and Jerusalem: Israel Universities Press, 1973), p. 180; (15) A. F. G. Scanlan, "The Energy Balance of the Comecon Countries," Round Table on the Exploitation of Siberia's Natural Resources, Brussels, January 30–February 1, 1974, pp. 3 and 12; (16) Soviet estimate, cited in "Is Siberia Really the Answer?," *The Economist* 250, no. 6809 (February 23, 1974): 47; (17) Soviet estimate, cited in *The Petroleum Economist* 41, no. 3 (March 1974): 100; (18) Soviet Five-Year Plan for 1976–80, *Pravda,* March 7, 1976, p. 3.

produced. In realistic terms it probably will not exceed 7 percent a year, and this would mean a production total of approximately 676 million tons in 1980. Looking at the various estimates shown in Table 13.1, and realizing that production increased by 9 percent in 1974 and by 7 percent in 1975, one can probably expect the growth rate to be at least 6 percent, resulting in the production of a minimum of 631 million tons in 1980. Apparent consumption in 1973 was 317.4 million tons and a yearly growth rate of 8 percent would mean oil consumption of 544 million tons in 1980. If consumption rises by as much as 10 percent per year, it will reach almost 619 million tons in 1980. In either case, production will exceed consumption and the Soviet Union will remain a net exporter of oil. It therefore has some leeway, but will run into trouble if production increases at only 5–5.5 percent per year and consumption at 9.5–10 percent. On the other hand, there should be no obstacle to the USSR's role as a net exporter of natural gas in 1980. The Soviet Union should produce about 550–600 billion cubic meters, import only 12.5 billion, and export at least 40 billion cubic meters.[6] Exports will be considerably greater during the following years if agreements are reached with the United States and Japan on the North Star and Yakutsk projects.

While the Soviet Union should not have a domestic oil shortage, it will encounter difficulties in maintaining its sizable oil export program. In 1973, it had net exports of 103.6 million tons (exports were 118.3 and imports 14.7), with roughly 3 million tons going to Third World states, 51 million to Western Europe (including Yugoslavia) and Japan, and 64 million to CMEA members plus North Korea and North Vietnam. However, if oil production in 1980 amounts to approximately 630 million tons and consumption reaches 550 million tons, the Soviet Union will be a net exporter of only 80 million tons. Perhaps this will break down into exports of about 100 million tons and imports of 20 million tons and, if production is indeed in this general area, the Soviet Union will have less oil available for export than it had in 1973 (provided that imports are not increased dramatically).

From looking at the figures in Table 13.2, one can estimate that Eastern Europe's oil production in 1980 will be approximately

Table 13.2. Estimates of East European Oil Resources in 1980 [a] (in millions of metric tons)

source	year estimate was made	estimated production	estimated consumption	estimated net imports
(1)	1966	23–33	170	137–47
(2)	1967	30	170	140
(3)	1969	30	117–35	87–105
(4)	1970	30	110	80
(5)	1970	30	140–70	110–40
(6)	1973	——	120–30	——
(7)	1974	20–25	100–150	75–130

SOURCES: (1) Stanislaw Albinowski, "Where is the Oil to Come From?," *Polityka,* September 24, 1966 (translated in Robert Ebel, *Communist Trade in Oil and Gas.* New York: Praeger, 1970, p. 251); (2) "The Communist Oil Conundrum," *The Economist* 222, no. 6437 (January 7, 1967): 46; (3) Stanislaw Wasowski, "The Fuel Situation in Eastern Europe," *Soviet Studies* 21, no. 1 (July 1969): 36, 43–44; (4) Robert Ebel, *Communist Trade in Oil and Gas* (New York: Praeger, 1970), pp. 89–91; (5) "When Oil Flows East," *The Economist* 234, no. 6594 (January 10, 1970): 51; (6) *Soviet Oil to 1980.* QER Special, no. 14, June, 1973 (London: The Economist Intelligence Unit), pp. 18 and 33; (7) A. F. G. Scanlan, "The Energy Balance of the Comecon Countries," Round Table on the Exploitation of Siberia's Natural Resources," Brussels, January 30–February 1, 1974, pp. 3 and 12.

[a] Eastern Europe includes Poland, Hungary, Czechoslovakia, East Germany, Rumania and Bulgaria.

30 million tons, its consumption 150 million tons, and its net imports 120 million tons. If the Soviet Union holds its exports to the Third World, Western Europe, and Japan constant at their 1973 levels and is able to export a total of only 100 million tons of oil in 1980, then 46 million tons will be available for all communist-ruled states (excluding Yugoslavia). If a total of 10 million tons is supplied to Cuba, Mongolia, North Korea, and Vietnam, then only 36 million tons can be delivered to Eastern Europe. East European states would therefore have to import more than 84 million tons from sources other than the USSR (only 84 million tons would be needed if Eastern Europe did not export as well as import).

Such a scenario, in which the Soviets would furnish less than 30 percent of Eastern Europe's oil imports (30 percent of net imports but less in terms of total imports since exports must be subtracted from total imports in order to arrive at net imports), would significantly reduce Soviet economic leverage and thus prove unacceptable to the USSR. At the same time, it is unlikely that Eastern Europe will be able to import so much oil from Arab states and Iran. A hard-currency shortage and declining barter demand for East European machinery and equipment in the oil-producing states will probably hold imports to approximately 50–60 million tons in 1980.[7] Soviet export limitations and East European import needs may combine to create a monumental oil problem within CMEA, but some options still remain open for softening the impact of this envisioned oil squeeze.

The Soviets will probably try to disengage themselves from the Cuban oil trade, thus freeing up to 8 million extra tons per year for delivery to Eastern Europe, and Cuba's present oil contacts with Venezuela and Mexico are apparently receiving the Soviet Union's blessing. The Soviets may also encourage a change in the East European consumption pattern, fostering the use of more gas, coal and atomic energy. They could then increase the supply of gas and cut back somewhat on expected deliveries of oil. Leonid Tomashpol'skii has estimated that Eastern Europe will be 11.5 percent dependent on gas and 8.5 percent on atomic energy as of 1980 but that the figures will rise to 20.5 percent and 28.5 percent in the year 2000.[8] The energy consumption pattern is evolving in this general direction and the Soviets could assist in speeding up the process. They could also refrain from concluding Tiumen oil agreements with Japan and the United States, thus reserving more oil for export to the East European states. For their part, the East European states could help alleviate the energy problem by slowing down their shift from coal to oil consumption.

In addition, the Soviets could increase their purchase of Arab oil in order to augment the quantity available for export to Eastern Europe. They would then be serving as middlemen and would retain a strong hold on the East European oil spigot. It has even been suggested that the Soviet Union could serve as a transit route for a Middle East to Eastern Europe pipeline.[9] Such a proposal would probably be acceptable to the USSR but Arab producers and Iran would prefer to transport the oil without having to rely on transit through the USSR and the Adriatica pipeline through Yugoslavia is indicative of the future course of events. The Soviets will continue to buy Arab oil, part of which they ship directly to Eastern Europe, but Arab hard-currency demands and high sale prices should limit the Soviet Union's purchases to a maximum of 20–25 million tons per year by 1980. In addition, the Soviets will have less of a geographical rationale for buying Persian Gulf or Gulf of Suez oil now that the Suez Canal is reopened. Some of this oil had been resold to Asian states but the Soviets can now ship their own oil directly from Black Sea ports without having to circumnavigate Africa.

Exports to Eastern Europe could be increased if the Soviets reduce deliveries to Third World states, Western Europe, and Japan, but such an event is not likely. Exports to the Third World are already minimal and any small quantity that could be diverted to Eastern Europe would just be a drop in the bucket (or should it be barrel?). Sales of oil to Western Europe are an important aspect of Soviet foreign trade since they acquire hard currency. The Soviets did cut down on these sales in 1969 when they were confronted with an oil availability problem but they would probably not resort to such a solution as a long-term policy.[10] At present, with the world price of oil increasing more rapidly than Soviet production costs, it would be economically unwise not to take advantage of the lucrative West European market. In regard to Japan, the Soviets will most likely maintain their modest level of oil exports so that the Chinese cannot secure too much control over the Japanese market.

Another questionable option is the conservation of oil within the USSR so that a greater quantity could be provided for export. There is already a campaign to combat wastage, but the Soviets are certainly not prepared to jeopardize economic growth by trying to hold back the yearly increase in consumption to less than 7 or 8 percent. The production of automobiles and trucks is expanding rapidly and the development of Siberia will require large amounts of energy. Greater use of gas would be helpful in limiting oil consumption, but much of the increased gas production will be exported to Western and Eastern Europe, and perhaps to Japan and the United States as well. Gas exports will be increasingly emphasized as the oil squeeze becomes more severe, and this will necessarily place some constraints on the domestic conversion from oil to gas usage.

The Soviet Union wants to preserve its pivotal role in East European oil markets in order to have an instrument available for the application of political pressure. On the other hand, it is not capable of supplying oil at a pace commensurate with Eastern Europe's staggering consumption growth rate, so it is encouraging East European purchases of Arab and Iranian oil. The Soviets would like to find some middle ground in which substantial oil leverage is kept over East European states but in which a critical drain is not developed on the Soviet oil supply. They therefore want these states to buy oil from other sources but only up to the point where the Soviet potential for exerting an influence effect is not seriously jeopardized. The Soviets realize that their political hegemony in Eastern Europe is based in part on the economic integration structure of CMEA and that a loosening of economic ties (and the lessening of the energy dependence of most of Eastern Europe on the USSR) could lead to greater political autonomy on the part of East European states. Albania and Rumania took advantage of their lack of oil dependence on the USSR to successfully challenge Soviet control mechanisms, and the Soviets want to make sure that any inroads made by Western oil companies into the oil-deficient East European states will not threaten the dominant Soviet position. Although the Soviets are faced with a burgeoning oil problem, they will strive to provide about 50 percent of Eastern Europe's oil imports in 1980 and this could mean 60 million or more tons. The task is difficult but not insurmountable, and the easiest solution would be to increase oil production at the rate of 7 percent annually. This may be possible and the fact that some East European states are beginning to provide capital for Soviet oil development clearly assists the Soviet effort.[11]

The Soviet Union will try to maintain the level of its oil exports to Western Europe or raise it slightly, but there should be no substantial increase in Soviet deliveries. Eastern Europe will have top priority on the limited Soviet oil supply, and the USSR therefore expects to emphasize gas exports to Western Europe in the coming years. Oil sales to Western Europe earn valuable hard currency and help secure needed pipe, so they will surely continue. However, the Soviets will probably not resort to price-cutting, as they have often done in the past, in order to gain access to West European markets. Their position is now secure since their trade reliability has been demonstrated and West European states are anxious to buy some Soviet oil to diversify their sources of supply. To some extent, the Soviets will be competing for markets with the Arab states and Iran, but this rivalry is not too significant since Western Europe is only 5 percent dependent on Soviet oil but about 80 percent dependent on oil from the Middle East and North Africa. The Soviet share of the market should even decrease as West European imports accelerate.

Soviet oil sales to the Third World are now running at less than 3 million tons per year. The Soviets do not want to supply more than this because they do not receive hard currency payments and they will probably shy away from sizable export commitments to states such as India. They will occasionally offer discount prices to maximize the political impact of their sales and they may possibly export small amounts to new Southeast Asian customers like Malaysia, Laos, and the Philippines to counter potential Chinese influence in the area. On the whole, the Third World will be of minimal importance in Soviet oil export plans, but the Soviets should continue to provide refineries, tankers, prospecting teams, and oil technicians to help reduce the dependence of Third World states on Western oil companies.

The Soviet Union may conclude small Siberian energy deals with the United States and Japan but major agreements are less likely than they were a few years ago. The Soviets are concerned about American political strings, they are in a better financial situation as a result of high world oil prices, and they cannot afford to export much Siberian oil to the United States or Japan because they need most of it for their own use and for export to Eastern Europe. They could possibly balance exports to the U.S. and

Japan with increased imports from Arab states but Arab prices are high and the Soviets do not want to become dependent on outside suppliers.

The Siberian carrot extended by the USSR did not discourage the United States and Japan from improving relations with China so the Soviets may be questioning the strategic efficacy of American and Japanese involvement in Siberian energy development. In addition, the USSR and China may possibly reach some reconciliation now that Mao has died and the need to gain the support of the United States and Japan for a policy of containing China may prove to be irrelevant. Therefore, the outlook is for continued small sales of oil to the United States and Japan and any potential deliveries of natural gas will not even begin until after 1980. In a twist which was probably unforeseen before 1973, the United States and Japan will not be major considerations as the Soviet Union contemplates its energy export policies for the remainder of the decade.

The Soviet Union is in a paradoxical, but not unique, position for an advanced industrial society as it is confronted with an energy problem despite its possession of abundant fuel resources. The geographical remoteness of oil and gas reserves and the growing energy needs of Eastern Europe have combined to create this problem and it could last into the 1980s and beyond if the Soviets want to maintain their dominant energy role in Eastern Europe. Soviet analysts dispute the existence of a world energy crisis, arguing that there is plenty of fuel but that the political and economic structures of capitalism lead to shortages. They point with pride to the energy self-sufficiency of the CMEA states, but their interpretation of the energy crisis seems to be becoming increasingly relevant to the Soviet–East European relationship within CMEA.

14 / Soviet Oil Politics Reconsidered

Oil sales enable the Soviet Union to secure economic benefits, such as hard currency and vitally needed imports of pipe and technology, but oil also contributes to the growth of Soviet state power. The basic self-sufficiency of the USSR provides very limited opportunities for other states to subject it to the influence effect of their oil export trade whereas large exports permit the USSR to exercise its influence effect to a substantial degree. In some cases, as in India and Sri Lanka (Ceylon), oil sales served to promote a general atmosphere of political good will (and additionally undercut the Western oil monopolies in these states) but the influence effect was clearly used to facilitate more specific power goals in Ghana and Finland. In the former case, the Soviets successfully brought about the release of Soviet trawlers and their crews, whereas in the latter situation they were able to influence the reorganization of the Finnish Cabinet to make it more pro-Soviet. The Soviets also registered some notable failures in attempting to exert their influence effect. Yugoslavia and China continued along their separatist paths and Iceland did not evict American troops from their bases.

The Soviet Union occasionally resorted to outright military force to gain control over oil fields, as in Rumania and Sakhalin during World War II, but it suffered a setback in northern Iran in 1946–47 when its troops were withdrawn and no oil concessions were acquired. The Soviet Union has not used such direct force to disrupt the flow of oil to Western states but it has assisted Arab states in the nationalization of Western oil properties and it has encouraged Arab embargoes. The Soviet Union has operated by proxy in interfering with the Western oil supply, thus taking little risk, but it has unintentionally fostered cooperative efforts on the part of Western oil-importing states under the aegis of the International Energy Agency. Arab embargoes may therefore be less effective in the future.

The Soviet Union is certainly not unique in its use of oil politics but it should be pointed out that all major powers except the Soviet Union and China have the disadvantage of being net importers of oil. The United States is additionally confronted with a conflict of interest between the welfare of the state and that of its privately owned oil companies. This was demonstrated during the Arab embargo of 1973–74 when some companies held back deliveries to the American military, kept oil in storage tanks or aboard tankers despite the energy shortage, and sold domestic oil at the price of foreign imports in order to maximize their profits. The Soviet system is not completely monolithic, as indicated by occasional bureaucratic differences between Soiuznefteeksport and the Council of Ministers during negotiations with Israel in the mid-fifties. However, Soiuznefteeksport has always been subordinate to the Council of Ministers once political considerations are involved and the latter's order to terminate deliveries to Israel because of her participation in the Suez War was dutifully carried out by Soiuznefteeksport. The oil policies of Soiuznefteeksport clearly conform to the needs of Soviet foreign policy.

Joseph Nye Jr., a Harvard political scientist, discusses the "private foreign policy" of American-based multinational corporations, such as oil companies, and he indicates that these corporations may also align with certain bureaucracies or interest groups to produce international policies representative of part of a state rather than the state itself.[1] The power interests of the United States and those of its oil companies do not always coincide and it is incorrect to view the actions of American oil companies as mere extensions of state policy. Aramco considered its own status in Saudi Arabia rather than American state interests when acceding to King Feisal's dictate that no oil should be supplied to the U.S. military during the 1973 Arab-Israeli war. Viewed from another perspective, the presence of American oil properties in a state does not necessarily provide the U.S. government with any leverage or political influence, as evidenced by the negligible American role in Iraq even before the nationalization of American oil properties in 1973.

Soviet analysts appear to oversimplify the situation by blurring over the important distinctions between the U.S. government and American oil companies and they therefore see the weakening position of American oil companies in the Middle East, as indicative of declining American power in the area. In fact, U.S. political influence in Saudi Arabia has not suffered despite the Saudis' gradual takeover of Aramco, and Arab threats to restrict or curtail the flow of oil have lead to an increase in the American naval presence in the Indian Ocean and Persian Gulf and to official Implications that the United States may possibly use force in order to assure itself of an adequate oil supply. Soviet efforts to limit American power in the Middle East through Arab nationalization and embargo tactics may therefore backfire as the reduction of American oil power may lead to the augmenting of American military power. Furthermore, the Arab embargo of 1973–74 emphasized the dichotomy between state and corporate interests and the U.S. government may try to exert greater control over American oil firms, synchronizing their actions with the supply effect energy needs of the United States. To the extent that oil contributes to state power, the United States may emerge in a more favorable position than it has occupied in recent years.

Much of the world was confronted with oil shortages during 1973 and 1974 but the increasing availability of oil is now creating a huge surplus on international markets. If oil prices go down, the Soviets will receive less revenue and will have difficulty in buying a significant amount of Western technology. Domestic oil development, including production at the Tiumen oil fields, could therefore suffer some setbacks. A world oil surplus could also blunt the effectiveness of any future Arab embargo, leading to a deemphasis of this indirect weapon in the Soviet arsenal of oil politics. On the other hand, the Soviets may possibly be able to build up their barter trade in the Middle East and North Africa, exchanging machinery and equipment for oil. A number of Arab states are now demanding hard currency rather than goods, but they may change their position once they have surplus oil on their hands. The Soviets will also benefit from the fact that they have not utilized supertankers as the growing oil surplus has led to a world supertanker glut. Importing states have large stockpiles of oil, and are decreasing their purchases, so hundreds of supertankers are standing idle. During the early sixties, the Soviets made a powerful political impact through oil sales despite the great oil abundance then in existence. They entered new markets, controlling a large percentage of the sales in many of them, and they also had a greatly increasing amount of oil available for export. These conditions no longer exist and a world oil surplus could therefore reduce the Soviet Union's potential to use its influence effect in states not under communist rule.

The Soviet Union does not really have one policy for its oil trade but a complex interaction of numerous subpolicies, which must mesh in an efficient manner. Imports must be harmonized with exports so that the Soviet Union is assured of an adequate supply of oil; the products received in exchange for oil exports must be related to the requirements of the Five-Year Plan; and exports to various states have completely different rationales. The oil trade must also be attuned to the Soviet gas trade and closely coordinated with domestic fuel development and energy consumption needs. The Soviet oil trade must also be consistent with the overall outlines of Soviet foreign trade in regard to the level of transactions, the choice of trading partners, and the timing of agreements.

The numerous aspects of Soviet oil trade policy must fit together in a fairly rational pattern since an economic commodity is involved. Planning, costs, and domestic energy requirements must therefore be taken into account and the room for political manuevering is somewhat restricted by the need for long-range and coherent economic planning. However, such planning can easily be thrown into disarray by the vagaries of the international oil trade since fluctuating prices, oil availability, embargoes, and the Western "energy crisis" definitely affect the Soviet Union's impact on world oil markets, as well as the willingness of other states to seek energy collaboration with the Soviet Union.

The effects of the energy trade on the Soviet system of rule can be the subject of much lively conjecture. When viewed in the context of reduced Soviet autarky and expanded trade relations with noncommunist states, many Western advocates of Soviet "liberalization" have come to believe that a "building bridges" approach on the part of Western states will lead to major de-authoritarian transformations within the Soviet system. The "containment doctrine" has been largely discarded as an instrument to encourage "liberalization" within the USSR, as détente and increased trade are now seen as effective antidotes to Soviet authoritarianism. In accord with this line of reasoning, growing economic prosperity in the USSR will lead to the rise of more pluralism, interest groups, and civil liberties, as well as to the relaxation of ideological controls. Technological and managerial skills will become more important than ideological purity, revolutionary fervor will subside as the standard of living improves, and "liberalization" of the system will become economically functional.

Western advocates of Soviet "liberalization" attach great importance to trade with the USSR, but the Soviets may be engaging in this trade for the completely opposite reason. As pointed out previously, they may be fostering such trade to promote economic development without effecting any significant reorganizations of their system. They may actually increase authoritarian controls to counteract any potential growth of "bourgeois" tendencies which could be brought about by the extension of trade contacts with Western states. Furthermore, Western advocates of liberalization are divided over the most efficacious tactical line to follow. Senator Henry Jackson calls for the use of pressure tactics, as increased trade makes the USSR more vulnerable to the influence effect of her trading partners, and his approach is endorsed by the dissident Soviet physicist, Andrei Sakharov. On the other hand, many Western analysts believe in the more automatic liberalizing effect of increased trade, and they predict Soviet retrenchment in the face of attempted Western trade pressure. Soviet historian Roy Medvedev adheres to this latter point of view.

The relationship between trade and the evolution of the Soviet system becomes particularly acute when related to the question of American and Japanese participation in Siberian energy development. Not only would there be extensive oil and gas trade but foreign corporations would be collaborating on projects within the USSR and foreign personnel would probably be involved in some of the decision-making. However, the Soviets do have some important safeguards against the potential influence which could be exerted by the Americans and the Japanese. All joint projects are to be owned by the Soviet state, commodities are to be imported or exported only with the approval of the Soviet government (assuring that economic planning will not be disrupted), and the geographical locations of the envisioned energy projects are to be so remote that the bulk of the Soviet population will scarcely be affected by the intrusion of foreign concepts or ideologies. Since the USSR is capable of developing Siberian resources without outside assistance, the ability of the United States and Japan to exert an influence effect through their economic participation is severely limited. Perhaps the more automatic liberalizing effect could be expected as energy development contributes to Soviet modernization and to an improvement in the standard of living, but a note of caution must be introduced: The Western economic role in the USSR during the New Economic Policy of the twenties produced no long-lasting liberalizing effects; NEP was followed by the coercive excesses of Stalinism.

Oil politics is a crucial aspect of the Soviet Union's foreign policy because it cuts across numerous dimensions of Soviet involvement in world affairs. For example, the Tiumen pipeline and BAM proposals are closely connected to Soviet strategic thinking about the Chinese border area and the northwest Pacific military balance. The Druzhba Pipeline is essential to Soviet and East European military capabilities in Central Europe while Soviet naval strength in the Indian Ocean is clearly dependent on the availability of refueling stations. In geopolitical terms, Soviet oil politics is integrally related to Soviet transportation and political interests in the Red Sea, Barents Sea, and Suez Canal areas and, from the standpoint of ideology, oil politics clearly underlines Soviet support for the nationalization of Western property by Third World states and the development of a state-controlled economic sector.

The Soviet Union has used oil in conjunction with political tactics toward Ghana, Cuba, Iceland, Israel, and other states but oil is also relevant to the strategy of Soviet foreign policy. Soviet political leverage over other CMEA members, long-term commercial relations with Western European states, and the reduction of Western influence in the Middle East are inextricably bound with the oil factor and negotiations with the United States and Japan on Siberian energy development are also related to long-range strategic concerns.

In some situations, it is difficult to reconcile oil policy with foreign policy. In early 1975, the Soviet Union wanted the Suez Canal to be opened to commercial traffic to facilitate its own oil trade, but at the same time it did not want to support Henry Kissinger's diplomatic effort to arrange a limited settlement between Egypt and Israel. Although such a settlement would have provided for the reopening of the Canal, the Soviets resented their exclusion from the negotiations and they also wanted to retain their credibility with the militant leadership of Syria and the Palestine Liberation Organization. In another case, Soviet foreign policy goals would seem to dictate continued maximum control over the East European oil supply but the realities of the growing oil squeeze and the desire to earn hard currency by maintaining sales to Western Europe have led the Soviets to favor East European oil purchases from Middle East and North African states. In regard to Japan, the Soviets wanted to conclude a Tiumen oil agreement before they changed their position in mid-1973, but they were unwilling to make the foreign policy concession of returning all four occupied islands in order to ensure Japanese participation.

The Soviets have naturally made some errors in judgment while engaging in oil politics. Their excessive use of the influence effect against Yugoslavia backfired, pushing this state toward the Western camp, and their dominance of the Cuban oil market has placed them in an economic bind from which they are now attempting to extricate themselves. They made mistakes in Iran as well; they overplayed their hand after World War II and emerged with no additional oil rights in northern Iran, and then underplayed their hand during the nationalization dispute of the early fifties and failed to gain any influence over Iranian oil operations. Occasionally, there appear to be discrepancies in Soviet oil policy but they are generally intentional and are not dysfunctional. The Soviet Union sold oil to Spain while supposedly supporting the Arab embargo of 1967 and then made sales to the United States and the Netherlands during the 1973–74 embargo. The motivation in these situations was purely economic, as the Soviets took advantage of high prices, and the size of their oil sales in no way offset the effect of the Arab embargoes. They therefore increased their oil profits and simultaneously furthered their political image among the Arabs. In other situations, the Soviets have kept their political options open by lending oil assistance to both parties engaged in an international dispute. They sold oil to Israel and many Arab states during the mid-fifties, explored for oil in India and Pakistan during the early sixties, and provided technical and construction assistance for a refinery in Ethiopia while selling oil to Somalia. By treading cautiously, the Soviets were able to maintain appropriate relations with all of these states.

The Soviets have been careful not to use oil so politically that other states are unwilling to trust them as a trading partner. They have used oil politics judiciously, exerting an influence effect through their export of oil and interfering with the supply of the West by acting indirectly through Arab intermediaries. At present, the Soviet Union also has to be conscious of his own supply effect (since it is partially dependent on Persian Gulf deliveries from Iraq and on oil transit rights through Syria), and its potential use of the influence effect against Third World or West European states may be reduced as oil shortages force it to limit exports to these areas.[2] If a buyers' market should develop in the international oil trade, the Soviet Union would have to stress its trade reliability when engaged in exporting oil and Arab states would be somewhat restricted in their use of the oil weapon against the West. Nevertheless, the selective application of Soviet oil politics would surely be continued.

Notes

1/Foreign Trade and State Power

1. Albert Hirschman, *National Power and the Structure of Foreign Trade* (Berkeley: University of California Press, 1969), pp. 4–5; and Philip Buck, *The Politics of Mercantilism* (New York: Octagon Books, 1964), pp. 1–2.

2. Joseph Nye, Jr. and Robert Keohane, "Transnational Relations and World Politics: An Introduction," in Keohane and Nye, eds., *Transnational Relations and World Politics* (Cambridge: Harvard University Press, 1972), p. xxvi.

3. Peter Wiles, *Communist International Economics* (New York and Washington: Praeger, 1969), p. 9 and; Vladimir Lenin, *Imperialism: The Highest Stage of Capitalism* (New York: International Publishers, 1939), p. 65.

4. For example, see Hirschman, *National Power,* pp. 14–15.

5. *Ibid.,* p. 34.

6. Benjamin Cohen, "Some General Principles of Analysis," in Cohen, ed., *American Foreign Economic Policy* (New York: Harper and Row, 1968), pp. 15–16.

7. Hirschman, *National Power,* p. 20.

8. The Soviet position, based on Marxism, is that foreign policy is a superstructure influenced by changes in the economic base. See V. Israelyan, "The Leninist Science of International Relations and Foreign Policy Reality," *International Affairs,* no. 6 (June 1967): 48.

9. Vernon Van Dyke, *International Politics,* 2nd edition (New York: Appleton-Century-Crofts, 1966), p. 91.

10. "Oil and U.S. Foreign Policy," *International Affairs,* no. 6 (June 1957): 131.

11. Nye and Keohane, "Transnational Relations," pp. xxiv–xxv, xvii.

12. Edward Morse, "Transnational Economic Processes," in Keohane and Nye, *Transnational Relations,* pp. 23–37; Werner Feld, *Nongovernmental Forces and World Politics* (New York: Praeger, 1972), p. 248; and Robert Gilpin, "The Politics of Transnational Economic Relations," in Keohane and Nye, *Transnational Relations,* p. 69.

13. Morse, "Transnational Economic Processes," p. 47.

14. James Reston, "The Moscow Tourists," *The New York Times,* July 21, 1972, p. 31.

15. On Yugoslavia, see Robert Freedman, *Economic Warfare in the Communist Bloc* (New York: Praeger, 1970), pp. 3–4.

16. Philip Buck, *The Politics of Mercantilism* (New York: Octagon Books, 1964), p. 1.

17. Lenin, *Imperialism,* pp. 65–66.

18. V. Rymalov, "The Struggle for Economic Emancipation," *International Affairs,* no. 2 (February 1968): 53.

19. Marshall Goldman, "A Balance Sheet of Soviet Foreign Aid," *Foreign Affairs* 43, no. 2 (January 1965): 357–58.

2/The Political Economy of Soviet Foreign Trade

1. Cited in Milton Kovner, *The Challenge of Coexistence: A Study of Soviet Economic Diplomacy* (Washington: Public Affairs Press, 1961), p. 54.

2. *Ibid.,* p. 53 and Abram Frumkin, *Modern Theories of International Economic Relations* (Moscow: Progress Publishers, 1969), p. 477.

3. R. Andreasian, "Arabskii vostok: novoe stolknovenie s neftianym imperializmom," (The Arab East: New Confrontation with Oil Imperialism) *Mirovaia Ekonomika i Mezhdunarodnye Otnosheniia* (World Economics and International Relations), no. 3 (March 1967): 112.

4. I. Motorin, "CMEA: Plan Co-ordination," *New Times,* no. 38 (September 24, 1969): 5.

5. Cited in the Foreword of Michael Sapir, *The New Role of the Soviets in the World Economy* (New York: Committee for Economic Development, 1958).

6. Frumkin, *Modern Theories,* p. 478.

7. James Schlesinger, "Strategic Leverage from Aid and Trade," in David Abshire and Richard Allen, eds., *National Security* (New York: Praeger, 1963), p. 701.

8. Nikolai Patolichev, *USSR Foreign Trade: Past, Present and Future* (Moscow: Novosti Press Agency Publishing House, 1967), p. 11.

9. Robert Strausz-Hupé and Stefan Possony, *International Relations* (New York: McGraw-Hill, 1954), p. 481 and Kovner, *Challenge of Coexistence,* p. 52.

10. Kovner, *Challenge of Coexistence,* p. 52.

11. Edward Taborsky, *Communist Penetration of the Third World* (New York: Robert Speller and Sons, 1973), p. 310.

12. Daniel Spencer, "The Role of Oil in Soviet Foreign Economic Policy," *American Journal of Economics and Sociology* 25, no. 1 (January 1966): 94.

13. Holland Hunter as cited in *Dimensions of Soviet Economic Power* (Washington: U.S. Government Printing Office, 1962), p. 54.

14. Robert Freedman, *Economic Warfare in the Communist Bloc* (New York: Praeger, 1970), pp. 7–8 and 10–12.

15. Jozef Wilczynski, *The Economics and Politics of East-West Trade* (New York: Praeger, 1969), p. 253.

16. Kovner, *Challenge of Coexistence*, pp. 54–55.

17. Taborsky, *Communist Penetration*, pp. 312–13; Wilczynski, *East-West Trade*, p. 253; Samuel Pisar, *Coexistence and Commerce* (New York: McGraw-Hill, 1970), p. 183; and Susan Strange, *The Soviet Trade Weapon* (London: Phoenix House, 1959), pp. 15 and 24.

18. Robert Loring Allen, *Soviet Economic Warfare* (Washington: Public Affairs Press, 1960), pp. 18–19 and Wilczynski, *East-West Trade*, p. 182.

19. Wilczynski, *East-West Trade*, p. 182 and Allen, *Soviet Economic Warfare*, pp. 18–19, 188 and 216.

20. George Liska, *The New Statecraft: Foreign Aid in American Foreign Policy* (Chicago: University of Chicago Press, 1960), p. 2.

21. Joan Nelson, *Aid, Influence, and Foreign Policy* (New York: Macmillan, 1968), p. 93.

22. Of course, Western states too use foreign aid for political purposes. For a discussion of the political aspects of American foreign aid, see *ibid.*

23. Strange, *Soviet Trade Weapon*, p. 17.

24. Leon Herman, "The Political Goals of Soviet Foreign Aid," in *Dimensions of Soviet Economic Power*, part 2, p. 477 and Taborsky, *Communist Penetration*, p. 306.

25. James Carter, *The Net Cost of Soviet Foreign Aid* (New York: Praeger, 1969), pp. 39 and 41.

26. For a discussion of these, and other, cases see Taborsky, *Communist Penetration*, pp. 312–13.

27. Alan Ford, *The Anglo-Iranian Oil Dispute of 1951–1952* (Berkeley: University of California Press, 1954), p. 123.

28. Wilczynski, *East-West Trade*, p. 245 and *Impact of Oil Exports From the Soviet Bloc*, vol. 2 (Washington: National Petroleum Council, 1962), p. 433.

29. *USSR and Third World* 1, no. 3 (February 15–March 21, 1971): 134.

30. Peter Wiles, *Communist International Economics* (New York: Praeger, 1969), p. 501 and Kovner, *Challenge of Coexistence*, p. 54.

31. Wilczynski, *East-West Trade*, p. 245.

32. Kovner, *Challenge of Coexistence*, p. 64; Wiles, *Communist International Economics*, p. 505; Pisar, *Coexistence and Commerce*, p. 183; and *Impact of Oil Exports From the Soviet Bloc*, vol. 2, p. 430.

33. John Griffiths, *Modern Iceland* (New York: Praeger, 1969), p. 58 and Wiles, *ibid.*, pp. 517–18.

34. Wiles, *ibid.*, and Kovner, *Challenge of Coexistence*, p. 54.

35. Icelandic imports of Soviet oil products in thousands of metric tons were 0 in *1951*, 0 in *1952*, 39 in *1953*, 218 in *1954*, 232 in *1955*, 265 in *1956*, 294 in *1957*, 322 in *1958*, and 347 in *1959*. See Wiles, *ibid.*, p. 517. Also see Michael Gehlen, "The

Politics of Soviet Foreign Trade," *The Western Political Quarterly* 18, no. 1 (March 1965): 111.

36. Wilczynski, *East-West Trade,* p. 251 and Griffiths, *Modern Iceland,* p. 140.

37. Wiles, *Communist International Economics,* p. 518.

38. On Cuba, see Gardner Patterson, *Discrimination in International Trade: The Policy Issues, 1945–1965* (Princeton: Princeton University Press, 1966), p. 15.

39. Iurii Kapelinskii, *Torgovlia SSSR s kapitalisticheskimi stranami posle vtoroi mirovoi voiny* (Trade of the USSR with Capitalist Countries After the Second World War) (Moscow: Izdatel'stvo "Mezhdunarodnye otnosheniia," 1970), pp. 60–61 and Halford Hoskins, "Problems Raised by the Soviet Oil Offensive," United States Senate, Committee on the Judiciary (Washington: U.S. Government Printing Office, 1962), p. 3.

40. Wilczynski, *East-West Trade,* p. 243 and Virgil Salera, "An Approach to Economic Strategy," in Abshire and Allen, *National Security,* pp. 657–70.

41. Kapelinskii, *Torgovlia SSSR,* ch. 2, P. N. Kumykin, ed., *50 let sovetskoi vneshnei torgovli* (50 Years of Soviet Foreign Trade) (Moscow: Izdatel'stvo "Mezhdunarodnye otnosheniia," 1967), pp. 84–85; and B. Vaganov, "The Leninist Foreign Trade Policy," *International Affairs,* no. 5 (May 1969): 53–54. Quotation is from Kapelinskii, p. 34.

42. Wilczynski, *East-West Trade,* p. 246.

43. *Ibid.,* pp. 178–79.

44. Mose Harvey, *East-West Trade and United States Policy* (New York: National Association of Manufacturers, 1966), p. 75.

45. Allen, *Soviet Economic Warfare,* p. 27.

46. Nicolas Spulber, "The Soviet-Bloc Foreign Trade System" *Law and Contemporary Problems,* State Trading, Part 2, School of Law, Duke University 24, no. 3 (Summer 1959): 432.

47. V. S. Pozdniakov, "The State Monopoly of Foreign Trade," *The Soviet Review* 9, no. 2 (Summer 1968): 45 (translated from *Sovetskoe Gosudarstvo i Pravo* (The Soviet State and Law) no. 10, 1967).

48. *Ibid.,* p. 48. Also see Vladimir Pozdniakov, *Gosudarstvennaia monopoliia vneshnei torgovli v SSSR* (The State Monopoly of Foreign Trade in the USSR) (Moscow: Izdatel'stvo "Mezhdunarodnye otnosheniia," 1969), pp. 106–16.

49. Pisar, *Coexistence and Commerce,* p. 147 and Glen Smith, *Soviet Foreign Trade: Organization, Operations, and Policy, 1918–1971* (New York: Praeger, 1973), p. 95.

50. United Nations, Economic Commission for Europe, "Trade Problems Between Countries Having Different Economic and Social Sytems," *Economic Bulletin for Europe* 16, no. 2 (November 1964): 41.

51. Pozdniakov, "State Monopoly of Foreign Trade," p. 46.

52. Wilczynski, *East-West Trade,* pp. 181 and 341.

53. B. Pichugin, "The Ninth Five-Year Plan and International Economic Cooperation," *International Affairs*, no. 2 (February 1972): 8.

54. Patolichev, *USSR Foreign Trade*, p. 14.

55. *23rd Congress of the CPSU* (Moscow: Novosti Press Agency Publishing House, 1966), pp. 261–62.

56. Iu. Kapelinskii, "Soviet Economic Relations with Developed Capitalist Countries," *International Affairs*, no. 3 (March 1968): 101.

57. U.S. Department of Commerce, Overseas Business Reports (OBR 70-52), "Trading With East Europe," rev. ed., October, 1972, pp. 6–7. The Department of Commerce views "compensatory trading" rather broadly, applying this term to non-cash trade transactions, but the Soviets use this term in a rather different context, referring to foreign credits for an enterprise which are repaid with future production from that enterprise. I use the Department of Commerce interpretation.

58. See Michael Tanzer, *The Political Economy of International Oil and the Underdeveloped Countries* (Boston: Beacon Press, 1969), p. 79.

59. Pisar, *Coexistence and Commerce*, p. 161.

60. Schlesinger, "Strategic Leverage," p. 702.

61. Taborsky, *Communist Penetration*, p. 304 and Allen, *Soviet Economic Warfare*, p. 14.

62. Wilczynski, *East-West Trade*, p. 206.

63. Mazanov, "International Settlements of CMEA Countries: Improvement Problems," *International Affairs*, no. 4 (April 1969): 72–73.

64. See Penelope Thunberg, "The Soviet Union in the World Economy," in *Dimensions of Soviet Economic Power*, part 2, p. 420 and V. Zolotarev, "Integration of CMEA Countries and the Development of the World Socialist Market," *International Affairs*, no. 1 (January 1972): 19. Beginning in 1975, CMEA began to move away from five-year fixed prices and started to make annual adjustments based on world market prices. See Radio Free Europe Research, "RAD Background Report 48 (Hungary)," March 14, 1975, p. 2.

65. United Nations, Economic Commission for Europe, p. 42 and Raymond Vernon, "Apparatchiks and Entrepreneurs: U.S.-Soviet Economic Relations," *Foreign Affairs* 52, no. 2 (January 1974): 252–53.

66. Wilczynski, *East-West Trade*, p. 170.

67. For Soviet comments on trade reliability, see P. Yurov, "Economic Co-operation: The Outlook," *New Times*, no. 7 (February 1974): 19.

68. J. H. Carmical, "Soviet Pushing Its Oil Exports," *The New York Times*, July 29, 1962, section 3, p. 14; *Impact of Oil Exports From the Soviet Bloc*, vol. 2, p. 432; and editorial, "Red is for Danger," *World Petroleum* 33, no. 10 (September 1962): 41.

69. On India, see "India Steps Up Pressure on Refiners," *Oil and Gas Journal* 67, no. 33 (August 18, 1969): 37. On Ceylon, see *Mizan*, Supplement B, no. 4 (July–

August, 1969): 2. Colombo Radio reported on July 16, 1969 that the USSR had failed to deliver refined oil products owing to the closure of the Suez Canal.

70. Editorial, *The Washington Post,* March 29, 1974, p. A30; *Platt's Oilgram News Service* 52, no. 14 (January 21, 1974): 4; Hedrick Smith, "Soviet Diplomacy: Waiting Game as Pendulum Swings Away From Moscow," *The New York Times,* November 26, 1973, p. 5; *Petroleum Intelligence Weekly* 13, no. 14 (April 8, 1974): 10; *Platt's Oilgram News Service* 52, no. 29 (February 11, 1974): 3; *Facts on File* 33, no. 1725 (November 18–24, 1973): 963; "Russian Oil: Sorry, Comrades," *The Economist* 250, no. 6812 (March 16, 1974): 92–93; and U.S. government memorandum, March 25, 1974.

71. Frumkin, *Modern Theories,* p. 483.

72. U.S. Department of State, *Background Notes: Union of Soviet Socialist Republics,* March 1973, p. 7 and U.S. Department of Commerce, Bureau of East-West Trade, *Selected U.S.S.R. and Eastern European Economic Data,* p. 4.

73. U.S. Department of Commerce, Bureau of East-West Trade, p. 4 and Frank Gardner, "Big Spurt in Income From Oil Sales Rescues Soviets," *Oil and Gas Journal* 72, no. 31 (August 5, 1974): 25.

74. Timothy Stanley and Darnell Whitt, *Detente Diplomacy: United States and European Security in the 1970's* (New York: Dunellen, 1970), p. 78.

75. U.S. Department of Commerce, Bureau of East-West Trade, p. 18. The "West" does not include the United States.

76. Vaganov, "Leninist Foreign Trade Policy," p. 51.

77. Wilczynski, *East-West Trade,* pp. 339–40.

78. For an analysis of price discrimination against CMEA members, see chapter 5.

79. Wilczynski, *East-West Trade,* p. 339.

80. John Hardt, George Holliday, and Young Kim, "Western Investment in Communist Economies," prepared for the Subcommittee on Multinational Corporations of the Committee on Foreign Relations, U.S. Senate, June 11, 1974, p. 6.

81. "Russia and the West: The Real Aims," *The Economist* 247, no. 6774 (June 23, 1973): 37.

82. Vernon, "Apparatchiks and Entrepreneurs," p. 254.

83. "Soviet Union: The Size of the Outstretched Hand," *The Economist* 248, no. 6779 (July 28, 1973): 41 and "New Venturers to Muscovy," *ibid.* 237, no. 6632 (October 3, 1970): 19.

84. Wolfgang Leonhard, "The Domestic Politics of the New Soviet Foreign Policy," *Foreign Affairs* 52, no. 1 (October 1973): pp. 59–74.

85. See Yurov, "Economic Co-operation," p. 18.

86. B. Svetlov, 'Soviet-US Relations Today," *International Affairs,* no. 3 (March 1973): 30.

87. Yurov, "Economic Co-operation," pp. 18–19.

88. Leonid Sabel'nikov, *Gosudarstvenno-monopolisticheskie sredstva torgovoi*

voiny (State-Monopoly Means of Trade War) (Moscow: Izdatel'stvo "Mezhdunarod-nye otnosheniia," 1973), pp. 191–200 and Vaganov, "Leninist Foreign Trade Policy," p. 53.

89. Pichugin, "Ninth Five-Year Plan," p. 14.

90. B. Svetlov, "USSR–USA: Possibilities and Reality," *International Affairs,* no. 2 (February 1972): 20.

91. Harvey, *East-West Trade and U.S. Policy,* p. 69.

92. Bazhenov, "Soviet-US Economic Relations," *International Affairs,* no. 6 (June 1972): 83.

93. V. Morozov, "CMEA Countries: Wide International Cooperation," *International Affairs,* no. 4 (April 1974): 15.

94. *23rd Congress of the CPSU,* p. 260.

3/Domestic Foundations of Soviet Energy Policies

1. "Is Siberia Really the Answer?" *The Economist* 250, no. 6809 (February 23, 1974): 47.

2. Robert Ebel, *Communist Trade in Oil and Gas* (New York: Praeger, 1970), p. 7; and Robert Campbell, *The Economics of Soviet Oil and Gas* (Baltimore: Johns Hopkins University Press, 1968), p. 157.

3. Boris Rachkov, *Oil Nationalism and Imperialism* (New Delhi: People's Publishing House, 1967), p. 70. For a Soviet analysis of Western oil interests in Russia from the 1880s until 1918, see Aleksandr Fursenko, *Neftianye tresty i mirovaia politika* (Oil Trusts and World Politics) (Moscow and Leningrad: Izdatel'stvo "Nauka," 1965).

4. Boris Rachkov, *Oil, Nations and Monopolies* (Moscow: Novosti Press Agency Publishing House), pp. 102–3.

5. Louis Fischer, *Oil Imperialism* (New York: International Publishers, 1926), p. 238; and Michael Tanzer, *The Political Economy of International Oil and the Underdeveloped Countries* (Boston: Beacon Press, 1969), p. 320.

6. See Fischer, *ibid.,* and E. P. Gurov, "The Export of Crude Oil and Petroleum Products," *Vneshniaia Torgovlia* (Foreign Trade), no. 8 (August, 1967), translated in Ebel, *Communist Trade,* p. 206.

7. Robert Loring Allen, *Soviet Economic Warfare* (Washington: Public Affairs Press, 1960), p. 261.

8. J. E. Hartshorn, *Politics and World Oil Economics,* rev. ed. (New York: Praeger, 1967), p. 235. The author is citing remarks made by E. P. Gurov in 1960. Gurov was the chairman of Soiuznefteeksport.

9. Gurov, "Export of Crude Oil," p. 207 and Jozef Wilczynski, *The Economics and Politics of East-West Trade* (New York: Praeger, 1969), p. 262.

10. Stephen Longrigg, *Oil in the Middle East,* 3rd ed. (London: Oxford University Press, 1968), p. 86.

11. Campbell, *Economics of Soviet Oil,* pp. 2 and 121.

12. Christopher Tugendhat, *Oil, the Biggest Business* (New York: Putnam, 1968), p. 115.

13. David Hooson, *A New Soviet Heartland?* (Princeton: Van Nostrand, 1964), p. 37 and Theodore Shabad, *The Basic Industrial Resources of the U.S.S.R.* (New York: Columbia University Press, 1969), p. 12.

14. Herbert Feis, *Three International Episodes* (New York: W. W. Norton, 1946), p. 176 and Ebel, *Communist Trade,* pp. 28–29. For a discussion of German damage to the Soviet oil industry, see "Oil on the Waters?" *The Economist* 150, no. 5353 (March 30, 1946): 482.

15. Ministerstvo Vneshnei Torgovli SSSR, *Vneshniaia torgovlia SSSR: statisticheskii sbornik, 1918–1966* (Ministry of Foreign Trade of the USSR, Foreign Trade of the USSR: Statistical Compendium, 1918–1966) (Moscow: Izdatel'stvo "Mezhdunarodnye otnosheniia," 1967), p. 134.

16. For a discussion of American and Iranian oil shipments to the USSR, see D. J. Payton-Smith, *Oil: A Study of War-time Policy and Administration* (London: Her Majesty's Stationery Office, 1971).

17. "Oil on the Waters?" p. 482.

18. Allen, *Soviet Economic Warfare,* p. 261.

19. Robert King, "Fossil Fuels," in *World Energy Demands and the Middle East,* part 1 (Washington: The Middle East Institute, 1973), pp. 56–57.

20. *International Economic Report of the President (February 1974)* (Washington: U.S. Government Printing Office, 1974) cited in *Middle East Information Series* 26–27 (Spring/Summer, 1974), p. 101 and R. M. Burrell, "Opportunity Knocks for the Kremlin's Drive East," *New Middle East,* no. 46 (July 1972): 11.

21. United Nations, Statistical Office, *Statistical Yearbook 1972* (New York: United Nations, 1973), pp. 180–81 and *Soviet Oil to 1980,* QER Special, no. 14, June 1973 (London: The Economist Intelligence Unit, 1973), p. 3. The United Nations figure for "proven" reserves is 5.716 billion tons. See United Nations, Statistical Office, *Statistical Yearbook 1973* (New York: United Nations, 1974), p. 171.

22. Lawrence Rocks and Richard Runyon, *The Energy Crisis* (New York: Crown Publishers, 1972), p. 137.

23. "Soviets Claim 35% of Global Gas as World Congress Opens," *Oil and Gas Journal* 68, no. 24 (June 15, 1970): 49 and "Now Those Gas Prices are Soaring Too," *The Economist* 252, no. 6835 (August 24, 1974): 72.

24. "Russians Claim World's Largest Gas Reserves," *Oil and Gas Journal* 66, no. 9 (February 26, 1968): 64, and United Nations, *Statistical Yearbook 1973,* p. 173.

25. Campbell, *Economics of Soviet Oil;* Shabad, *Basic Industrial Resources;* Violet Conolly, *Beyond the Urals: Economic Developments in Soviet Asia* (London: Oxford University Press, 1967), and Robert Ebel, *The Petroleum Industry of the Soviet Union* (Washington: American Petroleum Institute, 1961).

26. Hooson, *A New Soviet Heartland?*, p. 37.

27. Frank Gardner, "New Areas Spur Soviet Oil Gains," *Oil and Gas Journal* 66, no. 3 (January 15, 1968): 65.

28. Robert Campbell, "Some Issues in Soviet Energy Policy for the Seventies," *Middle East Information Series* 26–27 (Spring/Summer, 1974): 93.

29. Abraham Becker, "Oil and the Persian Gulf in Soviet Policy in the 1970s," in Michael Confino and Shimon Shamir, eds., *The U.S.S.R. and the Middle East* (New York: John Wiley and Sons and Jerusalem: Israel Universities Press, 1973), p. 177.

30. For Shashin's comments, see *Platt's Oilgram News Service* 52, no. 113 (June 12, 1974): 3.

31. A. F. Q. Scanlan, "The Energy Balance of the Comecon Countries," Round Table on the Exploitation of Siberia's Natural Resources, Brussels (January 30–February 1, 1974), p. 12.

32. Valentin Shashin, "The Soviet Oil Industry—Today and Tomorrow," *World Petroleum* 42, no. 5 (June, 1971): 40; Violet Conolly, "East Siberian Oil," *Mizan* 13, no. 1 (August 1971): 16; and Kosygin's report on the Tenth Five-Year Plan, *Pravda,* March 2, 1976, pp. 2–6.

33. "Russians Develop Siberian Fields," *The New York Times,* International Economic Survey, January 27, 1974, p. 41; and (for 1975) Albert Pin, "Grand Programme of Upbuilding," *New Times,* no. 11 (March 1976): 5.

34. Frank Gardner, "Soviets Aim High for 1974," *Oil and Gas Journal* 72, no. 2 (January 14, 1974): 19.

35. 230–260 million tons is cited in "Their Alaska," *The Economist* 234, no. 6596 (January 24, 1970): 32; 230–260 million is also cited in Shashin, "Soviet Oil," p. 38; 240–260 is cited in *Soviet Oil to 1980*, p. 13; 300 is cited in Valentin Shashin, "Soviet Oil," *New Times,* no. 15 (April 1974): 21; and 300–310 is cited in Pin, "Grand Programme," p. 5.

36. For a discussion of Soviet offshore oil programs, see A. Geodekian, "Skol'ko nefti u neptuna," (How Much Oil Neptune Has) *Pravda,* May 29, 1974, p. 3.

37. E. Sviridov, "Underwater Oil," *New Times,* no. 47 (November 1973): 28–29.

38. Seyom Brown and Larry Fabian, "Diplomats at Sea," *Foreign Affairs* 52, no. 2 (January 1974): 307 and Y. Igorev, "The Law of the Sea Conference," *New Times,* no. 36 (September 1974): 10–11.

39. King, "Fossil Fuels," pp. 63–64.

40. John Hardt, "West Siberia: The Quest for Energy," *Problems of Communism* 22, no. 3 (May–June 1973): 26; and "Soviets Speed Big Gas Arteries," *Oil and Gas Journal* 65, no. 9 (February 27, 1967): 86.

41. Shabad, *Basic Industrial Resources,* p. 6.

42. *Ibid.,* p. 4.

43. Campbell, *Economics of Soviet Oil,* p. 14.

308 / 3/Domestic Foundations of Energy Policies

44. U.S. Department of the Interior, Bureau of Mines, "The Mineral Industry of the U.S.S.R.," *Minerals Yearbook, Area Reports: International* 4 (Washington: U.S. Government Printing Office, 1971), p. 749.

45. Campbell, *Economics of Soviet Oil,* pp. 12–13.

46. Jaroslav Polach, "The Energy Gap in the Communist World," *East Europe* 18, no. 4 (April 1969): 24.

47. U.S. Department of the Interior, p. 749; Shabad, *Basic Industrial Resources,* p. 6; Leonid Tomashpol'skii, *Neft' i gaz v mirovom energeticheskom balanse (1900–2000 gg.)* (Oil and Gas in the World Energy Balance, 1900–2000) (Moscow: Izdatel'stvo "Nedra," 1968), p. 139; Hardt, "West Siberia," p. 26; John Hardt and George Holliday, *U.S.-Soviet Commercial Relations: The Interplay of Economics, Technology Transfer, and Diplomacy* (Washington: U.S. Government Printing Office, 1973), p. 17; Scanlan, "Energy Balance," p. 17; and B. Konovalov and I. Novodvorsky, "From Logs to Tritium," *Izvestiia,* February 2, 1974, p. 5 (*Current Digest of the Soviet Press* 26, no. 6 [March 6, 1974]: 7). It has been projected that American energy usage in 1980 will be oil, 42%; natural gas, 26%; coal, 20%; nuclear energy, 9%; and hydroelectric power, 4%. See J.M. Montgomery, "Capital Requirements and the Individual Company," in The Economist Intelligence Unit, *International Oil Symposium* (London: The Economist Intelligence Unit, 1972), p. 54.

48. R. S. Carlsmith, "Alternative Sources of Energy," in *World Energy Demands and the Middle East,* p. 69.

49. United Nations, Statistical Office, *Statistical Yearbook 1961* (New York: United Nations, 1961), p. 280 and United Nations, Statistical Office, *World Energy Supplies, 1961–70,* Statistical Papers, series J, no. 15 (New York: United Nations, 1972), p. 57.

50. *Statistical Yearbook 1973,* pp. 348 and 350.

51. Marshall Goldman, "With Russian Oil, Marketing Skill," *The New York Times,* January 21, 1972, p. 69.

52. Marshall Goldman, "The Soviet Role in Oil, Economics and the Middle East," *Middle East Information Series* 23 (May 1973): 89 and 'Russian Oil: Where Will They Get it From?" *The Economist* 249, no. 6797 (December 1, 1973): 40.

53. Christopher Wren, "Soviet Is Testing Propane Gas as Power for Vehicles," *The New York Times,* December 26, 1973, p. 65 and "U.S.S.R. to Get Gas-Driven Car," *International Herald Tribune,* September 25, 1974, p. 7.

54. For statistics on Soviet oil consumption, see "Russian Oil: Where Will They Get it From?" p. 40; Becker, "Oil and the Persian Gulf," p. 178; Campbell, *Economics of Soviet Oil,* p. 162; and U.S. Department of the Interior, p. 758.

55. "Is Siberia Really the Answer?" p. 47.

56. See *Soviet Oil to 1980,* p. 18. Soviet oil production in 1980 should be approximately 630 million tons. Soviet oil production statistics for 1974 and 1975 can be found in *Izvestiia,* January 25, 1975, p. 2 and *Pravda,* February 1, 1976, p. 1. Production amounted to 459 million tons in 1974 and 491 million tons in 1975.

57. Becker, "Oil and the Persian Gulf," p. 176.

58. Alexei Kosygin, *Directives of the Five-Year Economic Development Plan of the USSR for 1971–1975* (Moscow: Novosti Press Agency Publishing House, 1971), p. 40; and "Russian Headaches," *Petroleum Press Service* 40, no. 3 (March 1973): 87.

59. Hardt, "West Siberia," p. 29; "Soviet Union: The Size of the Outstretched Hand," *The Economist* 248, no. 6779 (July 28, 1973): 36; and J. Richard Lee, "The Soviet Petroleum Industry: Promise and Problems," in *Soviet Economic Prospects for the Seventies* (Washington: U.S. Government Printing Office, 1973), p. 285.

60. Lee, *ibid.,* p. 284 and *Platt's Oilgram News Service* 52, no. 20 (January 29, 1974): 3. Trying to paint a rosier picture of Soviet oil production in 1973, a Radio Moscow English language broadcast to Britain and Ireland on January 2, 1974 claimed that production had been 430 million tons. See Foreign Broadcast Information Service, *Soviet Union* 3, no. 2 (January 3, 1974), p. S1.

61. N. K. Baibakov, "On the State Plan for the Development of the U.S.S.R. National Economy in 1974," *Pravda,* December 13, 1973, pp. 2–3 (*Current Digest of the Soviet Press* 25, no. 50 [January 9, 1974]: 7) and Hedrick Smith, "Soviet Plan for 1974 Promises Faster Rise in Consumer Sector," *The New York Times,* December 13, 1973, p. 1.

62. For the *Tass* statement of January 7, 1974 see Foreign Broadcast Information Service, *Soviet Union* 3, no. 5 (January 8, 1974), p. S3. For Kosygin's remarks, see Christopher Wren, "Kosygin Says Soviet Energy Pool Buoys Economy," *The New York Times,* June 13, 1974, p. 5. For Shashin's use of the 458 figure, see Shashin, "Soviet Oil," p. 21 and Christopher Wren, "Soviet Increases Target for Oil Output," *The New York Times,* April 12, 1974, p. 43. For the Radio Moscow statement of January 1, 1974 see Foreign Broadcast Information Service, *Soviet Union* 3, no. 2 (January 3, 1974), p. S2.

63. Hardt, "West Siberia," p. 29; *Platt's Oilgram News Service* 52, no. 20 (January 29, 1974): 3; Theodore Shabad, "Reports By Soviet Indicate a Wide Lag in Production," *The New York Times,* December 24, 1972, p. 2: Lee, "Soviet Petroleum Industry," p. 284; and Hedrick Smith, "Position 'Tense' on Soviet Energy," *The New York Times,* November 26, 1973, p. 49.

64. Wren, "Kosygin Says Soviet Energy Pool Buoys Economy," p. 5 and *Izvestiia,* January 25, 1975, p. 2.

65. *Pravda,* February 1, 1976, p. 1.

66. Leslie Dienes, "Geographical Problems of Allocation in the Soviet Fuel Supply," *Energy Policy* 1, no. 1 (June 1973): 3–20.

67. For a discussion of how construction problems in the Tiumen region are hindering resource development, see A. Murzin and F. Chursin, "Offensive on the Ob," *Pravda,* July 10, 1974, p. 2 and July 13, 1974, p. 2 (*Current Digest of the Soviet Press* 26, no. 28 [August 7, 1974]: 11–12).

68. Dienes, "Geographical Problems," p. 12.

69. Lee, "Soviet Petroleum Industry," pp. 285–86.

70. Soviet oil minister Valentin Shashin complained about the pipe shortage. See *Platt's Oilgram News Service* 52, no. 113 (June 12, 1974): 3. See also "Soviet Oil: A Sticky Problem for U.K. Conservatives," *Oil and Gas Journal* 61, no. 7 (February 18, 1963): 72. For a discussion of the gas pipeline shortage, see "Soviets Speed Big Gas Arteries," pp. 84–87.

71. Alexei Kortunov, "Stupendous Pipeline Programme," *New Times,* no. 49 (December 1972): 14, and Hedrick Smith, "Building of Soviet Pipeline is Falling Behind Schedule," *The New York Times,* March 24, 1973, pp. 43 and 46.

72. Campbell, *Economics of Soviet Oil,* pp. 141–43 and Shabad, *Basic Industrial Resources,* p. 18.

73. Ebel, *The Petroleum Industry of the Soviet Union,* p. 75 and Shashin, "Soviet Oil," p. 21.

74. "Is Siberia Really the Answer?" p. 46.

75. T. Khachaturov, "Natural Resources and the Planning of the National Economy," *Voprosy Ekonomiki* (Questions of Economics), no. 8 (August 1973): 16–19 (*Current Digest of the Soviet Press* 25, no. 49 [January 2, 1974]: 6–7).

76. Conolly, "East Siberian Oil," p. 17.

77. Campbell, Economics of Soviet Oil, p. 137.

78. For a discussion of negotiations with the United States and Japan, see chapter 12. For a discussion of East European investments in the USSR, see chapter 9.

79. Conolly, *Beyond the Urals: Economic Developments in Soviet Asia,* p. 261.

80. Campbell, "Some Issues in Soviet Energy Policy for the Seventies," p. 98.

81. A. Krems, "Kladovye severa osvaivat' bystree" (Making Use of the Storehouses of the North More Rapidly), *Pravda,* May 6, 1974, p. 2.

82. *Facts on File* 33, no. 1727 (December 2–8, 1973): 1021; Smith, "Position 'Tense' on Soviet Energy," p. 49; *Facts on File, ibid.,* pp. 1021–22; Hedrick Smith, "Pravda Cautions on Wasting Fuel," *The New York Times,* November 28, 1973, p. 8 and Wren, "Kosygin Says Soviet Energy Pool Buoys Economy," p. 5.

4/Development of the Soviet Oil Trade

1. David Morison, "Soviet Interest in Middle East Oil," *Mizan* 10, no. 3 (May–June 1968): 79.

2. In 1972, the USSR ranked seventh as an exporter of crude oil after Saudi Arabia, Iran, Kuwait, Venezuela, Libya and Nigeria. It ranked fourth as an exporter of oil products after Venezuela, the Netherlands Antilles and the Netherlands, and it ranked fifth as a total exporter of oil after Saudi Arabia, Venezuela, Iran, and Kuwait. See United Nations, Statistical Office, *World Energy Supplies, 1969–1972,* Statistical Papers, Series J, no. 17 (New York: United Nations, 1974), pp. 50–57 and 77–88.

3. Robert Loring Allen, *Soviet Economic Warfare* (Washington: Public Affairs Press, 1960), p. 261; Mark Garrison and Morris Crawford, "Soviet Trade With the

Free World in 1961," in *Dimensions of Soviet Economic Power* (Washington: U.S. Government Printing Office, 1962), part 2, p. 448; "Soviet Oil Imports Jump 50,000 B/D," *Oil and Gas Journal* 71, no. 26 (June 25, 1973): 73; John Hardt, "West Siberia: The Quest for Energy," *Problems of Communism* 22, no. 3 (May–June 1973): 25; and Boris Rachkov, *Oil Nationalism and Imperialism* (New Delhi: People's Publishing House, 1967), p. 73.

4. Emile Bustani, "Soviet Oil Threatens the Middle East," *World Petroleum* 32, no. 2 (February 1961): 41.

5. Robert Ebel, *Communist Trade in Oil and Gas* (New York: Praeger, 1970), p. 210; *Soviet Oil to 1980,* QER Special, no. 14, June, 1973 (London: The Economist Intelligence Unit, 1973), pp. 31–32; "Soviet Trade in Slow Decline," *Petroleum Press Service* 39, no. 5 (May 1972): 162; and Iain Elliot, *The Soviet Energy Balance* (New York: Praeger, 1974), p. 253.

6. Michael Gehlen, "The Politics of Soviet Foreign Trade," *The Western Political Quarterly* 18, no. 1 (March 1965): 114.

7. Boris Rachkov, "Sovetskii Soiuz—krupnyi eksporter netti i nefteproduktov," (Soviet Union—Large Exporter of Oil and Oil Products) *Vneshniaia Torgovlia* (Foreign Trade), no. 3 (March 1964): 16, and Rachkov, *Oil Nationalism,* p. 74.

8. Harold Lubell, *The Soviet Oil Offensive and Inter-Bloc Economic Competition* (Santa Monica: Rand Corporation, 1961), pp. 54–55.

9. Frank Gardner, "Need for Cash Fires Soviet Export Drive," *Oil and Gas Journal* 71, no. 8 (February 19, 1973): 24 and "Russian Oil Exports—What to Do?" *World Petroleum* 32, no. 9 (August 1961): 27.

10. See "Russian Oil: Where Will They Get it From?" *The Economist* 249, no. 6797 (December 1, 1973): 40.

11. Samuel Nakaslan, *Soviet Oil in East-West Trade* (Washington: U.S. Government Printing Office, 1962), p. 13.

12. Lubell, *Soviet Oil Offensive,* p. 39 and Michael Tanzer, *The Political Economy of International Oil and the Underdeveloped Countries* (Boston: Beacon Press, 1969), p. 80.

13. Harold Lubell, "The Soviet Oil Offensive," *Quarterly Review of Economics and Business* 1, no. 4 (November 1961): 10 and "Russian Oil Competition," *World Petroleum* 31, no. 10 (September 1960): 52.

14. The Soviets hope to break the economic and political power of the major Western oil companies, the so-called "Seven Sisters," which include Exxon (formerly Standard Oil of New Jersey), the Royal Dutch Shell Group, Mobil, Texaco, Gulf, Standard Oil of California, and British Petroleum.

15. Cuba is an exception as the Soviets would probably like to reduce their role as an oil supplier. For a discussion of this issue, see chapter 9.

16. For statistical data on Soviet exports to communist-ruled states, see the yearly editions of *Vneshniaia torgovlia SSSR* (Foreign Trade of the USSR) as well as United Nations, Economic Commission for Europe, "Foreign Trade and Economic Development in Eastern Europe and the Soviet Union," *Economic Bulletin*

for Europe 11, no. 1 (June 1959): Appendix A, p. A28; P. Yurov, "Economic Cooperation: The Outlook," *New Times,* no. 7 (February 1974): 19; Ebel, *Communist Trade,* p. 44; and Robert Ebel, *The Petroleum Industry of the Soviet Union* (Washington: American Petroleum Institute, 1961), p. 156.

17. Abraham Becker, "Oil and the Persian Gulf in Soviet Policy in the 1970s," in Michael Confino and Shimon Shamir, eds., *The U.S.S.R. and the Middle East* (New York: John Wiley and Jerusalem: Israel Universities Press, 1973), p. 179.

18. *Vneshniaia torgovlia SSSR za 1973 god:statisticheskii obzor* (Foreign Trade of the USSR for 1973: Statistical Abstract) (Moscow: Izdatel'stvo "Mezhdunarodnye otnosheniia," 1974), pp. 70–71.

19. In 1973, Soviet oil exports, in millions of metric tons, went to Afghanistan (.165). Austria (1.250), Bangladesh (.048), Belgium (1.673), Bulgaria (9.322), Cuba (7.435), Cyprus (.122), Czechoslovakia (14.340), Denmark (.633), Egypt (.352), Finland (10.028), France (5.348), East Germany (12.985), West Germany (6.274), Ghana (.614), Great Britain (.834), Greece (.797), Guinea (.085), Hungary (6.294), Iceland (.468), India (.477), Ireland (.183), Italy (8.652), Japan (3.023), Mongolia (.323), Morocco (.943), the Netherlands (3.220), Nigeria (.002), North Korea (.585), North Vietnam (.230), Norway (.603), Poland (12.336), Senegal (.011), Sierra Leone (less than 500 tons), Somalia (.075), Spain (.510), Sweden (3.216), Switzerland (.658), Syria (.036), Yugoslavia (3.891). Total exports were 118.3 million tons. See *ibid.,* pp. 70–71.

20. Computed on the basis of West European import statistics cited in United Nations, Statistical Office, *World Energy Supplies, 1961–1964* (New York: United Nations, 1966), pp. 51–52, 60–62; *ibid., 1965–1968* (1970), pp. 53–54, 64–66; *ibid., 1969–1972* (1974), pp. 50–57, 77–88; Soviet export statistics cited in *Vneshniaia torgovlia SSSR za 1961 god: statisticheskii obzor* (Foreign Trade of the USSR for 1961: Statistical Abstract) (Moscow: Vneshtorgizdat, 1962), pp. 47–48; *ibid.,* 1969 (Moscow: Izdatel'stvo "Mezhdunarodnye otnosheniia, 1970), pp. 67–68; *ibid.,* 1973, pp. 70–71.

21. See Paul Swain, "Soviet Oil Exports Could Get Rough," *Oil and Gas Journal* 58, no. 28 (July 11, 1960): 77.

22. Christopher Tugendhat, *Oil, the Biggest Business* (New York: Putnam, 1968), pp. 249–50.

23. For statistics on Soviet oil exports to noncommunist states, see Ebel, *Communist Trade,* Table 53, pp. 386–88.

24. *Dimensions of Soviet Economic Power,* Part 2, pp. 734 and 742; "Soviet Oil Offensive Checked in Europe," *Oil and Gas Journal* 61, no. 37 (September 16, 1963): 84 and *Dimensions of Soviet Economic Power,* Part 2, pp. 736–42.

25. "Future of Russian Oil," *World Petroleum* 32, no. 10 (September 1961): 60–62.

26. N. Lyubimov, "Soviet Foreign Trade Problems," *International Affairs,* no. 8 (August, 1965): 14.

27. See "Say the Russians: We'll Take More of the Market, Please," *Oil and Gas Journal* 58, no. 43 (October 24, 1960): 54; Walter Laqueur, *The Struggle for the*

Middle East: The Soviet Union in the Mediterranean, 1958–1968 (New York: Macmillan, 1969), p. 120; and Benjamin Shwadran, "Middle East Oil in 1960," *Middle Eastern Affairs* 12, no. 6 (June–July 1961): 167.

28. Ebel, *Communist Trade*, p. 74.

29. "Russian Oil Exports—What to Do?" p. 27. Also see Gordon Reed, "Russia's Oil Drive," *World Petroleum* 32, no. 10 (September 1961): 55 and John Berry, "Oil and Soviet Policy in the Middle East," *Middle East Journal* 26, no. 2 (Spring 1972): 149.

30. Leon Herman, "The Soviet Oil Offensive," *Reporter* 26, no. 13 (June 21, 1962): 26 and Benjamin Shwadran, "Middle East Oil 1961," *Middle Eastern Affairs* 13, no. 8 (October 1962): 228.

31. "Russian Oil Competition," p. 52 and J. E. Hartohorn, *Politics and World Oil Economics,* rev. ed. (New York: Praeger, 1967), p. 236. For details on the sale to ENI, see chapter 10.

32. See Gurov's remarks at Beirut in "Say the Russians: We'll Take More of the Market, Please," p. 54; Laqueur, *Struggle,* p. 120; and Shwadran, "Middle East Oil in 1960," p. 167.

33. See Raymond Vernon, "Apparatchiks and Entrepreneurs: U.S.–Soviet Economic Relations," *Foreign Affairs* 52, no. 2 (January 1974): 257.

34. *Dimensions of Soviet Economic Power,* pp. 46 and 22.

35. Reed, "Russia's Oil Drive," pp. 54–55.

36. See Gurov's remarks in "Say the Russians: We'll Take More of the Market, Please," p. 55.

37. This is discussed in *The Mizan Newsletter* 2, no. 9 (October 1960): 13.

38. Benjamin Shwadran, "Middle East Oil 1962—II," *Middle Eastern Affairs* 14, no. 8 (October 1963): 234.

39. "Soviet Chalks Up Gains in Europe as It Drives for New Oil Markets," *Oil and Gas Journal* 63, no. 42 (October 18, 1965): 69; "Soviet Bloc Exports Climb Fast in '66," *Oil and Gas Journal* 64, no. 47 (November 21, 1966): 150; and J. H. Carmical, "Soviet May Press Oil Sales to West," *The New York Times,* August 23, 1965, p. 36.

40. Laqueur, *Struggle,* p. 136.

41. Theodore Shabad, "Soviet's Exports of Oil Show Drop," *The New York Times,* June 8, 1973, p. 51 and *Vneshniaia torgovlia* yearbooks for 1971 and 1972.

42. A. F. G. Scanlan, "The Energy Balance of the Comecon Countries," Round Table on the Exploitation of Siberia's Natural Resources, Brussels, January 30–February 1, 1974, pp. 21–22.

43. "Moscow Asks Its Allies to Buy Oil in Mideast and North Africa," *The New York Times,* November 24, 1969, p. 6 and *Facts on File* 29, no. 1520 (December 11–17, 1969): 814.

44. For a discussion of East European oil imports from the Middle East and North Africa, see chapter 9.

45. Editorial, "Moscow's Double Standard," *The New York Times,* December 6, 1969, p. 36.

46. See Ebel, *The Petroleum Industry of the Soviet Union,* p. 157 and *World Petroleum* 31, no. 12 (December 1960): 106.

47. "Soviet Bloc Turns to Middle East for Oil," *World Petroleum* 39, no. 10 (September 1968): 46 and Morison, "Soviet Interest," p. 82.

48. Robert North, "Soviet Northern Development: The Case of NW Siberia," *Soviet Studies* 24, no. 2 (October 1972): 195–96 and Jean-Jacques Berreby, "Oil in the Orient," *New Middle East,* no. 15 (December 1969): 44.

49. Cited in Frank Gardner, "Russians Will Endure the 'Injustices of Nature,' " *Oil and Gas Journal* 67, no. 43 (October 27, 1969): 51. See also David Morison, "Soviet Interest in Middle East Oil," *Mizan* 13, no. 1 (August 1971): 30.

50. Frank Gardner, "Big Spurt in Income from Oil Sales Rescues Soviets," *Oil and Gas Journal* 72, no. 31 (August 5, 1974): 25–26; "Russia: Cashing In," *The Economist* 252, no. 6832 (August 3, 1974): 67; and Marshall Goldman, "The Soviet Union and Its New Wealth," unpublished manuscript, 1974, p. 2. For an extensive analysis of Soviet activities during the Arab oil embargo, see chapter 8.

51. In 1974, Soviet oil exports decreased by two million tons but income from oil sales increased dramatically. See V. Klochek, "Vneshniaia torgovlia SSSR v 1974 godu" (Foreign Trade of the USSR in 1974) *Ekonomicheskaia Gazeta* (Economic Newspaper), no. 15 (April 1975): 20.

52. See Gardner, "Big Spurt in Income from Oil Sales Rescues Soviets," p. 26.

53. *Ibid.,* p. 25. Gardner maintains that the most accurate exchange rate for the ruble was $1.22 in 1972 and $1.38 in 1973. Differences in conversion to dollars are due to the declining value of the dollar during this period. Also see "Russia: Cashing In," p. 67. There is some disagreement as to whether the Soviet Union emerged with a positive balance of trade in 1973 but it is clear that high oil prices helped produce a large trade surplus during the last quarter of 1973. In 1974, the Soviet Union again had a positive balance of trade and earnings from energy exports increased from 3 billion rubles in 1973 to 5.3 billion rubles in 1974. See Klochek, "Vneshniaia torgovlia," p. 20. However, the need to import large quantities of grain in 1975 led to a negative balance of trade for that year. See Theodore Shabad, "Russians' Deficit in Trade Widens," *The New York Times,* March 6, 1976, pp. 1 and 37.

54. Hedrick Smith, "Moscow to Honor Western Oil Deal," *The New York Times,* December 21, 1973, p. 53.

55. Theodore Shabad, "Soviet Bars Increase in Exports of Oil," *The New York Times,* January 11, 1969, p. 39 and Hedrick Smith, "Soviets Sensitive to an Oil Issue," *The New York Times,* June 1, 1974, p. 35.

56. *The Petroleum Economist* 41 (January 1974): 33; Hedrick Smith, "Soviet Diplomacy: Waiting Game as Pendulum Swings Away from Moscow," *The New York Times,* November 26, 1973, p. 5; *Platt's Oilgram News Service* 52, no. 14 (January 21, 1974): 4; and editorial, *The Washington Post,* March 29, 1974, p. A30.

57. *Petroleum Intelligence Weekly* 12, no. 49 (December 3, 1973): 10 and *Petroleum Intelligence Weekly* 13, no. 16 (April 22, 1974): 12.

58. *Petroleum Intelligence Weekly* 13, no. 12 (March 25, 1974): 1–2; Hedrick Smith, "Confident Moscow Sends Gromyko to U.S.," *The New York Times,* February 3, 1974, p. 2; and Hedrick Smith, "French Say Moscow Sees Arabs in a Strong Negotiating Position," *The New York Times,* March 15, 1974, p. 8.

59. *Petroleum Intelligence Weekly* 13, no. 16 (April 22, 1974): 12.

60. Libya made its new policy effective immediately but Iraq applied it only to future agreements.

61. "New Trends in Soviet Trade," *The Petroleum Economist* 42, no. 8 (August 1975): 302.

62. See Radio Free Europe Research, "Hungarian Situation Report 10," March 11, 1975, p. 12; Radio Free Europe Research, "Czechoslovakia Situation Report 10," February 12, 1975, p. 1; and Malcolm Browne, "Soviet Doubles Oil Price in East Europe," *The New York Times,* January 28, 1973, p. 3.

63. "Russia Admits Grain Harvest Woes," *International Herald Tribune,* August 21, 1974, p. 1; Goldman, "New Wealth," p. 3; and "Brezhnev Seen Reaping Prestige Gain in Harvest," *The New York Times,* November 4, 1973, p. 3.

64. Soviet grain purchases from the United States were 17 million tons in 1972 and 7 million tons in 1973. In October 1974, the Soviets contracted for 2.2 million tons to be delivered through the summer of 1975, but additional purchases were also made in 1975. The disastrous grain harvest of 1975, amounting to only 140 million tons, then led to an October, 1975 agreement under which the Soviet Union would buy between 6 and 8 million tons of grain per year over a five-year period. See Dan Morgan, "U.S. Sets Grain Sale to Russia," *International Herald Tribune,* October 21, 1974, pp. 1–2; Clyde Farnsworth, "U.S.-Soviet Grain Accord Nearly Failed," *The New York Times,* October 25, 1975, pp. 37 and 42; and David Shipler, "Soviet Confirms Poor '75 Harvest, Lowest in Decade," *The New York Times,* February 1, 1976, pp. 1 and 8.

65. See "Russia: Cashing In," p. 67.

66. Goldman, "New Wealth," p. 2 and "Russodollars," *The Economist* 252, no. 6832 (August 3, 1974): 67. The USSR sold 250 tons of gold in 1974 and income was as great as in 1973 because the price of gold had risen. See Clyde Farnsworth, "Oil and Gold Price Increases Give Russians Windfall Profit," *International Herald Tribune,* January 11–12, 1975, p. 9.

67. Robert Kaiser, "Soviets Shift on Oil," *The Washington Post,* May 28, 1974, p. A1.

68. For a complete discussion of Soviet-Japanese and Soviet-American negotiations on Siberian oil and gas development, see chapter 12.

69. Gardner, "Big Spurt in Income from Oil Sales Rescues Soviets," p. 27.

70. Theodore Shabad, "Russia Seen Reaping Benefits from Increase in Oil Prices," *International Herald Tribune,* October 15, 1974, p. 2 and Theodore Sha-

bad, "The International Flavor of Moscow's New Plan," *The New York Times,* December 21, 1975, section 3, p. 3.

71. In 1974, Soviet sales to communist-ruled states increased by four million tons but sales to the rest of the world declined by six million tons. See Klochek, "Vneshniaia torgovlia," p. 20.

72. Soviet gas exports doubled in 1974 to approximately 14 billion cubic meters. See *ibid.,* p. 20.

73. Leslie Dienes, "Geographical Problems of Allocation in the Soviet Fuel Supply," *Energy Policy* 1, no. 1 (June 1973): 9–10.

74. Soviet sales of natural gas to communist-ruled states are analyzed in chapter 9, sales to Western Europe in chapter 10, and possible sales to Japan and the United States in chapter 12. Gas imports from Iran are analyzed in chapter 8 and those from Afghanistan in chapter 11.

75. "Russia: Cashing In," p. 67. *The Economist* cites statistics in thousands of cubic meters but they have been divided by 35.3 in order to be converted into thousands of cubic feet.

76. *Petroleum Intelligence Weekly* 12, no. 53 (December 31, 1973): 11. A similar decision was made regarding Finland.

77. Dienes, "Geographical Problems," p. 9.

78. *Platt's Oilgram News Service* 52, no. 40 (February 27, 1974): 5.

79. "Now Those Gas Prices are Soaring Too," *The Economist* 252, no. 6835 (August 24, 1974): 72. A. Hols maintains that the energy-unit cost of LNG tankers is four times that of oil tankers. He also points out the expense involved in constructing natural gas pipelines since a gas pipeline can transport only 20–30% of the energy carried by an oil pipeline of equal size. This is because gas occupies a greater volume for the same heat content. See A. Hols, "The Future Energy Supplies to the Free World," in The Economist Intelligence Unit, *International Oil Symposium* (London: The Economist Intelligence Unit, 1972), p. 8.

5/The Strategy and Tactics of Soviet Oil Politics

1. Jozef Wilczynski, *The Economics and Politics of East-West Trade* (New York: Praeger, 1969), p. 261.

2. Alawi Kayal, "The Control of Oil: East-West Rivalry in the Persian Gulf," doctoral dissertation, University of Colorado, 1972, p. 245.

3. Marshall Goldman, "With Russian Oil, Marketing Skill," *The New York Times,* January 21, 1972, p. 69. Also see Marshall Goldman, "The East Reaches for Markets," *Foreign Affairs* 47, no. 4 (July 1969): 731 and for a discussion of Soviet refining and marketing operations in Western Europe, see chapter 10.

4. "Canada Disturbed by Soviet Oil Bid," *The New York Times,* May 18, 1964, pp. 45–46.

5. Robert Ebel, *Communist Trade in Oil and Gas* (New York: Praeger, 1970), p. 62.

6. William Moskoff and G. William Benz, "The USSR and Developing Countries: Politics and Export Prices, 1955–1969," *Soviet Studies* 24, no. 3 (January 1973): 348–63.

7. *Ibid.,* p. 353.

8. See George Stocking, *Middle East Oil* (Nashville, Tenn.: Vanderbilt University Press, 1970), p. 196; Robert Ebel, *The Petroleum Industry of the Soviet Union* (Washington: American Petroleum Institute, 1961), p. 155; "Russian Exports Looming Larger," *Oil and Gas Journal* 59, no. 50 (December 11, 1961): 64; United Nations, Economic Commission for Europe, "Foreign Trade and Economic Development in Eastern Europe and the Soviet Union," *Economic Bulletin for Europe* 11, no. 1 (June 1959): 68; and "Satellites Get No Soviet Oil Bargains," *Oil and Gas Journal* 59, no. 3 (January 16, 1961): 64.

9. *Vneshniaia torgovlia SSSR za 1959 god: statisticheskii obzor* (Foreign Trade of the USSR for 1959: Statistical Abstract) (Moscow: Vneshtorgizdat, 1960), pp. 85, 95, 157, 167, and 181 and *Vneshniaia torgovlia SSSR za 1967 god: statisticheskii obzor* (Moscow: Izdatel'stvo "Mezhdunarodnye otnosheniia," 1968), pp. 137, 163, 199, and 205. The exchange value of the ruble was greatly increased in 1961, making one ruble equivalent to $1.11 in American currency. A ruble had previously been equivalent to 25 cents.

10. *Vneshniaia torgovlia SSSR za 1961 god: statisticheskii obzor* (Moscow: Vneshtorgizdat, 1962), pp. 99 and 132 and *Ibid., 1967,* pp. 145 and 189.

11. *Vneshniaia torgovlia SSSR za 1963 god: statisticheskii obzor* (Moscow: Vneshtorgizdat, 1964), p. 234 and *ibid., 1959 god,* pp. 141 and 167. Also see "It Would Be Foolhardy to Help Russia Develop Her Oil," *Oil and Gas Journal* 62, no. 13 (March 30, 1964): 53; "Russian Exports Looming Larger," p. 66; Paul Swain, "Soviet Oil Exports Could Get Rough," *Oil and Gas Journal* 58, no. 28 (July 11, 1960): 78 and "Soviet's Cheap Oil Gains Markets in Japan," *Oil and Gas Journal* 59, no. 21 (May 22, 1961): 62.

12. "The Communist Oil Conundrum," *The Economist* 222, no. 6437 (January 7, 1967): 47.

13. Gordon Reed, "Russia's Oil Drive," *World Petroleum* 32, no. 10 (September 1961): 58.

14. Raymond Vernon, "Apparatchiks and Entrepreneurs: U.S.-Soviet Economic Relations," *Foreign Affairs* 52, no. 2 (January 1974): 258.

15. M. A. Adelman, *The World Petroleum Market* (Baltimore: The Johns Hopkins University Press, 1972), pp. 201–2.

16. Paul Marer, *Postwar Pricing and Price Patterns in Socialist Foreign Trade (1946–1971)* (Bloomington, Indiana: International Development Research Center, 1972), p. 59.

17. *Ibid.,* p. 61.

18. Boris Rachkov, "Four ESSO Provocations," *New Times,* no. 39 (September 1960): 27 and 31.

19. Adelman, *Petroleum Market,* p. 201.

20. Congress of the United States, Joint Economic Committee, *Dimensions of Soviet Economic Power* (Washington: U.S. Government Printing Office, 1962), Part 1, pp. 22 and 46 and Samuel Pisar, *Coexistence and Commerce* (New York: McGraw-Hill, 1970), p. 237.

21. "BP Outbids Reds to Sell Crude," *Oil and Gas Journal* 60, no. 7 (February 12, 1962): 97.

22. Daniel Spencer, "The Role of Oil in Soviet Foreign Economic Policy," *American Journal of Economics and Sociology* 25, no. 1 (January 1966): 103 and Boris Rachkov, *Oil Nationalism and Imperialism* (New Delhi: People's Publishing House, 1967), pp. 74–75.

23. Marer, *Postwar Pricing,* p. 20.

24. Z. M. Fallenbuchl, "Comecon Integration," *Problems of Communism* 22, no. 2 (March-April, 1973): 35 and Stanislaw Wasowski, "Economic Integration in the Comecon," *Orbis* 16, no. 3 (Fall 1972): 764.

25. See Stanislaw Wasowski, "The Fuel Situation in Eastern Europe," *Soviet Studies* 21, no. 1 (July 1969): 45 and "The Communist Oil Conundrum," p. 46.

26. Wasowski, "Economic Integration in the Comecon," p. 764.

27. Y. Shiryayev, "Economic Levers of International Socialist Division of Labor," *International Affairs,* no. 11 (November 1966): 11–12.

28. Marer, *Postwar Pricing,* p. 33.

29. Ebel, *Communist Trade,* p. 63. Also see Walter Laqueur, *The Struggle for the Middle East: The Soviet Union in the Mediterranean, 1958–1968* (New York: Macmillan, 1969), p. 122 and "When Oil Flows East," *The Economist* 234, no. 6594 (January 10, 1970): 51.

30. "Billions for 'Black Gold'," *Sovetskaia Rossiia* (Soviet Russia), October 10, 1968, p. 3 (translated in Ebel, *ibid.,* pp. 197–98).

31. "Soviet Bloc Turns to Middle East for Oil," *World Petroleum* 39, no. 10 (September 1968): 48.

32. A. Zubkov, "CMEA Countries' Cooperation in the Fuel, Power and Raw-Material Industries," *International Affairs,* no. 12 (December 1971): 107.

33. See Radio Free Europe Research, "Hungarian Situation Report 10," March 11, 1975, p. 12; Radio Free Europe Research, "Czechoslovakia Situation Report 10," February 12, 1975, p. 1; and Malcolm Browne, "Soviet Doubles Oil Price in East Europe," *The New York Times,* January 28, 1975, p. 3.

34. "The Communist Oil Conundrum," p. 47.

35. See Dusko Doder, "Sharp Boost Feared," *The Washington Post,* March 4, 1974, pp. A1 and A13; "Eastern Europe: Ill-Effects of the Crisis," *The Petroleum Economist* 41, no. 1 (January 1974): 32; Ivan Semichastnov, "The Soviet Union's Foreign Economic Ties Today," *New Times,* no. 2 (January 1974): 8; and Radio Free Europe Research, "RAD Background Report 48 (Hungary)," March 14, 1975, p. 2.

36. *Platt's Oilgram News Service* 53, no. 204 (October 22, 1975): 1; *Platt's Oilgram News Service* 54, no. 34 (February 20, 1976): 2; and Jeremy Russell, "Energy Considerations in Comecon Policies," *The World Today* 32, no. 2 (February 1976): 42.

6/The Geopolitics of Middle East Oil

1. R. Andreasyan and D. Penzin, "Oil and the Anti-Imperialist Struggle," *International Affairs,* no. 8 (August 1971): 53.

2. "The Disruption of Middle East Oil Supplies," *The Economist* 181, no. 5907 (November 10, 1956): 525 and George Lenczowski, *Oil and State in the Middle East* (Ithaca: Cornell University Press, 1960), p. 45. The IPC pipeline begins in Kirkuk, Iraq and splits into two branches before reaching the Mediterranean. One terminates at Banias, Syria, and the other goes through Syria and terminates at Tripoli, Lebanon. The Tapline begins in the Saudi Arabian oil fields adjacent to the Persian Gulf and goes through Jordan, Syria (and now the Israeli-occupied Golan Heights), and Lebanon. It terminates at Sidon, Lebanon.

3. Harold Lubell, *Middle East Oil Crises and Western Europe's Energy Supplies* (Baltimore: Johns Hopkins University Press, 1963), p. 9 and Lenczowski, *Oil and State,* pp. 327–28.

4. Lenczowski, *ibid.,* p. 335; "The Disruption of Middle East Oil Supplies," p. 525; and Lubell, *Oil Crises,* p. 10.

5. See "The Disruption of Middle East Oil Supplies," p. 525; Lenczowski, *ibid.,* pp. 326–27; and Walter Laqueur, *The Struggle for the Middle East: The Soviet Union in the Mediterranean, 1958–1968* (New York: Macmillan, 1969), p. 126.

6. Lubell, *Oil Crises,* p. 15 and Lenczowski, *ibid.,* pp. 327–28.

7. Stephen Longrigg, *Oil in the Middle East,* 3rd ed. (London: Oxford University Press, 1968), p. 346 and Harry Schwartz, "Soviet Oil Trade Feels Suez Pull," *The New York Times,* September 16, 1956, p. 14.

8. See Halford Hoskins and Leon Herman, *Soviet Oil in the Cold War* (Washington: U.S. Government Printing Office, 1961), p. 4 and Schwartz, *ibid.,* p. 14.

9. S. Karpov, "Tankers and Arab Oil," *International Affairs,* no. 9, (September 1967): 116 and D.C. Watt, "Why There Is no Commercial Future for the Suez Canal," *New Middle East,* no. 4 (January 1969): 20. Also see Georgii Mirskii, "The Soviet View of the Future of the Suez Canal—and the Effects of Its Closure," *New Middle East,* no. 4 (January 1969): 16.

10. Watt, *ibid.,* p. 30. Also see Laqueur, *Struggle,* p. 128.

11. Gary Sick, "The USSR and the Suez Canal Closure," *Mizan* 12, no. 2 (November 1970): 91 and Watt, *ibid.,* p. 21.

12. Robert Ebel, *Communist Trade in Oil and Gas* (New York: Praeger, 1970), p. 181 and Sick, *ibid.,* p. 91.

13. "Bad Year Hits Soviet Export Program," *Oil and Gas Journal* 66, no. 25 (June 17, 1968): 44.

14. *Petroleum Intelligence Weekly,* December 4, 1967, p. 7 and *Vneshniaia torgovlia SSSR za 1967 god: statisticheskii obzor* (Foreign Trade of the USSR for 1967: Statistical Abstract) (Moscow: Izdatel'stvo "Mezhdunarodyne otnosheniia," 1968), p. 274.

15. *Vneshniaia torgovlia SSSR za 1967 god, ibid.,* pp. 231 and 273. Also see *Petroleum Intelligence Weekly,* June 3, 1968, p. 6; *Mizan,* Supplement B, no. 4 (July–August 1969): 2; and "Red Bloc Oil-Export Gains Slump," *Oil and Gas Journal* 65, no. 51 (December 18, 1967): 61.

16. Donald Mitchell, "The Soviet Naval Challenge," *Orbis* 14, no. 1 (Spring 1970): 150–51. Also see Iona Andronov, "The Black Gold of Indo-China," *New Times,* no. 52 (December 1971): 26.

17. *Vneshniaia torgovlia SSR za 1967 god,* p. 227. In 1972, the Soviets arranged to send oil to North Vietnam overland through China. See chapter 9.

18. "Bad Year Hits Soviet Export Program," p. 44 and Ebel, *Communist Trade,* p. 76.

19. *Petroleum Intelligence Weekly,* June 19, 1967, p. 5 and *Petroleum Intelligence Weekly,* June 26, 1967, p. 3.

20. "Mideast Losing European Oil Markets," *Oil and Gas Journal* 67, no. 15 (April 14, 1969): 100.

21. J. E. Hartshorn, "Oil and the Middle East War," *The World Today* 24, no. 4 (April 1968): 151.

22. See Ebel, *Communist Trade,* p. 63 and "Soviet Bloc Turns to Middle East for Oil," *World Petroleum* 39, no. 10 (September 1968): 46.

23. Ebel, *ibid.,* p. 102; *Petroleum Intelligence Weekly,* May 13, 1968, p. 2; Edward Hughes, "The Russians Drill Deep in the Middle East," *Fortune* 78, no. 1 (July 1968): 104; Marshall Goldman, "The East Reaches for Markets," *Foreign Affairs* 47, no. 4 (July 1969): 732; and Marshall Goldman, "The Soviet Role in Oil, Economics and the Middle East," *Middle East Information Series* 23 (May 1973): 91–92. Goldman cites 3.5 million tons as the quantity involved in the switch but Ebel's figure of 3.5 million barrels seems much more realistic.

24. Lincoln Landis, "Petroleum in Soviet Middle East Strategy," doctoral dissertation, Georgetown University 1969, p. 168; Ebel, *ibid.,* pp. 101–2; and Hughes, *ibid.,* p. 104. Ebel also reports that the Soviets arranged switch deals with both Shell and BP in 1967. They were concluded through a Swiss broker, Naftamondial, and oil was delivered to Ceylon to help fulfill a Soviet commitment there. Ebel does not indicate the origin of this oil.

25. "Oil Agreement with U.S.S.R.," *Middle East Economic Digest* 14, no. 43 (October 23, 1970): 1242; *Petroleum Intelligence Weekly* 9, no. 43 (October 26, 1970): 5; Alawi Kayal, "The Control of Oil: East-West Rivalry in the Persian Gulf," doctoral dissertation, University of Colorado, 1972, p. 239; and *Middle East Journal* 25, no. 1 (Winter 1971): 72.

26. Israel first shelled the Suez refinery complex on October 24, 1967, in retaliation for the Egyptian sinking of the Israeli destroyer *Eilat.* There was periodic

shelling thereafter and the Egyptians stopped repairing the damage and closed down the refinery in 1969 during the War of Attrition. There seemed to be a tacit understanding that Israel and Egypt would not attack each other's oil fields but Israel did not consider the Suez refinery complex to be covered under this protection. See Edward Luttwak and Dan Horowitz, *The Israeli Army* (New York: Harper and Row, 1975), pp. 316–17.

27. For a discussion of this point, as well as for further information on Soviet-Egyptian oil relations, see chapter 7.

28. *Platt's Oilgram News Service* 51, no. 215 (November 6, 1973): 3.

29. See Benjamin Shwadran, *The Middle East, Oil and the Great Powers,* 3rd ed. (New York: John Wiley and Jerusalem: Israel Universities Press, 1973), p. 466.

30. See R. M. Burrell, "Opportunity Knocks for the Kremlin's Drive East," *New Middle East,* no. 46 (July 1972): 13.

31. "China Blames Russia for Oil Troubles," *Oil and Gas Journal* 62, no. 1 (January 6, 1964): 110 and E. Primakov, "Economic Aspect of the Middle East Crisis," *International Affairs,* no. 6 (June 1972): 40. Curiously, the British magazine *The Economist* took a position very similar to that of the Soviets. See "Germany-Russia-Iran: Many-sided Deals," *The Economist* 250, no. 6805 (January 26, 1974): 34.

32. See Primakov, *ibid.,* p. 42.

33. See Yevgeny Primakov, "Why the Canal Must Be Re-opened: a Soviet View," *New Middle East,* no. 46 (July 1972): 7.

34. *Ibid.,* p. 8 and Karpov, "Tankers and Arab Oil," p. 116.

35. Sick, "Suez Canal Closure," p. 95.

36. *Middle-East Intelligence Survey* 1, no. 17 (December 1, 1973): 134.

37. See George Lenczowski, *Soviet Advances in the Middle East* (Washington: American Enterprise Institute for Public Policy Research, 1972), p. 157. In March 1976, Sadat revoked the Soviet-Egyptian friendship treaty; the following month he announced that Soviet naval vessels could no longer use Egyptian ports.

38. Drew Middleton, "Potential Reopening of the Suez Canal Raises Questions of Military Strategy," *The New York Times,* January 25, 1974, p. 6.

39. See Burrell, "Opportunity Knocks," pp. 9–10.

40. See Curt Gasteyger, "Moscow and the Mediterranean," *Foreign Affairs* 46, no. 4 (July 1968): 676–87.

41. Robert Hunter, "The Soviet Dilemma in the Middle East, Part II: Oil and the Persian Gulf," *Adelphi Papers,* no. 60 (October 1969): 7.

42. For an analysis of the strategic importance for Israel of the Strait of Tiran and the Bab el Mandeb Strait, see Mordechai Abir, "Sharm al-Sheikh—Bab al-Mandeb: The Strategic Balance and Israel's Southern Approaches," *Jerusalem Papers on Peace Problems,* no. 5 (March 1974).

43. See J. Bowyer Bell, "Bab el Mandeb, Strategic Troublespot," *Orbis* 16, no. 4 (Winter 1973): 984.

44. *Middle-East Intelligence Survey* 2, no. 5 (June 1, 1974): 37.

45. "Russian Aid: What's $60m Between Friends," *The Economist* 252, no. 6838 (September 14, 1974): 107.

46. Mogadishu radio, April 26, 1971 (*USSR and Third World* 1, no. 5, April 26–June 1, 1971, p. 269).

47. See Colin Legum, "Red Sea Politics: Implications Beyond the Fringe," *New Middle East,* no. 51 (December 1972): 8.

48. See Dana Adams Schmidt, "U.S.'s Quiet Role in Indian Ocean," *The Christian Science Monitor,* January 29, 1974 (*AF Press Clips* 9, no. 6, February 5, 1974, p. 21).

49. "Soviet Setback," *Washington Star-News,* March 4, 1974 (*AF Press Clips* 9, no. 11, March 10, 1974, p. 20).

50. In addition to naval collaboration, it is also possible that South Africa will share its process of making gasoline out of coal with the United States. See Jeff Wood, "Experts Tab Africa Gasoline-From-Coal Process Feasible," *American Metal Market,* January 29, 1974 (*AF Press Clips* 9, no. 6, p. 14).

51. See "The USSR and the Persian Gulf," *Mizan* 10, no. 2 (March–April 1968): 51–59.

52. *The Gulf: Implications of British Withdrawal* (Washington: Center for Strategic and International Studies, Georgetown University, 1969), p. 17.

53. For a discussion of this point, see David Morison, "Soviet Interest in Middle East Oil," *Mizan* 10, no. 3 (May–June 1968): 84.

54. For a discussion of the Soviet diplomatic initiative in the Persian Gulf, see *Middle-East Intelligence Survey* 1, no. 23 (March 1, 1974): 184.

55. See Hunter, "Soviet Dilemma," p. 14.

56. L. Tolkunov, *Izvestiia,* February 27, 1971 (*USSR and Third World* 1, no. 3, February 15–March 21, 1971, p. 121).

57. See the communique of the Shah's visit to the USSR, October 21, 1972, in *USSR and Third World* 2, no. 10 (October 23–December 3, 1972): 586; communique of Kosygin's visit to Iran, March 17, 1973, in *USSR and Third World* 3, no. 3 (February 19–April 8, 1973): 170; communique of Hoveyda's visit to the USSR, August 12, 1973, in *USSR and Third World* 3, no. 6 (July 16–September 2, 1973): 413; and Christopher Wren, "Brezhnev Adds Syria, Iraq to Itinerary," *International Herald Tribune,* November 22, 1974, p. 2.

58. *Pravda,* on December 2, 1971, reported that Iraq broke diplomatic relations with Iran over the seizure of Abu Musa and the Tumbs but *Pravda* offered no comments on these events. See *USSR and Third World* 1, no. 10 (October 25–December 5, 1971): 605.

59. See Robert Sullivan, "The Architecture of Western Security in the Persian Gulf," *Orbis* 14, no. 1 (Spring 1970): 75.

60. Radio Moscow, January 19, 1972 (*USSR and Third World* 1, no. 2, January 11–February 14, 1971, p. 67).

61. Radio Peace and Progress, January 19, 1972 (*USSR and Third World* 2, no. 2, January 17–February 13, 1972, p. 112).

62. *Middle-East Intelligence Survey* 1, no. 23 (March 1, 1974): 184.

63. Radio Moscow, January 9, 1973 (*USSR and Third World* 3, no. 1, December 4, 1972–January 14, 1973, p. 35).

64. Radio Moscow in Persian to Iran, February 23, 1974 (Foreign Broadcast Information Service, *Soviet Union* 3, no. 39, February 26, 1974, p. F8).

65. The Soviets also supported Kurdish efforts to gain autonomy from Iran after World War II.

66. Soviet support for the Iraqi plan for autonomy was indicated in Pavel Demchenko, "Avtonomiia Irakskikh Kurdov," (Autonomy of Iraq's Kurds) *Pravda,* March 14, 1974, p. 5.

67. Michael Getler, "Russian Pilots, in MiG-23s, Said to Attack Kurds for Iraq," *International Herald Tribune,* October 7, 1974, p. 2.

68. Paul Swain, "Soviet Oil Exports Could Get Rough," *Oil and Gas Journal* 58, no. 28 (July 11, 1960): 78 and Lenczowski, *Oil and State,* p. 34.

69. Hoskins and Herman, *Soviet Oil,* pp. 10–11; Halford Hoskins, "Problems Raised by the Soviet Oil Offense," United States Senate Committee on the Judiciary (Washington: U.S. Government Printing Office, 1962), p. 3; and Harvey O'Connor, *World Crisis in Oil* (New York: Monthly Review Press, 1962), p. 391.

70. Rudolf Sobotka, "Soviet Tanker Fleet Shows Large Growth Rate," *World Petroleum* 33, no. 6 (June 1962): 60 and O'Connor, *ibid.,* p. 391.

71. *World Petroleum* 31, no. 10 (September 1960): 104.

72. Sobotka, "Tanker Fleet," p. 60; Hoskins, "Soviet Oil Offensive," p. 3; and "Growing Soviet Tanker Fleet a Threat," *Oil and Gas Journal* 68, no. 4 (October 5, 1970): 80.

73. J. E. Hartshorn, *Politics and World Oil Economics,* rev. ed. (New York: Praeger, 1967), p. 239.

74. Lenczowski, *Soviet Advances in the Middle East,* p. 171.

75. *Petroleum Intelligence Weekly,* June 19, 1967, p. 5; *Petroleum Intelligence Weekly,* June 26, 1967, p. 3; and *USSR and Third World* 2, no. 1 (December 6, 1971–January 16, 1972): 36.

76. *Petroleum Intelligence Weekly* 12, no. 28 (July 9, 1973): 7.

77. Sick, "Suez Canal Closure," p. 97.

78. Lenczowski, *Soviet Advances in the Middle East,* p. 171; Sick, *Ibid.,* p. 91; and *The Gulf: Implications of British Withdrawal,* p. 91.

79. Since the USSR does not plan to emphasize supertankers, it points out that they increase sea pollution and should be controlled more carefully. See Leonid

Grankov and Pavel Pustovoi, "To Keep the Seas Clean," *New Times,* no. 4 (January 1974): 24–25.

80. Watt, "No Commercial Future," p. 20 and Jorgen Jahre, letter to the editor, *International Herald Tribune,* October 9, 1974, p. 6. Jahre is chairman of Intertanko in Oslo, Norway.

81. Christopher Hayman, "What to Do With All Those Tankers," *The New York Times,* April 14, 1974, Section 3, p. 2.

82. See R. M Burrell, "Canal, Pipeline or Cape?: Schemes for Oil Transportation," *New Middle East,* no. 41 (February 1972): 29.

7/The Middle East and North Africa

1. Victor Perlo, "American Oil Companies and the Middle East," *International Affairs,* no. 12 (December 1967): 44.

2. Ruben Andreasyan, "Arab Oil and Anti-Soviet Fabrications," *New Times,* no. 48 (November 1973):22.

3. See V. Shelepin, "Soviet-Moroccan Co-operation," *New Times,* no. 9 (March 1973): 24.

4. A. Ivanov, "Soviet Imports from the Developing Countries," *Foreign Trade,* no. 9 (1974): 39.

5. D. Kasatkin, "Assault on the Oil Monopolies," *International Affairs,* no. 1 (January 1967): 94.

6. R. Andreasyan, "New Developments on the Oil Front," *New Times,* no. 25 (June 1973): 23 and E. Primakov, "Economic Aspect of the Middle East Crisis," *International Affairs,* no. 6 (June 1972): 38.

7. Perlo, "American Oil Companies," p. 40.

8. Radio Moscow, December 15, 1971 (*USSR and Third World* 2, no. 1, December 6, 1971–January 16, 1972, pp. 28–29).

9. See B. Rachkov, "Oil, Trade and Politics," *International Affairs,* no. 4 (April 1966): 19.

10. "Adventures of the Oil Kings," *Izvestiia,* April 19, 1966, p. 2 (Translated in Robert Ebel, *Communist Trade in Oil and Gas,* New York: Praeger, 1970, p. 270).

11. Boris Rachkov, "Hazards of the Oil Battle," *International Affairs,* no. 11 (November 1969): 68–77. For a Soviet discussion of the role of oil companies in the formulation of American foreign policy, see B. Rachkov, "Oil in the U.S. External Economic Policy," *Foreign Trade,* no. 10 (1971): 38–41.

12. See Primakov, "Middle East Crisis," p. 37 and Perlo, "American Oil Companies," p. 40.

13. R. Andreasyan, "Middle Eastern Oil: Present and Future," *International Affairs,* no. 7 (July 1960): 23.

14. D. Volsky, "Iraq's Battle for Her Oil," *New Times,* no. 35 (August 1972): 9 and G. Starko, "How to Solve the Oil Problem," *New Times,* no. 35 (August 1958): 15. Also see Robert Engler, *The Politics of Oil* (New York: Macmillan, 1961), p. 264.

15. Boris Rachkov, "Neftianye monopolii i agressiia izrailia," (Oil Monopolies and the Aggression of Israel) *Kommunist,* no. 12 (August 1967): 109–17; Iu. Golovin, I. Matiukhin and B. Smirnov, "Imperializm i arabskaia neft'," (Imperialism and Arab Oil) *Mirovaia Ekonomika i Mezhdunarodnye Otnosheniia* (World Economics and International Relations) no. 9 (1967): 66–78; B. Rachkov, "The Middle East Crisis and U.S. Oil Monopolies," *International Affairs,* no. 4 (April 1969): 32; and S. Astakhov, "More About the Secret Springs of the Israeli Aggression," *International Affairs,* no. 10 (October 1967): 38. Also see Aryeh Yodfat, *Arab Politics in the Soviet Mirror* (New York: Halsted Press and Jerusalem: Israel Universities Press, 1973), p. 264 and David Morison, "Soviet Interest in Middle East Oil," *Mizan* 10, no. 3 (May–June 1968): 80.

16. Perlo, "American Oil Companies," p. 41.

17. V. Molchanov and Y. Osipov, "New Round in the Oil War," *New Times,* no. 48 (November 1971): 16.

18. *USSR and Third World* 1, no. 3 (February 15–March 21, 1971): 96.

19. See George Lenczowski, *Oil and State in the Middle East* (Ithaca: Cornell University Press, 1960), p. 42.

20. Y. Andreyanov, "The Oil Monopolies in the Persian Gulf Colonies," *International Affairs,* no. 10 (October 1962): 78 and Andreasyan, "New Developments on the Oil Front," p. 24.

21. Abram Frumkin, *Modern Theories of International Economic Relations* (Moscow: Progress Publishers, 1969), p. 256.

22. P. Demchenko, "Arab Oil for the Arabs," *New Times,* no. 25 (June 1972): 11.

23. See "Iraq: Down the Hole," *The Economist* 232, no. 6568 (July 12, 1969): 34.

24. Ruben Andreasyan, "The Energy Crisis and Mid-East Oil," *New Times,* no. 16 (April 1973): 25; D. C. Watt, "Russians Need Middle East Oil," *New Middle East,* no. 3 (December 1968): 23; and Marshall Goldman, "The Soviet Role in Oil, Economics and the Middle East," *Middle East Information Series* 25 (May 1973): 96.

25. Demchenko, "Arab Oil," p. 11 and Rachkov, "Oil, Trade and Politics," p. 15.

26. D. Penzin, "New Round in the Tussle With the Oil Magnates," *International Affairs,* no. 1 (January 1972): 53–54.

27. R. Andreasyan, "New Aspects of Middle East Countries' Oil Policy," *International Affairs,* no. 9 (September 1968): 29.

28. See Morison, "Soviet Interest," p. 82.

29. For example, see D. Penzin, "New Moves by Oil Imperialism," *International Affairs,* no. 5 (May 1973): 47–53.

30. See Kasatkin, "Oil Monopolies," pp. 93–94.

31. Andreasyan, "The Energy Crisis and Mid-East Oil," p. 25.

32. Igor Doronin, "Oil Money," *New Times,* no. 51 (December 1973): 20.

33. Penzin, "New Round in the Tussle With the Oil Magnates," p. 51.

34. Doronin, "Oil Money," p. 20.

35. For discussions of the Khoshtaria concession, see George Lenczowski, *Russia and the West in Iran, 1918–1948* (New York: Greenwood, 1968), pp. 81–82; Stephen Longrigg, *Oil in the Middle East,* 3rd ed. (London: Oxford University Press, 1968), pp. 38–39; Louis Fischer, *Oil Imperialism* (New York: International Publishers, 1926), pp. 210–36; and Alawi Kayal, "The Control of Oil: East-West Rivalry in the Persian Gulf," doctoral dissertation, University of Colorado, 1972, pp. 86–99.

36. Lenczowski, *ibid.,* p. 85.

37. Longrigg, *Oil in the Middle East,* p. 127 and *The Gulf: Implications of British Withdrawal* (Washington: Center for Strategic and International Studies, Georgetown University, 1969), p. 59.

38. Herbert Feis, *Three International Episodes* (New York: W. W. Norton, 1946), p. 176 and "Oil on the Waters?" *The Economist* 150, no. 5353 (March 30, 1946): 482.

39. Lenczowski, *Russia and the West,* pp. 216–17.

40. Longrigg, *Oil in the Middle East,* p. 130; Feis, *Three International Episodes,* pp. 175–77; and Lenczowski, *Russia and the West,* pp. 216–18 and 222.

41. Benjamin Shwadran, *The Middle East, Oil and the Great Powers* (New York: Praeger, 1955), p. 70.

42. *Ibid.,* pp. 75–78.

43. Lenczowski, *Russia and the West,* p. 300.

44. Benjamin Shwadran, *The Middle East, Oil and the Great Powers,* 3rd ed. (New York: John Wiley and Jerusalem: Israel Universities Press, 1973), pp. 104–6.

45. Peter Wiles, *Communist International Economics* (New York: Praeger, 1969), pp. 515–16.

46. Alan Ford, *The Anglo-Iranian Oil Dispute of 1951–1952* (Berkeley: University of California Press, 1954), p. 123 and John Donovan, ed., *U.S. and Soviet Policy in the Middle East, 1945–56* (New York: Facts on File, 1972), p. 94.

47. Donovan, *ibid.,* p. 98.

48. Rudolf Sobotka, "Russia Exports More Than Crude Oil," *World Petroleum* 34, no. 10 (September 1963): 49; Shoshana Klebanoff, *Middle East Oil and U.S. Foreign Policy* (New York: Praeger, 1974), p. 177; and Longrigg, *Oil in the Middle East,* p. 286.

49. Sobotka, "More Than Crude Oil," p. 49.

50. See Peter Odell, *Oil and World Power* (Baltimore: Penguin, 1970), p. 167.

51. Klebanoff, *Middle East Oil,* p. 178 and Sobotka, "More Than Crude Oil," p. 49.

52. D. Kasatkin, "Iran: Good-Neighborly Course," *International Affairs,* no. 4 (April 1968): 71.

53. "Oil Under the Caspian," *The Economist* 223, no. 6452 (April 22, 1967): 376 and *Facts on File* 27, no. 1377 (March 16–22, 1967): 83.

54. "Soviet Bloc Turns to Middle East for Oil," *World Petroleum* 39, no. 10 (September 1968): 48.

55. See *Facts on File* 27, no. 1404 (September 21–27, 1967): 407; D. C. Watt, "Soviet Presence in the Mediterranean," *New Middle East,* no. 1 (October 1968): 18; and Rouhollah Ramazani, *The Persian Gulf: Iran's Role* (Charlottesville: University Press of Virginia, 1972), p. 104.

56. William Smith, "Soviet Entry Into Mideast's Oil Affairs Has Some Pedestrian Trappings," *The New York Times,* May 5, 1968, section 3, p. 1.

57. Radio Moscow in Persian, August 7, 1974 (Foreign Broadcast Information Service, *Soviet Union* 3, no. 155, August 9, 1974, pp. F3–4).

58. "Iran, Soviet Sign Huge Trade Deal," *Oil and Gas Journal* 65, no. 17 (April 24, 1967): 72.

59. "Oil Pipelines Pose Dilemma for Iran," *Middle East Economic Digest* 14, no. 20 (May 15, 1970): 578.

60. T. B. Millar, "Soviet Policies South and East of Suez," *Foreign Affairs* 49, no. 1 (October 1970): 78; and Marshall Goldman, "With Russian Oil, Marketing Skill," *The New York Times,* January 21, 1972, p. 69.

61. Charles McLane, *Soviet-Middle East Relations* (London: Central Asian Research Centre, 1973), p. 14 and Frank Gardner, "Not a Bad Profit for the Soviets—300%," *Oil and Gas Journal* 72, no. 14 (April 8, 1974): 51. Robert Campbell also mentions Soviet oil purchases from Iran but he has informed me that a printing error was involved and the reference should actually have been to Iraq. See Robert Campbell, "Some Issues in Soviet Energy Policy for the Seventies," *Middle East Information Series* 27–28 (Spring/Summer, 1974): 99.

62. See "Oil Pipelines Pose Dilemma for Iran," p. 578; "Plan for Oil Pipeline to Soviet Union," *Middle East Economic Digest* 14, no. 16 (April 17, 1970): 470; and *Petroleum Intelligence Weekly* 9, no. 14 (April 6, 1970): 1.

63. Kayal, "Control of Oil," p. 235 and *Petroleum Intelligence Weekly* 9, no. 16 (April 20, 1970): 3.

64. *Petroleum Intelligence Weekly* 9, no. 19 (May 11, 1970): 4.

65. See Robert Campbell, *The Economics of Soviet Oil and Gas* (Baltimore: Johns Hopkins University Press, 1968), p. 207; Robert Ebel, "Two Decades of Soviet Oil and Gas," *World Petroleum* 42, no. 5 (June 1971): 79; and Theodore Shabad, *The Basic Industrial Resources of the U.S.S.R.* (New York: Columbia University Press, 1969), p. 151.

66. "Russian Gas: Pipes of Peace," *The Economist* 234, no. 6598 (February 7, 1970): 71.

67. "Russia: Cashing In," *The Economist* 252, no. 6832 (August 3, 1974): 67. *The Economist* gives the figures in thousands of cubic meters but they have been converted into thousands of cubic feet by dividing by 35.3.

68. See I. Savchenko, Radio Moscow in Persian, March 14, 1974 (*USSR and Third World* 4, no. 3, March 4–April 21, 1974, p. 152).

69. Christopher Lee, "The Soviet Contribution to Iran's Fourth Development Plan," *Mizan* 11, no. 5 (September–October, 1969): 241–42.

70. Goldman, "The Soviet Role in Oil, Economics and the Middle East," p. 94.

71. See Ramazani, *The Persian Gulf*, p. 77; Longrigg, *Oil in the Middle East*, p. 368; Morison, "Soviet Interest," p. 79; and George Lenczowski, *Soviet Advances in the Middle East* (Washington: American Enterprise Institute for Public Policy Research, 1972), pp. 32–33.

72. See Lee, "Soviet Contribution," p. 241; "Iranian-Soviet Gas Pipeline Agreement," *International Financial News Survey* 20, no. 18 (May 10, 1968): 149; and Lenczowski, *Soviet Advances in the Middle East*, p. 33.

73. See Morison, "Soviet Interest," p. 79 and Kayal, "Control of Oil," p. 234.

74. Abraham Becker, "Oil and the Persian Gulf in Soviet Policy in the 1970s," in Michael Confino and Shimon Shamir, eds., *The U.S.S.R. and the Middle East* (New York: John Wiley and Jerusalem: Israel Universities Press, 1973), p. 184 and Kayal, *ibid.*, p. 234.

75. "Iran, Soviet Sign Huge Trade Deal," p. 72.

76. *Mizan,* Supplement A, no. 5 (September–October, 1970): 7 and *Mizan,* Supplement A, no. 6 (November–December, 1970): 5.

77. *Vneshniaia torgovlia SSSR za 1971 god: statisticheskii obzor* (Foreign Trade of the USSR for 1971: Statistical Abstract) (Moscow: Izdatel'stvo "Mezhdunarodnye otnosheniia," 1972), p. 241; *ibid.,* 1972 (1973), p. 240; *ibid.* 1973 (1974), p. 239. In addition to gas deliveries from the Ahwaz area, the USSR may eventually assist Iran with gas exploitation and pipeline construction in return for gas at the Sarakhs gas fields near the Soviet-Iranian-Afghan border. See "Iran: Encircled Shah," *The Economist* 245, no. 6737 (October 7, 1972): 34.

78. *Petroleum Intelligence Weekly* 12, no. 31 (July 30, 1973): 9 and *Platt's Oilgram News Service* 52, no. 122 (June 25, 1974): 1. It should be pointed out that gas imports and exports are usually listed in terms of cubic meters while prices tend to be given in cubic feet.

79. *Middle East Economic Survey* 16, no. 40 (July 27, 1973): 5 and Frank Gardner, "Chinese Tattle on the Soviets," *Oil and Gas Journal* 71, no. 32 (August 6, 1973): 37.

80. U.S. government memorandum, June 24, 1974; "Money and Gas," *The Economist* 252, no. 6831 (July 27, 1974): 89; and *Platt's Oilgram News Service* 52, no. 122 (June 25, 1974): 1.

81. On the Soviet threat, see "Money and Gas," *ibid.,* p. 89.

82. Clyde Farnsworth, "Soviet-Iran Pact May Spur Other Prices," *International Herald Tribune,* August 21, 1974, p. 9.

83. "Money and Gas," p. 89.

84. *Platt's Oilgram News Service* 52, no. 143 (July 26, 1974): 1 and 3; *Platt's*

Oilgram News Service 52, no. 152 (August 8, 1974): 1; "Moscow Agrees to Pay Iran Nearly Double Price for Gas," *International Herald Tribune,* August 20, 1974, p. 2; and "Now Those Gas Prices Are Soaring Too," *The Economist* 252, no. 6835 (August 24, 1974): 72.

85. Eric Pace, "Iranian Gas Deal to Supply Europe," *The New York Times,* December 1, 1975, pp. 1 and 51.

86. *USSR and Third World* 3, no. 8 (October 22–December 2, 1973): 566 and *Middle East Economic Survey* 17, no. 2 (November 2, 1973): 5.

87. *Platt's Oilgram News Service* 52, no. 184 (September 24, 1974): 3.

88. "Soviet Gas Deal With Iran and W. Germany," *Chemical Age International,* June 1, 1973, p. 16.

89. "Germany-Russia-Iran: Many-sided Deals," *The Economist* 250, no. 6805 (January 26, 1974): 88.

90. It is possible that another Soviet–Iranian gas agreement will be worked out in which Sweden will be the recipient of Soviet gas and the Soviets will be compensated with Iranian gas. See *Platt's Oilgram News Service* 52, no. 16 (January 23, 1974): 4.

91. "Natural Gas: More, but at a Price," *The Petroleum Economist* 41, no. 8 (August 1974): 295 and "Now Those Gase Prices are Soaring Too," p. 72.

92. *Platt's Oilgram News Service* 52, no. 144 (July 29, 1974): 1.

93. Longrigg, *Oil in the Middle East,* p. 264; Sobotka, "More Than Crude Oil," p. 49; and Leon Herman, "The Soviet Oil Offensive," *Reporter* 26, no. 13 (June 21, 1962): 28. In addition to Soviet assistance, Czechoslovakia provided a credit of $33.6 million on October 23, 1960, to be used for building oil refineries and hydroelectric stations. See Oded Remba, "The Middle East in 1960—An Economic Survey," *Middle Eastern Affairs* 12, no. 3 (March 1961): 78.

94. George Stocking, Middle East Oil (Kingsport: Vanderbilt University Press, 1970), p. 314; Aryeh Yodfat, "Russia's Other Middle East Pasture—Iraq," *New Middle East,* no. 38 (November 1971): 26; Aryeh Yodfat, "Unpredictable Iraq Poses a Russian Problem," *New Middle East,* no. 13 (October 1969): 17; *Mizan* 10, no. 1 (January–February 1968): 45; and Kayal, "Control of Oil," p. 238.

95. Stocking, *Middle East Oil,* p. 315; Jean-Jacques Berreby, "Oil in the Orient," *New Middle East,* no. 12 (September 1969): 14; "Iraq-Soviet Pacts to Put INOC on its Feet," *Oil and Gas Journal* 67, no. 33 (August 18, 1969): 35; and Yodfat, "Unpredictable Iraq Poses a Russian Problem," p. 20.

96. Stocking, *ibid.,* 314–15; Yodfat, "Russia's Other Middle East Pasture—Iraq," p. 27; and Yodfat, "Unpredictable Iraq Poses a Russian Problem," p. 20.

97. Yodfat, "Russia's Other Middle East Pasture—Iraq," p. 27.

98. Roy Thoman, "Iraq Under Baathist Rule," *Current History* 62, no. 365 (January 1972): 36–37 and *Middle East Journal* 25, no. 3 (Summer 1971): 377.

99. Yodfat, "Russia's Other Middle East Pasture—Iraq," p. 27 and Elizabeth Kridl Valkenier, "Soviet Economic Relations With the Developing Nations," in Roger

Kanet, ed., *The Soviet Union and the Developing Nations* (Baltimore: Johns Hopkins University Press, 1974), p. 222. On the Mosul refinery, also see *USSR and Third World* 3, no. 3 (February 19–April 8, 1973): 175 and *USSR and Third World* 3, no. 2 (January 15–February 18, 1973): 98. It should also be pointed out that Czechoslovakia was helping to finance an oil refinery at Basra. See Larry Auldridge, "Soviet-Aided Iraq Shoots for the Big League in Oil," *Oil and Gas Journal* 69, no. 52 (December 27, 1971): 39.

100. "Russia: Cashing In," p. 67. On June 23, 1971, the Soviets made an additional commitment to North Rumailah oilfield development. See Thoman, "Iraq Under Baathist Rule," p. 37. On April 5, 1972, they agreed to build a refinery in the Hamman al-Alil area of northern Iraq. See *USSR and Third World* 2, no. 4 (March 13–April 17, 1972): 216. Also in 1972, Hungary provided a $50 million credit, part of which was for oilfield and refinery equipment. See U.S. Department of State, Bureau of Intelligence and Research, "Communist States and Developing Countries: Aid and Trade in 1972," RECS-10 (June 15, 1973): 3. On April 30, 1973, the Soviets agreed to provide equipment and build a pipeline at the Nahran Umar oil field in southern Iraq. See *USSR and Third World* 3, no. 4 (April 9–May 27, 1973): 250 and Foreign Broadcast Information Service, *Soviet Union,* May 1, 1973, p. B1.

101. *Middle East Journal* 27, no. 1 (Winter 1973): 62. Agreements on Iraq's debts were apparently made in both September and November, 1972. See Aryeh Yodfat, "Yahasey Brit-Hamoatsot-Irak" (Soviet-Iraqi Relations) (Yuli 1968–Mars 1973," *Hamizrah Hehadash* (New East) 24, no. 1–2 (1974): 42.

102. There seems to be some disagreement on the precise date of the first shipment. Benjamin Shwadran cites April 25, *Petroleum Press Service* cites April 12, and *The Economist* cites April 7. See Shwadran, *The Middle East, Oil and the Great Powers,* 3rd ed., p. 281; "Iraq: North Rumaila and the Russians," *Petroleum Press Service* 39, no. 5 (May 1972): 180; and "Iraq and Russia: The Tip of the Boot," *The Economist* 243, no. 6712 (April 15, 1972): 34.

103. Shwadran, *The Middle East, Oil and the Great Powers,* 3rd ed., p. 281.

104. "Iraq: North Rumaila and the Russians," p. 180.

105. B. Orekhov, "Vtoraia ochered' Rumeily," (Second Stage of Rumailah) *Pravda,* February 1, 1974, p. 5.

106. Becker, "Oil and the Persian Gulf," p. 174; Alvin Rubinstein, "The Soviet Union in the Middle East," *Current History* 63, no. 374 (October 1972): 169; and *Middle East Journal* 26, no. 4 (Autumn 1972): 442.

107. For a Soviet analysis of the Iraqi nationalization, see D. Penzin, "Oil and Independence," *International Affairs,* no. 10 (October 1972): 34–40.

108. *Middle East Journal* 26, no. 4 (Autumn 1972): 436. Also see R. M. Burrell, "Politics and Participation: Where Britannia Once Ruled," *New Middle East,* no. 51 (December 1972): 32; and Shelepin, "Soviet-Moroccan Co-operation," p. 24.

109. *Middle East Journal* 27, no. 3 (Summer 1973): 361.

110. See Radio Moscow in Arabic, June 8, 1972 (Foreign Broadcast Information Service, *Daily Report,* no. 113, June 9, 1972, p. B1); Radio Baghdad, June 7, 1972

(Foreign Broadcast Information Service, *Daily Report,* no. 112, June 8, 1972, pp. B1–2); "Consultations End," *Pravda,* June 8, 1972, p. 4 (*Current Digest of the Soviet Press* 24, no. 24, July 12, 1972, p. 11); and A. Petrushev, "Fruitful Cooperation," *Izvestiia,* July 22, 1972, p. 3 (*Current Digest of the Soviet Press* 24, no. 29, August 16, 1972, pp. 18–19).

111. Oleg Pilipets, Radio Moscow, Feburary 4, 1974 (Foreign Broadcast Information Service, *Soviet Union* 3, no. 27, February 27, 1974, pp. F9–10) and Volsky, "Iraq's Battle," p. 8.

112. See "Scant Market Seen for Iraqi Crude Oil," *Oil and Gas Journal* 70, no. 24 (June 12, 1972): 57.

113. *Middle-East Intelligence Survey* 1, no. 2 (April 15, 1973): 16.

114. See Juan de Onis, "Iraq Disregards Arab Oil Cutback," *The New York Times,* November 14, 1973, p. 17.

115. *Vneshniaia torgovlia SSSR za 1972 god,* p. 237; "New Trends in Soviet Trade," *The Petroleum Economist* 42, no. 8 (August 1975): 302 and *Vneshniaia torgovlia SSSR za 1973 god,* p. 237. Iraq exports approximately 70 million tons of crude oil per year.

116. *Soviet Oil to 1980,* QER Special, no. 14, June, 1973 (London: The Economist Intelligence Unit, 1973), p. 34; Hedrick Smith, "Moscow Wins an Oil Advantage," *The New York Times,* International Economic Survey, January 27, 1974, p. 39; R. M. Burrell, "Opportunity Knocks for the Kremlin's Drive East," *New Middle East,* no. 46 (July 1972): 12; and Odell, *Oil and World Power,* p. 168.

117. *Petroleum Intelligence Weekly* 13, no. 12 (March 25, 1974): 1–2; *Middle-East Intelligence Survey,* April 15, 1973, p. 16; and *Platt's Oilgram News Service* 53, no. 20 (January 29, 1975): 1.

118. Lenczowski, *Oil and State,* pp. 338–39.

119. Ibid., pp. 340–41.

120. *Platt's Oilgram News Service* 51, no. 222 (November 15, 1973): 4 and *Middle-East Intelligence Survey* 2, no. 1 (April 1, 1974): 8.

121. A dispute over transit tariffs, the Iraq-Kurdish conflict, and the instability of the Turkish government caused the Turkish legislature to delay ratification of the pipeline agreement. Some members of the legislature favored the use of tankers rather than the construction of a pipeline and there were strong Syrian objections to the Iraq-Turkey pipeline project. See *Middle-East Intelligence Survey* 2, no. 15 (November 1, 1974): 120 and Robert Freedman, *Soviet Policy Toward the Middle East Since 1970* (New York: Praeger, 1975), p. 132.

122. A. Zlatorunsky, "Algeria's Horizons," *International Affairs,* no. 11 (November 1973): 81–82.

123. Janos Horvath, "Economic Aid Flow From the USSR: A Recount of the First Fifteen Years," *Slavic Review* 29, no. 4 (December 1970): 625 and D. Chertkov, *The Soviet Union and Developing Countries* (Moscow: Novosti Press Agency Publishing House, 1972), p. 88.

124. David Ottaway and Marina Ottaway, *Algeria: The Politics of a Socialist Revolution* (Berkeley: University of California Press, 1970), p. 234 and Valkenier, "Soviet Economic Relations," p. 228.

125. *USSR and Third World* 31, no. 7 (September 3–October 21, 1973): 503; *USSR and Third World* 41, no. 3 (March 4–April 21, 1974): 167; and B. Peresada, " 'Arzev' —tanker iz SSSR," (The "Arzev," a Tanker from the USSR) *Pravda,* March 29, 1974, p. 5.

126. Imports were 61,300 tons in *1967;* 123,800 in *1968;* 495,400 in *1969;* 494,200 in *1970;* 749,000 in *1971* and 570,000 in *1972.* See *Vneshniaia torgovlia SSSR za 1967 god: statisticheskii obzor* (Moscow: Izdatel'stvo "Mezhdunarodnye otnosheniia," 1968), p. 278; *ibid.,* 1969 (1970), p. 259; *ibid.,* 1970 (1971), p. 262; and *ibid.,* 1972 (1973), p. 276.

127. See *Mizan,* Supplement A, no. 1 (January–February 1969): 13.

128. "Spain Buying Crude Oil From Russians," *Oil and Gas Journal* 69, no. 44 (November 1, 1971): 38.

129. Zuhayr Mikdashi, *The Community of Oil Exporting Countries* (Ithaca: Cornell University Press, 1972), p. 89.

130. "Algerian Gas: Behind the Row, the Russians," *The Economist* 222, no. 6441 (February 4, 1967): 433.

131. Soviet sales of crude oil to Egypt were 156,100 tons in 1955 and 295,400 in 1956. Sales of oil products were 173,400 in 1955 and 625,300 in 1956. See *Vneshniaia torgovlia SSSR za 1956 god* (Moscow: Vneshtorgizdat, 1958), p. 149. In 1955, the price charged to Egypt for crude oil was 57 rubles per ton, which was considerably less than the 72 rubles charged to the adjacent state of Israel. See *ibid.,* pp. 116 and 149.

132. See Susan Strange, *The Soviet Trade Weapon* (London: Phoenix House, 1959), p. 21;*Vneshniaia torgovlia SSSR: statisticheskii sbornik,* 1918–1966 (Foreign Trade of the USSR: Statistical Compendium, 1918–1966) (Moscow: Izdatel'stvo "Mezhdunarodnye otnosheniia," 1967), pp. 218–19; and Harold Lubell, *The Soviet Oil Offensive and Inter-Bloc Economic Competition* (Santa Monica: Rand Corporation, 1961), p. 43.

133. During the late fities, there were numerous agreements involving credits and technicians for work on the Suez and Alexandria refineries. See Sobotka, "More Than Crude Oil," p. 48; Horvath, "Economic Aid Flow," p. 629; Longrigg, *Oil in the Middle East,* p. 345; and Charles McLane, "Foreign Aid in Soviet Third World Policies," *Mizan* 10, no. 6 (November–December, 1968), p. 215. There were also oil prospecting agreements in 1960 and 1966 and arrangements for the training of Egyptian oil technicians. See McLane, *ibid.,* p. 214; Longrigg, *ibid.,* p. 457; "UAR Plans 7-Year Soviet-Assisted Oil and Gas Search," *Oil and Gas Journal* 64, no. 39 (September 26, 1966): 71; and Edward Hughes, "The Russians Drill Deep in the Middle East," *Fortune* 78, no. 1 (July 1968): 102.

134. "Economic Relations Between U.A.R. and Eastern Bloc," *International Financial News Survey* 20, no. 6 (February 16, 1968), p. 48; *USSR and Third World* 3, no. 6 (July 16–September 2, 1973), p. 408; John Berry, "Oil and Soviet Policy in the

Middle East," *Middle East Journal* 26, no. 2 (Spring 1972): 157; Berreby, "Oil in the Orient," p. 14; and "Egypt: Russians Withdraw From Exploration," *Petroleum Press Service* 40, no. 9 (September 1973): 344.

135. Soviet purchases of Egyptian crude oil were 943,800 tons in *1969;* 2,022,100 in *1970;* 2,040,000 in *1971;* 971,000 in *1972;* and 209,000 in *1973.* See *Vneshniaia torgovlia SSSR za 1969 god,* p. 271; *ibid.,* 1970, p. 274; *ibid., 1972,* p. 282; and *ibid., 1973,* p. 280. Soviet exports of crude oil and oil products to Egypt were 963,500 tons in *1966;* 1,003,500 in *1967;* 1,033,100 in *1968;* 1,018,600 in *1969;* 1,638,600 in *1970;* 1,604,400 in *1971;* 1,442,100 in *1972;* and 352,300 in *1973.* See *Vneshniaia torgovlia SSSR za 1967 god,* p. 288; *ibid.,* 1969, p. 270; *ibid.,* 1970, p. 273; *ibid.,* 1972, p. 281; *ibid.,* 1973, p. 279.

136. These figures are calculated on the basis of the volume of crude oil sold and the ruble value for this oil, as indicated in *Vneshniaia torgovlia SSSR za 1973 god.*

137. Egypt imported Soviet kerosene since its own oil was more suitable for refining into fuel oil. As Egypt became more industrialized, it had less of a need for kerosene and this may help explain reduced purchases from the USSR.

138. *Middle East Economic Digest* 18, no. 18 (May 3, 1974): 509.

139. Lincoln Landis, "Petroleum in Soviet Middle East Strategy," doctoral dissertation, Georgetown University, 1969, p. 86 and Halford Hoskins and Leon Herman, *Soviet Oil in the Cold War* (Washington: U.S. Government Printing Office, 1961), p. 16.

140. Soviet exports of crude oil and oil products to Syria were 252,100 tons in *1968;* 63,200 in *1969;* 46,800 in *1970;* 13 in *1971;* and 220 in *1972.* See *Vneshniaia torgovlia SSSR za 1967 god,* p. 250; *Vneshniaia torgovlia SSSR za 1970 god,* p. 253; and *ibid.,* 1972 p. 266.

141. *Vneshniaia torgovlia SSSR za 1973 god,* p. 265.

142. *Petroleum Intelligence Weekly* 13, no. 12 (March 25, 1974): 1–2.

143. Longrigg, *Oil in the Middle East,* p. 336 and Lenczowski, *Soviet Advances in the Middle East,* p. 105.

144. Sobotka, "More Than Crude Oil," p. 49; Shwadran, *The Middle East, Oil and the Great Powers,* 3rd ed., p. 466; and Lenczowski, *Soviet Advances in the Middle East,* p. 112.

145. Walter Laqueur, *The Struggle for the Middle East: The Soviet Union in the Mediterranean, 1958–1968* (New York: Macmillan, 1969), p. 133. The USSR also had an agreement with Syria to develop oil fields in the Jezira region. See Hughes, "Russians Drill Deep," p. 102.

146. Radio Moscow, February 17, 1971 (*USSR and Third World* 1, no. 3, February 15–March 21, 1971, p. 125).

147. *Mizan,* Supplement A, no. 5 (September–October, 1970): 22.

148. Frank Gardner, "A Mission to Moscow," *Oil and Gas Journal* 70, no. 11 (March 13, 1972): 35 and Hedrick Smith, "Soviet Announces Pact to Develop Libya's Oil Fields," *The New York Times,* March 5, 1972, p. 1.

149. *Middle East Journal* 26, no. 3 (Summer 1972): 299.

150. Christopher Wren, "Soviet Pledges to Help the Palestinians," *The New York Times,* May 22, 1974, p. 18 and "Russia's New Pasture," *Petroleum Press Service* 39, no. 9 (September 1972): 325.

151. *Vneshniaia torgovlia SSSR za 1973 god,* p. 284.

152. *Petroleum Intelligence Weekly* 13, no. 18 (May 6, 1974): 6.

153. Robert Brougham, "An Oil Company View," *Middle East Information Series* 23 (May 1973): 59.

154. *Vneshniaia torgovlia SSSR za 1973 god,* p. 286. For the Soviet claims, see Shelepin, "Soviet-Moroccan Co-operation," p. 27 and Radio Moscow, May 4, 1974 (*USSR and Third World* 4, no. 4, April 22–June 9, 1974, p. 255). The claims appear to be exaggerated as it is likely that Morocco received slightly under 50% of its oil needs from the USSR. Morocco probably consumed almost two million tons of oil in 1973.

155. *Mizan,* Supplement A, no. 1 (January–February 1968): 10 and Rabat radio, May 23, 1974 (*USSR and Third World* 4, no. 4, April 22–June 9, 1974, p. 255).

156. "USSR Loan to Turkey for Steel Plant," *International Financial News Survey* 21, no. 42 (October 24, 1969): 339; Jozef Wilczynski, *The Economics and Politics of East-West Trade* (New York: Praeger, 1969), p. 262; Lenczowski, *Soviet Advances in the Middle East,* p. 52; and *Facts on File* 27, no. 1404 (September 21–27, 1967): 407.

157. *USSR and Third World* 3, no. 4 (April 9–May 27, 1973): 263.

158. Dwight Simpson, "Turkey: A Time of Troubles," *Current History* 62, no. 365 (January 1972): 40. Soviet exports of crude oil and oil products to Turkey were 123,000 tons in *1968; 297,500* in *1969; 184,700* in *1970; 68,900* in *1971; 300* in *1972;* and 400 in *1973.* See *Vneshniaia torgovlia SSSR za 1969 god,* p. 253; *Vneshniaia torgovlia SSSR za 1970 god,* p. 255; *Vneshniaia torgovlia SSSR za 1971 god,* p. 271; *Vneshniaia torgovlia SSSR za 1972 god,* p. 269; and *Vneshniaia torgovlia SSSR za 1973 god,* p. 267.

159. See "Greco-Turkish Dispute," *New Times,* no. 16 (April 1974): 9.

160. Soviet purchases of oil products from South Yemen were 31,100 tons in *1969;* 8,000 in *1970;* 100 in *1971;* 200 in *1972;* and 200 in *1973.* See *Vneshniaia torgovlia SSSR za 1969 god,* p. 228; *ibid.,* 1970, p. 231; *ibid.,* 1971, p. 243; *ibid.,* 1972, p. 242; and *ibid.,* 1973, p. 242. On Soviet prospecting assistance, see Berry, "Oil and Soviet Policy," p. 157.

161. Watt, "Soviet Presence in the Mediterranean," p. 18.

162. Soviet purchases of diesel fuel from Kuwait were 11,200 tons in 1970 and 21,200 tons in 1971. See *Vneshniaia torgovlia SSSR za 1970 god,* p. 240 and *ibid.,* 1971, p. 253. The Soviets also sold oil rigs to Kuwait. See Stephen Page, "Moscow and the Persian Gulf Countries, 1967–1970," *Mizan* 13, no. 2 (October 1971): 77. For the Soviet purchase from Saudi Arabia, see *Vneshniaia torgovlia SSSR za 1969 god,* p. 249.

163. The Soviets frequently leave certain trade statistics out of their foreign trade yearbooks. For example, the Soviets do not want to publicize their oil sales to the United States or their purchases of American wheat so statistics on these transactions have been conveniently left out of the yearbooks at certain times.

164. Page, "Persian Gulf Countries," p. 75.

165. *Izvestiia,* February 10, 1972, p. 3 (*Current Digest of the Soviet Press* 24, no. 6, March 8, 1972, p. 16). Plans for oil exploration were also discussed in 1973. See Radio Moscow, August 21, 1973 (*USSR and Third World* 3, no. 6, July 16–September 2, 1973, pp. 417–18).

166. Israel is very sensitive about revealing information on its oil imports and very little has been written on this topic. The author secured the following information from interviews with many Israeli oil specialists, academicians, and political figures but, owing to the sensitivity of the issues involved, footnotes will not be used to cite specific sources. In addition to those Israelis mentioned in the acknowledgments, many other Israelis were also very helpful but it is preferable not to mention their names.

167. See "Israel Assured Supplies of Oil by Rumanian Deal," *The New York Times,* May 30, 1948, p. 6.

168. See "Oil Prospects for Israel," *The Israel Economist* 5, no. 1 (January 1949): 8.

169. Mordechai Namir, *Shlichut Bemoskva* (Mission in Moscow) (Tel Aviv: Oved Publishers, 1971), p. 28.

170. For a discussion of the Soviet role in the Rumanian oil industry, see chapter 9.

171. Namir, *Shlichut Bemoskva,* p. 155.

172. Sydney Gruson, "Israel Signs Pact With Oil Concerns," *The New York Times,* October 9, 1948, p. 2.

173. "Oil Prospects for Israel," p. 8.

174. Gruson, "Israel Signs Pact," p. 2.

175. Shwadran, *The Middle East, Oil and the Great Powers,* 3rd ed., p. 454.

176. Eliezer Shinnar, *Beol Korach Urgashot* (Under the Yoke of Necessity and Feeling) (Tel Aviv: Schocken, 1967), pp. 34–56.

117. *Ibid.,* pp. 46–47 and 55.

178. Donovan, *U.S. and Soviet Policy,* p. 128 and "Israelis Sue Arm of Soviet on Oil," *The New York Times,* November 3, 1957, p. 21.

179. See "Soviet Agrees to Increase Shipments of Oil to Israel," *The New York Times,* July 18, 1956, pp. 1 and 8 and William Jorden, "Oil Exports Seen as Soviet Weapon," *The New York Times,* November 29, 1956, p. 4.

180. Jack Raymond, "Soviet Seeking to Assure Arabs," *The New York Times,* July 27, 1956, p. 2 and Sam Pope Brewer, "2 Setbacks Augur Review by Arabs," *The New York Times,* July 20, 1956, p. 3.

181. Milton Kovner, *The Challenge of Coexistence: A Study of Soviet Economic Diplomacy* (Washington: Public Affairs Press, 1961), p. 56.

182. See "Israelis Sue Arm of Soviet on Oil," p. 21 and Max Frankel, "Israeli's Oil Suit Opens in Moscow," *The New York Times,* December 5, 1957, p. 21.

183. Kovner, *Challenge of Coexistence,* p. 57 and "Moscow Rejects Israeli Oil Suit," *The New York Times,* June 20, 1958, p. 1.

184. "Israelis May Seek Trade with Soviet," *The New York Times,* February 8, 1962, p. 9.

185. The Soviet request to Iran was carried on Radio Moscow in a Persian language broadcast on January 9, 1969. See *Mizan,* Supplement A, no. 1 (January–February 1969): 4.

186. "Soviet Trade in Slow Decline," *Petroleum Press Service* 39, no. 5 (May 1972): 163 and R. M. Burrell, "Canal, Pipeline or Cape?: Schemes for Oil Transportation," *New Middle East,* no. 41 (February 1972): 29.

187. "Eastern Europe: Ill-Effects of the Crisis," *The Petroleum Economist* 41, no. 1 (January 1974): 13.

188. *Petroleum Intelligence Weekly* 10, no. 52 (December 27, 1971): 7 and *Platt's Oilgram News Service* 54, no. 50 (March 15, 1976): 1.

189. See Walter Laqueur and Edward Luttwak, "Oil," *Commentary* 56, no. 4 (October 1973): 41; Leonard Binder, "Transformation in the Middle Eastern Subordinate System After 1967," in Confino and Shamir, *USSR and Middle East,* p. 271; and P. J. Vatikiotis, "Notes for an Assessment of the Soviet Impact on Egypt," in *ibid.,* p. 274. Note that all three of these analyses were written before the 1973 Arab-Israeli war.

190. It has been reported that Poliansky and Kirilenko, members of the Soviet Politburo, have warned against overreliance on the more radical Arab states since these states now have sources of arms other than the USSR and are less dependent than previously on the USSR. These men want a more multi-optioned policy which would include the renewal of ties with Israel and improved relations with generally pro-Western, oil-producing states. See *Middle-East Intelligence Survey* 2, no. 2 (April 15, 1974): 14. Poliansky was removed from the Politburo in 1976.

191. See "Rethinking Soviet Policies," *The Petroleum Economist* 41, no. 3 (March 1974): 99.

192. See George Weber, "Cracks Developing in U.S., Soviet Oil-Trade Barriers," *Oil and Gas Journal* 69, no. 31 (August 2, 1971): 23.

193. See Frank Gardner, "Soviets Score String of Historic Oil Penetrations," *Oil and Gas Journal* 68, no. 14 (April 6, 1970): 59.

194. Another possibility is to construct pipelines from the Middle East to Eastern Europe which pass through the Soviet Union. See *Soviet Oil to 1980,* p. 42.

195. Campbell, "Soviet Energy Policy," p. 100.

196. J. C. Hurewitz, *Soviet-American Rivalry in the Middle East* (New York:

Praeger, 1969), p. 116 and "Russian Oil: Sorry, Comrades," *The Economist* 250, no. 6812 (March 16, 1974): 93.

197. Becker, "Oil and the Persian Gulf," pp. 189–90.

198. Marshall Goldman, "The Asset We Have in Soviet Oil," *The New York Times,* March 4, 1973, section 3, p. 15.

199. Andreasyan, "New Aspects of Middle East Countries' Oil Policy," p. 33 and Boris Rachkov, *Oil Nationalism and Imperialism* (New Delhi: People's Publishing House, 1967), pp. 76–77.

200. See Boris Rachkov, "The Russian Stake in the Middle East," *New Middle East,* no. 8 (May 1969): 37.

8/Oil Embargoes and the Energy Crisis

1. Maxwell Taylor, "The Legitimate Claims of National Security," *Foreign Affairs* 52, no. 3 (April 1974): 593. Also see Arnold Horellck, *The Soviet Union, the Middle East, and the Evolving World Energy Situation* (Santa Monica: Rand Corporation, 1973), p. 7.

2. Thomas Ronan, "Britons Willing to Buy Soviet Oil," *The New York Times,* November 30, 1956, p. 3.

3. William Jorden, "Oil Exports Seen as Soviet Weapon," *The New York Times,* November 29, 1956, p. 4; "Soviet Offer Clarified," *The New York Times,* December 1, 1956, p. 4; and "Soviet Denies Offering Oil," *The New York Times,* December 2, 1956, p. 35.

4. Soviet sales of crude oil to France rose from 199,000 tons in 1955 to 262,000 tons in 1956. Sales of oil products rose from 69,400 tons to 146,900 tons. See *Vneshniaia torgovlia SSSR za 1956 god: statisticheskii obzor* (Foreign Trade of the USSR for 1956: Statistical Abstract) (Moscow: Vneshtorgizdat, 1958), p. 93.

5. Dana Adams Schmidt, "Soviet Reported Offering French and Arabs Its Oil," *The New York Times,* November 28, 1956, pp. 1 and 5 and Halford Hoskins, "Problems Raised by the Soviet Oil Offensive," United States Senate, Committee on the Judiciary (Washington: U.S. Government Printing Office, 1962): 2. Soviet sales of crude oil to Egypt rose from 156,100 tons in 1955 to 295,400 tons in 1956. Sales of oil products rose from 173,400 tons to 625,300 tons. In the case of Syria, there were no Soviet oil deliveries in 1955 but 26,000 tons of oil products were supplied in 1956. See *Vneshniaia torgovlia SSSR za 1956 god,* pp. 145 and 149.

6. G. Starko, "How to Solve the Oil Problem," *New Times,* no. 35 (August 1958): 15.

7. Abraham Becker, "Oil and the Persian Gulf in Soviet Policy in the 1970s," in Michael Confino and Shimon Shamir, eds., *The U.S.S.R. and the Middle East* (New York: John Wiley and Jerusalem: Israel Universities Press, 1973), p. 193 and J. E. Hartshorn, "Oil and the Middle East War," *The World Today* 24, no. 4 (April 1968): 152.

8. Y. Dmitriyev, "Arab Oil Resources," *International Affairs,* no. 8 (August 1967): 102.

9. L. Sedin, "The Arab Peoples' Just Cause," *International Affairs,* no. 8 (August 1967): 28. Also see G. Drambyants, "The Oil Embargo," *New Times, no. 26 (June 28, 1967): 4–5.*

10. K. Vishnevetsky, *Izvestiia,* June 9, 1967, p. 2 (*Current Digest of the Soviet Press* 19, no. 23, June 28, 1967, p. 7).

11. Cited in Becker, "Oil and the Persian Gulf," p. 212.

12. *Ibid.,* p. 191.

13. *Pravda,* September 3, 1967, p. 1 (*Current Digest of the Soviet Press* 19, no. 35, September 20, 1967, p. 21).

14. See V. Kudriavtsev, *Izvestiia,* September 5, 1967, p. 2 (*Current Digest of the Soviet Press* 19, no. 36, September 27, 1967, p. 20) and Igor Belyaev and Evgeny Primakov, "The Situation in the Arab World," *New Times,* no. 39 (September 27, 1967): 10. For an analysis of the Soviet reaction to the ending of the embargo, see David Morison, "Soviet Interest in Middle East Oil," *Mizan* 10, no. 3 (May–June 1968): 81–85.

15. R. Andreasyan, "New Aspects of Middle East Countries' Oil Policy," *International Affairs,* no. 9 (September 1968): 35–36.

16. *Petroleum Intelligence Weekly,* June 26, 1967, p. 3 and *Petroleum Intelligence Weekly,* February 26, 1968, p. 3.

17. *Petroleum Intelligence Weekly,* March 10, 1969, pp. 6–7.

18. "Arabs Mull Total Crude Embargo," *Oil and Gas Journal* 65, no. 32 (August 7, 1967): 98.

19. *Petroleum Intelligence Weekly,* June 19, 1967, p. 5; "Oil: A New War Nasser is Losing," *U.S. News and World Report* 63, no. 1 (July 3, 1967): 66; and Lincoln Landis, "Petroleum in Soviet Middle East Strategy," doctoral dissertation, Georgetown University, 1969, p. 152.

20. *Vneshniaia torgovlia SSSR za 1967 god: statisticheskii obzor* (Moscow: Izdatel'stvo "Mezhdunarodnye otnosheniia," 1968), p. 162. Sales of oil products to Britain jumped in 1967 and fell back in 1968 and this may have indicated increased sales during the embargo. See *ibid.,* p. 129.

21. Translation of "Soviet Oil on the World Market," *Ekonomicheskaia gazeta* (Economic Newspaper) no. 39, September, 1967, p. 44 in Robert Ebel, *Communist Trade in Oil and Gas* (New York: Praeger, 1970), p. 204.

22. Boris Rachkov, "The Russian Stake in the Middle East," *New Middle East,* no. 8 (May 1969): 37.

23. Soviet sales of oil products to India fell from 1,213,700 tons in 1966 to 468,700 tons in 1967. Sales of oil products to Ceylon fell from 644,600 tons to 564,800 tons and sales of crude oil to Japan fell from 2,786,200 tons to 1,798,100 tons. Sales of oil products to Japan rose slightly from 1,363,500 tons to 1,474,700 tons. See *Vneshniaia torgovlia SSSR za 1967 god,* pp. 231, 273, and 274.

24. Rachkov, "Russian Stake," p. 36.

25. Ruben Andreasyan, "Battle of Oil," *New Times*, no. 6 (February 10, 1971): 5 and Ruben Andreasyan, "Offensive on the Oil Front," *New Times*, no. 11 (March 17, 1971): 26.

26. E. Primakov, "Economic Aspect of the Middle East Crisis," *International Affairs*, no. 6 (June 1972): 39.

27. Radio Peace and Progress, February 24, 1973 (*USSR and Third World* 3, no. 3, February 19–April 8, 1973, pp. 159–60).

28. Ruben Andreasyan, "The Energy Crisis and Mid-East Oil," *New Times*, no. 16 (April 1973): 24.

29. Radio Moscow in Arabic, August 30, 1973 (Foreign Broadcast Information Service, *Soviet Union* 3, no. 172, September 5, 1973, p. F6).

30. Iurii Glukhov, "Important Lever," *Pravda*, September 5, 1973, p. 5 (*Current Digest of the Soviet Press* 25, no. 36, October 3, 1973, p. 10).

31. D. Volsky and A. Usvatov, "Israeli Expansionists Miscalculate," *New Times*, no. 42 (October 1973): 10.

32. C. L. Sulzberger, "Having and Eating Oilcake," *The New York Times*, December 29, 1973, p. 25.

33. V. Lobachenko, "Operation Oil Boom," *New Times*, no. 18 (May 1973): 14–15; V. Grigorovich, "Ishchut neft'," (Looking for Oil) *Pravda*, April 9, 1974, p. 5; and Valerian Skvortsov, "Neftianoi grabezh," (Oil Plunder) *Pravda*, June 9, 1974, p. 5.

34. William Smith, "The Search Widens for More Oil," *The New York Times*, December 16, 1973, section 3, p. 1.

35. Boris Orekhov, "Neft' i politika," (Oil and Politics) *Pravda*, November 20, 1973, p. 5; Ruben Andreasyan, "Middle East: The Oil Factor," *New Times*, nos. 45–46 (November 1973): 18; and Vladimir Peresada, "Neft' i politika," (Oil and Politics) *Pravda*, October 29, 1973, p. 5.

36. A. Vasil'ev, "Neftianoi krizis," (Oil Crisis) *Pravda*, December 6, 1973, p. 4.

37. Boris Orekhov, "Edinstvennyi put' k miru," (The Only Road to Peace) *Pravda*, December 4, 1973, p. 5 and M. Mikhailov, "Facets of the Oil Crisis," *Izvestiia*, November 22, 1973, p. 4 (*Current Digest of the Soviet Press* 25, no. 47, December 19, 1973, pp. 11–12).

38. Andreasyan, "Middle East: The Oil Factor," p. 18.

39. A Vasil'ev, "Neftianoi krizis," p. 4.

40. Radio Moscow in Arabic, December 26, 1973 (Foreign Broadcast Information Service, *Soviet Union* 3, no. 250, December 28, 1973, p. F10).

41. M. Fyodorov, "Oil—The Arabs' Weapon," *New Times*, no. 50 (December 1973): 14 and Iona Andronov, "Why They Will Have to Shiver This Winter," *New Times*, nos. 45–46 (November 1973): 13.

42. Valentin Korovikov, "Boikot—rasistam," (Boycott the Racists) *Pravda*, De-

cember 3, 1973, p. 3 and Fedor Tarasov, "Deistvennaia solidarnost'," (Active Solidarity) *Pravda,* December 25, 1973, p. 5.

43. Radio Moscow in Arabic, December 20, 1973 (*USSR and Third World* 4, no. 2, January 14–March 3, 1974, p. 53).

44. Radio Peace and Progress, December 1, 1973 (*USSR and Third World* 4, no. 1, December 3, 1973–January 13, 1974, p. 43).

45. Juan de Onis, "Iraq Disregards Arab Oil Cutback," *The New York Times,* November 14, 1973, p. 17.

46. "Iraqis Increasing Oil Production," *The New York Times,* December 19, 1973, p. 13.

47. *Pravda,* November 9, 1973, p. 1.

48. Boris Rachkov, "The 'Oil Weapon' and the Imperialist Slanderers," *Mezhdunarodnaia Zhizn'* (International Life) December 19, 1973, pp. 118–19 (Foreign Broadcast Information Service, *Soviet Union* 3, no. 18, January 25, 1974, p. F9).

49. Radio Moscow in Arabic, January 8, 1974 (Foreign Broadcast Information Service, *Soviet Union* 3, no. 6, January 9, 1974, pp. F1–2).

50. Rachkov, "The 'Oil Weapon' and the Imperialist Slanderers," p. F9.

51. "Soviet Radio Beamed to Arabs Backs Those Favoring Oil Ban," *The New York Times,* March 13, 1974, p. 24.

52. *Pravda,* March 14, 1974, p. 5.

53. Tomas Kolesnichenko, "Mezhdunarodnaia nedelia" (International Week) *Pravda,* March 17, 1974, p. 4.

54. Christopher Wren, "Soviet Stresses U.S.-Allied Split," *The New York Times,* March 20, 1974, p. 4.

55. Vladimir Bol'shakov, "Mezhdunarodnaia nedelia," (International Week) *Pravda,* March 24, 1974, p. 4.

56. See "Moscow Assails U.S. Oil Concerns," *The New York Times,* March 24, 1974, p. 10.

57. See Robert Freedman, *Soviet Policy toward the Middle East Since 1970* (New York: Praeger, 1975), p. 140.

58. See Clyde Farnsworth, "Shah and Faisal Were Prime Movers in Strategy on Oil," *The New York Times,* December 29, 1973, p. 11.

59. Members of OPEC are Abu Dhabi, Algeria, Ecuador, Indonesia, Iran, Iraq, Kuwait, Libya, Nigeria, Qatar, Saudi Arabia and Venezuela, while Gabon is an associate member. Members of OAPEC are Algeria, Bahrain, Egypt, Iraq, Kuwait, Libya, Qatar, Saudi Arabia, Syria and the United Arab Emirates.

60. R. Andreasyan, "Oil Barons in Trouble," *New Times,* no. 43 (October 28, 1964): 18.

61. B. Rachkov, "Oil and Arab Solidarity," *Foreign Trade,* no. 2 (1968): 56. Also see Stephen Page, "Moscow and the Persian Gulf Countries, 1967–1970," *Mizan* 13, no. 2 (October 1971): 79.

62. On the issue of prices, see Viktor Maevskii, "Neft' i Tretii Mir" (Oil and the Third World) *Pravda*, April 3, 1974, p. 4; Y. Yershov, "The 'Energy Crisis' and Oil Diplomacy Manoeuvres," *International Affairs*, no. 11 (November 1973): 4; and Igor Doronin, "Oil Money," *New Times*, no. 51 (December 1973): 20.

63. See R. Andreasyan, "New Developments on the Oil Front," *New Times*, no. 25 (June 1973): 24 and Theodore Shabad, "Russia Seen Reaping Benefits From Increase in Oil Prices," *International Herald Tribune*, October 15, 1974, p. 2.

64. See Ia. Bronin, "Arabskaia neft'—SShA—Zapadnaia Evropa," (Arab Oil—USA—Western Europe) *Mirovaia Ekonomika i Mezhdunarodnye Otnosheniia* (World Economics and International Relations), no. 2 (February 1972): 31–42 and Alawi Kayal, "The Control of Oil: East-West Rivalry in the Persian Gulf," doctoral dissertation, University of Colorado, 1972, p. 300.

65. See Radio Moscow in Arabic, February 7, 1974 (USSR and Third World 4, no. 2, January 14–March 3, 1974, p. 53); Alexei Vasilyev, "Persian Gulf : Where Epochs Meet," *New Times*, no. 5 (February 1974): 25; Yershov, "Energy Crisis," p. 59; and Stanislav Vasilyev, "Africa, the Monopolies and Arab Oil," *New Times*, no. 6 (February 1974): 15.

66. Vladlen Kuznetsov, "Battle for Oil," *New Times*, no. 4 (January 1974): 14–15 and Iurii Kharlanov, "Kozni 'Semi sester,'" (Intrigues of the "Seven Sisters") *Pravda*, March 23, 1974, p. 5. This Soviet claim conflicts with another Soviet claim that Western oil companies are raising prices as much as possible in order to maximize their profits during a period of energy shortages.

67. Felix Goryunov and Alexander Kazyukov, "Oil Magnates under Crossfire," *New Times*, no. 20 (May 1974): 23.

68. Andronov, "Shiver This Winter," p. 12; S. Safronov, "The Capitalist Economy 1973," *New Times*, no. 52 (December 1973): 19; Ivan Semichastnov, "The Soviet Union's Foreign Economic Ties Today," *New Times*, no. 2 (January 1974): 8; and Dmitry Kostyukhin, "Boom Giving Way to Slump," *New Times*, nos. 18–19 (May 1974): 26.

69. See "Neftianye monopolii nazhivaiutsia," (Oil Monopolies Prosper) *Pravda*, February 27, 1974, p. 5.

70. L. Tomashpol'skii, "Mirovoi energeticheskii balans: problemy poslednei treti veka," (World Energy Balance: Problems of the Last Three Centuries) *Mirovaia Ekonomika i Mezhdunarodnye Otnosheniia*, no. 2 (1967): 15–29 and Semichastnov, "Foreign Economic Ties," pp. 7–8. Also see "Russia Says It'll Be Leading Oil Nation by 2000," *Oil and Gas Journal* 65, no. 17 (April 24, 1967): 67.

71. Kostyukhin, "Boom," p. 27 and Yershov, "Energy Crisis," pp. 57–58.

72. Y. Yershov, "A Closer Look at the Energy Crisis," *New Times* no. 37 (September 1973): 18–20.

73. L. Lobanov, "Raw Materials and Politics," *International Affairs*, no. 7 (July 1974): 23.

74. Cited in A. Manzhulo and V. Polezhayev, "The 6th Special Session of the U.N. General Assembly on the Study of Problems of Raw Materials and Development," *Foreign Trade*, no. 9 (1974): 17.

75. "Eastern Europe: Ill-Effects of the Crisis," *The Petroleum Economist* 41, no. 1 (January 1974): 13; Christopher Wren, "Now Soviet, Too, Wages Electricity Conservation," *The New York Times,* January 14, 1974, p. 21; and *Facts on File* 33, no. 1727 (December 2–8, 1973): 1021–22.

76. Goryunov and Kazyukov, "Oil Magnates," p. 21.

77. Aleksandr Zholkver, Radio Moscow in Turkish to Cyprus, February 26, 1974 (Foreign Broadcast Information Service, *Soviet Union* 3, no. 40, February 27, 1974, pp. CC1–2).

78. Tomas Kolesnichenko, "Pirshestvo tsen," (Price Bonanza) *Pravda,* February 2, 1974, p. 5 and Konstantin Geivandov, "Komu pribyli, komu infliatsiia" (Those Who Profit Create Inflation) *Pravda,* May 2, 1974, p. 5.

79. Lev Bezymensky, "The Oil Crisis Bonanza," *New Times,* no. 51 (December 1973): 8–9; V. Pronin, "Vexing Problems," *New Times,* no. 47 (November 1973): 12; I. Latyshev, "Zagovor spekuliantov," (Conspiracy of the Speculators) *Pravda,* January 25, 1974, p. 5; and Vladimir Ermakov, "Podkontrolem monopolii," (Under Monopoly Control) *Pravda,* May 5, 1974, p. 5.

80. Radio Moscow in Arabic, October 17, 1973 (*USSR and Third World* 3, no. 8, October 22–December 2, 1973, p. 562); Ruben Anreasyan, "Arab Oil and Anti-Soviet Fabrications," *New Times,* no. 48 (November 1973): 21; and Radio Moscow in Arabic, August 30, 1973 (Foreign Broadcast Information Service, *Soviet Union* 3, no. 172, September 5, 1973, p. F6). The Soviets never really explain how American oil profits are supposedly forwarded to Israel.

81. B. Strel'nikov, "SShA: Kakoi budet zima," (USA: What a Winter It Will Be) *Pravda,* December 4, 1973, p. 4; Viktor Maevskii, "Monopolii i krizis" (Monopolies and the Crisis) *Pravda,* February 8, 1974, p. 4; and Viktor Maevskii, "Izoliatsiia agressorov" (Isolation of the Aggressors) *Pravda,* November 23, 1973, p. 4.

82. Safronov, "Capitalist Economy, pp. 19–20; Andronov, "Shiver This Winter," p. 12; Kuznetsov, "Battle for Oil," p. 15; Iurii Kharlanov, "Korni krizisa" (Roots of the Crisis) *Pravda,* January 14, 1974, p. 3; T. Kolesnichenko, "SShA: skvoz' prizmu neftianogo krizisa" (USA: Through the Prism of the Oil Crisis) *Pravda,* December 16, 1973, p. 4; *Pravda,* November 4, 1973, p. 5; *Pravda,* November 10, 1973, p. 5; *Pravda,* November 12, 1973, p. 5; and *Pravda,* November 18, 1973, p. 5.

83. Igor Ornatsky, "Co-operation of Equals, Not 'Partnership,' " *New Times,* no. 40 (October 1974): 21.

84. Pronin, "Vexing Problems," p. 12 and Felix Goryunov, "Money Market Ups and Downs," *New Times,* no. 3 (January 1974): 8.

85. For some American comments, see Clyde Farnsworth, "U.S. Advantage in Oil Helps Lift Dollar," *The New York Times,* December 28, 1973, p. 1 and Leonard Silk, "The Dollar's Comeback" *The New York Times,* January 16, 1974, p. 36.

86. Andreasyan, "Middle East: The Oil Factor," p. 18; Vladimir Mikhailov, "Mezhdunarodnaia nedelia," (International Week) *Pravda,* November 25, 1973, p. 4; and Boris Strel'nikov, "Partnery—soperniki," (Partners—Competitors) *Pravda,* November 25, 1973, p. 4.

87. For Western accounts, see Walter Laqueur, "The Idea of Europe Runs Out of Gas," *The New York Times Magazine,* January 20, 1974, pp. 12, 13, 36, 39, 41, 43, and 46; Martin Mauthner, "The Politics of Energy," *Middle East Information Series* 26–27 (Spring/Summer, 1974): 61–66; and Louis Turner, "Politics of the Energy Crisis," *International Affairs* (London) 50, no. 3 (July 1974): 404–15.

88. Vladimir Bol'shakov, "Mezhdunarodnaia nedelia," (International Week) *Pravda,* January 20, 1974, p. 4 and Ruben Andreasyan, Radio Moscow in Arabic, February 10, 1974 (Foreign Broadcast Information Service, *Soviet Union* 3, no. 29, February 11, 1974, p. CC2).

89. Radio Moscow in Arabic, January 14, 1974 (Foreign Broadcast Information Service, *Soviet Union* 3, no. 10, January 15, 1974, pp. A2–3).

90. Aleksandr Zholkver, Radio Moscow, p. CC2.

91. Reuters, January 16, 1974 (Foreign Broadcast Information Service, *Soviet Union* 3, no. 12, January 17, 1974, pp. A7 8); Radio Moscow in English to North America, January 19, 1974 (Foreign Broadcast Information Service, *Soviet Union* 3, no. 14, January 21, 1974, p. A12); and Radio Moscow in Arabic, February 14, 1974 (Foreign Broadcast Information Service, *Soviet Union* 3, no. 33, February 15, 1974, pp. CC5–6).

92. Y. Primakov, "The Fourth Arab-Israeli War," *World Marxist Review* 16, no. 12 (December 1973): 58 and Peresada, "Neft' i politika," p. 5.

93. A. Valentinov, "Soviet-Italian Co-operation: Results and Prospects," *New Times,* no. 8 (February 1974): 21 and E. Grigor'ev, "Neftianye nevzgody" (Oil Misfortunes) *Pravda,* November 25, 1973, p. 5.

94. Igor Latyshev, "Ishchut vykhod," (Looking for a Way Out) *Pravda,* December 18, 1973, p. 5 and Vadim Kassis, "Neon Blackout in Tokyo," *New Times,* no. 50 (December 1973): 21. Also see *Pravda,* November 22, 1973, p. 1 and *Pravda,* November 23, 1973, p. 1. For the Radio Moscow statement in Persian, January 5, 1974, see Foreign Broadcast Information Service, *Soviet Union* 3, no. 8 (January 11, 1974): A6.

95. Primakov, "The Fourth Arab-Israel War," p. 60 and Radio Peace and Progress in English to Africa, January 17, 1974 (Foreign Broadcast Information Service, *Soviet Union* 3, no. 13, January 18, 1974, p. F2).

96. For an analysis of the effect of the 1973–74 oil embargo on Soviet oil policies, see Chapter 4.

97. Semichastnov, "Foreign Economic Ties," p. 8. Also see Hedrick Smith, "Moscow to Honor Western Oil Deal," *The New York Times,* December 21, 1973, p. 53.

98. Radio Moscow in Arabic, December 27, 1973 (Foreign Broadcast Information Service, *Soviet Union* 3, no. 250, December 28, 1973, p. F11) and Christopher Wren, "Moscow Angrily Denying Role in Arab Oil Embargo," *The New York Times,* December 6, 1973, p. 40.

99. See Theodore Shabad, "Soviet Held Unaffected by Arab Oil Cuts," *The New York Times,* November 16, 1973, p. 22.

100. See Frank Gardner, "Not a Bad Profit for the Soviets—300%," *Oil and Gas Journal* 72, no. 14 (April 8, 1974): 51.

101. *Platt's Oilgram News Service* 52, no. 14 (January 21, 1974): 4; editorial, *The Washington Post,* March 29, 1974, p. A30; and Hedrick Smith, "Soviet Diplomacy: Waiting Game as Pendulum Swings Away From Moscow," *The New York Times,* November 26, 1973, p. 5.

102. See *The Petroleum Economist* 41 (January 1974): 33.

103. Christopher Wren, "Soviet Links U.S. Oil Shortage to 'Subversive Zionist Lobby,' " *The New York Times,* December 14, 1973, p. 14.

104. Frank Gardner, "Big Spurt in Income From Oil Sales Rescues Soviets," *Oil and Gas Journal* 72, no. 31 (August 5, 1974): 27 and Benjamin Shwadran, "Middle East Oil," *Current History* 66, no. 390 (February 1974): 82.

105. *Vneshniaia torgovlia SSSR za 1973 god: statisticheskii obzor* (Moscow: Izdatel'stvo "Mezhdunarodnye otnosheniia," 1974), p. 168.

106. *Ibid.,* p. 157. It is also possible that oil was diverted to Britain since British imports of Soviet oil were 267,400 tons in 1972 but 833,800 tons in 1973. See *ibid.,* p. 70.

107. Vladimir Pozner, Radio Moscow in English, November 4, 1973 (*USSR and Third World* 3, no. 8, October 22–December 2, 1973, p. 563).

108. U.S. government memorandum, April 18, 1974, p. 3.

109. *Ibid.,* pp. 1–3.

110. Radio Moscow in Arabic, December 27, 1973 (Foreign Broadcast Information Service, *Soviet Union* 3, no. 250, December 28, 1973, p. F11). It could also be added that Polish coal shipments to the United States began during the embargo but these deliveries had been planned earlier. See Gerd Wilcke, "Coal From Poland," *The New York Times,* December 13, 1973, p. 73.

111. See Jean Heller, "Soviets Shipped Oil to U.S. During Arab Embargo," *The Washington Post,* April 2, 1974, p. A13; Werner Bamberger, "U.S. Awaits First Soviet Oil Since '45," *The New York Times,* January 6, 1973, p. 58; and *Platt's Oilgram News Service* 52, no. 101 (May 24, 1974): 1.

112. Marshall Goldman, "The Asset We Have in Soviet Oil," *The New York Times,* March 4, 1973, section 3, p. 15.

113. Harry Schwartz, "In Place of Euphoria," *The New York Times,* October 30, 1973, p. 43.

114. "U.S.–Soviet Trade Rising: Moscow Assails Bill on Oil," *The New York Times,* December 8, 1973, pp. 49 and 51.

115. John Finney, "U.S. Dips into War Reserve to Supply Oil for Indochina," *The New York Times,* December 13, 1973, p. 3.

116. Drew Middleton, "Oil-Related Cut in Training Worries U.S. Military," *The New York Times,* December 1, 1973, p. 10.

117. John Finney, "Military Raising Domestic Oil Use," *The New York Times,* No-

vember 16, 1973, p. 20 and Drew Middleton, "Overseas Forces Get Oil Supplies," *The New York Times,* February 3, 1974, p. 9.

118. "Faisal Threatened U.S. Oil Firms to Campaign Against Israel," *The Jerusalem Post,* August 9, 1974, p. 5.

119. "Jackson Accuses Company: Cut to Military Charged," *The New York Times,* January 24, 1974, p. 1.

120. Robert McFadden, "Aramco Concedes Denying Oil to U.S. Military Since October," *The New York Times,* January 26, 1974, p. 14.

121. Kassis, "Neon Blackout," p. 21 and *Pravda,* December 26, 1973, p. 4.

122. "Philippines: Control Over Oil," *New Times,* no 51 (December 1973): 13.

123. New China News Agency dispatch of November 17, 1973 (*USSR and Third World* 3, no. 8, October 22–December 2, 1973, pp. 565–66) and New China News Agency dispatch of March 31, 1974 (U.S. government memorandum, April 1, 1974).

124. "Chinese Oil Lures Far East Consumers," *Oil and Gas Journal* 72, no. 8 (February 25, 1974): 84 and "Deal Has Been Closed," *Pravda,* December 31, 1973, p. 5 (*Current Digest of the Soviet Press* 25, no. 52, January 23, 1974, p. 11).

125. Radio Peace and Progress, November 24, 1973 (*USSR and Third World* 3, no. 8, October 22–December 2, 1973, p. 542).

126. *Pravda,* December 15, 1973, p. 5 and Radio Peace and Progress in Mandarin to Southeast Asia, January 31, 1974 (Foreign Broadcast Information Service, *Soviet Union* 3, no. 24, February 4, 1974, p. C3).

127. Smith Hempstone, "The War against America," *Washington Star-News,* January 4, 1974 (*AF Press Clips* 9, no. 3, January 15, 1974, p. 6). The U.S. imports a majority of the aluminum, chromium, manganese, nickel, tin and zinc it consumes.

128. See Edwin Dale, "Oil Increases Seen Offsetting Foreign Aid," *The New York Times,* January 1, 1974, pp. 27 and 30; Bernard Weinraub, "India to Cut Back on Oil Purchases," *The New York Times,* February 4, 1974, p. 9; Bernard Weinraub, "India, Pakistan, Bangladesh—On the Edge of Hunger," *The New York Times,* International Economic Survey, January 27, 1974, p. 46; Walter Sullivan, "Parley Says Oil Cut Reduces Fertilizer," *The New York Times,* January 26, 1974, p. 1; and Bernard Weinraub, "India, Slow to Grasp Oil Crisis, Now Fears Severe Economic Loss," *The New York Times,* January 20, 1974, p. 2.

129. Iurii Potemkin, "Solidarnost' v deistvii," (Solidarity in Action) *Pravda,* April 18, 1974, p. 5 and Iurii Potemkin, "Konstruktivnye resheniia," (Constructive Decisions) *Pravda,* January 30, 1974, p. 5.

9/Communist-Ruled States

1. Sources for Soviet-Rumanian oil relations are Anthony Sutton, *Western Technology and Soviet Economic Development 1945–1965* (Stanford: Hoover Institution Press, 1973), pp. 38–39; Margaret Dewar, *Soviet Trade With Eastern Europe, 1945–1949* (London: Royal Institute of International Affairs, 1951), pp. 78–79; Con-

stantin Jordan, *The Romanian Oil Industry* (New York: New York University Press, 1955), pp. 5–6, 42, 284–85 and 290–91; Glen Smith, *Soviet Foreign Trade: Organization, Operations, and Policy, 1918–1971* (New York: Praeger, 1973), p. 198; and John Montias, *Economic Development in Communist Rumania* (Cambridge: M.I.T. Press, 1967), pp. 19–20.

2. "Austria: Let's Talk It Over," *The Economist* 248, no. 6779, supplement (July 28, 1973): 6. Also see Robert Campbell, *The Economics of Soviet Oil and Gas* (Baltimore: Johns Hopkins University Press, 1968), pp. 244–45.

3. *Vneshniaia torgovlia SSSR: statisticheskii sbornik, 1918–1966* (Foreign Trade of the USSR: Statistical Compendium, 1918–1966) (Moscow: Izdatel'stvo "Mezhdunarodnye otnosheniia," 1967), pp. 163–65 and Robert Ebel, *The Petroleum Industry of the Soviet Union* (Washington: American Petroleum Institute, 1961), p. 157. Also see *Vneshniaia torgovlia SSSR za 1959 god: statisticheskii obzor* (Foreign Trade of the USSR for 1959: Statistical Abstract) (Moscow: Vneshtorgizdat, 1960), pp. 39 and 41; *ibid.*, 1961 (1962), pp. 70 and 72; and *ibid.*, 1963 (1964), pp. 87 and 89.

4. See Jan Triska and David Finley, *Soviet Foreign Policy* (New York: Macmillan, 1968), pp. 208–10.

5. See Alawi Kayal, "The Control of Oil: East-West Rivalry in the Persian Gulf," doctoral dissertation, University of Colorado, 1972, p. 253. Despite a decrease in Soviet oil exports in 1974, oil deliveries to CMEA members increased.

6. See United Nations, Statistical Office, *Statistical Yearbook 1972* (New York: United Nations, 1973): 354–56.

7. J. Richard Lee, "Petroleum Supply Problems in Eastern Europe," unpublished paper, March 1974, pp. 5–6.

8. "The Communist Oil Conundrum," *The Economist* 222, no. 6437 (January 7, 1967): 46.

9. Frank Gardner, "Russian Oil Exports Head for Squeeze," *Oil and Gas Journal* 67, no. 42 (October 20, 1969): 59; Lee, "Petroleum Supply," p. 6; and *Statistical Yearbook 1972,* pp. 180–81.

10. *Statistical Yearbook 1972,* pp. 180–81 and Montias, *Economic Development,* p. 290.

11. Jordan, *The Romanian Oil Industry,* pp. 1 and 243; Montias, *ibid.,* p. 6; and United Nations, Statistical Office, *World Energy Supplies, 1969–1972,* Statistical Papers, Series J, no. 17 (New York: United Nations, 1974): 50–57 and 77–88.

12. Campbell, *Economics of Soviet Oil,* p. 243; *Statistical Yearbook 1972,* p. 356; and United Nations, Statistical Office, *Statistical Yearbook 1973* (New York: United Nations, 1974): 350.

13. Leonid Tomashpol'skii, *Neft' i gaz v mirovom energeticheskom balanse (1900–2000gg.)* (Oil and Gas in the World Energy Balance, 1900–2000) (Moscow: Izdatel'stvo "Nedra," 1968), p. 141 and A. F. G. Scanlan, "The Energy Balance of the Comecon Countries," Round Table on the Exploitation of Siberia's Natural Resources," Brussels, January 30–February 1, 1974, pp. 17 and 20.

14. North Vietnam and North Korea import Soviet oil products but the demand has not escalated in recent years and, in the case of North Vietnam, it has decreased somewhat since the more active years of the Vietnam war. Soviet exports to these two states are on a small scale; North Vietnam received 229,800 tons in 1973 and North Korea 585,000 tons. See *Vneshniaia torgovlia SSSR za 1973 god: statisticheskii obzor* (Moscow: Izdatel'stvo "Mezhdunarodnye otnosheniia," 1974), pp. 227 and 246. Mongolia, a member of CMEA, received 323,100 tons in 1973. See *ibid.*, p. 71.

15. V. Zolotarev, "Integration of CMEA Countries and the Development of the World Socialist Market," *International Affairs,* no. 1 (January 1972): 21; Lee, "Petroleum Supply," pp. 8–9; United Nations, Economic Commission for Europe, "Recent Changes in Europe's Trade," *Economic Bulletin for Europe* 23, no. 2 (1972): 30; and Abraham Becker, "Oil and the Persian Gulf in Soviet Policy in the 1970s," in Michael Confino and Shimon Shamir, eds., *The USSR and the Middle East* (New York: John Wiley and Jerusalem: Israel Universities Press, 1973), p. 177.

16. "Russian Oil: Hammering Away," *The Economist* 244, no. 6726 (July 22, 1972): 82.

17. *Soviet Oil to 1980,* QER Special, no. 14, June 1973 (London: The Economist Intelligence Unit, 1973): 49 and Stanislaw Albinowski, "Where Is the Oil to Come From?" *Polityka,* September 24, 1966 (translated in Robert Ebel, *Communist Trade in Oil and Gas,* New York: Praeger, 1970, p. 251).

18. Valentin Shashin, "Soviet Oil," *New Times,* no. 15 (April 1974): 21.

19. "Moscow Asks Its Allies to Buy Oil in Mideast and North Africa," *The New York Times,* November 24, 1969, p. 6 and *Facts on File* 29, no. 1520 (December 11–17, 1969): 814.

20. Campbell, *Economics of Soviet Oil,* p. 248. There were numerous oil import agreements between East European states and Middle East and North African producers prior to the Czechoslovak announcement in November, 1969. The earliest was between Rumania and Iran on October 25, 1965 and all East European states followed suit. See George Stocking, *Middle East Oil* (Nashville, Tennessee: Vanderbilt University Press, 1970), p. 197; Robert Sullivan, "The Architecture of Western Security in the Persian Gulf," *Orbis* 14, no. 1 (Spring 1970): 75; R. Andreasyan, "New Aspects of Middle East Countries' Oil Policy," *International Affairs,* no. 9 (September 1968): 33; George Lenczowski, *Soviet Advances in the Middle East* (Washington: American Enterprise Institute for Public Policy Research, 1972), pp. 34–35; Stanislaw Wasowski, "The Fuel Situation in Eastern Europe," *Soviet Studies* 21, no. 1 (July 1969): 49; David Morison, "Soviet Interest in Middle East Oil," *Mizan* 13, no. 1 (August 1971): 31; Stephen Page, "Moscow and the Persian Gulf Countries, 1967–1970," *Mizan* 13, no. 2 (October 1971): 75; and Benjamin Shwadran, *The Middle East, Oil and the Great Powers,* 3rd ed. (New York: John Wiley and Jerusalem: Israel Universities Press, 1973), p. 378.

21. Morison, *ibid.,* p. 33.

22. Yu. Belayev, "CMEA Cooperation Today," *International Affairs,* no. 12 (December 1968): 8–9.

23. N. Korniyenko, "Friendship Oil Pipeline in Operation," *Foreign Trade,* no. 6 (1973): 14.

24. In addition to all of the sources cited in note 20, see Kayal, "Control of Oil," p. 240; "Russia's New Pasture," *Petroleum Press Service* 39, no. 9 (September 1972): 325; "East Germany to Get Iraq Oil," *Oil and Gas Journal* 70, no. 28 (July 10, 1972): 38; Ebel, *Communist Trade in Oil and Gas,* pp. 100–101; "Yugoslavs to Trade Tankers for Saudi Oil," *Oil and Gas Journal* 70, no. 26 (June 26, 1972): 40; Christopher Tugendhat, *Oil, The Biggest Business* (New York: G. P. Putnam's Sons, 1968), p. 253; Shwadran, *Oil and the Great Powers,* p. 442; "Soviet Bloc Turns to Middle East for Oil," *World Petroleum* 39, no. 10 (September 1968): 48 and 65; Lee, "Petroleum Supply," p. 11; "Eastern Europe: Ill-Effects of the Crisis," *The Petroleum Economist* 41, no. 1 (January 1974): 32; R. M. Burrell, "Canal, Pipeline or Cape?: Schemes for Oil Transportation," *New Middle East,* no. 41 (February 1972): 29; "Iraq: North Rumaila and the Russians," *Petroleum Press Service* 39, no. 5 (May 1972): 180; "Soviet Trade in Slow Decline," *Petroleum Press Service* 39, no. 5 (May 1972): 163; United Nations, Statistical Office, *World Energy Supplies, 1961–70,* Statistical Papers, Series J, no. 15 (New York: United Nations, 1972): 120–21; Becker, "Oil and the Persian Gulf," p. 181, "When Oil Flows East," *The Economist* 234, no. 6594 (January 10, 1970): 51–52; Marshall Goldman, "The Soviet Role in Oil, Economics and the Middle East," *Middle East Information Series* 23 (May 1973): 90–91; *Middle East Journal* 26, no. 4 (Autumn 1972): 439; *Middle East Journal* 26, no. 1 (Winter 1972): 44; *Middle East Journal* 25, no. 3 (Summer 1971): 379; *Petroleum Intelligence Weekly* 13, no. 1 (January 7, 1974): 9; *Petroleum Intelligence Weekly* 13, no. 9 (March 4, 1974): 11; *Oil and Gas Journal* 72, no. 7 (February 18, 1974): 56; *Middle-East Intelligence Survey* 1, no. 23 (March 1, 1974): 184; "Oil to Yugoslavia," *The Journal of Commerce,* November 23, 1973 (*AF Press Clips* 8, no. 48, November 27, 1973, p. 6); and *Platt's Oilgram News Service* 52, no. 245 (December 23, 1974): 2.

Rumania has arranged to import oil from Saudi Arabia, Libya, Iraq, Iran, Abu Dhabi, Kuwait, and Egypt; Bulgaria from Algeria, Syria, Iraq, Iran, Libya, and Egypt; East Germany from Egypt, Syria, Iraq, Algeria and Iran; Poland from Iran, Iraq, Algeria, Saudi Arabia, and Libya; Czechoslovakia from Iraq, Iran, Libya, Syria, and Egypt; and Hungary from Iraq, Iran, Libya, Egypt, and Syria. Yugoslavia, which is not a regular member of CMEA, concluded agreements with Iran, Libya, Saudi Arabia, Algeria, Iraq, Kuwait and Oman.

25. George Lenczowski, *Oil and State in the Middle East* (Ithaca, New York: Cornell University Press, 1960), p. 344; Burrell, "Oil Transportation," p. 31; Rouhollah Ramazani, *The Persian Gulf: Iran's Role* (Charlottesville: University Press of Virginia, 1972), p. 80; Ann Schulz, "A Leadership Role for Iran in the Persian Gulf?," *Current History* 62, no. 365 (January 1972): 26; and "Iran: Encircled Shah," *The Economist* 245, no. 6737 (October 7, 1972): 34.

26. Theodore Shabad, "Pipeline for Arab Oil Is Set for Eastern Europe," *The New York Times,* February 23, 1974, p. 41; B. Dudoladov, "Adriatika Oil Pipeline," *International Affairs,* no. 6 (June 1974): 112; and "Adrijatika Oil Pipeline," *New Times,* no. 8 (February 1974): 23.

27. *Middle-East Intelligence Survey* 2, no. 2 (April 15, 1974): 16; Dusko Doder,

"Kuwait to Help Finance East-Bloc Pipeline," *International Herald Tribune,* January 11–12, 1975, p. 9; *Petroleum Intelligence Weekly* 13, no. 9 (March 4, 1974): 11, and "Iraq: North Rumaila and the Russians," p. 180.

28. *Petroleum Intelligence Weekly* 9, no. 26 (June 29, 1970): 3 and *Petroleum Intelligence Weekly* 10, no. 28 (July 12, 1971): 3.

29. Goldman, "Soviet Role," p. 91.

30. James Feron, "Poland Signs Pact to Buy Oil from British Concern," *The New York Times,* July 3, 1971, p. 3; "East European Oil: Poland Turns West," *The Economist* 240, no. 6672 (July 10, 1971): 90; John Berry, "Oil and Soviet Policy in the Middle East," *Middle East Journal* 26, no. 2 (Spring 1972): 153; Becker, "Oil and the Persian Gulf," p. 181; and Goldman, *ibid.,* p. 91.

31. "Snam Gets Contract for Polish Refinery," *Oil and Gas Journal* 70, no. 29 (July 17, 1972): 64.

32. *Platt's Oilgram News Service* 51, no. 224 (November 19, 1973): 4.

33. Brian Hague, "Hungary—A Marketing Foothold for Western Companies," *World Petroleum* 42, no. 5 (June 1971): 68; Ebel, *Communist Trade in Oil and Gas,* p. 126; and George Weber, "Cracks Developing in U.S., Soviet Oil-Trade Barriers," *Oil and Gas Journal* 69, no. 31 (August 2, 1971): 25.

34. Hague, *ibid.,* p. 68 and Weber, *ibid.,* p. 25.

35. David Binder, "U.S. and Rumania Pledge Firmer Links," *The New York Times,* December 6, 1973, p. 3.

36. *Petroleum Intelligence Weekly* 12, no. 13 (March 26, 1973): 1.

37. U.S. government memorandum, January 14, 1974 and *Petroleum Intelligence Weekly* 13, no. 22 (June 3, 1974): 12.

38. For an analysis of Soviet negotiations with the United States and Japan on Siberian development, see Chapter 12.

39. Y. Zhuravlev, "Finland and CMEA," *New Times,* no. 51 (December 1973): 11 and "The 25th Anniversary of the Council for Mutual Economic Assistance," *Foreign Trade,* no. 9 (1974): 6. Also see "Accelerator of Progress," *New Times,* no. 51 (December 1973): 16.

40. The Soviet Union also helps East European states by building refineries, such as at Plock, Poland and by assisting in oil prospecting, as in Poland and East Germany. See N. Syomin, "Co-operation of CMEA Countries Advances the People's Living Standard," *International Affairs,* no. 9 (September 1964): 5 and S. Skachkov, "Economic and Technological Co-operation Between the Soviet Union and the Other CMEA Countries," *Foreign Trade,* no. 8 (1974): 5.

41. Heinz Kohler, *Economic Integration in the Soviet Bloc* (New York: Praeger, 1965), pp. 107–8 and Michael Kaser, *Comecon: Integration Problems of the Planned Economies* (London: Oxford University Press, 1967), p. 81.

42. Kaser, *ibid.,* pp. 55 and 81 and Andrzej Korbonski, "Comecon," *International Conciliation,* no. 549 (September 1964): 41.

43. D. Parondzhanov, "The Friendship Pipeline," *International Affairs,* no. 10 (October 1968): 120 and Theodore Shabad, *The Basic Industrial Resources of the U.S.S.R* (New York: Columbia University Press, 1969), p. 18.

44. Kohler, *Economic Integration,* pp. 108–9.

45. *Soviet Oil to 1980,* p. 20 and A. Zimin and L. Nikolayev, "Joint Construction Projects of CMEA Countries," *International Affairs,* no. 10 (October 1974): 137.

46. Lee, "Petroleum Supply," p. 10 and *Soviet Oil to 1980, ibid.,* p. 20.

47. Parondzhanov, "The Friendship Pipeline," p. 121 and Zimin and Nikolayev, "Joint Construction," p. 137.

48. The Druzhba Pipeline has branches going to the ports of Ventspils, Latvia and Klaipeda, Lithuania and oil is exported to Western Europe from these locations.

49. Alec Nove and Desmond Donnelly, *Trade with Communist Countries* (London: Hutchinson, 1960), p. 133.

50. Belayev, "CMEA Cooperation Today," p. 9.

51. L. Valentinovich and I. Motorin, "CMEA: Fuel and Raw Materials," *New Times,* no. 7 (February 17, 1970): 24.

52. Nikolai Patolichev, "Our Trade with Other CMEA Countries," *New Times,* no. 5 (February 17, 1974): 15.

53. Wasowski, "Fuel Situation," p. 48.

54. See V. Zolotaryov, "Economic Co-operation Between the CMEA Countries," *Foreign Trade,* no. 4 (1968): 27, and Y. Shmakova, "The CMEA Countries' Co-operation in Developing Fuel and Power Resources," *Foreign Trade,* no. 2 (1973): 5.

55. Belayev, "CMEA Cooperation Today," p. 10; A. Ivanov and Y. Semyonov, "Socialist Countries' Industrial Cooperation and Progress," *International Affairs,* no. 8 (August 1968): 38; and *Petroleum Intelligence Weekly,* June 24, 1968, pp. 5–6.

56. Otakar Simunek, "Czechoslovakia in the CMEA System," *International Affairs,* no. 3 (March 1968): 25; A. Shiryayev, "Soviet-Czechoslovak Economic Co-operation," *Foreign Trade,* no. 5 (1970): 17; and A. Zubkov, "CMEA Countries' Cooperation in the Fuel, Power and Raw-Material Industries," *International Affairs,* no. 12 (December 1971): 107–8.

57. Y. Akimov, "Problems of CMEA Countries' Economic Integration," *International Affairs,* no. 12 (December 1969): 10 and P. Yurov, "Socialist Economic Integration," *New Times,* no. 33 (August 1971): 7.

58. Khristo Konsulov and Albert Pin, "Bulgarian Workers in the Kara Kum," *New Times,* no. 22 (June 1974): 24.

59. Valentinovich and Motorin, "CMEA," p. 24; Zubkov, "Cooperation," p. 108; G. Kartsev, "U.S.S.R—Finland: Friendship and Trust," *New Times,* no. 38 (September 1974): 7; and Alan Tillier, "Finland in a Squeeze," *The Washington Post,* March 4, 1974, p. A12.

60. "East Germans in Soviet to Lay Pipeline," *The New York Times,* April 5, 1975, p. 2.

61. See Robert Freedman, *Economic Warfare in the Communist Bloc* (New York: Praeger, 1970), p. 28 and Milton Kovner, *The Challenge of Coexistence: A Study of Soviet Economic Diplomacy* (Washington: Public Affairs Press, 1961), p. 69.

62. Freedman, *ibid., p.* 28 and Marshall Goldman, *Soviet Foreign Aid* (New York: Praeger, 1967), p. 16.

63. *Vneshniaia torgovlia SSSR: statisticheskii sbornik, 1918–1966,* pp. 198–99.

64. For a discussion of the steps toward rapprochement between the USSR and Yugoslavia in late 1954, see Richard Lowenthal, *World Communism: the Disintegration of a Secular Faith* (New York: Oxford University Press, 1966), p. 10.

65. Freedman, *Economic Warfare,* p. 38 and Ebel, *Communist Trade in Oil and Gas,* p. 35.

66. For the 1973 statistic, see *Vneshniaia torgovlia SSSR za 1973 god,* p. 218. Soviet exports of crude oil and oil products to Yugoslavia were 456,400 tons in *1960;* 153,000 tons in *1961;* and 465,900 tons in *1962. Ser Vneshniaia torgovlia SSSR za 1961 god,* p. 157 and *ibid.,* 1963, p. 181.

67. For an excellent analysis of Soviet-Chinese political relations during this period, see Donald Zagoria, *The Sino-Soviet Conflict, 1956–1961* (Princeton: Princeton University Press, 1962).

68. T. R. Tregear, *An Economic Geography of China* (New York: American Elsevier, 1970), p. 194 and "China Blames Russia for Oil Troubles," *Oil and Gas Journal* 62, no. 1 (January 6, 1964): 49.

69. Pauline Lewin, *The Foreign Trade of Communist China* (New York: Praeger, 1964), p. 47.

70. Oleg Hoeffding, "Sino-Soviet Economic Relations, 1959–1962," *The Annals of the American Academy of Political and Social Science* 349 (September 1963): 95–96. Hoeffding argues that the Soviets did not use economic warfare and that they maintained trade relations despite political differences. He claims that the reduction in trade was due to China's inability to produce enough goods for export. However, he does admit that Soviet technicians were withdrawn in 1960 and that Soviet oil supplies were reduced after 1961 but he fails to point out that no crude oil was delivered after 1960.

71. *Dimensions of Soviet Economic Power* (Washington: U.S. Government Printing Office, 1962), Part 2, p. 738 and Alexander Eckstein, *Communist China's Economic Growth and Foreign Trade* (New York: McGraw-Hill, 1966), p. 151.

72. China's approximate oil production and her imports from sources other than the USSR are derived from statistics appearing in Chang Chun, "Peiping's Petroleum Industry: Growth and Future Development," *Issues and Studies* 10, no. 8 (May 1974): 53. For Soviet oil exports to China, see Table 9.1.

73. See Lewin, *Foreign Trade,* p. 48.

74. "China: How Much Oil?," *The Economist* 218, no. 6384 (January 8, 1966): 97; Michael Tanzer, *The Political Economy of International Oil and the Underdeveloped Countries* (Boston: Beacon Press, 1969), pp. 411–12; and Wu Yuan-li, *Eco-*

nomic Development and the Use of Energy Resources in Communist China (New York: Praeger, 1963), p. 180.

75. Chang Chun, "Peiping's Petroleum," p. 53; "Red China Battles for Oil Status," *Oil and Gas Journal* 65, no. 8 (February 20, 1967): 36; Sevinc Carlson, "China's Urgent Need for Stability in the Middle East," *New Middle East,* no. 36 (September 1971): 28; Lewin, *Foreign Trade,* p. 47; Freedman, *Economic Warfare,* pp. 136–38; and Tregear, *Economic Geography,* p. 195.

76. "China: How Much Oil?," p. 96; Freedman, *ibid.,* p. 14; and Eckstein, *Economic Growth,* p. 17.

77. "Turmoil Cripples Red Chinese Oil," *Oil and Gas Journal* 66, no. 22 (May 27, 1968): 74.

78. See John Gittings, *Survey of the Sino-Soviet Dispute* (London: Oxford University Press, 1968), pp. 230–31.

79. Tad Szulc, "U.S. Officials Say Soviet is Delivering Oil to China," *The New York Times,* September 1, 1972, p. 2 and "Openings in China," *Petroleum Press Service* 39, no. 10 (October 1972): 360.

80. L. Nikolayev and Y. Mikhailov, "China's Foreign Economic Policy," *International Affairs,* no. 9 (September 1973): 46.

81. "Letter of the Central Committee of the C.P.C. of February 29, 1964, to the Central Committee of the C.P.S.U.," *Peking Review* 7, no. 19 (May 8, 1964): 15.

82. Chin Wei-tung, "Following Our Own Road of Industrial Development," *Peking Review,* no. 24 (June 13, 1969): 12.

83. See Freedman, *Economic Warfare,* pp. 67–70 and 76–77.

84. "Albania: Big Brother's Helping Hand," *The Economist* 230, no. 6545 (February 1, 1969): 30.

85. Soviet imports of crude oil from Albania were 73,600 tons in *1958;* 70,900 tons in *1959;* 163,000 tons in *1960;* and 115,000 tons in *1961.* See *Vneshniaia torgovlia SSSR za 1959 god,* p. 45 and *Vneshniaia torgovlia SSSR za 1961 god,* p. 77. The Soviet Union also regularly imported Albanian crude oil before 1958.

86. Ivanov and Semyonov, "Industrial Cooperation," p. 38. Also see "Rouble Roulette," *The Economist* 228, no. 6519 (August 3, 1968): 17 for a discussion of Soviet threats against Czechoslovakia.

87. See Ebel, *Communist Trade in Oil and Gas,* pp. 92 and 180.

88. For the *Tass* report of September 6, 1968, see Frank Gardner, "Czech Blitz Craters Soviet Gas Deals," *Oil and Gas Journal* 66, no. 42 (October 14, 1968): 74.

89. *Vneshniaia torgovlia SSSR za 1967 god: statisticheskii obzor* (Moscow: Izdatel's tvo "Mezhdunarodnye otnosheniia," 1968), p. 205 and ibid., 1969 (1970), p. 195.

90. Belayev, "CMEA Cooperation Today," p. 9.

91. "Unready for Dubcek," *The Economist* 228, no. 6518 (July 27, 1968): 11–12.

92. "Rouble Roulette," p. 19.

93. Freedman, *Economic Warfare,* pp. 173–75.

94. Philip Bonsal, *Cuba, Castro and the United States* (Pittsburgh: University of Pittsburgh Press, 1971), pp. 44, 97, and 145–47.

95. *Ibid.,* p. 147; Anna Schreiber, "Economic Coercion as an Instrument of Foreign Policy: U.S. Economic Measures Against Cuba and the Dominican Republic," *World Politics* 25, no. 3 (April 1973): 391; and A. G. Mezerik, *Cuba and the United States* (New York: International Review Service, 1960), p. 7.

96. Edward Boorstein, *The Economic Transformation of Cuba* (New York and London: Monthly Review Press, 1968), p. 28 and Tanzer, *Political Economy,* pp. 328 and 344.

97. Bonsal, *Cuba,* p. 144.

98. Mezerik, *Cuba and the United States,* p. 7.

99. "Soviet Oil for Cuban Refineries?," *Oil and Gas Journal* 58, no. 22 (May 30, 1960): 72 and Cole Blasier, "The Elimination of United States Influence," in Carmelo Mesa-Lago, ed., *Revolutionary Change in Cuba* (Pittsburgh: University of Pittsburgh Press, 1971), p. 59.

100. Bonsal, *Cuba,* p. 148 and "Soviet Oil for Cuban Refineries?" p. 71. The Western oil companies may have believed that if they succumbed to Cuban pressure, they would have been faced with a similar situation in India. See "Suspense Mounts for Refiners in Cuba," *Oil and Gas Journal* 58, no. 25 (June 20, 1960): 95.

101. Tanzer, *Political Economy,* p. 346.

102. "Cuba Won't Press Soviet Crude on Refiners," *Oil and Gas Journal* 58, no. 24 (June 13, 1960): 82.

103. "Suspense Mounts for Refiners in Cuba," p. 95.

104. "Castro's Militia Takes Texaco Refinery," *Oil and Gas Journal* 58, no. 27 (July 4, 1960): 76.

105. Andres Suarez, *Cuba: Castroism and Communism, 1959–1966* (Cambridge: M.I.T. Press, 1967), p. 93.

106. K. S. Karol, *Guerrillas in Power: The Course of the Cuban Revolution* (New York: Hill and Wang, 1970), p. 26.

107. Mezerik, *Cuba and the United States,* pp. 6 and 40.

108. See Blasier, "Elimination of Influence," p. 69.

109. See Rudolf Sobotka, "Russia Exports More Than Crude Oil," *World Petroleum* 34, no. 10 (September 1963): 50 and Bonsal, *Cuba,* p. 148.

110. Jacinto Torres, *Cuba Socialista,* no. 10, June 1962 (translated in Stephen Clissold, ed., *Soviet Relations With Latin America, 1918–1968: A Documentary Survey,* London: Oxford University Press, 1970, p. 267).

111. Gardner Patterson, *Discrimination in International Trade: The Policy Issues, 1945–1965* (Princeton: Princeton University Press, 1966), p. 15.

112. Suarez, *Castroism and Communism,* p. 218.

113. See Desmond Wilson, Jr., "Strategic Projections and Policy Options in the Soviet-Cuban Relationship," *Orbis* 12, no. 2 (Summer 1968): 507.

114. See Frank Gardner, "Soviets Seen Cutting Off Cuban Oil," *Oil and Gas Journal* 66, no. 26 (June 24, 1968): 47.

115. Castro's contention was made in a speech on January 2, 1968. See Juan de Onis, "Castro Announces Curbs in Oil Crisis," *The New York Times,* January 3, 1968, p. 1. The Soviet claim had appeared in *Pravda* on December 29, 1967. See Clissold, *Soviet Relations,* p. 56.

116. Robert Lamberg, "The Cuban Economy and the Soviet Bloc, 1963–1968: A Commentary," in J. Gregory Oswald and Anthony Strover, eds., *The Soviet Union and Latin America* (New York: Praeger, 1968), p. 123 and Freedman, *Economic Warfare,* pp. 7–8.

117. Karol, *Guerrillas in Power,* p. 439 and de Onis, "Castro Announces Curbs," p. 1.

118. Leon Gouré and Julian Weinkle, "Cuba's New Dependency," *Problems of Communism* 21, no. 2 (March–April 1972): 73.

119. "Castro Says Cuba Plans Oil Search," *The New York Times,* April 20, 1968, p. 14. While oil relations with the Soviet Union were at a low point, Rumania came to Cuba's aid by providing a $30 million loan for the purchase of Rumanian oil-drilling equipment. See Lamberg, "Cuban Economy," p. 123 and Schreiber, "Economic Coercion," p. 402.

120. Edward Gonzalez, "Relationship With the Soviet Union," in Mesa-Lago, *Revolutionary Change,* p. 94.

121. Gouré and Weinkle, "Cuba's New Dependency," p. 73 and Gonzalez, *ibid.,* pp. 93–94.

122. Gonzalez, *ibid.,* 93–94. For a quantitative analysis of the lack of cooperation between the Soviet Union and Cuba during 1967–1969, see Daniel Tretiak, "Cuba and the Communist System: The Politics of a Communist Independent, 1967–1969," *Orbis* 14, no. 3 (Fall 1970): 740–64.

123. Gouré and Weinkle, "Cuba's New Dependency," p. 73.

124. Schreiber, "Economic Coercion," p. 388.

125. "Reds Busy Lining Up Tankers for Cuban Run," *Oil and Gas Journal* 58, no. 34 (August 22, 1960): 52.

126. "British Charter Ships to Reds," *Oil and Gas Journal* 58, no. 37 (September 12, 1960): 84.

127. Wilson, "Strategic Projections," p. 507.

128. *Petroleum Intelligence Weekly* 10, no. 19 (May 10, 1971): 5.

129. *Platt's Oilgram News Service* 51, no. 163 (August 22, 1973): 2.

130. "Soviets Push Cuban Exploration Effort," *Oil and Gas Journal* 62, no. 16 (April 20, 1964): 86; "Cuba: A Dry-Hole Satellite for Russia," *Oil and Gas Journal* 63, no. 26 (June 28, 1965): 70; "Russian Balk Tightens Cuba Fuel Pinch," *Oil and*

Gas Journal 68, no. 50 (December 14, 1970): 64; and "Cuba Comes Up Dry in Expensive Search," *Oil and Gas Journal* 70, no. 23 (June 5, 1972): 34.

131. See United Nations, Statistical Office, *World Energy Supplies, 1961–70,* Statistical Papers, Series J, no. 15 (New York: United Nations, 1972): 32–33 and *Statistical Yearbook 1973,* p. 348.

132. Gouré and Weinkle, "Cuba's New Dependency," p. 69.

133. See Suarez, *Castroism and Communism,* p. 182.

134. J. H. Carmical, "Soviet Pushing Its Oil Exports," *The New York Times,* July 29, 1962, section 3, p. 14.

135. "Brezhnev Believed Using Cuba Trip against China," *The New York Times,* January 22, 1974, p. 6, and "Brezhnev Promises to Help Cubans Search for Oil," *The New York Times,* February 1, 1974, p. 3.

136. *Platt's Oilgram News Service* 52, no. 164 (August 26, 1974): 3.

137. H. J. Maidenberg, "Venezuela Is Aiding Poor Nations on Oil," *The New York Times,* September 15, 1975, pp. 27–28.

138. "Mexico, Now Oil-Rich, Seeks to Align Itself with the OPEC," *International Herald Tribune,* October 17, 1974, p. 2 and "Oil Trading Deal Set by Cuba, Mexico, Soviet and Venezuela," *The New York Times,* March 26, 1975, p. 67.

139. Campbell, *Economics of Soviet Oil,* p. 242 and Rudolf Sobotka, "Policy Factors Affect East Europe Oil Industry Outlook," *World Petroleum* 42, no. 5 (June 1971): 250.

140. Lee, "Petroleum Supply," p. 16.

141. *Ibid.,* p. 19 and "Recent Changes in Europe's Trade," p. 30.

142. *Vneshniaia torgovlia SSSR za 1973 god,* p. 71. Some Soviet gas deliveries to Czechoslovakia pay for transit rights since Soviet gas is piped through Czechoslovakia to other states. See Radio Free Europe Research, "Czechoslovakia Situation Report 10," February 12, 1975, p. 4.

143. Lee, "Petroleum Supply," p. 20; "U.S.S.R.-Bulgaria Gas Pipeline," *New Times,* no. 36 (September 1974): 7; and *Platt's Oilgram News Service* 52, no. 172 (September 6, 1974): 4.

144. E. Shmakova, "The Comprehensive Programme in Action," *Foreign Trade,* no. 12 (1973): 6; R. Takhnenko, "Soviet Gas Goes to Europe," *International Affairs,* no. 3 (March 1973): 117; and *Platt's Oilgram News Service* 52, no. 42 (March 1, 1974): 3.

145. Theodore Shabad, "Soviet Opens Big Natural-Gas Field Relatively Near Markets in Europe," *The New York Times,* February 20, 1974, p. 51.

146. See Korbonski, "Comecon," p. 50.

147. Lee, "Petroleum Supply," p. 25.

10/Western Europe

1. A. Hols, "The Future Energy Supplies to the Free World," in *International Oil Symposium* (London: The Economist Intelligence Unit, 1972), p. 17.

2. See chapter 2 for a discussion of the Icelandic and Finnish cases.

3. Tonne Huitfeldt, "A Strategic Perspective on the Arctic," *Cooperation and Conflict,* no. 2–3 (1974): 93.

4. *Platt's Oilgram News Service* 52, no. 10 (January 15, 1974): 2 and *ibid.,* no. 163 (August 23, 1974): 5.

5. *Ibid.,* no. 215 (November 7, 1974): 1.

6. "Norway and Russia: No Piece of Cake," *The Economist* 253, no. 6849 (November 30, 1974): 45 and "Norway, Russia to Open Talks Today on Sharing Barents Sea," *International Herald Tribune,* November 25, 1974, p. 5.

7. Kim Traavik and Willy Ostreng, "The Arctic Ocean and the Law of the Sea," *Cooperation and Conflict,* no. 2–3 (1974): 59 and Huitfeldt, "Strategic Perspective," p. 92.

8. "Norway Set for Continental Shelf Negotiations," *Newsweek,* International Edition (November 25, 1974): 42.

9. Drew Middleton, "Four Problems Beset NATO: In North, South and Within," *International Herald Tribune,* September 10, 1974, p. 2.

10. Traavik and Ostreng, "Arctic Ocean," p. 58. For an excellent analysis of the strategic importance of the Arctic and of Soviet military strategy in the area, see Huitfeldt, "Strategic Perspective," pp. 83–99.

11. Drew Middleton, "NATO Seeks Ways to Defend North Sea Oil-Pumping Rigs," *International Herald Tribune,* December 27, 1974, p. 5.

12. For a complete, although somewhat outdated, analysis of the strategic importance of the Soviet-Norwegian border area, see Nils Orvik, *Europe's Northern Cap and the Soviet Union,* Harvard University Center for International Affairs, Occasional Papers in International Affairs, no. 6 (September 1963).

13. Finn Sollie, "Norway's Continental Shelf and the Boundary Question on the Seabed," *Cooperation and Conflict,* no. 2–3 (1974): 111–13.

14. *Ibid.,* and Finn Sollie, "New Territories and New Problems in Norwegian Foreign and Security Policy," *Cooperation and Conflict,* no. 2–3 (1974): 149.

15. Sollie, "New Territories," pp. 148–49.

16. Middleton, "NATO Seeks Ways," p. 5.

17. Halford Hoskins, "Problems Raised by the Soviet Oil Offensive," United States Senate, Committee on the Judiciary (Washington: U.S. Government Printing Office, 1962), p. 14 and J. H. Carmical, "Common Market Seeks Oil Policy," *The New York Times,* March 4, 1962, section 3, p. 1.

18. See Benjamin Welles, "U.S. May Accede on Sales of Pipe," *The New York Times,* September 17, 1966, p. 10.

19. *Ibid.,* p. 10 and Michael Gehlen, "The Politics of Soviet Foreign Trade," *The Western Political Quarterly* 18, no. 1 (March 1965): 112.

20. Michael Tanzer, *The Political Economy of International Oil and the Underdeveloped Countries* (Boston: Beacon Press, 1969), p. 193.

21. V. Butrin, "Japan, Winter 1963," *New Times,* no. 10 (March 13, 1963): 11 and V. Spandaryan, "New Soviet-Japanese Trade Agreement," *New Times,* no. 6 (February 13, 1963): 8.

22. B. Rachkov, "Oil, Trade and Politics," *International Affairs,* no. 4 (April 1966): 19.

23. Philip Shabecoff, "Bonn Is Reported Seeking End of NATO Ban on Pipe for Soviet," *The New York Times,* September 8, 1966, p. 14; Richard Mooney, "Allies Irritated by Soviet Pipe Bid," *The New York Times,* April 1, 1963, p. 60; Abram Frumkin, *Modern Theories of International Economic Relations* (Moscow: Progress Publishers, 1969), p. 487; and "Bonn Delivers Note to Soviet," *The New York Times,* April 12, 1963, p. 3.

24. Shabecoff, "Bonn Seeking End," p. 14 and "Soviets Plan World's Biggest Pipeline," *Oil and Gas Journal* 64, no. 45 (November 7, 1966): 70.

25. Welles, "U.S. May Accede," p. 10 and "Soviets Plan World's Biggest Pipeline," p. 70.

26. "NATO Lifts Its Ban on Sale of Large Pipe to Red Bloc," *The New York Times,* November 11, 1968, p. 8.

27. Peter Odell, *Oil and World Power* (Baltimore: Penguin, 1970), p. 175. NATO states have been exporting pipe to the Soviet Union ever since and, in October 1974, West Germany concluded a large transaction with the Soviet Union in which the Soviets were given a $575 million credit for the purchase of 950,000 tons of large-diameter steel pipe to be delivered over a ten-year period. See Christopher Wren, "Berlin Issue is Hampering Talks by Schmidt, Brezhnev," *International Herald Tribune,* October 30, 1974, p. 4. The largest suppliers of pipe to the USSR are West Germany, Italy and France. See Frank Gardner, "Big Spurt in Income From Oil Sales Rescues Soviets," *Oil and Gas Journal* 72, no. 31 (August 5, 1974): 27.

28. For a discussion of Soviet exports to Western Europe as part of the Soviet "oil offensive," see chapter 4. Also see Tables 9.3 and 9.4. It should be pointed out that the dependence of NATO states on Soviet oil was somewhat less than the overall dependence of Western Europe since Finland and Yugoslavia were included in the statistics for Western Europe. Together, they received about 25% of Soviet oil exports to Western Europe and they had a high degree of dependence on the USSR.

29. *Petroleum Intelligence Weekly* 10, no. 6 (February 8, 1971): 5.

30. "Soviet Oil: A Sticky Problem for U.K. Conservatives," *Oil and Gas Journal* 61, no. 7 (February 18, 1963): 72.

31. *Petroleum Intelligence Weekly* 10, no. 6 (February 8, 1971): 5; *Facts on File* 31, no. 1591 (April 22–28, 1971): 319; and Marshall Goldman, "The Soviet Role in Oil, Economics and the Middle East," *Middle East Information Series* 23 (May 1973): 88.

32. *Platt's Oilgram News Service* 51, no. 127 (July 2, 1973): 3 and *Vneshniaia torgovlia SSSR za 1973 god: statisticheskii obzor* (Foreign Trade of the USSR for 1973: Statistical Abstract) (Moscow: Izdatel'stvo "Mezhdunarodnye otnosheniia," 1974), p. 130.

33. Odell, *Oil and World Power,* p. 54.

34. "United Kingdom's East-West Trade," *East-West Trade News* (May 29, 1974): 2.

35. For an analysis of the role of ENI and its conflicts with the major Western oil companies, see P. H. Frankel, *Mattei: Oil and Power Politics* (New York: Praeger, 1966).

36. Boris Rachkov, *Oil Nationalism and Imperialism* (New Delhi: People's Publishing House, 1967) p. 59.

37. See Walter Laqueur, *The Struggle for the Middle East: The Soviet Union in the Mediterranean, 1958–1968* (New York: Macmillan, 1969), p. 121 and J. E. Hartshorn, *Politics and World Oil Economics*, rev. ed. (New York: Praeger, 1967), p. 236. The Soviet Union sold modest amounts of both crude oil and oil products to Italian firms before the agreements with ENI but the large sales to ENI greatly increased the Soviet presence in the Italian market.

38. Hartshorn, *ibid.,* p. 236.

39. Gehlen, "Soviet Foreign Trade," p. 111.

40. *Ibid.,* p. 111; Daniel Spencer, "The Role of Oil in Soviet Foreign Economic Policy," *American Journal of Economics and Sociology* 25, no. 1 (January 1966): 100; and Iurii Kapelinskii, *Torgovlia SSSR s kapitalisticheskimi stranami posle vtoroi mirovoi voiny* (Trade of the USSR with Capitalist Countries after the Second World War) (Moscow: Izdatel'stvo "Mezhdunarodnye otnosheniia," 1970), p. 61.

41. Halford Hoskins and Leon Herman, *Soviet Oil in the Cold War* (Washington: U.S. Government Printing Office, 1961), p. 6; Spencer, "Role of Oil," pp. 100–101; "Russian Oil Competition," *World Petroleum* 31, no. 10 (September 1960): 53; and Stefan Stolte, "Oil as a Weapon in the Cold War," *Bulletin of the Institute for the Study of the USSR* 8, no. 9 (September 1961): 11.

42. See *Vneshniaia torgovlia SSSR za 1973 god*, pp. 70–71. In November 1974, the USSR agreed in principle to start supplying oil for the post-Spinola government of Portugal but no specific commitment was made. The Soviet offer coincided with a great improvement in Soviet-Portuguese political relations. See *Platt's Oilgram News Service* 52, no. 220 (November 14, 1974): 2.

43. Goldman, "Soviet Role," p. 92 and N. Markov and L. Savitsky, "The Teboil and Suomen Petrooli Joint-Stock Companies on the Finnish Oil Market," *Foreign Trade,* no. 5 (1974): 29.

44. Markov and Savitsky, *ibid.,* p. 30 and Frank Gardner, "Russian Capitalism Works Well . . . In Finland," *Oil and Gas Journal* 72, no. 30 (July 29, 1974): 111.

45. "Soviet to Join in Building of a French Oil Refinery," *The New York Times,* June 2, 1971, p. 6 and Goldman, "Soviet Role," p. 92.

46. J. H. Carmical, "Soviet May Press Oil Sales to West," *The New York Times,* August 23, 1965, p. 36.

47. Goldman, "Soviet Role," p. 93.

48. *Ibid.*, p. 93; Samuel Pisar, *Coexistence and Commerce* (New York: McGraw-Hill, 1970), p. 153; and Harvey Shapiro, "Alexei Kosygin Has a Friend at Chase Manhattan . . ." *The New York Times Magazine,* February 24, 1974, p. 67.

49. Robert Ebel, *Communist Trade in Oil and Gas* (New York: Praeger, 1970), p. 125 and "Putting a Bear in Britain's Tank," *Business Week,* July 20, 1968, p. 80.

50. "A Bar to Soviet Oil is Asked in Belgium," *The New York Times,* May 31, 1968, pp. 41–42.

51. Goldman, "Soviet Role," p. 93 and "Putting a Bear in Britain's Tank," p. 80. The Soviets have suggested to Chancellor Schmidt of West Germany that they participate in the operation of a joint refinery, to be built near Kassel, West Germany. See *Platt's Oilgram News Service* 52, no. 214 (November 6, 1974): 1.

52. Marshall Goldman, "With Russian Oil, Marketing Skill," *The New York Times,* January 21, 1972, p. 69 and Goldman, "Soviet Role," pp. 92–93.

53. Goldman, "Soviet Role," p. 92 and *Petroleum Intelligence Weekly* 12, no. 28 (July 9, 1973): 4.

54. *Facts on File* 31, no. 1591 (April 22–28, 1971), p. 319; *Petroleum Intelligence Weekly* 10, no. 6 (February 8, 1971): 5; and *Petroleum Intelligence Weekly* 12, no. 28 (July 9, 1973): 4.

55. "Putting a Bear in Britain's Tank," p. 80; Pisar, *Coexistence and Commerce,* p. 153; and Shapiro, "Kosygin Has a Friend," p. 67. The Soviets have oil marketing networks in Britain, Belgium, and Finland but many other West European states import Soviet crude oil or oil products. This oil is therefore marketed by Western firms. For example, Soviet oil products in Iceland are marketed by Exxon, BP and Shell. See John Griffiths, *Modern Iceland* (New York: Praeger, 1969), pp. 58–59.

56. Hols, "Future Energy Supplies," pp. 20–21.

57. Elizabeth Kridl Valkenier, "Soviet Economic Relations With the Developing Nations," in Roger Kanet, ed., *The Soviet Union and the Developing Nations* (Baltimore: Johns Hopkins University Press, 1974), p. 222 and Frank Gardner, "Czech Blitz Craters Soviet Gas Deals," *Oil and Gas Journal* 66, no. 42 (October 14, 1968): 75.

58. Gardner, *ibid.*, p. 74 and *Keesing's Contemporary Archives* (February 19–25, 1973): 25748.

59. *Platt's Oilgram News Service* 52, no. 227 (November 25, 1974): 1.

60. *Vneshniaia torgovlia SSSR za 1973 god,* p. 71.

61. *Facts on File* 29, no. 1520 (December 11–17, 1969): 814.

62. Alawi Kayal, "The Control of Oil: East-West Rivalry in the Persian Gulf," doctoral dissertation, University of Colorado, 1972, p. 248; *Facts on File, ibid.,* p. 814; and A. Grigoryev, "USSR–FRG Economic Relations," *International Affairs,* no. 10 (October 1974): 48.

63. Pisar, *Coexistence and Commerce,* p. 60; "Russian Gas: Pipes of Peace," *The Economist* 234, no. 6598 (February 7, 1970): 71; and "Now Those Gas Prices Are Soaring Too," *The Economist* 252, no. 6835 (August 24, 1974): 72.

64. Grigoryev, "USSR–FRG," p. 48.

65. See *Facts on File* 34, no. 1732 (January 19, 1974): 35 and "Russian Oil: Sorry, Comrades," *The Economist* 250, no. 6812 (March 16, 1974): 93.

66. Iu. Kuznetsov, "Cooperation Strengthens," *Pravda,* January 10, 1974, p. 5 (*Current Digest of the Soviet Press* 26, no. 2, February 6, 1974, p. 16).

67. "Russian Gas Market Expands to Finland," *Oil and Gas Journal* 69, no. 51 (December 20, 1971): 18.

68. U.S. government memorandum, January 11, 1974.

69. *Ibid.*

70. "Soviet Gas for Italy," *New Times,* no. 24 (June 1974): 12 and U.S. government memorandum, June 13, 1974.

71. Nikolai Osipov, "Soviet Natural Gas for France," *New Times,* no. 34 (August 1971): 5 and "France, Soviets Sign Gas Deal," *Newsweek,* International Edition, December 16, 1974, p. 46.

72. Christopher Tugendhat, *Oil, the Biggest Business* (New York: G. P. Putnam's Sons, 1968), p. 255.

73. "The Great Gas Swap," *The Economist* 244, no. 6728 (August 5, 1972): 85.

74. *Press Bulletin,* April 11, 1973, p. 10.

75. See *Platt's Oilgram News Service* 51, no. 220 (November 13, 1973): 3.

76. *Platt's Oilgram News Service* 52, no. 212 (November 4, 1974): 2.

11/The Third World

1. During the period 1955–1961, oil constituted about 20% of total Soviet exports to the Third World. See *Dimensions of Soviet Economic Power* (Washington: U.S. Government Printing Office, 1962), Part 2, p. 742.

2. See Robert Campbell, *The Economics of Soviet Oil and Gas* (Baltimore: Johns Hopkins University Press, 1968), p. 251 and "Skilled Oil-Worker Shortage Hits Soviet," *Oil and Gas Journal* 65, no. 31 (July 31, 1967): 98.

3. See Stephen Clarkson, "Manicheism Corrupted: The Soviet View of Aid to India," *International Journal* 22, no. 2 (Spring 1967): 257–58.

4. D. Chertkov, *The Soviet Union and Developing Countries* (Moscow: Novosti Press Agency Publishing House, 1972), pp. 37–38.

5. See Michael Tanzer, *The Political Economy of International Oil and the Underdeveloped Countries* (Boston: Beacon Press, 1969), p. 181 and J. A. Naik, *Soviet Policy Towards India: From Stalin to Brezhnev (Delhi: Vikas Publications, 1970), p. 168.*

6. *Arthur Stein, India and the Soviet Union: The Nehru Era* (Chicago: University of Chicago Press, 1969), pp. 79–80 and Geoffrey Jukes, *The Soviet Union in Asia* (Sydney: Angus and Robertson, 1973), p. 114.

55. "Soviets Boast of Major Afghanistan Strike," *Oil and Gas Journal* 58, no. 22 (May 30, 1960): 76.

56. John Griffiths, *Afghanistan* (New York: Praeger, 1967), p. 124.

57. U.S. Department of State, Bureau of Intelligence and Research, "Communist States and Developing Countries: Aid and Trade in 1972," RECS–10 (June 15, 1973): 2.

58. Robert Ebel, *Communist Trade in Oil and Gas* (New York: Praeger, 1970), p. 160 and Violet Conolly, *Beyond the Urals: Economic Developments in Soviet Asia* (London: Oxford University Press, 1967), p. 139.

59. Goldman, *Soviet Foreign Trade*, p. 118.

60. Y. Nadezhdin, "Soviet-Afghan Trade," *Foreign Trade*, no. 9 (1969): 19; Theodore Shabad, *The Basic Industrial Resources of the U.S.S.R.* (New York: Columbia University Press, 1969), p. 319; and Elizabeth Kridl Valkenier, "Soviet Economic Relations With the Developing Nations," in Roger Kanet, ed., *The Soviet Union and the Developing Nations* (Baltimore: Johns Hopkins University Press, 1974), p. 222.

61. Griffiths, *Afghanistan*, p. 128.

62. Nadezhdin, "Soviet-Afghan Trade," p. 19.

63. V. Shelepin, "The Socialist World and the Developing Countries," *New Times*, no. 9 (March 3, 1970): 21.

64. See Leslie Dienes, "Geographical Problems of Allocation in the Soviet Fuel Supply," *Energy Policy* 1, no. 1 (June 1973): 12.

65. See Robert Ebel, "Two Decades of Soviet Oil and Gas," *World Petroleum* 42, no. 5 (June 1971): 79.

66. "Russia to Import Gas It Doesn't 'Need,'" *Oil and Gas Journal* 64, no. 4 (January 24, 1966): 63 and "Gas in Afghanistan," *Petroleum Press Service* 39, no. 5 (May 1972): 174.

67. Afghan gas exports to the USSR were 1,500,000,000 cubic meters in *1968*; 2,029,700,000 in *1969*; 2,590,700,000 in *1970*; 2,513,000,000 in *1971*; 2,849,400,000 in *1972*; 2,734,900,000 in *1973*; and approximately 2,800,000,000 in *1974*. See *Vneshniaia torgovlia SSSR za 1969 god: statisticheskii obzor* (Moscow: Izdatel'stvo "Mezhdunarodnye otnosheniia," 1970), p. 211; *ibid.*, 1970 (1971), p. 215; *ibid.*, 1971 (1972), p. 226; *ibid.*, 1972 (1973), p. 223; *ibid.*, 1973 (1974), p. 223; and *USSR and Third World* 4, no. 5 (June 10–July 18, 1974), p. 283.

68. Marshall Goldman, "The Soviet Role in Oil, Economics and the Middle East," *Middle East Information Series* 23 (May 1973): 95.

69. "Money and Gas," *The Economist* 252, no. 6831 (July 27, 1974): 89; "Natural Gas: More, but at a Price," *The Petroleum Economist* 41, no. 8 (August 1974): 295; and *USSR and Third World* 4, no. 5 (June 10–July 28, 1974): 283.

70. *Vneshniaia torgovlia SSSR za 1965 god: statisticheskii obzor* (Moscow: Izdatel'stvo "Mezhdunarodnye otnosheniia," 1966), p. 292. Also see "Ghana, U.S. Firms Eye Offshore Terms," *Oil and Gas Journal* 66, no. 38 (September 16, 1968): 56 and Ebel, *Communist Trade*, p. 409.

7. Rudolf Sobotka, "Russia Exports More Than Crude Oil," *World Petroleum* 34, no. 10 (September 1963): 48; Harvey O'Connor, *World Crisis in Oil* (New York: Monthly Review Press, 1962), p. 396; and Stein, *ibid.*, pp. 178–79.

8. Sobotka, *ibid.*, p. 48.

9. Charles McLane, "Foreign Aid in Soviet Third World Policies," *Mizan* 10, no. 6 (November–December 1968): 224.

10. Janos Horvath, "Economic Aid Flow from the USSR: A Recount of the First Fifteen Years," *Slavic Review* 29, no. 4 (December 1970): 627 and McLane, *ibid.*, p. 225.

11. McLane, *ibid.*, p. 25 and Sobotka, "More Than Crude Oil," p. 48.

12. Harish Kapur, *The Soviet Union and the Emerging Nations* (London: Michael Joseph, 1972), p. 63 and Biplab Dasgupta, *The Oil Industry in India* (London: Frank Cass, 1971), p. 68.

13. The offer was made early in 1960 but it is difficult to ascertain the precise date. See Dasgupta, *ibid.*, p. 185; Tanzer, *Political Economy,* p. 179; Naik, *Soviet Policy*, p. 172; and Edith Penrose, "International Economic Relations and the Large International Firm," in E. F. Penrose, Peter Lyon and Edith Penrose, eds., *New Orientations* (London: Frank Cass, 1970), p. 126.

14. Penrose, *ibid.*, p. 126; Tanzer, *ibid.*, p. 179; and Dasgupta, *ibid.*, p. 185. Tanzer indicates that the Soviets offered 18 million barrels of crude oil per year (slightly under 2.5 million tons) while Dasgupta maintains that the offer was for 3.5 million tons.

15. See "India Pushes Coexistence in its Oil Program," *Oil and Gas Journal* 58, no. 29 (July 18, 1960): 80.

16. The amount of the discount during the period 1960–65 varied and the conflicting figures offered by various sources may reflect the discount at different points in time. The crux of the matter, however, was that India received a discount after the Soviet crude oil offer of 1960, whereas it had paid world market prices up to that time. See O'Connor, *World Crisis in Oil*, p. 397; Naik, *Soviet Policy*, p. 172; Marshall Goldman, *Soviet Foreign Aid* (New York: Praeger, 1967), p. 96; Dasgupta, *Oil Industry*, p. 186; and Tanzer, *Political Economy*, p. 184.

17. "Russian Oil Competition," *World Petroleum* 31, no. 10 (September 1960): 134 and Harold Lubell, *The Soviet Oil Offensive and Inter-Bloc Economic Competition* (Santa Monica: Rand Corporation, 1961), pp. 47–48.

18. Tanzer, *Political Economy*, p. 179 and Y. Yershov, "Soviet Oil Products for India," *Foreign Trade*, no. 1 (1971): 28–29.

19. Tanzer, *ibid.*, pp. 179 and 204.

20. "Soviet Prices Curdle Indian Oil Deal," *Oil and Gas Journal* 62, no. 7 (February 17, 1964): 84.

21. Anthony Lukas, "Oil Imports Stir Dispute in India," *The New York Times,* July 5, 1965, p. 3 and Tanzer, *Political Economy*, p. 204.

22. McLane, "Foreign Aid," pp. 226–27; Derek Davies, ed., *Far Eastern Economic*

Review, 1967 Yearbook (Hong Kong: Far Eastern Economic Review, 1966), p. 116; Harish Kapur, "India and the Soviet Union," *Survey* 17, no. 1 (Winter 1971): 213; and *Keesing's Contemporary Archives* (February 25–March 3, 1974): 26372.

23. Naik, *Soviet Policy,* pp. 172–73 and Georgii Kudin, "Foundation of Soviet-Indian Friendship," *New Times,* no. 32 (August 1974): 8.

24. Sobotka, "More Than Crude Oil," p. 48 and Stein, *Nehru Era,* p. 179.

25. *USSR and Third World* 3, no. 6 (July 16–September 2, 1973): 385–86; *USSR and Third World* 3, no. 7 (September 3–October 21, 1973): 466; and Nikolai Baibakov, "New Stage in Soviet-Indian Co-operation," *New Times,* no. 50 (December 1973): 9.

26. G. Kudin, "Industrial India," *New Times,* no. 47 (November 1973): 7 and Kudin, "Soviet-Indian Friendship," p. 8.

27. Chertkov, *Developing Countries,* p. 74.

28. Goldman, *Soviet Foreign Aid,* pp. 98–99; Kapur, *Emerging Nations,* p. 64; New Delhi radio, January 12, 1974 (*USSR and Third World* 4, no. 2, January 14–March 3, 1974, p. 59); Baibakov, "New Stage," p. 9 and Ivan Shchedrov, "Ukrepliaia nezavisimost' " (Strengthening Independence) *Pravda,* January 22, 1974, p. 5.

29. *Vneshniaia torgovlia SSSR za 1973 god: statisticheskii obzor* (Foreign Trade of the USSR for 1973: Statistical Abstract) (Moscow: Izdatel'stvo "Mezhdunarodnye otnosheniia," 1974), p. 231.

30. See Bernard Weinraub, "India, Slow to Grasp Oil Crisis, Now Fears Severe Economic Loss," *The New York Times,* January 20, 1974, p. 2.

31. U.S. government memorandum, April 11, 1974; "India: Russia to Supply Crude Oil," *The Petroleum Economist* 41, no. 1 (January 1974): 13; and Bernard Weinraub, "India and Soviet Will Expand Ties," *The New York Times,* November 29, 1973, p. 9.

32. U.S. government memorandum, *ibid.;* New Delhi radio, April 5, 1974 (*USSR and Third World* 4, no. 3, March 4–April 21, 1974, p. 132); and New Delhi radio, May 23, 1974 (*USSR and Third World* 4, no. 4, April 22–June 9, 1974, p. 200).

33. "Soviet-Indian Trade," *International Herald Tribune,* December 31, 1974, p. 2.

34. *USSR and Third World* 4, no. 2 (January 14–March 3, 1974): 59.

35. *Platt's Oilgram News Service* 52, no. 15 (January 22, 1974): 5.

36. Sobotka, "More Than Crude Oil," p. 49.

37. Irving Brecher and S. A. Abbas, *Foreign Aid and Industrial Development in Pakistan* (Cambridge: Cambridge University Press, 1972), p. 79; O'Connor, *World Crisis in Oil,* p. 399; Horvath, "Economic Aid Flow," p. 628; Arthur Stein, "India's Relations with the USSR, 1953–1963," *Orbis* 8, no. 1 (Spring 1964): 367; Goldman, *Soviet Foreign Aid,* pp. 97 and 145; and Paul Swain, "Soviet Aid May Be Greater Menace than Cheap Crude," *Oil and Gas Journal* 59, no. 26 (June 26, 1961): 134.

38. Chertkov, *Developing Countries,* p. 78; Radio Moscow, September 5, 1971 (*USSR and Third World* 1, no. 8, August 16–September 19, 1971, p. 443); and Igor Voltsev, "Nationalization in Pakistan," *New Times,* no. 3 (January 1974): 26–27.

39. "Pakistan May Shift Loan to Red China," *Oil and Gas Journal* [Se]ptember 30, 1968): 60.

40. Jukes, *The Soviet Union in Asia,* p. 140; Lubell, *Soviet Oil Of[fensive]* Penrose, "International Economic Relations," p. 128; S. Arasara[tnam,] (Englewood Cliffs: Prentice-Hall, 1964), p. 37; "Ceylon Will Accept [Oil] Russia," *Oil and Gas Journal* 60, no. 1 (January 1, 1962): 69; Boris [Ponomarev,] *Nationalism and Imperialism* (New Delhi: People's Publishing House, [1962);] Jukes, *ibid.,* pp. 140–41 and Rachkov, *ibid.,* pp. 55–56.

41. Penrose, *ibid.,* p. 128 and Arasaratnam, *ibid.,* p. 38.

42. Joan Nelson, *Aid, Influence and Foreign Policy* (New York: Macmilla[n, 1968),] p. 109 and Rachkov, *ibid.,* p. 56.

43. Goldman, *Soviet Foreign Aid,* p. 144 and Colombo radio, July 16, 1969 [(BBC,] Supplement B, no. 4, July–August, 1969, p. 2).

44. Michael Gehlen, "The Politics of Soviet Foreign Trade," *The Western Po[litical]* *Quarterly* 18, no. 1 (March 1965): 112; *USSR and Third World* 1, no. 4 (M[arch] 22–April 25, 1971): 162; *USSR and Third World* 1, no. 3 (February 15–Marc[h 21,] 1971): 99; and *USSR and Third World* 3, no. 1 (December 4, 1972–January [14, 1973]) 1973): 15.

45. *Vneshniaia torgovlia SSSR za 1973 god,* p. 324; Chertkov, *Developing Cou[n-]* *tries,* p. 79; *USSR and Third World* 3, no. 1 (December 4, 1972–January 14, 1973) 4; *USSR and Third World* 3, no. 5 (May 28–July 15, 1973): 303; and Radio Moscow, April 7, 1974 (*USSR and Third World* 4, no. 4, April 22–June 9, 1974, p. 197).

46. Gehlen, "Soviet Foreign Trade," p. 112; *USSR and Third World* 1, no. 6 (June 2–July 4, 1971): 288; *USSR and Third World* 3, no. 7 (September 3–October 21, 1973): 472; and McLane, *Foreign Aid,* p. 238.

47. See Peter Howard, "Soviet Relations with Malaysia and Singapore," *Mizan* 10, no. 1 (January–February 1968): 32–33.

48. See T. B. Millar, "Soviet Policies South and East of Suez," *Foreign Affairs* 49, no. 1 (October 1970): 70–80.

49. *Mizan* 9, no. 5 (September–October 1967): 229 and Howard, "Soviet Rela[tions," p. 33.

50. Robert Loring Allen, *Soviet Economic Warfare* (Washington: Public Affairs Press, 1960), pp. 181–82.

51. Peter Wiles, *Communist International Economics* (New York: Praeger, 1969), pp. 518–22.

52. "Afghanistan: His Rich Friends," *The Economist* 252, no. 6832 (August 3, 1974): 30.

53. Sobotka, "More Than Crude Oil," p. 49; Horvath, "Economic Aid Flow," p. 625; Aloys Michel, "Foreign Trade and Foreign Policy in Afghanistan," *Middle Eastern Affairs* 12, no. 1 (January 1961): 12; and Goldman, *Soviet Foreign Trade,* p. 117.

54. Sobotka, *ibid.,* p. 49.

71. *Vneshniaia torgovlia SSSR za 1967 god: statisticheskii obzor* (Moscow: Izdatel'stvo "Mezhdunarodnye otnosheniia," 1968), p. 279. Also see "Soviet Bloc Exports Climb Fast in '66," *Oil and Gas Journal* 64, no. 47 (November 21, 1966): 150.

72. P. N. Kumykin, ed., *50 let sovetskoi vneshnei torgovli* (50 Years of Soviet Foreign Trade) (Moscow: Izdatel'stvo "Mezhdunarodnye otnosheniia," 1967), p. 197.

73. *Ibid.*, p. 197; *Vneshniaia torgovlia SSSR za 1965 god,* pp. 291–92; and *Vneshniaia torgovlia SSSR za 1967 god,* pp. 279–80. Kumykin claims that Ghanaian exports to the USSR fell slightly from 28 million rubles in 1965 to 22 million rubles in 1966 but Soviet trade statistics reported an increase from 18.7 million rubles to 21.8 million rubles.

74. *Vneshniaia torgovlia SSSR za 1967 god,* p. 279.

75. "Ghana, U.S. Firms Eye Offshore Terms," p. 56 and *Petroleum Intelligence Weekly,* September 2, 1968, p. 3. Since Soviet deliveries before September were rather small, total Soviet oil exports to Ghana were only 225,700 tons in 1968. See *Vneshniaia torgovlia SSSR za 1969 god,* p. 260.

76. "Ghana and Russia: One Pueblovsky of a Fishing Trip," *The Economist* 230, no. 6550 (March 8, 1969): 31 and *Keesing's Contemporary Archives* (January 31–February 7, 1970): 23803.

77. Radio Moscow, September 12, 1968 (*Mizan,* Supplement A, no. 5, September-October, 1968, p. 10).

78. *Mizan,* Supplement A, no. 6 (November–December 1968): 18.

79. "Ghana and Russia: One Pueblovsky of a Fishing Trip," p. 31 and Ebel, *Communist Trade,* pp. 178–79.

80. "Ghana and Russia: One Pueblovsky of a Fishing Trip," p. 31 and *Petroleum Intelligence Weekly,* July 7, 1969, p. 2.

81. *Vneshniaia torgovlia SSSR za 1969 god,* p. 260.

82. See *Petroleum Press Service* 39, no. 8 (August 1972): 289 and *Vneshniaia torgovlia SSSR za 1973 god,* p. 70.

83. *Keesing's Contemporary Archives* (January 31–February 7, 1970), p. 23803.

84. Accra radio, March 3, 1969 (*Mizan,* Supplement A, no. 2, March–April, 1969, p. 12).

85. For a discussion of Soviet-Nigerian relations before the war with Biafra, and for an analysis of the Soviet Union's motivation in supporting the central government against Biafra, see Arthur Jay Klinghoffer, "The Nigerian War: Why the Soviets Chose Sides," *Africa Report* 13, no. 2 (February 1968): 47–49.

86. See Victor Sidenko, "Oil War in Nigeria," *New Times,* no. 11 (March 15, 1967): 21–22; A. Osipov, "Neft' Nigerii," (The Oil of Nigeria) *Mirovaia Ekonomika i Mezhdunarodnye Otnosheniia* (World Economics and International Relations) no. 5 (1967): 125; V. Laptev, "From Katanga to Biafra," *New Times,* no. 52 (December 27, 1967): 17–18; "Soviet Views on Nigeria," *Mizan* 9, no. 2 (March–April 1967): 72;

and David Morison, "The USSR and the War in Nigeria," *Mizan* 11, no. 1 (January–February 1969): 33–35.

87. Radio Moscow, August 26, 1968 (*Mizan*, Supplement A, no. 5, September–October 1968, p. 13). Also see A. Tryasunov, "Nigeria: War or Peace?" *International Affairs*, no. 7 (July 1968): 90.

88. V. Laptev, "Lessons of the Nigerian Tragedy," *International Affairs*, no. 4 (April 1969): 53.

89. *USSR and Third World* 3, no. 5 (May 28–July 15, 1973): 359; Radio Peace and Progress, May 20, 1974 (*USSR and Third World* 4, no. 4, April 22–June 9, 1974, p. 260); and M. Zenovich, "At New Frontiers," *Pravda,* April 12, 1973, p. 4 (*Current Digest of the Soviet Press* 25, no. 15, May 9, 1973, p. 22). The Soviets also agreed to build another oil training center. See Radio Moscow, January 23, 1974 (*USSR and Third World* 4, no. 2, January 14–March 3, 1974, p. 101).

90. See Karen Pennar, "Nigeria Boosts Oil Production," *The Journal of Commerce,* January 9, 1974 (*AF Press Clips* 9, no. 3, January 15, 1974, p. 7).

91. See Henry Hayward, "Oil-Rich Nigeria Still Buys Foreign Gasoline," *The Christian Science Monitor,* January 18, 1974 (*AF Press Clips* 9, no. 4, January 22, 1974, p. 17).

92. On Soviet deliveries of oil products to Nigeria, see *Vneshniaia torgovlia SSSR za 1973 god,* p. 287.

93. V. Baryshnikov and N. Volkov, "Soviet-Nigerian Trade, Its State and Prospects," *Foreign Trade,* no. 6 (1974): 21.

94. Leon Herman, "The Soviet Oil Offensive," *The Reporter* 26, no. 13 (June 21, 1962): 27. The Soviets also supplied some oil products to Ethiopia during the early sixties.

95. See Chertkov, *Developing Countries,* pp. 102–3; Horvath, "Economic Aid Flow," p. 626; "Russia Expands Its Oil Markets in Ethiopia," *Oil and Gas Journal* 58, no. 23 (June 6, 1960): 89; and Goldman, *Soviet Foreign Aid,* pp. 178–79.

96. Radio Moscow, July 14, 1974 (*USSR and Third World* 4, no. 5, June 10– July 28, 1974, p. 319).

97. See Jozef Wilczynski, *The Economics and Politics of East-West Trade* (New York: Praeger, 1969), p. 261 and Frank Gardner, "Soviets Score String of Historic Oil Penetrations," *Oil and Gas Journal* 68, no. 14 (April 6, 1970): 59.

98. See Goldman, *Soviet Foreign Aid,* pp. 156–59; Susan Strange, *The Soviet Trade Weapon* (London: Phoenix House, 1959), p. 24; and "Rio to Get Soviet Oil," *The New York Times,* June 5, 1960, p. 3.

99. Stephen Clissold, ed., *Soviet Relations With Latin America, 1918–1968: A Documentary Survey* (London: Oxford University Press, 1970), p. 183; Horvath, "Economic Aid Flow," p. 625; Gardner, "String of Historic Oil Penetrations," p. 59; Herman, "The Soviet Oil Offensive," p. 28; and Gehlen, "Soviet Foreign Trade," p. 112.

100. Sobotka, "More Than Crude Oil," p. 50 and Goldman, *Soviet Foreign Aid,* p. 97.

101. G. Terekhov, "Soviet-Argentine Trade Relations," *Foreign Trade,* no. 6 (1974): 15.

12/The Pacific Connection: Japan, the United States and China

1. See Jon Halliday and Gavan McCormack, *Japanese Imperialism Today* (New York: Monthly Review Press, 1973), p. 234.

2. "Is Siberia Really the Answer?," *The Economist* 250, no. 6809 (February 23, 1974): 46–47.

3. For example, see Y. Shipov, "Economic Relations between the USSR and Japan," *International Affairs,* no. 12 (December 1969): 90–91.

4. D. Petrov, "Japan in Quest of a New Course," *Mirovaia Ekonomika i Mezhdunarodnye Otnosheniia,* (World Economics and International Relations) no. 9, 1973 (translated in *International Journal of Politics* 3, no. 4, Winter, 1973–74, p. 116).

5. Y. Shipov and Y. Sorokin, "Economic Relations with Japan," *Foreign Trade,* no. 8 (1970): 9–10.

6. See I. Latyshev, "Khokkaido—severnyi krai Iaponii," (Hokkaido—Northern Territory of Japan) *Pravda,* March 12, 1974, p. 4.

7. See John Hardt, George Holliday and Young Kim, "Western Investment in Communist Economies," prepared for the Subcommittee on Multinational Corporations of the Committee on Foreign Relations, U.S. Senate (June 11, 1974): 90.

8. See John Surrey, "Japan's Uncertain Energy Prospects: The Problem of Import Dependence," *Energy Policy* 2, no. 3 (September 1974): 228.

9. Savitri Vishwanathan, *Normalization of Japanese-Soviet Relations, 1945–1970* (Tallahassee: Diplomatic Press, 1973), p. 100 and "Soviet's Cheap Oil Gains Markets in Japan," *Oil and Gas Journal* 59, no. 21 (May 22, 1961): 63.

10. Vishwanathan, *ibid.,* pp. 101–2 and "U.S. Stops Buying Japan's Jet Fuel," *The New York Times,* December 22, 1961, p. 6.

11. *Vneshniaia torgovlia SSSR za 1973 god: statisticheskii obzor* (Foreign Trade of the USSR for 1973: Statistical Abstract) (Moscow: Izdatel'stvo "Mezhdunarodnye otnosheniia," 1974), p. 269.

12. Violet Conolly, "East Siberian Oil," *Mizan* 13, no. 1 (August 1971): 19.

13. Eduardo Lachica, "Between Russia and China," *International Herald Tribune,* December 23, 1974, p. 10.

14. See N. Nikolayev, "Expansion of Soviet-Japanese Relations," *International Affairs,* no. 8 (August 1973): 44 and N. Nikolayev, "Japanese-Soviet Relations and Peking Mischief-Making," *New Times,* no. 3 (January 1974): 12.

15. David Hitchcock, Jr., "Joint Development of Siberia: Decision-Making in Japanese-Soviet Relations," *Asian Survey* 11, no. 3 (March 1971): 281–82.

16. Kenzo Kiga, "Russo-Japanese Economic Cooperation and Its International Environment," *Pacific Community* 4, no. 3 (April 1973): 457 and Kiichi Saeki, "Toward

Japanese Cooperation in Siberian Development," *Problems of Communism* 21, no. 3 (May–June 1972): 5.

17. Petrov, "Japan in Quest," p. 117.

18. Elizabeth Pond, "Japan and Russia: The View from Tokyo," *Foreign Affairs* 52, no. 1 (October 1973): 147; Hedrick Smith, "Soviet Opens a Wharf in Pacific Built with Help of Japanese," *The New York Times,* December 28, 1973, pp. 43 and 50; and Christopher Wren, "Soviet Building Port in Far East," *The New York Times,* November 11, 1975, p. 47.

19. Theodore Shabad, "Japan and Soviet in Coal Agreement," *The New York Times,* March 18, 1974, p. 45 and "Tokyo and Moscow in Coal Venture," *The New York Times,* March 10, 1974, p. 9.

20. Ivan Semichastnov, "U.S.S.R.-Japan: Big Economic Projects," *New Times,* no. 14 (April 1974): 12.

21. For discussions of many of these points, see Saeki, "Siberian Development," p. 10 and Hitchcock, "Joint Development," pp. 285–86.

22. See *Platt's Oilgram News Service* 52, no. 129 (July 8, 1974): 5.

23. Hitchcock, "Joint Development," p. 296.

24. Violet Conolly, "Soviet-Japanese Economic Cooperation in Siberia," *Pacific Community* 2, no. 1 (October 1970): 63.

25. "Russia-America: Hot Air," *The Economist* 248, no. 6776 (July 1973): 76.

26. See "Sino-Soviet Clashes Spur Sakhalin Hunt," *Oil and Gas Journal 67, no. 18 (May 5, 1969): 98; Conolly, "East Siberian Oil," p. 17; John Stephan, "Sakhalin Island: Soviet Outpost in Northeast Asia," Asian Survey* 10, no. 12 (December 1970): 1093; and Theodore Shabad, "Soviet Woos Gulf Oil in Drilling Deal," *The New York Times,* February 22, 1975, p. 35.

27. Theodore Shabad, *The Basic Industrial Resources of the U.S.S.R.* (New York: Columbia University Press, 1969), p. 282.

28. "Sino-Soviet Clashes Spur Sakhalin Hunt," p. 98 and Conolly, "East Siberian Oil," p. 17.

29. See Conolly, "East Siberian Oil," pp. 17–18.

30. See Violet Conolly, *Beyond the Urals: Economic Developments in Soviet Asia* (London: Oxford University Press, 1967), p. 322 and V. Savin, A. Osorgin and N. Shlyk, "U.S.S.R.'s Far Eastern Export Base," *Foreign Trade,* no. 11 (1974): 28.

31. Saeki, "Siberian Development," p. 8; Hardt, Holliday and Kim, "Western Investment," p. 76; Vishwanathan, *Normalization,* p. 110; and Conolly, "Soviet-Japanese Economic Cooperation in Siberia," p. 56.

32. "Eastern Siberian Gas Gets Hard Sell," *Oil and Gas Journal* 68, no. 10 (March 9, 1970): 26 and John Hardt, "West Siberia: The Quest for Energy," *Problems of Communism* 22, no. 3 (May–June 1973): 27.

33. "Eastern Siberian Gas Gets Hard Sell," pp. 26–27 and Ivan Semichastnov, "Soviet-Japanese Economic Conference," *New Times,* no. 9 (March 3, 1970): 19.

34. Junnosuke Ofusa, "Japan and Soviet Agree on Joint Oil-Gas Project," *The New York Times,* November 25, 1972, p. 41 and "Japan, Russia Set Oil Search Accord," *International Herald Tribune,* December 12, 1974, p. 9.

35. "Japan, Russia Set Oil Search Accord," p. 9; Shabad, "Soviet Woos Gulf Oil," p. 35; "Japanese in Siberian Venture," *International Herald Tribune,* October 2, 1974, p. 7 and *Platt's Oilgram News Service* 52, no. 238 (December 12, 1974): 1.

36. See Ira Nambeil, "Soviet Offshore Oil May Be Used to Supply West Coast of U.S.," *Journal of Commerce, March 27, 1974,* p. 1 and Theodore Shabad, "Soviet and China in Oil Search," *The New York Times,* March 12, 1974, p. 49.

37. Frank Gardner, "Big E. Siberian Gas Exports Years Away," *Oil and Gas Journal* 71, no. 23 (June 4, 1973): 24–25 and Conolly, "East Siberian Oil," p. 19.

38. See Hardt, Holliday and Kim, "Western Investment," p. 77 and *Platt's Oilgram News Service* 52, no. 229 (November 27, 1974): 4. One estimate has placed the eventual cost at $10 billion. See *East-West Trade Council Newsletter* 2, no. 2 (February 7, 1974): 3.

39. Hardt, Holliday and Kim, *ibid.,* p. 77; editorial, "The Siberation Gas Deal," *The Washington Post,* May 4, 1974, p. A14; Theodore Shabad, "Americans Visiting Soviet Gas Fields," *The New York Times,* December 4, 1973, p. 61; and G. Bazhenov, "USSR-USA: Businesslike Cooperation," *International Affairs,* no. 7 (July 1974): 17.

40. See Gardner, "Years Away," p. 24 and Ofusa, "Joint Oil-Gas Project," p. 41.

41. "Russia–America: Hot Air," p. 76 and Bazhenov, "USSR–USA," p. 17.

42. Pond, "Japan and Russia," p. 148 and Shabad, "Americans Visiting Soviet Gas Fields," p. 61.

43. Ivan Semichastnov, "Soviet-Japanese Economic Ties," *New Times,* no. 38 (September 1973): 16.

44. "In the Interests of Developing Friendly Relations," *Pravda,* August 19, 1973, p. 4 (*Current Digest of the Soviet Press* 25, no. 33, September 12, 1973, p. 12).

45. See Dan Morgan, "U.S. Officials Doubt Shift on Natural Gas," *The Washington Post,* May 28, 1974 and "Senate Unit Hits Siberia Gas Plan," *International Herald Tribune,* December 26, 1974, p. 7.

46. *Platt's Oilgram News Service* 52, no. 228 (November 26, 1974): 1.

47. See Surrey, "Energy Prospects," p. 228.

48. See Robert Ebel, *The Petroleum Industry of the Soviet Union* (Washington: American Petroleum Institute, 1961), p. 152; Conolly, "Soviet-Japanese Economic Cooperation," p. 55; and Saeki, "Siberian Development," pp. 7–8.

49. See Ivan Semichastnov, "Soviet-Japanese Economic Co-operation," *New Times,* no. 11 (March 1972): 15 and Petrov, "Japan in Quest," p. 117.

50. Abraham Becker, "Oil and the Persian Gulf in Soviet Policy in the 1970s," in Michael Confino and Shimon Shamir, eds., *The U.S.S.R. and the Middle East* (New York: John Wiley and Jerusalem: Israel Universities Press, 1973), p. 211; Pond,

"Japan and Russia," p. 147; and "Japan Said to Cool to Siberian Oil Project," *International Herald Tribune,* August 31-September 1, 1974, p. 9.

51. M. V. Nesterov, "Doing Business with Japan," *New Times,* no. 25 (June 22, 1966): 15; Saeki, "Siberian Development," pp. 7–8; Junnosuke Ofusa, "Soviet-Japanese Talks Set on Oil Pipeline," *The New York Times,* June 28, 1971, p. 47; Semichastnov, "Soviet-Japanese Economic Cooperation," p. 15; "Soviet Union: Japan's Tiumen Scheme in Jeopardy," *Petroleum Press Service* 40, no. 10 (October 1973): 389; and James Simon, "Japan's Ostpolitik and the Soviet Union," *The World Today* 30, no. 4 (April 1974): 166.

52. See Geoffrey Jukes, *The Soviet Union in Asia* (Sydney: Angus and Robertson, 1973), p. 61.

53. Semichastnov, "Soviet-Japanese Economic Cooperation," p. 15 and Saeki, "Siberian Development," p. 7.

54. "W. Siberian Fields Seen Able to Supply Japanese Oil Needs," *Oil and Gas Journal* 70, no. 29 (July 17, 1972): 66–67 and "Russia and Japan: Linked by a Pipe," *The Economist* 244, no. 6730 (August 19, 1972): 82.

55. Rinjiro Harako, "Prospects for Relations with the USSR," *Survey* 18, no. 4 (Autumn 1972): 52.

56. Frank Gardner, "Russian LNG Coming to U.S.? Probably," *Oil and Gas Journal* 70, no. 22 (May 29, 1972): 13.

57. See "Siberian Oil: East or West," *The Economist* 245, no. 6742 (November 11, 1972): 95 and Alexander Young, "Energy: View from Tokyo," *The New York Times,* August 22, 1973, section 3, p. 6.

58. See "Siberian Oil: East or West," p. 95.

59. Richard Halloran, "Japan–U.S. Links Termed Strained," *The New York Times,* August 25, 1972, p. 43 and Richard Halloran, "Japanese Feel Nixon Accepts Their Policy of Ties With China," *The New York Times,* September 3, 1972, p. 16. In August 1973, the USSR and Japan agreed that they would include the United States in any Tiumen deal but would offer the U.S. only 10–20% of the investment. This would serve the political ends of both the USSR and Japan but would also reserve the bulk of the oil for themselves. See *Platt's Oilgram News Service* 51, no. 154 (August 9, 1973): 1.

60. Hardt, Holliday and Kim, "Western Investment," p. 85.

61. Richard Halloran, "Japan's Premier to Visit Soviet to Meet Brezhnev," *The New York Times,* March 29, 1973, p. 3 and "Japan: We're on Our Own, Sort of," *The Economist* 247, no. 6772 (June 9, 1973): 49. Chinese oil exports to Japan and the Soviet-Japanese controversy over the islands are discussed later in this chapter.

62. "Japan: We're on Our Own, Sort of," p. 49 and "Soviet Talks on Siberian Oil Development Stalled," *Journal of Commerce,* June 11, 1973, p. 14A.

63. B. Pishchik and B. Smirnov, "From Niigata to Nagoya," *New Times,* no. 25 (June 1973): 8–9 and P. Dolgorukov, "Our Neighbor Japan," *Pravda,* June 15, 1973, p. 5 (*Current Digest of the Soviet Press* 25, no. 24, July 11, 1973, p. 7).

64. Frank Gardner, "Big Spurt in Income from Oil Sales Rescues Soviets," *Oil and Gas Journal* 72, no. 31 (August 5, 1974): 27.

65. See "Soviet Union: Japan's Tiumen Scheme in Jeopardy," p. 389 and Simon, "Japan's Ostpolitik," p. 166.

66. Surrey, "Energy Prospects," p. 218.

67. "Japan's Tanaka Visits the U.S.S.R.," *Current Digest of the Soviet Press* 25, no. 41 (November 7, 1973): 3–4.

68. See V. Pronin, "Useful Dialogue," *New Times,*no. 42 (October 1973): 12–13.

69. "Japan and Siberia: Is This What It Was All About?" *The Economist* 251, no. 6815 (April 6, 1974): 44. According to another account, Tanaka received a similar letter from Brezhnev in early April so there were apparently two letters from Brezhnev to Tanaka. See "Japan and Soviet Plan Siberian Loan," *The New York Times,* April 23, 1974, p. 1.

70. Hedrick Smith, "Brezhnev Unveils a Vast Effort to Farm Steppes of Northern Russia," *The New York Times,* March 16, 1974, p. 6 and *Pravda,* March 16, 1974, p. 2.

71. See Semichastnov, "U.S.S.R.-Japan," pp. 12–13. Kosygin met with the Japanese on March 22 and Brezhnev on March 25. See *Pravda,* March 23, 1974, p. 1 and *Pravda,* March 26, 1974, p. 1.

72. Semichastnov, *ibid.,* p. 12 and *Platt's Oilgram News Service* 52, no. 73 (April 16, 1974): 2.

73. "Soviet Seeks $500-Million of New Deals with U.S.," *The New York Times,* May 28, 1974, p. 59 and Robert Kaiser, "Soviets Shift on Oil," *The Washington Post,* May 28, 1974, pp. A1 and A18.

74. Robert Kaiser, "Moscow Reassures Tokyo on Oil," *The Washington Post,* June 1, 1974, p. F1.

75. *Ibid.,* p. F1 and "USSR Stresses Willingness to Trade Oil," *East-West Trade News,* June 6, 1974, p. 2. Also see Don Oberdorfer, "Oil 'Shift' Surprises Japanese," *The Washington Post,* May 29, 1974, p. A1.

76. V. Molchanov, "From Lake Baikal to the Amur," *Pravda,* July 25, 1974, pp. 1 and 3 (*Current Digest of the Soviet Press* 26, no. 30, August 21, 1974, p. 19); Albert Pin, "Baikal–Amur Railway," *New Times,* no. 49 (December 1974): 18 and 21; and Theodore Shabad, "Soviet Building New Siberian Rail Line," *The New York Times,* July 5, 1974, p. 31.

77. Shabad, "Soviet Building New Siberian Rail Line," p. 31.

78. Molchanov, *ibid.,* p. 19.

79. See *The Petroleum Economist* 41, no. 5 (May 1974): 177–78.

80. Bazhenov, "USSR–USA," pp. 15–21.

81. "U.S.S.R.—Japan: Large-Scale Co-operation," *New Times,* no. 32 (August 1974): 20–21.

82. "Kosygin Said to Press Japan on Siberia Oil," *International Herald Tribune,* November 1, 1974, p. 7.

83. *Platt's Oilgram News Service* 52, no. 211 (November 1, 1974): 1.

84. *Ibid.,* 52, no. 214 (November 6, 1974): 1; *Ibid.,* 52, no. 208 (October 29, 1974): 2; and "Kosygin Said to Press Japan on Siberia Oil," p. 7.

85. Hardt, Holliday and Kim, "Western Investment," p. 91 and "Japan and Siberia: Is This What It Was All About?" p. 44.

86. Sheldon Simon, "The Japan-China-USSR Triangle," *Pacific Affairs* 47, no. 2 (Summer 1974): 130; Hardt, Holliday and Kim, *ibid.,* p. 91; and Nikolayev, "Expansion of Soviet-Japanese Relations," p. 44.

87. Simon, *ibid.,* p. 130; Petrov, "Japan in Quest," pp. 118–19; Nikolayev, "Expansion of Soviet-Japanese Relations," p. 44; and Richard Halloran, "Japan's Asia Plan Is Merely an Idea," *The New York Times,* March 16, 1973, p. 7.

88. Petrov, *ibid.,* pp. 118–19.

89. See Koji Nakamura, "Treading the Siberian Tightrope," *Far Eastern Economic Review* 80, no. 19 (May 14, 1973): 7.

90. See O. Borisov and B. Koloskov, "Peking's Foreign Policy After the 10th Congress of the CPC," *International Affairs,* no. 7 (July 1974): 37.

91. Vishwanathan, *Normalization,* pp. 76 and 79.

92. James Simon, "Japan's Ostpolitik," p. 165 and Morinosuke Kajima, *Modern Japan's Foreign Policy* (Rutland and Tokyo: Charles E. Tuttle, 1969), p. 141.

93. Hitchcock, "Joint Development," p. 281.

94. For an analysis of the Soviet "collective security" proposal, see Arnold Horelick, "The Soviet Union's Asian Collective Security Proposal: A Club in Search of Members," *Pacific Affairs* 47, no. 3 (Fall 1974): 269–85.

95. James Simon, "Japan's Ostpolitik," p. 163.

96. Pond, "Japan and Russia," p. 141 and Nakamura, "Siberian Tightrope," p. 6.

97. Nikolayev, "Expansion of Soviet-Japanese Relations," p. 44. Also see Boris Pishchik, "Japan in the Changing World," *New Times,* no. 23 (June 1973): 12.

98. James Simon, "Japan's Ostpolitik," p. 168 and *Facts on File* 33, no. 1720 (October 14–20, 1973): 874. Also see "Japan's Tanaka Visits the U.S.S.R.," p. 4.

99. Pronin, "Useful Dialogue," p. 13.

100. For a thorough discussion of the anti-hegemony issue, see Joachim Glaubitz, "Anti-Hegemony Formulas in Chinese Foreign Policy," *Asian Survey* 16, no. 3 (March 1976): 205–15.

101. Richard Halloran, "Japan to Sign China Pact Despite Soviet Warnings," *The New York Times,* January 14, 1976, pp. 1–2.

102. United States Department of State, "The United States and Japan: Prime Minister Tanaka's Washington Visit, July 31–August 1, 1973 and the Tokyo Meeting of the Joint U.S.-Japan Committee on Trade and Economic Affairs, July 16–17,

1973," Department of State Publication 8740 (Washington: U.S. Government Printing Office, 1973): 14.

103. For Japanese and Soviet support for tripartite cooperation, see "Three-Country Soviet Gas Deal Pushed," *Oil and Gas Journal* 70, no. 41 (October 9, 1972): 40; Young, "View from Tokyo," p. 6; "In the Interests of Developing Friendly Relations," p. 12; and Semichastnov, "U.S.S.R.-Japan," p. 13.

104. "Red Bloc Market No Longer Off Limits," *Oil and Gas Journal* 68, no. 1 (January 5, 1970): 59.

105. "Soviet Oil Minister Sees 10 Million B/D Flow by 1975," *Oil and Gas Journal* 68, no. 34 (August 24, 1970): 22; "Russia Buys More U.S. Equipment, Technology," *Oil and Gas Journal* 70, no. 44 (October 30, 1972): 25; and "Byron Jackson to Sell Pumps to Soviets," *Oil and Gas Journal* 71, no. 5 (January 29, 1973): 77. Among the American companies selling oil equipment to the USSR were Caterpillar Tractor Company, ARCO Chemical Company, Gearhart-Owen Industries, Reda Pump Company, and the Byron Jackson pump division of Borg-Warner.

106. See *Facts on File* 33, no. 1727 (December 2–8, 1973): 1022.

107. See Christopher Wren, "Russia Asserts It Surpasses U.S. in Production of Oil," *International Herald Tribune,* November 14, 1974, p. 7.

108. Bazhenov, "USSR-USA," p. 17.

109. "Oxy, Soviets Sign 5-Year Business Deal," *Oil and Gas Journal* 70, no. 30 (July 24, 1972): 14; Michael Stern, "Soviet Trade Set by Occidental Oil," *The New York Times,* July 19, 1972, p. 1; Bazhenov, *ibid.,* p. 16; and M. Zakhmatov, "USSR-USA: Prospects for Economic Cooperation," *International Affairs,* no. 11 (November 1973): 45.

110. See Clyde Farnsworth, "U.S.-Soviet Grain Accord Nearly Failed," *The New York Times,* October 25, 1975, pp. 37 and 42.

111. "Podpisan protokol," (A Protocol is Signed) *Pravda,* June 30, 1973, p. 4.

112. "Russia-America: Hot Air," p. 76; Nikolai Gladkov, "U.S.S.R.-U.S.A.: Mutually Advantageous Business Ties," *New Times,* no. 33 (August 1973): 26; and "Signing Near for Big Russia LNG Deal," *Oil and Gas Journal* 70, no. 46 (November 13, 1972): 97–99.

113. "North Star Project," report issued by Tenneco, p. 10.

114. Gardner, "Russian LNG Coming to U.S.? Probably.," p. 15.

115. John Hardt and George Holliday, *U.S.-Soviet Commercial Relations: The Interplay of Economics, Technology Transfer, and Diplomacy* (Washington: U.S. Government Printing Office, 1973), p. 71.

116. Bazhenov, "USSR–USA," pp. 16–17 and *Platt's Oilgram News Service* 52, no. 40 (February 27, 1974): 5.

117. Bernard Gwertzman, "U.S. Is Cautioned in Soviet on Gas," *The New York Times,* March 27, 1974, p. 57; Hardt and Holliday, *Commercial Relations,* p. 71; "North Star Project," p. 7; and Bazhenov, *ibid.,* pp. 16–17.

18. *East-West Trade Council Newsletter* 2, no. 2 (February 7, 1974): 2 and Robert :ing, "Fossil Fuels," in *World Energy Demands and the Middle East,* part I (Wash-¬gton: Middle East Institute, 1973), p. 65.

19. "North Star Project," p. 10.

20. *East-West Trade Council Newsletter,* p. 2.

21. Theodore Shabad, "Loan Snag Fails to Deter Soviet Energy Projects," *The ‚Jew York Times,* December 14, 1973, p. 71.

122. Gwertzman, "U.S. Is Cautioned," p. 57.

123. U.S. Department of Commerce, Bureau of East-West Trade, "Selected U.S.S.R. and Eastern European Economic Data," p. 21 and "Trade with Soviet Up by 120% in '73," *The New York Times,* February 16, 1974, p. 43.

124. "Trade with Soviet Up by 120% in '73," p. 43; "Selected U.S.S.R. and Eastern European Economic Data," p. 21 and "USSR: Recent Commercial Agreements Set Stage for U.S.–Soviet Trade Growth," *Commerce Today,* July 23, 1973, p. 43.

125. See M. Trush, "Soviet-American Relations as Viewed by Lenin," *International Affairs,* no. 7 (July 1974): 18 and Bazhenov, "USSR–USA," p. 19.

126. Bazhenov, *ibid.,* p. 18.

127. Hardt and Holliday, *Commercial Relations,* p. 74.

128. Hardt, Holliday and Kim, "Western Investment," p. CRS-121.

129. Office of the White House Press Secretary, "Trade Agreement, Lend Lease Settlement, Reciprocal Credit Arrangements, Joint US–USSR Commercial Commission," October 18, 1972.

130. Ivan Ivanov, "Soviet-American Economic Cooperation: Recent Development, Prospects and Problems," *The Annals of the American Academy of Political and Social Science* 414 (July 1974): 24.

131. *Ibid.,* p. 23.

132. See "Senate Unit Hits Siberia Gas Plan," *International Herald Tribune,* December 26, 1974, p. 7 and "Trade and Emigration: Next Phase," editorial, *The Washington Post* (*International Herald Tribune,* December 24, 1974, p. 4).

133. Even before the Arab embargo, former U.S. Ambassador to the Soviet Union Foy Kohler pointed out while addressing a Congressional hearing that the Soviets did embargo manganese deliveries to the United States in March 1949. They resumed some shipments in September but the U.S. had already contracted to get most of its manganese from other sources. At the time of the embargo, almost all U.S. manganese imports came from the Soviet Union. See *Soviet Economic Outlook,* hearings before the Joint Economic Committee, July 17–19, 1973 (Washington: U.S. Government Printing Office, 1973), p. 126.

134. Harry Schwartz, "In Place of Euphoria," *The New York Times,* October 20, 1973, p. 43.

135. "Trade and Emigration: Next Phase," p. 4. Also see editorial, *The Washington Post,* March 22, 1974, p. A38.

136. See "Is Siberia Really the Answer?" p. 47.

137. Bernard Gwertzman, "Senator Opposes Soviet Gas Deals," *The New York Times,* June 20, 1974, p. 5.

138. Theodore Shabad, "U.S.-Soviet Trade Progress: So Far So Good," *The New York Times,* June 23, 1974, section 3, p. 1.

139. "The Siberation Gas Deal," editorial, *The Washington Post,* May 4, 1974, p. A14.

140. "Siberian Gas," editorial, *The New York Times,* March 14, 1974, p. 36.

141. Nicholas Fedoruk and Barry Smernoff, "LNG: A Hazard for U.S.-Soviet Relations," Hudson Institute Paper, July 13, 1973 in *Soviet Economic Outlook,* pp. 178–80.

142. Hardt and Holliday, *Commercial Relations,* p. 71.

143. "The Siberation Gas Deal," p. A14.

144. See "Senate Unit Hits Siberia Gas Plan," p. 7. The 10–15% figure was presented by Senator Church. Also see Robert Ebel, "Gas in the Soviet Union," Paper No. SPE 4561 (Dallas: Society of Petroleum Engineers of AIME, 1973) p. 6.

145. Marshall Goldman, "The Soviet Union and Its New Wealth," unpublished manuscript, 1974, p. 5.

146. United Nations, Statistical Office, *Statistical Yearbook 1973* (New York: United Nations, 1974), p. 170 and Chang Chun, "Peiping's Petroleum Industry: Growth and Future Development," *Issues and Studies* 10, no. 8 (May 1974): 44.

147. Chang Chun, *ibid.,* p. 49.

148. Yoshio Koide, "China's Crude Oil Production," *Pacific Community* 5, no. 3 (April 1974): 469.

149. On the controversy surrounding China's oil production in 1973, see "Chou En-lai's Million B/D," *The Petroleum Economist* 41, no. 2 (February 1974): 49; Chang Chun, "Peiping's Petroleum," p. 49; and Koide, *ibid.,* p. 469. On the 1974 controversy, see Alexander Eckstein, "China's Trade Policy and Sino-Soviet Relations," *Foreign Affairs* 54, no. 1 (October 1975): 141; Selig Harrison, "Time Bomb in East Asia," *Foreign Policy,* no. 20 (Fall 1975): 5; and Choon-ho Park and Jerome Alan Cohen, "The Politics of China's Oil Weapon," *Foreign Policy,* no. 20 (Fall 1975): 32.

150. *Platt's Oilgram News Service* 52, no. 160 (August 20, 1974): 2.

151. *Statistical Yearbook 1973,* pp. 348 and 350.

152. Koide, "Oil Production," p. 468; Genevieve Dean, "Energy in the People's Republic of China," *Energy Policy* 2, no. 1 (March 1974): 39; and Chang Chun, "Peiping's Petroleum," p. 56.

153. "China's Forward Leap," *The Petroleum Economist* 41, no. 11 (November 1974): 409.

154. Chang Chun, "Peiping's Petroleum," p. 53; Sevinc Carlson, "China's Urgent Need for Stability in the Middle East," *New Middle East,* no. 36 (September 1971):

25 and 28; and "Openings in China," *Petroleum Press Service* 39, no. 10 (October 1972): 360.

155. "China Gets into Tanker Business," *Newsweek*, International Edition, September 30, 1974, p. 52.

156. Dean, "Energy in China," p. 39. Also see "Chinese Oil Lures Far East Consumers," *Oil and Gas Journal* 72, no. 8 (February 25, 1974): 85.

157. See "China Gets into Tanker Business," p. 52.

158. *Petroleum Intelligence Weekly* 12, no. 48 (November 26, 1973): 15 and "China Gets Into Tanker Business," p. 52.

159. "China: How Much Oil?" *The Economist* 218, no. 6384 (January 8, 1966): 97 and Joseph Lelyveld, "China Is Increasing Oil-Export Deals," *The New York Times,* January 5, 1974, p. 40.

160. "Chinese Oil Lures Far East Customers," p. 85 and James Sterba, "Peking Purchasing U.S. Oil Equipment to Step Up Output," *The New York Times,* November 28, 1975, pp. 1 and 63. Kissinger may have asked Chou En-lai for American participation in the development of oil in the Gulf of Chihli. This was reported in the *Tokyo Shimbun* and discussed in *Pravda,* September 7, 1971, p. 5.

161. "Openings in China," pp. 360–61.

162. *Platt's Oilgram News Service* 52, no. 155 (August 13, 1974): 4. In another strange episode, it was reported that China sold oil to Sweden in 1970. See Dean, "Energy in China," p. 42.

163. *Petroleum Intelligence Weekly* 13, no. 6 (February 11, 1974): 7 and *Platt's Oilgram News Service* 52, no. 177 (September 13, 1974): 2.

164. "Philippines Takes Control of Oil Operations in Crisis," *The New York Times,* December 11, 1973, p. 37 and *Platt's Oilgram News Service* 51, no. 223 (November 16, 1973): 2. No oil export agreement was reached between the Soviet Union and the Philippines.

165. *USSR and Third World* 4, no. 5 (June 10–July 28, 1974), p. 290 and "Philippines Cites China Oil Accord," *International Herald Tribune,* October 1, 1974, p. 4.

166. *Platt's Oilgram News Service* 52, no. 191 (October 3, 1974): 2 and "China's Forward Leap," p. 410.

167. On North Korea and North Vietnam, see "Openings in China," p. 360; "China's Forward Leap," p. 410; and Nicholas Ludlow, "U.S. Companies and China's Oil Development," *The New York Times,* March 3, 1974, section 3, p. 2. On Laos, see *The New York Times,* February 5, 1976, p. 11.

168. Koide, "Oil Production," p. 468.

169. See "Chou En-lai's Million B/D," p. 50 and Chang Chun, "Peiping's Petroleum," p. 54.

170. Lelyveld, "Oil Export Deals," p. 35.

171. Nakamura, "Siberian Tightrope," p. 7; "Russia and Japan: Oil from China?," *The Economist* 246, no. 6754 (February 3, 1973): 64; "China: Export of Crude Oil,"

Petroleum Press Service 40, no. 2 (February 1973): 69; and Chang Chun, ping's Petroleum," p. 53. Chang Chun claims that Chinese oil began arrivi Japan on May 12, Yoshio Koide cites June 21 and Nicholas Ludlow points to tember 17. See Chang Chun, *ibid.,* p. 53; Koide, "Oil Production," p. 463; Ludlow, "U.S. Companies," p. 2.

172. "Japanese Foreign Minister and Chou Confer 3 Hours," *The New York Time* January 5, 1974, p. 11; *Petroleum Intelligence Weekly* 13, no. 6 (February 1 1974): 7; *ibid.,* 13, no. 14 (April 8, 1974): 10; and *ibid.,* 13, no. 25 (June 24, 1974), p. 11.

173. Lachica, "Between Russia and China," p. 10.

174. *Platt's Oilgram News Service* 52, no. 189 (October 1, 1974): 2 and "China's Forward Leap," p. 409.

175. *Petroleum Intelligence Weekly* 13, no. 11 (March 18, 1974): 10.

176. "Japan to Get Chinese Oil," *International Herald Tribune,* October 23, 1974, p. 9 and *Platt's Oilgram News Service* 52, no. 245 (December 23, 1974): 4.

177. Another important development in Pacific oil politics is China's entry into territorial disputes over offshore oil rights. China used military force in January 1974 to occupy the Paracel Islands, which had also been claimed by South Vietnam, and the Senkaku Islands are involved in a controversy between China, Japan, and Taiwan. China and Japan are also contesting offshore rights near South Korea while China, Vietnam, Taiwan, and the Philippines all make claims on the Spratly Islands.

13/The Future of Soviet Energy Policies

1. See A. F. G. Scanlan, "The Energy Balance of the Comecon Countries," Round Table on the Exploitation of Siberia's Natural Resources, Brussels, January 30–February 1, 1974, p. 12.

2. Valentin Shashin, "The Soviet Oil Industry—Today and Tomorrow," *World Petroleum* 42, no. 5 (June 1971): 38 and Boris Belitzky, "USSR's Bright Energy Prospects," *Energy Policy* 2, no. 4 (December 1974): 350. Shashin is cited by Belitzky. The Economist Intelligence Unit estimates Western Siberian production in 1980 at 240–260 million tons. See *Soviet Oil to 1980,* QER Special, no. 14, June 1973 (London: The Economist Intelligence Unit, 1973): 13.

3. See Leonid Tomashpol'skii, *Neft' i gaz v mirovom energeticheskom balanse (1900–2000gg.)* (Oil and Gas in the World Energy Balance, 1900–2000) (Moscow: Izdatel'stvo "Nedra," 1968), p. 139 and Jaroslav Polach, "The Energy Gap in the Communist World," *East Europe* 18, no. 4 (April 1969): 25.

4. Belitzky, "Energy Prospects," p. 349.

5. See Samuel Pisar, *Coexistence and Commerce* (New York: McGraw-Hill, 1970), p. 237; Jean-Jacques Berreby, "Oil in the Orient," *New Middle East,* no. 15 (December 1969): 44; and John Hardt, "West Siberia: The Quest for Energy," *Problems of Communism* 22, no. 3 (May–June 1973): 35.

6. See J.V. Licence, "Siberia in the Context of World Natural Gas Supplies," Round Table, p. 8; Robert Ebel, "Gas in the Soviet Union," Paper No. SPE 4561 (Dallas: Society of Petroleum Engineers of AIME, 1973), p. 8; and *The Petroleum Economist* 41, no. 3 (March 1974): 100.

7. For some pertinent comments on Eastern Europe's import problem, see P. H. Frankel, "The Economic Relationship of Siberian Resources and World Demand," Round Table, p. 3.

8. Tomashpol'skii, *Neft' i gaz,* p. 141.

9. *Soviet Oil to 1980,* p. 42.

10. In 1974, total Soviet oil exports to Western Europe, Japan, and the Third World did decline slightly but earnings from these sales were much greater than in 1973 as a result of higher oil prices.

11. The economic picture brightened even more in 1976 when new prices went into effect on oil exports to Eastern Europe, replacing the anomalously low prices charged since the Arab embargo of 1973–74.

14/Soviet Oil Politics Reconsidered

1. Joseph Nye, Jr., "Multinational Corporations in World Politics," *Foreign Affairs* 53, no. 1 (October 1974): 155–56.

2. The IPC pipeline running from Kirkuk, Iraq, to Banias, Syria, and Tripoli, Lebanon, ceased operations, at least temporarily, on April 12, 1976 as a consequence of economic and political squabbles between Iraq and Syria. However, Iraq had already completed a new pipeline network linking the Kirkuk oil fields with the Persian Gulf port of Fao. The first exports via this route were on January 6, 1976.

Index